Contents

Illustrations

FOREWORD

THIS COLLECTION OF ESSAYS by an eminent group of historians and political scientists significantly expands understanding of the influential roles certain first ladies have played throughout U.S. history. Discussions of the women show how they have been integral to their husbands' presidencies. This volume describes not only how first ladies influenced their times, but also how the position has evolved.

I had the privilege of serving as chief of staff to one of the most activist first ladies, Hillary Rodham Clinton. From that vantage point I observed some distinctive features about the office of first lady: the unique nature of the position, the power it conveys, the controversy it attracts, and society's role in shaping its dynamic and evolving character.

The position is unique in that it derives its raison d'être from the first lady's marriage to the president. As such, there is no job description, no salary, no appointment, no election. The position is affected by tradition but also by conflicting expectations from the public. How the job is performed depends on the interests, background, and professional experience of the occupant and the priorities of her husband and his administration.

The power of the office comes from each first lady's relationship to her husband, the president—their personal and political partnerships. Many first ladies functioned as their husbands' trusted counselors for years prior to their coming to the White House. As did Mrs. Clinton, they debated policy, held appointive office (Governor Clinton named his wife to head Arkansas's education reform effort), campaigned endlessly (Mrs. Clinton was front and center in twenty of her husband's campaigns, from Arkansas attorney general to president), and weighed in on key decisions about their husbands' political careers. Every White House staff member recognizes that the president spends more time with his wife than with any appointee and is likely to hear her views on a vast array of issues. I know from experience how keenly the power of this relationship is understood. Administration colleagues, including cabinet secretaries, lobbied me to convey information to the first lady, to urge her to weigh in on an impending presidential decision, to solicit her opinion, and to schedule meetings with her. She was perceived as either the solution to a problem or a problem to be solved. The first lady can help or hurt the president's administration. As a result, staffs of the president and first lady today are more integrated in an effort to avoid difficulties and achieve optimal efficiency and benefits.

The Office of the First Lady provides a national (and increasingly international) platform to further projects and policies. The possibilities are fairly unlimited. The first lady functions as the president's eyes and ears. She can translate problems she learns about from the people into programmatic solutions. For example, if she learns that a particular disease is not receiving its fair share of research dollars, she can push for an increase. (Mrs. Clinton did so with regard to childhood asthma, juvenile diabetes, and epilepsy.) If the first lady becomes concerned about the large number of children languishing in foster care, she can push for new federal incentives to the states to encourage adoptions. (Mrs. Clinton played a critical role in adoption reform.) If the first lady thinks an issue, such as balancing work and family, deserves more attention, she can use her national platform to elevate the issue. (Mrs. Clinton organized the first-ever White House Conference on Child Care, in which the president and the secretary of the treasury participated.) A first lady can testify before Congress, inspire and inaugurate public/private collaborations, hold press briefings, convene public hearings and events across the country, and make hundreds of speeches to state her case. In a telling example of the power of the first lady, when her husband's presidency was threatened with the prospect of impeachment, Mrs. Clinton rallied the party by barnstorming across the country to forestall what was expected to be a huge loss for the Democratic Party in the off-year election. As the votes were counted, she was credited with playing the pivotal role. In fact, *Time* magazine weighed naming her "Person of the Year."

One of the innovative essays in this book deals with "First Ladies and U.S. Foreign Policy." The wielding of global power is a more recent development in the evolution of the Office of the First Lady, but as the chapter demonstrates, presidential wives have always played some role, albeit perhaps limited, in this sphere. The essay focuses on the more prominent roles of Mrs. Carter and Mrs. Clinton and their significance to foreign policy development. Hillary Clinton's international accomplishments may prove to be her most lasting contribution; yet, until now, they received little analysis or discussion. While much more work on the role and involvement of first ladies in foreign affairs is warranted, this chapter breaks new ground.

The American public seems divided about what it expects from our first ladies or what it considers their appropriate involvement in the presidential administration. As societal views about the status of women, power, and marriage have evolved, so too has the role of first lady. This gives first ladies a Rorschach test–like quality—the American public sees what it wants to see. Perhaps that is why the public (and the media) have so much difficulty with any but single-dimensional views of the women who have occupied this position. For example, how can a first lady testify before Congress as well as plan the menu for a state dinner? How can she go before the United Nations and give an eloquent speech on human rights while also worrying about redecorating the Blue Room? Reporters candidly told me that during Mrs. Clinton's first weeks as first lady they had heated discussions in their newsrooms over whether stories about her should appear in the "news" section or in the "personalities" section. Reflecting on this very complexity, Mrs. Clinton once remarked: "We expect so much of the woman who is married to the President, but we don't really know what it is we expect. There is something about the position itself which raises in Americans' minds concerns about hidden power, about influence behind the scenes, about unaccountability, yet if you try to be public about your interests and concerns, then that is equally criticized. I think the answer is just to be who you are and do what you can do and get through it and wait for the First Man to hold the position."

First ladies have attracted controversy throughout history, and Mrs. Clinton, as a quintessential transitional first lady, drew a great deal of fire over what critics perceived to be a usurpation of power. When she took a small office on the second floor of the West Wing near the domestic policy director (instead of in the traditional East Wing or residence section), critics had a field day. One cartoonist drew a skyscraper addition over the West Wing of the White House as his depiction of ambition out of control. In their times Abigail Adams was called "Mrs. President" and Edith Wilson was referred to as "the 28th and a half President" for the same reasons. Nancy Reagan was resented for her behind-the-scenes clout. Eleanor Roosevelt was vilified for her public activities, such as taking a job with the Office of Civilian Defense, which she eventually had to abandon. She once remarked that a first lady needed to have the "skin of a rhinoceros."

Increasingly, thoughtful observers are calling for a more realistic expectation of the first lady's role. In January 1993 even the conservative editorial page of the *Wall Street Journal* opined: "It may well be that the time has come to rethink the First Lady model that we've lived with for some 200 years. . . . If Mrs. Clinton is going to revise the way we think about First Ladies, it is better it should be in an assignment like this (health care reform task force head) as a public equal of her administration peers, than as a figure in the shadows." As modern first ladies enlarge the scope of the office, each will do so in a way that best suits her. Each successive first lady, however, will have more choices in the process. In time a new model may be created. Certainly this will be the case when the occupant of the office is the "first man."

This is a fascinating topic that is critical to an understanding of American history, the presidency, and women's progress in this country. This collection of essays does justice to its topic. It provides a distinct lens with which to view history. The research and thoughtful analyses presented chart the past and in the process help us to understand the future better.

MELANNE VERVEER
*Former assistant to the president and former chief
of staff to First Lady Hillary Rodham Clinton*

Preface

First ladies have emerged as powerful forces in White House politics. Whether campaigning for their husbands, promoting social causes, presiding over official state dinners, or testifying before Congress, first ladies have wielded their influence in many ways. Indeed, the first ladyship has become an institution of the White House and U.S. politics. Chief among the manifestations of influence is that first ladies have generally functioned as their husbands' most trusted political confidantes. As partners in the presidency, first ladies have influenced politics, policy, and the history of the country. Yet the presidential spouses have generally been overlooked in scholarly research, in textbooks, and in the classroom.

The Presidential Companion attempts to remedy this general neglect. The book features a collection of readings on the many facets, challenges, and complexities of the first ladyship. Two themes run through the essays in the book. The first is that the first ladies are politically and socially influential in and beyond the White House. The second examines the partnership found in the presidency. The book is also intended to introduce readers to first ladies in a general sense by offering a variety of essays on individual first ladies and topics pertaining to the first ladyship. It is not possible in a book of this length, nor is it the intention of the editors, to present every one of the first ladies. As such, the number of first ladies featured is limited and includes some well-known and some not so well-known occupants of the White House. Perhaps even more so than in the Executive Office of the President, there has been great diversity in the first ladyship in terms of style, approach, and even the degree of enthusiasm for the office. Some first ladies embraced their public responsibilities and pursued active political roles, while others were reluctant to enter public life. This range in approaches is reflected in the essays, some of which are devoted to politically powerful first ladies and others of which describe those whose foci were restricted to the social and family arenas. The topical essays all relate to the book's themes of influence in the office and partnership in the presidency.

Following an introduction, the essays are organized into four sections and are followed by a conclusion. Each section contains three or four essays and begins with a brief overview that presents the main themes under analysis in the section. Section topics include: the founding and development of the office;

the social and behind-the-scenes influence of first ladies; the political and policy influence of first ladies; and the modern first ladyship.

Both scholars and students should find the book useful, and the essays are appropriate for students of history, women's studies, and political science at the undergraduate and graduate levels. The contributing authors, from a range of backgrounds and disciplines, committed themselves to producing thought-provoking and original, yet highly readable essays. A comprehensive list of sources appears in the bibliography, should the reader want to explore the topic in greater detail.

We would like to thank editor Alexander Moore, Scott Evan Burgess, and the rest of the staff at the University of South Carolina Press, as well as copyeditors Patricia L. Coate and Jennifer Reid, for their support and excellent work on this book.

The presidential spouses had front-row seats to the momentous events and decisions of history, and much can be learned from the study of first ladies. Indeed, we believe that the first ladies are worthy of scholarly attention in and of themselves and that to ignore their roles in presidential affairs is to overlook an important component of the presidency and nation's history. We hope that you find this book to be informative.

ROBERT P. WATSON
ANTHONY J. EKSTEROWICZ

PART ONE

Introduction

The first ladies deserve attention if for no other reason than they have been part of the presidency since the nation's founding. Because George Washington served his inaugural presidency in the cities of New York and Philadelphia while the "federal city" was being planned and developed, the first ladyship can be said to have predated the completion of the White House. The first presidential spouse, Martha Washington, served through two presidential terms without ever actually stepping foot in the building now known as the White House. The first presidential spouse to reside in the White House was Abigail Adams, wife of John Adams, the second president.

The service of presidents' wives also predates the use of the title "first lady," which was not a part of the early office. For instance, the term was not used at the time of Martha Washington's service; rather, she was known as "Lady Washington." Early first ladies were known by a variety of titles, including "Lady Presidentress" and even "Queen." It was not until the mid-nineteenth century that the title "first lady" was initially used and not until the early twentieth century that the term gained widespread acceptance, although scholars remain divided as to the exact date of the title's first use.[1]

Regardless of the origins of the title, the first ladyship has been an important component of the American presidency. To begin with, the majority of presidents served with their spouses at their side. Only two bachelors have been elected president, James Buchanan and Grover Cleveland, although Cleveland married Frances Folsom during his first presidential term. James Buchanan relied on his niece Harriet Lane to function as White House hostess, a task she performed so admirably that her service was one of the few bright spots in Buchanan's otherwise unsuccessful tenure in office. Five spouses of men who would go on to become president died prior to their husbands' service as commander in chief. This list includes Martha Jefferson, Rachel Jackson, Hannah Van Buren, Ellen Arthur, and Alice Roosevelt, the first wife of Theodore Roosevelt. Although she never served as first lady, Rachel Jackson had been married to her husband for nearly four decades at the time of her death and was at his side during his political ascension from the frontier to the pinnacle of power. In fact, Rachel died in the short interim between Andrew Jackson's election and his inauguration as president.

Three first ladies died while serving beside their husbands in the presidency: Caroline Harrison, Letitia Tyler, and Ellen Wilson. All three of these women enjoyed close relationships with their husbands and were valued confidantes throughout their spouses' political careers. The presidents who became widowers in office all remarried, with Presidents John Tyler and Woodrow Wilson marrying again while serving as president. Most first ladies, however, outlived their husbands, although only two widowed former first ladies would later remarry. These two—Frances Cleveland and Jacqueline Kennedy—were much younger than their first husbands.

A total of four wives of presidents had previously been married and widowed before marrying their presidential husbands. Three of these widows were from the founding period of the nation's history: Martha Washington, Martha Jefferson, and Dolley Madison. All three were young widows when they met their second husbands. The fourth was Edith Wilson, a wealthy widow living in the nation's capital city when she met then-president Woodrow Wilson, a recent widower. There have been several divorces associated with the presidency and first ladyship. Rachel Donelson (Jackson), Florence Kling (Harding), and Betty Bloomer (Ford) were divorcees when they married men who would one day become president. President Ronald Reagan remains the only president to have been divorced. His first wife, Jane Wyman, was a divorcee when she married Reagan. Martha Washington, Martha Jefferson, Dolley Madison, and Florence Harding had children from their first marriages whom they brought into their presidential marriages.

In sum, wives served in thirty-eight of the first forty-three presidencies. When a presidential spouse was either deceased or incapacitated due to poor health, a hostess was called on to function in her absence. Typically, these "surrogate first ladies" were young daughters, daughters-in-law, or nieces of the president and first lady.[2] Their service points not only to the public's expectations about the office, but to the valuable role fulfilled by first ladies, one deemed necessary even when the president's wife was unable to fulfill the role's responsibilities.

It is clear that the first ladyship has emerged as a dominant institution of the White House. Over the years first ladies have fulfilled an array of roles and responsibilities, some informal and others that approach a quasi-official capacity. The great diversity in first ladies' roles coexists with little consensus about the roles assumed by first ladies, a paradox that is the by-product of several factors. The fact that few constitutional or legal guidelines exist governing what the first ladies may and may not do has been a mixed blessing for the presidential spouses.[3] On one hand, most anything they choose to do is open to questioning. Yet, within the parameters established by precedent and public opinion, first ladies have had a range of options available to them as they contemplated the nature of their approaches to the office. In developing these approaches first ladies have also taken their cues from public opinion, the preferences of the presidents, historical precedent, the prevailing views on the status of women in society, and, of course, their own inclinations and abilities.

POLITICAL OFFICE

Initially, because the responsibilities of the president's wife had not been contemplated, each decision and action performed by Martha Washington served to lay the foundation of the office and establish precedents that are followed to the present time. Even before she arrived in the new, temporary presidential residence in New York City, Martha realized that she had become a public figure, as she had experienced crowds of curious well-wishers in every town she passed during the long trip from her home in Virginia to meet her husband in the new capital city.[4] From that moment Lady Washington responded to her public celebrity and thus fulfilled an important role within the first presidency, one that gave further credibility to her position, the presidency, and the new nation. The task of hosting a social reception each week also fell to Washington's wife. Martha's weekly "levees" were enormously popular affairs that successfully balanced the competing pressures from those advocating democratic simplicity with those expecting a more regal manner befitting the courts of Europe. From the outset the presidential residence was Martha's domain, and she picked up where she had left off in private life, functioning as her husband's household manager and social hostess.

With a long married life behind them, the Washingtons brought with them to the presidency their experiences running a successful Mount Vernon home and plantation. By the time the Washingtons entered the presidency, they had hosted the leading public figures in the land at their estate and were well practiced in the social graces. They had also forged a close working relationship and a shared dependency on one another, to the extent that it resembled what today might be deemed a partnership. Accordingly Martha, always concerned about her husband's health and reluctant to leave their beloved Mount Vernon for the turmoil of public office, fulfilled perhaps her most important task: functioning as the president's supporter and guardian.[5] The president relied on her calm steadfastness, and when Washington was ill, Martha reduced his workload, demanded quiet at the presidential residence (and even in the street fronting the home), and nursed him back to strength.

The tenure of Martha Washington thus initiated at least three identifiable roles for the first lady: public figure, social hostess, and presidential helpmate. The first ladyships of subsequent spouses would further reflect the precedents and direction of Lady Washington's service. Abigail Adams continued the first lady's status as public figure, hostess, and certainly her husband's helpmate, if not his most influential political adviser. Dolley Madison would go on to become perhaps the most beloved of all first ladies and the most successful presidential social hostess of all time. The near-universal admiration of Dolley Madison and legendary accounts of her warmth, character, and social acumen brought further credibility to the spousal role and assured the continuation of a public first ladyship.

The office would receive a challenge, however, in the mid-nineteenth century, as the wives of Presidents Martin Van Buren and Andrew Jackson had passed away prior to their presidencies and several other first ladies either suffered from poor health or were reluctant to participate fully in the public dimensions of the office. This list includes Anna Harrison, Letitia Tyler, Margaret Taylor, Jane Pierce, and Eliza Johnson. Even in the absence of healthy, enthusiastic first ladies, the roles framed by the "founding mothers" of the first ladyship endured those trying times. By the latter 1800s, thanks to the capable first ladyships of Julia Grant, Lucy Hayes, Frances Cleveland, and Caroline Harrison, the office was again popular and fully engaged in the aforementioned roles of the presidential spouse.

By the late nineteenth century two additional roles had become established parts of the first ladyship: White House renovator-preservationist and campaigner. Given the established gender roles of U.S. society, first ladies quite naturally continued the role of homemaker once in the presidential residence. The years of wear and tear on the executive mansion eventually required consideration of how the building would be refurbished, and again responsibility fell to the first ladies. But more than simply decorating the building, first ladies oversaw several major historic restorations of the president's home. The presidents' wives had also become managers of the White House, overseeing social events, guest lists, protocol, and menus; acquiring state china; and eventually giving tours of the building. Thanks to the efforts of first ladies, the White House remains today a living museum of U.S. history that is open and accessible to the public.

The other nineteenth-century development within the office was the role of campaigner. Frances Cleveland, Caroline Harrison, Ida McKinley, and other spouses of political candidates in the late nineteenth century found themselves entertaining guests, posing for the media, and even becoming focal points of the literally named "front porch campaigns" of the day. Both the public and the press expected the candidates and their wives to open their homes to them and willingly to greet the electorate from their front porches. Once again political spouses served by enhancing the family image of the candidates.

The advent of new media technologies such as the radio and television and such campaign developments as the whistle-stop train tour and the modern, media-saturated presidential campaign only furthered first ladies' involvement in presidential campaigns. The twentieth century witnessed Lou Hoover addressing large radio audiences; Eleanor Roosevelt speaking as a stand-in for her husband at the 1940 Democratic National Convention; Lady Bird Johnson campaigning solo on a whistle-stop train tour through the South in an effort to offset any ill will toward the president by southern whites caused by Johnson's support of the 1964 Civil Rights Act; and, with her husband preoccupied with the Iranian hostage crisis, Rosalynn Carter traveling across the country shouldering much of the weight of her husband's 1980 reelection campaign. Indeed, recent first ladies have been expected to campaign, answer questions from the press, and deliver speeches at their parties' national conventions. First ladies have become well-known fixtures on the campaign stump and have not been given the luxury of declining to participate in the campaigns.

By the close of the twentieth century at least three additional characteristics had become core components of the office of the first lady. The first of these is the advent of a formal office complete with staff, office space, and resources. Several spouses have enjoyed office space in the East Wing of the White House, and Hillary Rodham Clinton worked out of several offices, including one in the West Wing. Indeed, the modern first lady's office rivals that of senior presidential advisers in terms of its size and importance. The development of a professional staff began during the service of Edith Roosevelt at the dawn of the twentieth century when a clerk in the Department of War was reassigned to Mrs. Roosevelt to assist the first lady with her correspondence and schedule. As the roles and scope of activities of first ladies grew, the addition of staff became as much a practical necessity as it might have been a strategic move for power. In recent years this office has grown to average over twenty employees, with staff positions responsible for press relations, special projects, schedule and advance, and other duties central to the functioning of the modern first ladyship.

The first lady's duties have also expanded to include her own social activism and advocacy. In this capacity first ladies have become identified with a particular social cause or pet project. For instance, Lady Bird Johnson led a highly successful beautification and conservation program, promoting the planting of trees and flowers, urban renewal, and the protection of natural areas. Nancy Reagan became a well-known point person for the war against drugs through her high-profile "Just Say No" campaign aimed at preventing drug use among youths. Barbara Bush advanced the crusade of adult and family literacy through her work as first lady and her personal literacy foundation. The public has grown to expect first ladies to champion social issues, and in turn recent first ladies have been quite successful in lending their support to important social causes.

A final key development in the office during the last century was the emergence of the first lady as a formal actor in the policy process. Even as early as the first ladyship of Eleanor Roosevelt in the 1930s and 1940s, the first lady testified before Congress, conducted investigations of public facilities on behalf of the president, and assumed a leadership position in the Office of Civilian Defense. However, Mrs. Roosevelt was ahead of her time, and such official policy roles did not become commonplace in the office until much later in the century. For example, during the Carter administration first lady Rosalynn Carter headed her husband's task force charged with studying mental health care reform, and she was instrumental in producing mental health legislation that was ultimately signed into law. Mrs. Carter also traveled throughout Latin America, meeting with heads of state in her role as official presidential envoy. Hillary Rodham Clinton followed in her predecessor's footsteps by leading the Clinton administration's health care reform efforts. Rosalynn Carter and Hillary Rodham Clinton, along with Laura Bush, testified before Congress in the capacity of policy experts. Additionally, spouses of vice presidents, including Joan Mondale, Marilyn Quayle, and Tipper Gore, testified before Congress.

The first ladyship of the twenty-first century inherits a history rich in activism, and the future direction of this complex, challenging, and powerful office will be in part shaped by its past. As such, in spite of the unelected and unappointed status of the first lady and the controversy the office has attracted, the first ladyship has assumed responsibility for several highly public roles.

Presidential Partner

Despite the many contributions made by first ladies to their husbands' public careers and the country, the press and popular magazines often depict the first ladies as little more than window dressing on the arms of the presidents, focusing their coverage on their clothing and hairstyles. Remarkably, irrespective of the activist first ladyship of Eleanor Roosevelt five decades before her and the close partnership of the Carters in the late 1970s and early 1980s, Hillary Rodham Clinton was described in the news as a "new type" of first lady, and her political activism was seen as "unprecedented."[6] Of course, such assessments of the first lady are typically untrue and fail to capture the complex nature of the office. To be sure, a closer inspection of the office reveals a history of influence and power. First ladies dating to Abigail Adams, and even possibly the inaugural first ladyship of Martha Washington, exhibited interest in their husbands' political careers and presidencies, showed talent for hosting social events, and functioned as trusted political confidantes to their president husbands.

In this capacity first ladies might be better understood as presidential partners. As such, each first lady has functioned in a variety of roles, but perhaps none is more important to the president than that of trusted personal confidante. Given the tumultuous experience of serving as president, the commander in chief has often turned to the person closest to him for support. Indeed, presidents have long taken assurance from the counsel and support of their spouses. The first lady is, after all, family. Moreover, the first lady has typically known her husband longer than any of even his most senior aides have known him and, more often than not, has been with him since before the start of his political career. So too have the demands of politics and campaigns forced spouses to participate in all facets of their partners' careers, whereby political careers have evolved into co-careers shared by both spouses.

Few, if any, members of any presidential staff can claim such familiarity with a president's career or a president's personality as can the first lady. In fact, the majority of presidential couples had been married at least twenty years before entering the White House. Andrew and Eliza Johnson, Benjamin and Caroline Harrison, the Eisenhowers, and the Carters were all married over thirty years before their periods of presidential service. The Washingtons, John and Abigail Adams, William and Anna Harrison, and George and Barbara Bush had spent over four decades together as husband and wife.

Many first ladies functioned as close political advisers and active participants in all aspects of their husbands' presidencies. The list includes Abigail Adams, Sarah Polk, Helen Taft, Caroline Harrison, Ellen Wilson, Edith Wilson, Florence Harding, Eleanor Roosevelt, Lady Bird Johnson, Rosalynn Carter, Nancy Reagan, and Hillary Rodham Clinton, to name a few. Likewise, many first ladies have been extremely popular with the public and the capital city's politicians. As the nation's social hostesses, many spouses literally charmed the public and won the support of dignitaries visiting the White House. As popular public figures and capable hostesses, first ladies have thus benefited presidents' images and popularity. For instance, first ladies Martha Washington, Dolley Madison, Julia Grant, Lucy Hayes, Frances Cleveland, Grace Coolidge, Mamie Eisenhower, Jacqueline Kennedy, Barbara Bush, and Laura Bush were easily among the most well-liked women of their times.

Paradoxical Position

Of course, the extent of first ladies' activism and influence with their husbands has not always been received with open arms. One thing all first ladies have in common is that they have been the targets of personal and often hostile criticism. These attacks have come from many sources, including the public, the press, and the presidents' political enemies. There are many paradoxes concerning the criticism of first ladies, not the least of which is the fact that a first lady's activism is often in response to public expectations. The public has, after all, in recent years grown to expect first ladies to champion social causes, participate in political campaigns, maintain a high profile, provide intimate access to the press, and perform a wide array of additional political and social functions within and beyond the White House. Yet she risks criticism if she does these things. First ladies are not free to refuse active service. As a result, the manner in which a first lady defines the parameters of her first ladyship are not hers alone to decide. Numerous media, public, and gendered forces continue to act on the first ladyship.

Public opinion polls reveal that the public remains uncertain as to the exact roles and responsibilities desired of first ladies.[7] Paradoxically, the result is that first ladies are criticized if they are too active and criticized if they are too passive. While Betty Ford received criticism for being too outspoken, her immediate predecessor, Pat Nixon, was criticized for not being outspoken enough. The appearance of first ladies has been a regular source of fodder for the public and the press. Eleanor Roosevelt and Rosalynn Carter, for example, were ridiculed for dressing too drably and plainly, while others such as Mary Lincoln and Nancy Reagan were assailed for dressing too regally and expensively.

Possibly the most common basis for such criticism is power. Dating all the way back to Abigail Adams, whose husband's political opponents lampooned her with names such as "Her Majesty" and "Madame President," first ladies have been accused of possessing too much power or giving the appearance of possessing too much power. In recent years Nancy Reagan was vilified as "Queen Nancy" and the "Dragon Lady," largely because of questions about the extent of her power inside the White House. Hillary Rodham Clinton's first ladyship experienced near daily condemnation from her husband's political opponents for an array of charges, most centering on perceived political influence and power.

At times the attacks on first ladies have transcended all sense of decency and fair play, becoming highly personal and destructive. For example, political satirists of the day depicted Margaret Taylor as a "country hick" smoking a corncob pipe, and Eleanor Roosevelt was drawn by cartoonists with oversized buckteeth. Some critics insensitively used Julia Grant's crossed eye and Ida McKinley's epilepsy as sources of criticism. Even when their actions have been performed under the most noble of intentions, first ladies have not been spared controversy. When Lou Hoover and Eleanor Roosevelt invited African-American guests to the White House, the southern press and politicians viciously attacked them. First lady Betty Ford, appearing for an interview on a popular television show, was ambushed by the host with questions about such sensitive and taboo topics as abortion, teen sex, and drug use. The first lady's thoughtful and frank responses to the questions became the source of brutal criticism directed at both her and the president.

Even with periodic criticism coming from a variety of sources, public opinion polls have found first ladies to enjoy rather impressive ratings that often exceeded the approval ratings of their husbands.[8] For instance, the annual Gallup Poll of the country's most admired women, conducted since the 1940s, has been dominated by first ladies. Many years two, three, or four first ladies have been featured among the country's top ten most admired women, and several first ladies have topped the poll.[9]

First ladies have often gone beyond the call of duty by putting in long and tiring hours on the campaign trail, enduring personal criticism and a variety of demands from the public, and working with intrusive media. The office has its rewards, but it is not without its challenges. A few first ladies, such as Margaret Taylor, Anna Harrison, Jane Pierce, and Eliza Johnson, showed little interest in the office and any responsibility associated with it. Other first ladies have lost spouses and children while serving in the White House, often the direct results of their public service. Yet, for the most part first ladies have served admirably and selflessly, accomplishing much on behalf of their president husbands. Countless contributions to the country are included among the numerous facets of their legacy. In recognition of their contributions, several first ladies have transcended identity merely as wives and have emerged from their husbands' shadows. For instance, Eleanor Roosevelt, Betty Ford,

Rosalynn Carter, and Hillary Rodham Clinton all carved out successful post–White House careers for themselves independent of their husbands. Other first ladies and former first ladies are newsworthy for their own lives and accomplishments.

A FIELD OF STUDY

Until the late 1980s and 1990s the first ladies had largely been omitted from serious scholarly attention. Rarely were spouses of presidents even mentioned in American politics or U.S. history textbooks or in the pages of political science or history journals. Remarkably, even books on the presidency —including the main texts in the field—neglected any viable consideration of the persons married to the presidents.[10] However, beginning in the late 1980s with the publication of Betty Boyd Caroli's *First Ladies* and Myra Gutin's *The President's Partner: The First Lady in the Twentieth Century* that all changed.[11] These two books ushered in a new wave of scholarship devoted to the first ladies. Over the course of the 1990s several additional books were published on the first ladies, papers and panels at academic conferences focused on the topic, and articles appeared in scholarly journals, with *Presidential Studies Quarterly* devoting half an issue to the first ladies at the outset of the decade.[12] At the outset of the following decade, the first journal to devote an entire issue to first-lady scholarship was *The Social Science Journal.*[13] This was followed a year later by the Organization of American History's *Magazine of History,* which also published an issue dedicated to first-lady scholarship.[14] Other journals such as *White House Studies* regularly publish scholarly articles on the first ladies.

Yet, in spite of the growth in scholarly interest on the first ladies and the promising state of scholarship at the dawn of the twenty-first century, a field of study on the topic is still in its infancy and widespread misrepresentation of the first ladyship by the public, the press, and professors alike remains a problem. Moreover, as is the case with any emerging discipline, there exists the need for additional development and testing of theory and models. Curricular aids and materials suitable for the classroom are also needed, along with further incorporation of studies of first ladies into the political science and U.S. history curricula, especially at the graduate level, so as to train researchers and future teachers on the subject.

Numerous additional challenges face those studying the first ladies. As is the case with the field of presidential studies, students of the first ladyship are provided with a small number of cases to study, with much variation among those cases in terms of approach to the office, roles undertaken, personal ability, interest in the office, and degree of success or failure experienced in office. Unlike the presidency, however, for which parameters of the office are discussed in Article 2 of the Constitution, the first ladyship lacks constitutional guidelines. Accordingly, there is much disagreement as to what the first lady should do and should not do, and no agreed-upon body of criteria presents itself for those attempting to study or rate the first ladies. Because first ladies are unelected and unappointed, even the existence of the institution as an office, much less the scope and duties of that office, remains a point of debate.

The reality of the matter, however, is that the first ladyship has emerged as an institution, not only in the White House but as an institution of the American political system and the nation. But because of the inherent conflicts presented when, in a democratic system, power is based solely through the wedding band and not the electorate, and because the first lady has been married to the president, her influence has often been wielded in private. This behind-the-scenes manifestation of power clearly exists, but it is next to impossible to assess. Furthermore, given the nature of politics and the continued struggles women in power face in U.S. society, the first lady must often deny her role and any influence in her husband's presidency, fail to claim credit for her accomplishments, and project a public image that is less her own than it is a seemingly antiquated archetype of the dutiful spouse.

Those seeking to study first ladies' views and political influence are presented with a daunting challenge. Nevertheless, a field of study has emerged. A truly interdisciplinary and multidisciplinary undertaking, first-lady studies promise to inform other disciplines such as presidential studies, U.S. history, social history, and women's studies. The study of first ladies is also developing an identity as a separate field of inquiry. A dynamic and complex institution, the office will continue to be shaped by a host of social and political forces. So too will the office undergo major changes when the first married, heterosexual female is elected president. The only certainties are that the office of the first spouse will continue to evolve, will continue to face criticism and an array of difficult public and political pressures, and will continue to make important contributions to the presidency and the nation. The story is yet unfolding.

THE PRESIDENTIAL COMPANION

This collection of essays on the first ladies brings together a diverse group of highly capable scholars from such backgrounds as history, political science, communication, journalism, women's studies, and the presidency.

The authors' goals include filling in the gaps in the literature base and providing a comprehensive analysis of the first ladyship. This will be accomplished by combining historical, political, and policy approaches to the study of the first ladies into a series of essays that examine the history and development of the institution and both the social and political facets of the office. The essays feature case studies of individual first ladies, research assessments of some of the major topics and themes in first ladyship studies, and theoretical and conceptual explorations of the nature of the office. The book is thus intended to serve an interdisciplinary audience of scholars interested in original and theoretical scholarship and also to function as one of the first textbooks on the subject matter.

NOTES

1. Several dates have been given for the first use of the title "first lady," but there is no consensus among scholars as to which one is correct. In 1849 President Zachary Taylor, when giving a eulogy for Dolley Madison, referred to her as "our first lady for a half-century." In 1860 *Frank Leslie's Illustrated Newspaper* called President James Buchanan's niece and hostess, Harriet Lane, the first lady. During the Civil War the *New York Herald* and *Sacramento Union* used the term to describe Mary Lincoln, while British journalists used it to describe the wife of Jefferson Davis, president of the Confederacy. Julia Grant was on a rare occasion called "first lady" by the press after the Civil War, and Lucy Hayes was deemed "First lady of the land" a few years later. In the early 1900s the term became widely used.

2. A few presidents lost their wives before or during their presidencies, while the spouses of a few others were either ill during the years in the White House or unwilling to perform the duties of first lady. As such, the presidents called on young daughters, daughters-in-law, nieces, or sisters to serve as White House hostesses. For instance, Thomas Jefferson's daughters Martha ("Patsy") and Mary ("Polly") served for their widowed father. Andrew Jackson's niece Emily Donelson and daughter-in-law Sarah Yorke Jackson both served for the widower. For a full discussion of such hostesses see Robert P. Watson, *The Presidents' Wives: Reassessing the Office of First Lady* (Boulder, Colo.: Lynne Rienner Publishers, 1999).

3. One of the few legal restrictions on the roles first ladies can perform is known as the "Bobby Kennedy Rule," named for President John F. Kennedy's younger brother and attorney general. The clause precludes presidents from hiring immediate family members. A court challenge to this was brought against Hillary Clinton by the Association of American Physicians and Surgeons (997 F. 2nd 898, 904, U.S. App. DC, 22 June 1993) in 1993 over the first lady's leadership in the Clinton administration's health care reforms. The DC Court of Appeals ruled in

favor of Mrs. Clinton, recognizing the public service and many roles performed by first ladies.

4. Surviving letters by Mrs. Washington and Mr. Lewis, a young relative who accompanied her to meet the president in the new, temporary capital city, New York, reflect her views. See the collection of Mrs. Washington's surviving letters in Joseph E. Fields, *"Worthy Partner:" The Papers of Martha Washington* (Westport, Conn.: Greenwood Press, 1994).

5. See Watson, "Remembering Martha," *Magazine of History* 14, no. 2 (2000): 54–57; and Watson, *Martha Washington: "Mother of Her Country"* (New York: Longman, 2002).

6. Several books present Mrs. Clinton as a new type of first lady, nearly unprecedented in her political and policy activism. See, for instance, Barbara Burrell, *Public Opinion, the First Ladyship, and Hillary Rodham Clinton* (New York: Garland Publishers, 1997); Joyce Milton, *The First Partner: Hillary Rodham Clinton* (New York: William Morrow, 1999); Peggy Noonan, *The Case against Hillary Clinton* (New York: Regan Books, 2000); Barbara Olson, *Hell to Pay: The Unfolding Story of Hillary Rodham Clinton* (Washington, D.C.: Regnery Publishing, 2000); Gail Sheehy, *Hillary's Choice* (New York: Random House, 1999).

7. Polls on the "proper" roles for first ladies have been commissioned by all the leading polling organizations and reflect hugely mixed results and much uncertainty about what first ladies should and should not do. For a good discussion of recent polls see Burrell, *Public Opinion*.

8. Most recent polls (from Betty Ford on) show that first ladies often have approval ratings higher than those experienced by the presidents.

9. Gallop's "Most Admired Woman" poll has been taken nearly every year since the 1940s. Most first ladies in that time period have headed the poll at one point, and the top ten spots in the poll often feature two, three, or four former and current first ladies. Eleanor Roosevelt headed or appeared in the poll for over two decades.

10. Scholars noting the lack of scholarship on the first ladies and calling for more include Lewis L. Gould, "Modern First Ladies and the Presidency," *Presidential Studies Quarterly* 20 (1990): 677–83; Hoxie R. Gordon, "About This Issue," *Presidential Studies Quarterly* 20 (1990): 672–75; Karen O'Connor, Bernadette Nye, and Laura Van Assendelft, "Wives in the White House: The Political Influence of First Ladies," *Presidential Studies Quarterly* 26 (1997): 835–53; and Watson, *Presidents' Wives*, 3–6, 22–26.

11. Betty Boyd Caroli, *First Ladies* (New York: Oxford University Press, 1987); Myra G. Gutin, *The President's Partner: The First Lady in the Twentieth Century* (Westport, Conn.: Greenwood Press, 1989).

12. Subsequent books include Carl Sferrazza Anthony, *First Ladies: The Saga of the First Ladies and Their Power* (New York: Quill, 1991); Gould, *American First Ladies: Their Lives and Their Legacy* (New York: Garland, 1996); Gil Troy, *Affairs*

of State: The Rise and Rejection of the Presidential Couple Since World War II (New York: Free Press, 1997); Watson, *Presidents' Wives* and *First Ladies of the United States: A Biographical Dictionary* (Boulder, Colo.: Lynne Rienner Publishers, 2001). The special issue of *Presidential Studies Quarterly* appeared in volume 20 in 1990.

13. The special issue of *The Social Science Journal,* vol. 37, appeared in 2000 and was titled "Focus on the First Ladies."

14. The special issue of *Magazine of History,* vol. 15, no. 3, appeared in 2001.

Part Two

Founding and Development of the First Ladyship

Overview

It is important to consider the history and development of the office, as many of the protocols surrounding the first ladyship and approaches by early presidential spouses to their duties are still very much part of the office. As is examined by Patricia Brady in the first essay, "Martha Washington and the Creation of the Role of First Lady," when Lady Washington first joined her husband for his inaugural presidency, she found that there were no precedents for her to follow. Few details of the day-to-day operations of the presidency or social protocols of official entertaining for the new country had been worked out by the Founding Fathers. And even less thought had been given to the roles and duties of the president's spouse. Although it contained guidelines for the presidency, the Constitution provided no guidance to spouses, who were, after all, unelected and unappointed.

Brady examines the legacy of the first presidential spouse, Martha Washington, who set precedents with her every action. Mrs. Washington confronted numerous challenges during her time of service, including a loss of her cherished privacy and the prospect of attempting to appease those desiring democratic simplicity in the formal affairs of state as well as those favoring a style more suited to the courts of Europe. Dr. Brady's essay makes a case for the selfless public service and devotion to duty exhibited by Lady Washington and her legacy as a most worthy partner to her husband.

In the second essay Dr. Catherine Allgor looks at the contributions of the early first ladies in establishing the social and political protocols of the capital city and federal government. Through the social arena and, in Allgor's words, the "Parlor Politics" that hearkened back to the customs of the courts of Europe, these political spouses established vital political connections, bringing together opponents and supporters of their husbands. They also provided a forum through which official Washington was legitimized. Allgor's keen insights trace the various contributions of, among others, first lady Dolley Madison, the nation's foremost social hostess and celebrity in the early nineteenth century.

From the contributions of the "Founding Mothers," the third essay moves to the first ladyship of Betty Ford, who in the 1970s contributed to the development of the office—for better or for worse—by defining herself as an individual. Mrs. Ford emerged as her own person, much as Eleanor Roosevelt had earlier in the century, transcending her status solely as spouse. Betty Ford brought a degree of celebrity to the office, much as Jacqueline Kennedy had in the early 1960s, and her life became a source of media attention. Yet, in the essay by Dr. Mary Linehan one sees how Betty Ford transformed the role of first lady and how her celebrity was different from such twentieth-century precedent setters as Eleanor Roosevelt and Jackie Kennedy, in that she merged the public and personal realms of her life. Through her famous candor and openness, Betty Ford quite possibly became a political liability to her husband, marking one of the few times a first lady may have factored into presidential voting. Yet, while she was demonized by her enemies, she was perhaps more popular than the president was among her supporters, and her service forever changed the nature of the office and prefigured the modern first ladyship of Hillary Rodham Clinton.

The first ladyship has endured the test of time, from impeachments and constitutional crises in the presidency, to wars, to deaths and tragedies in the White House. Presidential spouses have passed away in the White House, and a few presidents have served without their wives, who died prior to their husbands' elections. Still, to the present time the first lady remains a powerful presence in presidential politics and is responsible for, among other things, White House social functions, serving as the nation's hostess. As was discussed in the book's introduction, there are several reasons why the office has emerged as an institution and endures. One of the main reasons has to do with the personalities of the first ladies. Individual first ladies such as Martha Washington, Dolley Madison, and other early "mothers of the country," as well as more recent presidential spouses such as Betty Ford have contributed to the development of the office through sheer charisma and energy. The three essays in part one of this book provide snapshots of key moments in the history and development of the first ladyship, events critical for an appreciation of the complexities, roles, and nature of the modern office.

ONE

Martha Washington and the Creation of the Role of First Lady

Patricia Brady

What has been will be again, what has been done will be done again;
There is nothing new under the sun.
Is there anything of which one can say, "Look! This is something new"?
It was here already, long ago; it was here before our time.

Ecclesiastes 1:9–10

INTRODUCTION

Today's savaging of presidential families—the obsession of press and public with the tiniest detail of what the naive might consider their personal lives—is grossly uncivil. Particularly vulnerable are the wives of presidents, who seem to have stumbled into a bizarre Mrs. America pageant in which contestants are judged for womanly perfection and everyone comes up losers. Whether they are professional or domestic, outspoken or discreet, shy or sophisticated, frumpy or chic, thin or fat, distant or visibly devoted to their husbands, vocal commentators will find fault. But while the multiplying means of communication are new, the content is not. Since the birth of the nation friends and critics alike have kept close eye on the first ladies, feeling free to praise or carp at will. There has never been a truly private life for the presidential family; for them the social *is* the political.

Today's presidents, of course, are generally professional politicians who have spent their careers in the public spotlight, becoming accustomed to the constant attention and criticism. Their wives have also spent their marriages sharing the stage, while generally attempting to shield themselves and their children from the most hurtful attacks. But George Washington did not seek the presidency, and Martha Washington strongly opposed his acceptance of the position and public life in general.

Washington felt, and his wife agreed with him, that his many years in the field during the American Revolution with the consequent neglect of their financial affairs entitled him to a peaceful retirement. Martha Washington was already cozily ensconced at Mount Vernon, their plantation home, when following the news of peace with Britain her husband rushed home in time for Christmas in 1783. Both in their early fifties, it was time to retire happily "under their vine and fig tree," a biblical phrase often used by Washington. He would restore the worn-out land and make needed repairs, as well as elegant architectural additions, to his beloved Mount Vernon. She would provide a satisfying domestic and active social life, which included their large extended family and many friends.[1]

But the tranquil life of retirement would not last long, as George Washington, along with his wife, would again be swept up by the momentous events of the nation's founding. When Washington assumed the inaugural presidency in 1789, Martha Washington would be at his side, serving as the first presidential spouse and, with her every action, shaping the nature of the role of first lady.

CALLED TO PUBLIC SERVICE

In the period after the Revolutionary War the Washingtons welcomed a return to private life and, equally important to them, a return to Mount Vernon. Two lively little additions to the household increased their enjoyment. The Washingtons were unhappily childless, and Mrs. Washington's children by a first marriage were all dead. Her last surviving son, "Jacky" Custis, had died only two years before, leaving a widow and four children. On their return to Virginia the Washingtons decided to adopt Jacky's two younger children, Eleanor "Nelly" Parke Custis and George Washington Park "Wash" Custis, who had already lived at Mount Vernon for most of their young lives. Their mother and two older sisters, as well as their new stepfather, were frequent and welcome guests. Assorted nieces, nephews, cousins, friends' children, secretaries, and aides enlarged the family circle for months or even years at a time.

It was an attractive and sociable household, hospitable in the colonial Virginia way, with friends and relatives appearing with or without notice for long visits. It quickly became clear, however, that the general's celebrity (the common public perception of his status as the world's greatest living hero) was a magnet drawing many uninvited guests. George Washington had become an international icon—the object of interest and admiration at home and abroad. A pilgrimage to pay their respects to the hero of the American Revolution was de rigueur for many: foreign visitors came to take a look at the colonies that had cast off a king; former colleagues in arms, acquaintances, and strangers who could scrape up even a shadow of an introduction traveled to Mount Vernon and frequently stayed for days. The Washingtons' social code called for their entertainment, sometimes to the generals exasperation, as he remarked on various occasions in his diaries along with the comments that he and Mrs. Washington had not dined alone for twenty years and that his home had come to resemble "a well resorted tavern."[2]

Increasingly over the next four years these visitors, as well as Washington's correspondents, were politicians discussing American affairs and angling for his return to the national scene. The Federalists, those who considered the Articles of Confederation an instrument of government too weak for a successful nation, triumphed with the writing and ratification of the new Constitution; it provided a strengthened federal government headed by an elected chief executive. Most Americans agreed that there was only one possible president for this new form of government and for the new nation. Again duty called, and when Washington was informed of his election on 14 April 1789, he set off within days for New York City, the temporary capital of the United States, where he was sworn into office on 30 April. On 16 April he had noted in his diary, "About ten o'clock I bade adieu to Mount Vernon, to private life, and to domestic felicity."[3]

Mrs. Washington, dreaming of a permanent retirement in which they would "grow old in solitude and tranquility together," was not at all pleased by this honor. She wrote to her nephew, "I am truly sorry to tell that the General is gone to New York . . . when, or wheather he will ever come home again god only knows. I think it was much too late for him to go in to publick life again, but it was not to be avoided, our family will be deranged as I must soon follow him." She acquiesced as always, however, in his—and her— devotion to the nation. After all, she was a resolute patriot with convictions firmly fixed in America's favor. For example, she wrote to a friend returning from a European sojourn, "I think our country affords every thing that can give pleasure or satisfaction to a rational mind."[4]

FRAMING THE PRESIDENCY: SOCIAL CHALLENGES, SOCIAL ROLES

In New York, Washington found that even the smallest detail of the day-to-day business of the new republican government was to be invented, and he felt his way slowly setting precedents for the future. He was deeply aware that an ill-considered decision could reverberate for years and that the numerous enemies of the nation looked for the slightest stumble or misstep. There was no extant model to promise that this new government would not promptly disintegrate—reverting to royal control, fragmenting into tiny nations without economic viability, or falling under the sway of dictatorship, as later came to pass with the republics of Latin America. He saw his responsibility as ensuring the continued existence of the government by creating examples that would stand the test of time.[5]

It would take more than a month for Mrs. Washington to pack up the household and join him in the rented presidential mansion. There were the Custis children (now eight and ten years old) to be considered, as well as the multitude of items she was planning to transport for the family's comfort and pleasure. Decisions about endless matters had to be mulled over with Mount Vernon's manager, Washington's nephew George Augustine Washington, and his wife, Martha Washington's favorite niece, Fanny Bassett Washington. The younger couple had generally resided at Mount Vernon during the years of their marriage. Fanny would oversee the household in her aunt's absence, also looking after Washington's orphaned niece, Hariot, who was something of a problem child, and arranging for another niece, Fanny's cousin, to go home after a visit of nearly one year.

In the meantime Washington's governmental burden was almost immediately complicated by unforeseen social problems. There were many who believed that the citizens of a republic had an inalienable right to communicate in person with their president at will. Always hospitable, Washington found, however, that this republican propensity for intruding on the president on the smallest excuse—or indeed none at all—made it almost impossible for him to carry out the work he had been elected to perform.

After consultation with trusted friends and advisers, he fixed on a formal schedule of public entertaining and refused to receive guests at other times. To limit intrusive visitors Washington inaugurated weekly Tuesday afternoon levees that any respectable-looking man was welcome to attend without appointment. He delegated domestic arrangements to the indispensable Tobias Lear, who had joined the Mount Vernon household in the mid-1780s as family secretary and the children's tutor. To republican critics, such as the hypercritical senator William Maclay of Pennsylvania, all this smacked of aping royalty, a despicable attempt to set up a court and favor a set of "courtiers."

Maclay noted in his journal on 4 May 1789, just after the plan for presidential levees had become known, that crowds of visitors would tire Washington but that "for him to be seen only in public on stated times, like an Eastern Lama, would be equally offensive. If he was not to be seen but in public, where nothing confidential could pass between him and any individual, the business would, to all appearance, be done without him, and he could not escape the charge of favoritism."[6] As always, Maclay and increasingly radical republicans such as Edmund Randolph and Thomas Jefferson feared a tendency toward royalty.

That same month the president sent back the family horses and coach that he had earlier used to travel north. Another of his many useful nephews, Robert Lewis, was on hand to help with the tears and farewells, the excitement, and the confusion, as well as the overwhelming number of boxes and trunks still to be secured. Since all was not packed, Fanny Washington was requested to send such important items as a black lace apron and some fine net handkerchiefs, which her aunt planned to convert into borders for the caps generally worn by older ladies. On the day of departure it was not until three o'clock in the afternoon that the normally punctual Washington party set off in Lewis's charge, and they arrived in New York on 28 May 1789.[7]

That journey and Martha Washington's arrival in New York may be seen as the honeymoon of her sojourn as first lady. Although she had been dubious, the universal acclaim (almost adulation) that she received on this trip— "the great parade that was made for us all the way we come"—reflecting as it did the nation's respect for her husband, could not help but please. In Philadelphia, then the nation's most prominent city, the party was received by its leading citizens. Her account of formal and complimentary ceremonies is interlaced with her usual domestic concerns—Nelly's touch of coach sickness, corset stays ordered for Fanny and fashionable shoes for Nelly's mother and sisters, Wash's amazement at everything. They were met at Elizabethtown Point, New Jersey, by the president in a fine new barge originally commissioned for his reception; twenty-six men rowed the party the fifteen miles to the tip of Manhattan Island.[8]

Mrs. Washington, however, soon discovered the tedium of constant public attention. Contrary to her usual habit at home, her hair had to be set and dressed every day, and she attended much more to her clothes, putting on white muslin habits for the summer. As she reported to her niece: "You would I fear think me a good deal in the fashion if you could but see me," clearly not meaning to imply satisfaction with the arrangement.[9] Even when she was an attractive young woman of elite social position, she had never prided herself on modishness.

The boundaries of social life to be observed by the president's lady were just being defined, and often the definition arrived at by her husband was not to her liking. Washington had decided that she should preside at a weekly "drawing room" for both men and women on Friday evenings. On only the second day after her arrival in New York she was the hostess at the first of these parties, marking perhaps the first "official" duty of a presidential spouse. These drawing-room affairs would continue throughout Washington's presidency. Seated, she received her guests, who were greeted by the president and then were free to circulate among the other visitors. In addition the Washingtons gave dinner parties on Thursday evenings for government officials, members of Congress, and foreign dignitaries, invited in rotation. Limiting their social life to official entertainments, Washington had announced that he and his wife would not accept invitations to private gatherings, nor would they return social calls.

Of all the roles expected of the first lady, that of being the nation's hostess has been one of the most onerous for presidents' wives throughout U.S. history. As the first to fill the position, however, Martha Washington had not foreseen the formality of the rules that would come to govern the role, nor that her own private socializing would be so curtailed. Like many a subsequent first lady, Mrs. Washington was considerably disgruntled to find herself so fettered by political considerations. She repined and stayed at home, pouting: "I never goe to the publick place—indeed I think I am more like a state prisoner than anything else, there is certain bounds set for me which I must not depart from—and as I can not doe as I like I am obstinate and stay at home a great deal."[10]

One might have expected that such a social woman would have settled easily into the routine of presidential entertainments. But she liked to visit friends and to invite family and friends to her home. A situation in which her normal social habits were forbidden because guests were chosen in a fairly rigid rota by political position, not by social desirability or friendship, and in which the preponderance of guests were strangers, men whose wives were back home, was not appealing to Martha Washington.

And there was, of course, the damned-if-you-do, damned-if-you-don't factor, the hypercritical attention lavished on every aspect of presidential entertainment—too lavish, too formal, too free. William Maclay was an unusually biased observer determined not to fall under the spell of "the greatest Character of the world" and to maintain the purity of his republican ideals, immune to the influences of the presidential "court." Nevertheless, his comments may be cited as extreme examples of what many were saying.

Although Maclay was insulted and annoyed that others were invited before him, when he was invited to join the president and party at the theater, he complained of the company and the indecency of the play, *The School for Scandal*. Socially uncomfortable, he lamented that the major qualifications necessary for presidential entertainment were those "that flow from the tailer, barber, or dancing-master. To be clean shaved, shirted, and powdered, to make your bows with grace, and to be master of small chat on the weather, play, or newspaper anecdote of the day are the highest qualifications necessary."[11]

Maclay found little to admire, other than the food "all in the taste of high life," at Mrs. Washington's dinner parties, and he generally left without joining the ladies upstairs for after-dinner coffee. He complained of the heaviness of the conversation, jokes that fell flat, and the president's habit of drumming on the table with a fork or knife. One can only imagine his contributions to social gaiety. As a loyal Pennsylvanian, he considered the milk available in New York unhealthy and quoted with glee a tale by Mary White (Mrs. Robert) Morris about a dinner with the Washingtons. She had taken a bite of a large, fine-looking trifle but had to spit it into her handkerchief because the cream in it was "unusually(!) stale and rancid." "But," she added with a titter, "Mrs. Washington ate a whole heap of it."[12]

Abigail Adams, a much more vigorous correspondent than Martha Washington, enlarged on the drudgery of routinely giving official dinners. "Indeed I have been fully employed in entertaining company, in the first place all the Senators who had ladies & families, then the remaining Senators, and this week we have begun with the House, and tho we have a room in which we dine 24 persons at a Time, I shall not get through them all, together with the publick Ministers for a month to come. The help I find here is so very indifferent to what I had in England, the weather so warm that we can give only one dinner a week. I cannot find a cook in the whole city but what will get drunk."[13]

Washington had certainly been wise in declaring that he and Mrs. Washington would not return social calls. The ceremonial of making and receiving formal calls could have engulfed their lives. Although the etiquette of calling was not as rigid in the new American nation as in England or much of Europe, members of the social elite, which by courtesy included the nation's elected officials, were still governed by severe rules. This social quadrille was largely an urban phenomenon; poor communications and great distances meant that entertaining in the country must be a much more relaxed and friendly affair.

There were questions involved in calling: Who was (and, more important, was not) considered an equal in the calling order? Who called on whom first? When (and if) a call was to be returned, how long should a call last? When was leaving an engraved calling card a substitute for a call? How did ladies determine their days for receiving calls? Abigail Adams lamented "the splendid misery" of this round, remarking that she had returned more than sixty visits in three or four days, stopping to drink tea only at the president's home and two others. She wrote:

> I could give an account of visiting and receiving visits, but in that there is so little variety that one Letter only might consider the whole History. For Instance on Monday Evenings Mrs. Adams Receives company. That is her Rooms are lighted & put in order. Servants & Gentlemen and Ladies, as many as inclination, curiosity or Fashion tempts, come out to make their Bow & Curtzy, take coffee & Tea, chat an half hour, or longer, and then return to Town again. On Tuesday the same Ceremony is performed at Lady Temple's [Elizabeth Bowdoin Temple, wife of John Temple], on Wednesday at Mrs. Knox's [Lucy Flucker Knox, wife of Gen. Henry Knox], on Thursdays at Mrs. Jays [Sarah Livingston Jay, wife of John Jay] and on Fryday at Mrs. Washingtons, so that if any person has so little to employ themselves in as to want an amusement five Evenings in a week, they may find it at one or other of these places. To Mrs. Washingtons I usually go as often as once a fortnight, and to the others occasionally.[14]

Among Martha Washington's sparse surviving correspondence from the first year of the presidency are two social notes to the wives of cabinet members. Because of the pressure of creating a government from scratch, the Washingtons remained in New York during the summer of 1789. In August, in the polite third person of urban society, she inquired if Mrs. Hamilton, that is, Elizabeth Schuyler Hamilton, the wife of Secretary of the Treasury Alexander Hamilton, would be "disengaged" that evening; if so, Mrs. Washington would like to call. In October she wrote to invite Mrs. Adams and her family to dinner and an evening concert. Almost her entire social life during the year that the capital city was in New York involved the wives of government officials.[15]

Fortunately, Lucy Knox, the wife of the secretary of war, was an old friend from the Revolutionary War days. An unexpected new friend, given the differences in their personal styles, was the outspoken New Englander Abigail Adams. Mrs. Adams, generally more inclined to critical observance, wrote soon after meeting her that "Mrs. Washington is one of those unassuming characters which create Love & Esteem. A most becoming pleasantness sits upon her countenance & an unaffected deportment which renders her the object of veneration and Respect."[16]

Finding teachers and entertaining and caring for the children took up a great deal of Martha Washington's time. Like their grandmother, the children were accustomed to country living and found the city of New York fascinating, spending hours at the window watching carriages and passers-by.[17] Befriending government ladies and their children was all very well, but Martha Washington was bored and lonely for the circle of devoted and compatible women friends who had surrounded her all her adult life. As the eldest of a large family, she was accustomed to daily companionship. After her marriage to Washington her younger sisters, nieces from both sides of the family, her daughter-in-law, and the wives of military officers and aides had shared her cozy domestic life; together they sewed endlessly (the ultimate ladylike task), looked after the children, and discussed friends and relatives with all their infinite variety of interests, including illnesses, marriages—happy and strained—childbirth, death, celebrations, and the rest of the spectrum of human existence. This was the life that Martha Washington knew and loved. At the presidential mansion she missed this web of feminine support, particularly as critics multiplied.

But no one who attended the presidential entertainments would have known of her dissatisfaction. Although George Washington was sometimes criticized for stiff ceremoniousness, Martha Washington was praised for her charm and graciousness. Even her husband's political enemies succumbed to the effortless kindness with which she made all her guests feel at ease.

Living arrangements for the presidential family were makeshift in the temporary capital. They rented a three-story house on Cherry Street that was large but still cramped with all the staff and servants to house; it also served as the working office of the president and his staff. Mrs. Washington mothered not only her grandchildren but also the several young gentlemen who were the president's secretaries and aides. In addition to their official duties, these amiable bachelors escorted Mrs. Washington and the children on their excursions and acted as deputy hosts on all social occasions.

There were grave doubts at home and abroad about the long-term success of the American governmental experiment. Only Washington, it was believed, enjoyed the solid popular respect needed to lead the new nation through these years. But Washington, as his worried wife pointed out, was not a young man, even though he was still vigorous. During the first two years of his presidency illness threatened both his life and the shaky new government. He was so gravely ill in 1789 and again in 1790 that he nearly died. Although he recovered completely in both cases, Mrs. Washington was convinced that long hours, worry, and lack of regular country exercise were undermining her husband's health.

THE PHILADELPHIA YEARS

At the end of 1790, after a holiday at Mount Vernon, the family moved to the interim capital, Philadelphia. There they rented the large Morris mansion on High Street, and the president busied himself with household alterations and improvements, one of his abiding interests. The Custis children were settled in school, and the Washingtons again took up their schedule of official entertaining. But in Philadelphia there were many old friends and some engaging new ones. Gradually, under his wife's influence, the president's strictures against accepting private invitations were informally relaxed, and the seven years they spent in Philadelphia were filled with pleasurable social activities as they attended parties, the theater, church, concerts, and everything else of interest, from balloon ascensions to a circular panorama of Westminster and London.

Some of the family's Philadelphia friends were extremely wealthy, well educated, and sophisticated, to the disgust of voluble republican critics. Martha Washington, however, with her simple dignity, self-confidence, and graceful manners, never found herself at a loss socially. Only about her writing ability did the rather uneducated first lady suffer from any sense of diffidence. When she wanted to shine, certain letters—to the wives of foreign officials or to the formidably accomplished, prominent socialite Elizabeth Powel or her official responses to tendered gifts—were drafted at her request by Washington or Tobias Lear. She then copied the drafts and signed them as her own. But the formal correspondence, with its attention to grammar and consciously literary turns of phrase, lacks the charm of her own letters to her intimates, which are sensible, homely, and frequently lightened with self-deprecating humor.

As far as Martha Washington was concerned, her sixty-year-old husband had done all that could be expected for his country by 1792, toward the end of his first term as president. Their neglected acres at Mount Vernon needed attention, and the rising tide of partisan political attacks distressed them both. It was time for him to retire and let a younger generation of political leaders take command. Unfortunately, those politicians were not yet prepared to do so, and both factions begged Washington to accept a second term for the good of the country. It was almost unbearably disappointing to Martha Washington when her aging husband again bowed to duty. After the simple inauguration that she and the children attended, the problems of the second term rapidly multiplied, becoming far worse than she could ever have anticipated.

The deadly yellow fever epidemic that struck Philadelphia in 1793, forcing the Washington family to take refuge in Germantown, was an ominous opening note to the troubled second presidential term. Those years saw the Whiskey Rebellion, a major international crisis with Great Britain, Indian attacks on the frontier, and the tumultuous intrusion of French revolutionary influence into American politics. Most discouraging of all to Washington was the ferocity of partisan infighting, as Alexander Hamilton and Thomas Jefferson emerged as leaders of contending political factions. Republican newspaper attacks on the president grew more virulent, wounding him terribly. The family formed a lasting dislike of Jefferson for his deliberate orchestration of the attacks on Washington.

Under Their Vine and Fig Tree

Martha Washington also feared that her husband would not survive his second term in office. When he wrenched his back while riding during a 1794 trip to Mount Vernon, she was beside herself with anxiety. The disappointments of those years caused the president and his wife to long for their well-earned retirement. Washington had spent weary years building a government that could now survive a change of executive while avoiding the cycles of revolution and dictatorship that would plague future republics. Martha Washington had set precedents for future first ladies. Although it soon became obvious that their social life was seen as political and thus fair game for public discussion and criticism, Mrs. Washington attempted to maintain some degree of familial and personal privacy. Her warmth and charm in welcoming the public to official entertainments disarmed all but her husband's most dedicated enemies. Like the president, she both belonged to and represented the nation. Unlike some of her successors, she stayed firmly aloof from the day-to-day business of government.

Remaining only to attend the inauguration of John Adams as president in 1797, they bade farewell to their friends in Philadelphia and loaded the family, staff, servants, Nelly's dog and parrot, and mountains of baggage into two groaning coaches. The overflow—furniture and yet more baggage—was sent by ship to Mount Vernon. Despite a heavy cold and cough, Martha Washington would hear of no delay in setting anxiously off for Virginia.

Like many a later first lady, she was exhausted by the calls on her time and angered by the attacks on her husband. She looked forward to leaving the presidential mansion as though they were departing for the promised land. Although she wished for many years of peaceful retirement, Martha and George Washington would only enjoy two and one-half more years together. Yet the retirement was delightful, filled with solid content after the uncertainties and doubtful pleasures of the presidency.

She never forgave her husband's political enemies and their attacks. The habit of visiting Mount Vernon as a political shrine did not cease with Washington's death in 1799. Visitors from far and wide continued to flock to pay their respects. Martha Washington, aided by Nelly Custis (now married with children), continued to receive them graciously. Visibly aged by sorrow, she was a short, stout figure dressed in black and with a ruffled white cap. When Thomas Jefferson was elected to the presidency in 1800, Mrs. Washington commented freely and critically on his administration. She would never forgive the former intimate who, in her eyes, had gained her husband's love and confidence and then betrayed him for partisan advantage.

As one visitor wrote about a visit to Mount Vernon and his discussion with Martha Washington: "We were all federalists, which evidently gave her particular pleasure. Her remarks were frequently pointed and sometimes very sarcastic on the new order of things and present administrations."[18] The idea of an independent view of politics was completely beyond her personal view.

CONCLUSION

Until her death in 1802 Martha Washington remained the first lady of the American nation. She took seriously her role as representative of her husband and his achievements. In the dark days right after Washington's death, there was a flood of letters of condolence and requests for mementos. She was fortunate in having the assistance of Tobias Lear, who answered or drafted her answers for much of the official correspondence. The correspondence grew so heavy that official means were taken to ease the financial burden. Washington's old friend Henry Lee, now a congressman, and Timothy Pickering, the secretary of state, were able to see that the widow enjoyed the privilege of "franking," or sending free, letters and packages for her lifetime.[19] The tenor of many of the condolence letters was not just sympathy for personal loss but of the loss to the country. After 1775 George Washington had never again belonged solely to his family, but he was "Father of His Country."

Many of the letters representing the public aspect of mourning came from total strangers and often included requests for keepsakes. To visitors to Mount Vernon, Martha frequently gave small mementos in remembrance of the great man. She also responded generously to mail requests. For instance, a committee of the Grand Lodge of Massachusetts, whose membership included the patriot Paul Revere, wrote in early January 1800 requesting a lock of Washington's hair to be preserved in a gold urn with jewels and regalia of the lodge. Two weeks later Tobias Lear responded on her behalf with a letter enclosing the requested lock and indicated that Mrs. Washington "views with gratitude, the tributes of respect and affection paid to the memory of her dear deceased husband, and receives with a feeling heart, the expressions of sympathy contained in your letter."[20]

In February the members of a "Society of Females" in Providence, Rhode Island, wrote extolling Washington's many virtues as a warrior, expressing gratitude for his protection of them from their enemies and for his contributions as leader of the country. They also requested "a lock (however small) of his invaluable hair," which they proposed to wear "as a charm to deter us from ill and while gazing on it, think on the bright perfections of its former owner." If their request were granted, they planned to bequeath "the sacred talisman of virtue" to their children. In a postscript they also requested a lock of Martha Washington's hair, writing, "altho we have not the happiness of being personally acquainted with you Madam, yet the chosen Friend of Washington, will ever be dear to our Hearts." Like the others, this request was graciously granted.[21] Martha Washington had by this time taken the position beside her husband as a symbol of the nation and as the foremost woman of her times.

Although Washington had passed on the office of the presidency, no future president could achieve the almost mythical status of being *the* founding and first president. Nor could any future first lady replace Martha Washington in the public's esteem.

NOTES

1. For an overview of Martha Washington's life, see Patricia Brady's "Martha Washington," in *American First Ladies: Their Lives and Their Legacy*, ed. Lewis L. Gould (New York: Garland, 1996), 2–15.

2. Donald Jackson and Dorothy Twohig, *The Diaries of George Washington,* 6 vols. (Charlottesville: University of Virginia Press, 1979).

3. Ibid., 5:445.

4. Martha Washington to Mercy Otis Warren, 26 Dec. 1789; to John Dandridge, 20 Apr. 1789; to Janet Livingstone Montgomery, 29 Jan. 1791, in Joseph E. Fields, *"Worthy Partner": The Papers of Martha Washington* (Westport, Conn.: Greenwood Press, 1994), 223, 213, 229.

5. For details of Washington's presidency, see James T. Flexner, *George Washington,* vols. 3, 4 (Boston: Houghton Mifflin, 1969); and Richard Norton Smith, *Patriarch: George Washington and the New American Nation* (Boston: Houghton Mifflin, 1993).

6. Edgar S. Maclay, *Journal of William Maclay: United States Senator from Pennsylvania, 1789–1791* (1890; reprint, New York: Reprint Services Corporation, 1991), 15–16.

7. Ellen McCallister Clark, "The Life of Martha Washington," in Fields, *"Worthy Partner,"* xxv.

8. Martha Washington to Fanny Bassett Washington, 8 June 1789, in Fields, *"Worthy Partner,"* 215.

9. Ibid.

10. Martha Washington to Fanny Bassett Washington, 23 Oct. 1789, in Fields, *"Worthy Partner,"* 220.

11. Maclay, *Journal,* 30–31, 69.

12. Ibid., 73–74.

13. Abigail Adams to Mary Smith Cranch, 9 Aug. 1789, in Steward Mitchell, *New Letters of Abigail Adams, 1788–1801* (New York: Reprint Services, 1947), 18–20.

14. Abigail Adams to Mary Smith Cranch, 24 Jan. 1789, in Mitchell, *New Letters,* 7–8.

15. Martha Washington to Elizabeth Schuyler Hamilton, 30 Aug. 1789; to Abigail Smith Adams, Oct. 1789, in Fields, *"Worthy Partner,"* 218–19.

16. Abigail Adams to Mary Smith Cranch, 12 July 1789, in Mitchell, *New Letters,* 15.

17. Martha Washington to Fanny Bassett Washington, summer 1789, in Fields, *"Worthy Partner,"* 217.

18. Fields, *"Worthy Partner,"* xxvi.

19. Ibid., 373–74.

20. Ibid., 337–38, 344.

21. Ibid., 351–52, 363–64, 369.

Two

Political Parties

*First Ladies and Social Events in the Formation
of the Federal Government*

Catherine Allgor

Introduction

Even before they were dubbed "first ladies," presidential wives and companions have drawn the attention of historians and other journalists. For the most part, examinations of these women and their roles have tended to be more anecdotal than scholarly. With the exception of Eleanor Roosevelt, historians, political scientists, and biographers have studied a first lady only for insights into her husband's personality or to make a general statement about American women in her era. However, bringing tools of historical and political analysis to a close examination of these women's work and lives can enrich our understanding of politics far beyond insight into the presidential character.

This is especially true when studying the presidential wives and hostesses of the early republic—the first three or four decades of the nineteenth century. During this formative period many significant characters crossed the national stage. Male members of the founding generation—Thomas Jefferson, James Madison, James Monroe, among others—assumed positions of importance, while newer politicians who would profoundly shape the coming democracy—Henry Clay, Andrew Jackson, John C. Calhoun—made their entrances. One of the most famous and well-regarded participants was Dolley Payne Todd Madison, who served as the widower Jefferson's hostess from 1801 to 1809 and then as the wife of President Madison and the capital's official social leader from 1809 to 1817.

So influential was she that upon the widowed Dolley's return to Washington in 1837, her home was second only to the White House as a place for important people to gather. Congress granted her a seat on the floor of the House, and famed orator Daniel Webster declared Dolley to be "the only permanent power in Washington, all others are transient." Dolley Madison had almost single-handedly created the position of the "President's Lady," setting a model that would go unchallenged until the twentieth century. At her funeral in 1848, then president Zachary Taylor pronounced: "She will never be forgotten because she was truly our First Lady for a half-century." Thanks to Dolley's inspiration, the unofficial, unmandated, untitled job of the president's wife now had a title, "First Lady."[1]

Taylor was right; Dolley Madison's name is still familiar. Even twentieth-century historians who sometimes grudgingly acknowledge Dolley's fame and popularity—evidence for her renown is too present in the sources to ignore—cannot comprehend how she attained this prominence and why it lasted so long. Left to their own devices, modern scholars attribute the persistent power she had in Washington City solely to "charm and popularity," which seems even to them a rather weak explanation. Dolley Madison, they conclude with puzzlement, achieved renown as *hostess,* an occupation that seems to belong to private life, to the frivolous, to the marginal, to the female, and thus to the powerless.[2] The truth is paradoxical. While Dolley Payne Todd Madison *was* powerful *and* did indeed gain her power by being a hostess and a wife, this seeming contradiction may be resolved with a reevaluation of the meaning of that womanly role in the political culture of the early republic.

The political model formed by Dolley as first lady, and expanded by her early republican successors Elizabeth Kortwright Monroe and Louisa Catherine Johnson Adams, may be analyzed as relevant to a number of historical issues. For instance, one could examine the role of president's wife as the charismatic figure for the administration, or how the first lady functioned as a mediator in the political and cultural debate over the place of aristocracy in a republic. But perhaps the most overtly political function of the early first ladies lies in the centrality of social events in the early federal government.

The paradoxical fact that Dolley achieved such renown as a "mere" wife and hostess requires an understanding of her historical context. Dolley Madison, Elizabeth Monroe, and Louisa Adams reigned over the brand-new capital of the new United States, Washington City, during a formative time in the development of the city and the new government.[3] During the years 1800–1828, not only was the fate of the new capital city in question, but the whole republican experiment in federal union seemed a shaky proposition to Americans and European observers alike. The new Americans had won their Revolution, but no one was sure what was going to come next.[4]

FORMING A REPUBLIC

Elected in the "republican revolution of 1800," Thomas Jefferson was convinced that the previous Federalist administrations had drifted toward the very monarchical and aristocratic forms that the colonists had rebelled against. Only his firm hand on the tiller could restore the nation to "a republican tack"; he and his republican followers were the last, best hope of the republic. As president, Jefferson could begin what he called the "second American revolution" in a setting uncontaminated by the corruption and politics-as-usual of more established eastern seaboard cities that had served as Federalist capitals.[5] In 1800 the federal government moved to the new capital, Washington City, where the city and the government could be built from the ground up according to a particular ideology.

The political theory of "republicanism" had fueled the American Revolution and informed the drafting of the new Constitution, which served as the blueprint for constructing the capital and the federal government. Republicanism was a theory with long roots; at its heart was a fear of the absolute power that an abusive monarch could wield. In fact, republican theory decried everything associated with courts—not just kings and what republicans called "consolidated power," but the way politics was conducted in court systems. Particularly abhorrent were the face-to-face transactions among elites, who exchanged favors and worked for their own personal and family interests. The displays of luxury and material culture that characterized courts provoked republican horror, as did the presence and power of "unofficial characters," including designing ministers, scheming courtiers, and women.[6]

As ambassador to France and a European traveler, Thomas Jefferson had many opportunities to observe the depravity and corruption of real courts. The constant presence of women at the French court sparked his particular revulsion. Women dominated social events, and according to Jefferson, in their capacities as social leaders they exerted a destructive effect on the government's decisions, "their solicitations bid[ding] defiance to laws and regulations." In a letter to George Washington, Jefferson detailed the plans for reform after the French Revolution, gloomily adding that female influence proved so powerful that it would negate any attempts at official reform.[7]

In his quest to create a government of "pure republicanism," then, President Jefferson banished women from the halls of power in the new capital by doing away with the receptions, called levees, that had characterized European courts and the Washington and Adams administrations. Instead he instituted a regular series of small dinner parties, usually for congressmen of a single party only, where he could indirectly exert his influence over political processes, legislative and otherwise. Women could only visit the "President's House" occasionally as dinner partners for male guests and at the large celebrations on New Year's Day and the Fourth of July.[8]

But there existed a formidable obstacle to the project of building a government based on an antipower, antipolitical political theory. A government, a nation, and a capital city *need* power and politics, the networks of interests that characterize any government, including royal courts. In order to secure the future of the republic, the women and men of the founding generation had to make the United States *real* in the eyes of its own citizens and other nations, and they had to create a governmental system. To accomplish these two goals they had to build a practical, workable federal government, and they had to create a capital city, a seat of governance and center for federal power.

HIGH SOCIETY AND HIGH POLITICS

That the Washington ruling class succeeded, in spite of the burden of republicanism, was due largely to the work of Washington women—white, elite, and middling-class members of families for whom politics was the family business. These mothers, wives, sisters, and daughters of political families used a variety of time-honored techniques that created bonds among rulers, the networks and structures that the infant federal government lacked. Their work was encouraged and advanced by Dolley Madison's position as the head of official society, the most visible indicator and manifestation of this alternative political culture.

James and Dolley Madison came to the capital with Thomas Jefferson in 1800, when James took up his duties as Jefferson's secretary of state. Both products of a southern culture that prized hospitality, James and Dolley Madison understood the importance of social events, and early in their partnership Dolley took charge of this element of their personal and political lives. Thomas Jefferson had no official hostess, and so Dolley served in that capacity on mixed-sex occasions. More important, in the social vacuum that Jefferson created, Dolley set about making the Madison home on F Street a center for Washington City society and making herself (and thus James) a presence in Washington City.

And she succeeded. During the Jefferson administration the Madison home became the place where visitors and travelers called first, where the local elite mingled with the official community, where official families formed bonds. The crucial nature of this work became increasingly clear as James Madison's bid for the presidency drew nearer. In 1807 Samuel Latham Mitchill, representative from New York, evaluated for his wife, Catharine, James's chances for election: "Mr. Madison and Mr. Clinton are the two prominent characters talked of to succeed [Mr. Jefferson]. The former gives dinners and makes generous displays to the members." In contrast, "the latter lives snug at his lodgings and keeps aloof from such captivating exhibitions." Mitchill pinpointed the decisive factor in the two candidates' camps: "The secretary of state has a wife to aid his pretensions. The vice president has nothing of female succor on his side. And in these two respects [the wife and the social events], Mr. Madison is going greatly ahead of him." Musing upon his own defeat in the election of 1808, Charles Cotesworth Pinckney concluded: "I was beaten by Mr. and Mrs. Madison. I might have had a better chance had I faced Mr. Madison alone."[9]

Her efforts did not cease when James won the presidential election. Indeed the stakes were higher once the Madisons moved into the President's House. Dolley's list of assignments included legitimizing her husband's administration and the national capital (for both Americans and outsiders), helping the president deal with one of the worst Congresses in American history and a tense relationship with France and Great Britain, personifying the American war effort when hostilities were declared in 1812, and imparting to the citizenry a sense of Americanness.

Social Strategies

Accordingly, during her tenure Dolley lengthened the social season from six weeks to ten. She began her husband's administration with a dramatic flourish, giving her consent for the first inaugural ball, to be held at Long's Hotel. At the event Dolley "looked a queen," moving among the over four hundred guests resplendent in "a pale buff colored velvet . . . and a beautiful pearl necklace, earrings, and bracelets." In a style that would become both identifiably hers and endlessly copied, Dolley wore a turban made of the same buff velvet and white satin and decorated with "two superb plumes" of bird of paradise. She doubtless was the main attraction of the evening and "was almost pressed to death" by the crowd, anxious to have "a peep at her."[10]

Domestic Policy

Dolley Madison also dominated a more ordinary social form, the state dinner. Thomas Jefferson held his small dinners frequently, but the Madisons' versions were more lavish events, held once a week, and included as many as thirty guests—congressmen, distinguished visitors, and members of the diplomatic corps. These occasions took time and money, but all Washington hosts and guests recognized them as "powerful political factors . . . and even more so under the tactful sway of 'Queen Dolly [sic].'"[11]

At these official dinners Dolley, quite contrary to custom, took the seat at the head of the table, placing Edward Coles, James's secretary and her kinsman, at the foot. Surprisingly, though many observers commented on this startling sight, none expressed censure or disapproval. Several pointed out that the arrangement spared the president from leading the conversation, pouring wine, or seeing to his guests' needs. Casual observers and close friends agreed that James, quite convivial in small groups, fell silent in large companies. Dolley, on the other hand, flourished as the leader of the table, directing the flow of conversation, expressing her own opinions to legislators, and persuading them to accept her husband's views. If she was not always successful in this endeavor, she went far toward softening her husband's rivals. Guests commented positively on "the ease with which she glided into the stream of conversation and accommodated herself to its endless variety." A chronicler pronounced approvingly, "In the art of conversation she is truly distinguished."[12]

An accomplished hostess at her estate in Virginia, Dolley differentiated these dinners as "official" by a conscious invocation of "Americanness." Though the Madisons served continental food on occasion and French wine frequently, she actively sought recipes from all over the country to feature on her table. Some guests expressed surprise that though "the dinner was certainly very fine," it was not as fancy as they had expected or, as one guest commented, "not surpass[ing] some I have eaten in Carolina." The exchange of recipes between women of that time, especially southern women, served as an invitation to and a reinforcement of intimacy. In her quest for regional dishes Dolley built bridges with elite families throughout the infant United States. She offered her "receipts" as part of the transaction, including the exotic ice cream wrapped in warm pastry, a forerunner to the dish called baked Alaska. Perhaps this small part Dolley played in introducing ice cream to families across the country explains why popular lore ascribes the invention of this most American of desserts to her.[13]

Party Politics

Elites in Europe and colonial America had long used social events, personal influence, and the display of material luxury to assert, negotiate, and secure status and power. Dolley and James Madison were merely adapting time-honored techniques, then, to anchor their own administration. But the situation in early republican Washington made their efforts remarkable for two reasons. First, more traditional elite groups were normally involved in a city's overlapping networks of influence, including political, cultural, and economic power. In Washington City, however, a town built by, for, and about politics, Dolley's efforts can only be seen in a context of national and international politics. Second, in a republican culture that frowned upon official men engaging in such old-fashioned aristocratic politicking, women assumed more responsibility for creating the political machine and keeping its operations smooth.

Though obviously skilled at adapting time-honored social customs, Dolley also invented the most important social institution of the early Republic, one that most directly contrasts with Jefferson's exclusive dinner parties. "Mrs. Madison's" Wednesday night drawing rooms began on 30 March 1809 and lasted through both administrations. At some points before and during the War of 1812, they provided the only place where political enemies met and talked civilly. Dolley accomplished and extended many of her goals and projects with these soirees, for they integrated official and local elites, as well as providing an event for visitors, distinguished and ordinary, that allowed them to feel part of the national scene. Above all, Dolley's drawing rooms created a new kind of political space, one that afforded access to men in power and, like European court events, allowed for the participation of women and other political family members.

Housekeeping and Nation Building

The first step in Dolley's plan was her famous "redecorating" of the President's House. More accurately, Dolley and architect Benjamin Henry Latrobe *restructured* the shabby executive mansion, but not to create a habitable home or a haven from public life for the president. Rather, in creating a state dining room, a parlor, and a grand receiving room, they established public spaces in which the ceremonies suitable for a new republic could take place.[14] Colonial and European gentry had always seen the construction of houses as public acts, ways literally to dominate the landscape of an area. Consequently, gentry men (such as George Washington at Mount Vernon) involved themselves in choosing paint colors and silverware to a degree puzzling to us in the twentieth-first century, who think of these activities as private and the province of women.[15] Though such acts are always about power, Dolley's house-building project in the milieu of the capital city was more specific; it was about politics. The need for James to maintain a pose of republican simplicity shifted the responsibility for creating this public statement of power to Dolley.

The choices of decor and function for these rooms reflect an important tension in American culture between aristocratic-monarchical impulses and republican-democratic energies. In a political context that repudiated anything that smacked of court practices, Dolley should simply have banished all aristocratic forms and ideals. This would have been no easy task, as no forms existed that were not some version of an aristocratic practice, and some of those were extremely useful in keeping order. American people also craved honors and dignities and thrilled at displays of pomp and luxury. The adoption of republican ideals at the time of the American Revolution did not eliminate the attraction of these hierarchical forms. Indeed, the American Revolution and its resulting cultural chaos created a need for the stability and dignity that status symbols carried. Revolution can destroy aristocracy or appropriate it.[16]

Dolley chose to appropriate it. She and Latrobe created a gorgeous set of rooms, the finest interiors in nineteenth-century America. They were filled with rich fabrics, dazzling mirrors and silver pieces that reflected light and color, as well as signifiers of cultural superiority, such as musical instruments. But Dolley and Latrobe also chose nationalistic art to adorn the walls and used American manufactures, including furniture and decorations with a Greek theme, as befitting a government that involved its citizenry.[17]

The Madisons and Benjamin Latrobe knew that their audience would be composed of European diplomats, accustomed to refinement and convention; federalists, for whom formality and elegance signaled a proper attitude toward tradition and power; and more democratically minded Americans from across the country. Dolley's genius lay not in her taste but in her ability to combine republican simplicity with federalist high style. With the objects she chose, she created a public space for the executive that reassured both Federalists and Republicans, while impressing European visitors and officials with the sophistication of the new nation.[18]

The new "White House," as it was increasingly called, was a triumph. In a culture that understood the powerful symbolism of architecture, the White House became a focus for visitors of all nationalities and all classes. This period marks the beginning of the American people's identification with "their" house, an identification that would prove critical when the British torched Dolley's magnificent achievement in 1814.

But these sumptuous rooms were not just a symbol for nationality, the capital's stability, and the Madisons' right to rule. They were a stage setting for Dolley's primary mission, which was to counteract a constitutionally weak presidency by establishing her White House as the focal center of Washington, creating a practical place for politics. Dolley blended the pull of aristocracy with the push of what would become known as "democracy." She created a palace and then invited the whole world to use it.

Social Work

Dolley's Wednesday night drawing rooms were differentiated from every other party in town by dint of their regularity, their lavishness, and the numbers of enthusiastic participants. Each session also went by the nicknames "Wednesday Night" and "Mrs. Madison's crush" or "squeeze." It is notable that, in an era so patriarchal that a husband referred to "*my* child" even when discussing the child with his/her mother, people identified these parties as "Mrs. Madison's."

In the beginning Dolley placed announcements of the drawing rooms in the newspapers as a general invitation. Technically no one could attend the drawing room without having been introduced to James and Dolley Madison, but visitors also came with written introductions. These restrictions were no more onerous than those "prevailing in private drawing rooms."[19] However, even these rudimentary rules may have fallen by the wayside. Later sources indicate that the drawing rooms were open to Americans from many classes.

Precursors to the modern cocktail parties, these soirees required that the majority of guests stand throughout. A few chairs were scattered about for ladies who needed a respite. Martha Washington's (and later Abigail Adams's) levees had been held in fairly informal settings but were characterized by more courtly procedures and postures. In contrast, Dolley's events combined the most formal of settings with extensive freedom of movement. During the evenings groups of guests formed, broke up, and reformed as people moved through the three large public rooms Dolley had created. Sometimes there would be music, instrumental and vocal, while black slaves and possibly white servants carried huge waiters, or serving trays, through the crowd serving coffee, tea, wines, punch, and light foods.

Dolley created a social milieu peculiar to Washington City, one which English traveler and observer Frances Trollope would later describe as having "so little attention to ceremony . . . [that] it is possible that many things may be permitted there, which would be objected to elsewhere."[20] This power of possibility did very nicely for a political environment of bureaucrats, legislators, and other officials trying to create a working structure. By inventing these soirees, Dolley constructed a political space unlike any other in Washington. In contrast to Jefferson's rigidly controlled dinner tables, which accommodated no private conversations, Dolley's soirees allowed for a fluid, freewheeling atmosphere of political activity that could take in all numbers and combinations of folks, encouraging display and providing ample opportunity for private conversation. By regularly providing a large space everyone could count on, a place "to see and be seen," as one female visitor proclaimed, Dolley ensured that political business of all kinds could take place.[21]

Unlike Jefferson's dinners, the Wednesday Nights included Republicans and Federalists, cabinet secretaries, and members of Congress. In addition to accommodating partisan government officials, the "open house" nature of the events allowed for visitors, "gentlemen from New York" and other parts of the country in Washington on "visits of business or pleasure"; wives, daughters, and other female members of political families; and kin from across the country.[22] Margaret Bayard Smith, early Washington's best chronicler, estimated that "seldom . . . less than two or three hundred, and generally more" people attended the Wednesday night sessions during the winter after the 1812 war. Little wonder attendees dubbed them "squeezes"![23]

Not everyone loved Dolley's drawing rooms, and though many described the events with enthusiasm, negative accounts exist as well. Some hated the crush, the noise, or the kinds of people one met. In 1810 a newcomer to the city, Abijah Bigelow, representative from Massachusetts, attended "Mrs. Madison's levée" for the first time and left declaring, "Once more will suffice for me." He elaborated on his dissatisfactions, which included the refreshments, "Wine and Punch, neither very good"; the company, "that infamous scoundrel Turreau" (Louis Marie Turreau de Garambouville, the French minister); and the physical appearance of the presidential couple.[24] The very regularity of the events wearied other congressmen, but even as they complained repeatedly, everyone continued to attend. They could not afford not to go, as the drawing rooms offered rare political opportunities.

The chief commodity supplied by these weekly gatherings was *access*—the building block of interest groups, the first step toward fashioning a working political culture. Access begins the process of communication and then nurtures the personal relationships that keep the politics going. It is part of the unofficial sphere of politics, as important an aspect of the political process as the official sphere of documents and office-holding. Studying only the formal structural arrangements in the political process cannot but generate a skewed picture. "Official channels" cannot accurately describe "all the meanderings of the stream of politics." In the American federal system the separation of powers, especially between the executive and legislative branches, and the system of checks and balances do not guarantee that access to one branch of the government is access to all. Neither does membership in one area automatically ensure a tie or obligation to another.[25]

In such a governmental system, access to officeholders in all branches is central to all of the activities undertaken by politicians to get things done. These activities could include, but are not limited to, obtaining, giving, or disseminating information; proposing future legislation or political projects; office-seeking and patronage; mediating conflicts and compromises; and "horse-trading" of all kinds. At her drawing rooms Dolley was successful in facilitating all of these activities.[26]

Obviously, attending "Mrs. Madison's crush" provided access to the president. James attended these drawing rooms as faithfully as he performed his other duties, shaking hands with everybody. Governmental players from all regions of the country and branches of the government had the chance, once a week, for a personal discussion during the course of the evening. They also had access to each other, both before the critical decision to go to war with England in 1812 and throughout the war. Diplomatic dispatches explicitly discussed the political maneuverings in the drawing room. Dolley invited the minister of Spain to her drawing room especially to reconcile a diplomatic conflict.[27] Correspondence from congressmen and visitors also demonstrates that plenty of Americans did their politicking surrounded by the music, refreshments, and noisy chat of the squeezes.

The atmosphere and access Dolley created quickly became so crucial to the everyday workings of the government that even the death of Vice President George Clinton in 1812 did not distract from this activity. Two days after Clinton's death, Sophia May, a visitor to the city, observed, "It was generally thought upon the Hill there would not be any levées altogether, but they would not pay even that poor compliment to his memory."[28] The drawing rooms were too important. Even as Clinton lay dying, according to Dolley, "electioneering for his office goes on beyond description."[29]

COURTING RITUALS

While Dolley's political parties offered the opportunity to participate in politics to a wide group of citizens and partisans, she had her own particular mission, to deal with and guide a fractious Congress, a body which James Madison described as "unhinged."[30] Historians generally agree that no president has ever had a worse Congress. Part of the problem lay in the growing institutionalization of what had been in Jefferson's time a motley crew of individuals. Congress, like a rebellious adolescent, was discovering its own power, and its members were fighting against the president and among themselves over the declaration of war. Once Madison declared war, the legislators' hostility escalated. Several times the infighting threatened to split the

Union, culminating in the Hartford Convention's unsuccessful bid for seces-
sion in 1815.

In an effort to curb executive power, the framers of the Constitution had
deliberately provided no legislative representation for the president. Ordinary citizens had a far better chance of influencing legislators, by their votes
and their formal and informal petitions, than did the president. The living
and social spaces of Washington City mirrored the constitutional separation
of powers; until Dolley's tenure in the White House, the congressional communities had conducted a separate social life.[31]

When official channels fail or do not exist, however, social settings assume
an even greater importance. Dolley's soirees allowed James to interact with
congressmen and contributed mightily to the formation of the alliances and
structures that sent Congress into preeminence immediately following the
war. The emergence of "stars," such as Webster, Calhoun, and Clay, testifies
to the body's growing importance in the 1810s, but the less celebrated members' ability to build their own power structures also demonstrates the increasing influence of the legislature. This was a pivotal time in the development
of that institution, and Dolley played a part, both intended and unintended.
However, her primary motivation in establishing good relations with the
members of Congress undoubtedly stemmed from her desire to help her
husband.

Social events could cut both ways as a method of communication between
Congress and the executive branch. During the election of 1812 the Federalists decided to boycott Dolley's parties en masse as a show of solidarity against
James Madison. Republicans responded in kind, using attendance to make
their statement by flooding the President's House with their social presence.
Dolley saw the Federalists' act and another similar attempt by the Republican faction that supported DeWitt Clinton for president as attempts "to
break us." However, the social machinery Dolley set in place did its job, and
only a short while later she reported smugly that "such a rallying of our party
had alarmed [the Federalists] into a return."[32] Congressman John Harper
noted that nothing in the entire session had distressed and mortified the Federalists more than "finding that the Republicans, in consequence of their conduct, paid their respects to Mrs. Madison almost to a man."[33]

During her social events Dolley gathered and gave information, made
connections between people, and secured offices for her friends and family.
But her principal goal was to bind people to her and her husband, which she
did both by force of personality, a politician's greatest asset, and by willingness
to play politics. Contemporary observers agree that the "Lady Presidentess"

secured a second term for her husband by her social lobby.[34] James Madison was elected under the old system before congressional reforms, when the president was nominated or renominated by a party caucus, making the president a creation of Congress.[35] In this system cultivation of individual members made the difference, and that was Dolley's job. Among the members of the 1810 Congress, it was no coincidence that her closest new friend was the rising power Henry Clay, and she counted John C. Calhoun among her intimates as well. When Dolley and Henry Clay began sharing a snuff-box, they signaled their new political intimacy to insiders.[36]

Petticoat Politicking

Contemporaries and later writers often praised Dolley Madison for her "good heart" and told stories that showcased her generous, inclusive nature. For instance, Dolley has long been lauded for her welcome and tolerance of families and men of both parties at her social events. Jonathan Roberts, representative from Pennsylvania, commented: "Mrs. Madison has acted with singular discreetness during a very embarrassing season. By her deportment in her own house you cannot discover who is her husband's friends or foes."[37] To historians and biographers who have viewed this tolerance as a personal quality, her ability to welcome men of the rival party into her home, ignoring their public vilification of the president, was natural and certainly not political. For a wife who deeply loved her husband, a woman whose actions demonstrated her fierce loyalty and protective devotion, surely the natural response would have been to forbid those men to enter her door. Her ability to suppress anger and express warmth lay not in her good heart, though her personality provided a beguiling mask. She disguised her emotions, providing enemies with access to her, her husband, and other officials because she was a master politician. Her ability to create a bipartisan milieu of cooperation marks her as the member of the founding generation most like present-day politicians.

Such stories show that she foreshadowed a modern attitude toward politics, one that anticipated the need to negotiate within a two-party system. In an age characterized by "passion," by heated all-or-nothing rhetoric, Dolley's assumption that compromise would be the salvation of the system marks her as one of the most sophisticated politicians of her time. Power sharing and compromise—essentials for an effective democratic political culture—seemed inconceivable to the men who held office, but not to Dolley, who built coalitions and connections every week in her drawing rooms. Dolley's techniques, in some ways reminiscent of old-fashioned court styles, did not encompass violent expression, unlike the male political culture that incorporated dueling and fisticuffs on the floors of Congress.[38] Instead she accepted the inevitability of partisanship and used it to her husband's advantage.

During the war of 1812 Dolley intensified her efforts to create compromise, community, and united national sentiment by enlarging the scope of her parties. Her entertaining efforts became more purposeful in the months leading up to the invasion, as James Madison had to cope with enormous pressure from Congress and the country. Her parties gave an increasingly divided Congress a place to work out their troubles and presented a reassuring face to the American public. Her job was to keep the capital of the nation calm and hopeful, and she rallied her troops to the cause. Sarah Gales Seaton, wife and sister of the local newspaper editors, reported that Dolley had called on her to ensure her presence at the next drawing room, urging Gales Seaton, with a military metaphor, "not to desert the standard altogether."[39]

On the very day that the British invaded Washington City and Dolley ensured her husband's place in history by saving his cabinet papers and her own fame by rescuing the portrait of George Washington, she had prepared another in a series of dinner parties designed to reassure members of the Washington community. Ironically, the first White House's last moments were a social event; before they burned the building, the British commander and his officers sat and enjoyed her feast.

When Dolley and James Madison returned to the smoking ruins of the city a few days later, Dolley determined to rally the capital and the nation. Under impoverished conditions, she resumed her entertaining and her role as the charismatic figure of her husband's administration. As Congress convened to discuss whether or not to move the capital of the United States to another city, she enlisted her network of women from influential families to forestall this radical change. By her efforts the federal government managed to hang on long enough to reassert itself as the power center of the nation. By the end of her husband's administration, observers said that she was the most popular person in the United States. Dolley had succeeded in making the President's House and the capital city a presence in many Americans' minds. Her flight from the White House and her preservation of the icon of America set the tone of renewed patriotism and anchored the capital firmly in Washington.[40]

Conclusion

Even after Dolley and James set out for retirement at their Virginia estate, the social model Dolley had forged remained in Washington City. Its characteristics—the participation of women and families, the building of extraofficial structures in the absence of official ones, the focus on building coalitions and consensus among legislators, the growing relationship between the local and official communities—contributed to the institutionalization and growth of the government.

First ladies Elizabeth Monroe, who served from 1817 to 1825, and Louisa Adams, who occupied the position from 1825 to 1829, also used social events to strengthen and facilitate their husbands' respective presidencies. They, too, reigned as charismatic figures for their sober republican men, and they pushed the capital city closer to the model of European power centers. However, both Elizabeth and Louisa were limited in their roles by their husbands' weak presidencies—Monroe's by choice and Adams's by ill-fortune. Unlike Dolley, they were not able or willing to exploit their own power fully.

But the system set in place by Dolley had implications all the way down the political food chain. Women of political families at all levels grew increasingly important in the political culture of Washington City. Individually and in groups they contributed to the growth of Congress and the power of the cabinet. Through extensive patronage activities they literally staffed the halls of power. This era would end abruptly in 1829, when an outsider, Andrew Jackson, came to the White House without a wife and the ladies of Washington contended over his substitute, a local woman named Margaret Eaton. In an ironic negative proof of female influence, the "Peggy Eaton Affair" brought down the president's cabinet for the first and only time in United States history.[41]

Even in this brief treatment, it should be apparent that the unofficial office of first lady, like the office of president, is a historical phenomenon and changes over time. In the early nineteenth century, when Euro-American culture had not yet developed a clear delineation between a private sphere of home, emotion, and family and a public sphere of office, bureaucracy, and business, "work" happened in all arenas of life, especially in a town such as Washington. In a government with little mandated structure, the unofficial sphere proved as crucial as the official one.

The ideology of republicanism precluded the assertion of authority and legitimacy, as well as the institution and coalition building that the embryonic federal government required to grow and thrive. Using social events, Dolley Madison and other political women transmuted the abstractions and ideals of republicanism through selective borrowing from court culture. They adapted republicanism for political needs, created a governmental configuration, secured the capital, and, overall, moved the processes of democracy and government growth forward while providing legitimacy and an image of stability.

Paradoxically, women's work in the unofficial sphere also preserved republicanism in its purest form. By taking on the pragmatic work of politics, Dolley Madison and her set allowed their husbands and male kin—the official, public figures—to remain virtuous, struggling to maintain pure republicanism in an increasingly power-driven political system. But when republicanism failed as a practical system, as it would in the 1830s, the structures built by the political families of Washington would remain as the foundation for the future nation-state and a government based on the new notion of democracy.

Notes

1. Daniel Webster and Zachary Taylor cited in Paul F. Boller Jr., *Presidential Wives: An Anecdotal History* (New York: Oxford University Press, 1988), 43, 46.

2. There are some exceptions to this rule. Several fine studies of Dolley's work exist, though mostly in brief treatment. For a full-length work that is absorbing, though dated, see Ethel Stephens Arnett, *Mrs. James Madison: The Incomparable Dolley* (Greensboro, N.C.: Piedmont Press, 1972). For more modern treatments, see Holly Cowan Shulman, "Dolley (Payne Todd) Madison," in *American First Ladies: Their Lives and Their Legacy,* ed. Lewis L. Gould (New York: Garland, 1996), 45–68; and Carl Sferrazza Anthony, *First Ladies: The Saga of the Presidents' Wives and Their Power, 1789–1961,* vol. 1 (New York: Quill/William Morrow, 1991), 73–98.

3. The classic examination of government formation in early Washington City remains James Sterling Young's *The Washington Community, 1800–1828* (New York: Columbia University Press, 1966). The inclusion of women and gender analysis not available to Young deepens and enriches some of his key arguments.

4. For the uncertainty of the republican era, see John R. Howe Jr., "Republican Thought and Political Violence of the 1790s," *American Quarterly* 19 (summer 1967), 147–65; James Roger Sharp, *American Politics in the Early Republic: The New Nation in Crisis* (New Haven, Conn.: Yale University Press, 1993); Joanne B. Freeman, "Slander, Poison, Whispers, and Fame: Jefferson's 'Anas' and Political Gossip in the Early Republic," *Journal of the Early Republic* 15 (spring 1995), 25–27; and Marshall Smelser, "The Federalist Period as an Age of Passion," *American Quarterly* 10 (winter 1958): 391–419.

5. Thomas Jefferson to Joseph Priestley, 21 Mar. 1801, in Paul Leicester Ford, *The Writings of Thomas Jefferson* (New York: G. P. Putnam's, 1892–99), 8:21–23; Joseph J. Ellis, *American Sphinx: The Character of Thomas Jefferson* (New York: Alfred A. Knopf, 1993), 133, 184.

6. Lance Banning, *The Jeffersonian Persuasion: Evolution of a Party Ideology* (Ithaca, N.Y.: Cornell University Press, 1978), 59, 83, 201. The literature on republicanism and its role in the founding era is extensive, but Banning remains one of the best sources; see also Stanley Elkins and Eric McKitrick, *The Age of Federalism: The Early American Republic, 1788–1800* (New York: Oxford University Press, 1993), 6–21.

7. Thomas Jefferson to George Washington, 4 Dec. 1788, in Julian P. Boyd, *Papers of Thomas Jefferson* (1950; reprint, Princeton, N.J.: Princeton University Press, 1972), 14:330.

8. Young, *Washington Community,* 168, 190–91; Ellis, *American Sphinx,* 191; Joanne B. Freeman, "Jefferson and Political Combat" (presentation at "New Horizons in Jefferson Scholarship" conference, International Center for Jefferson Studies, Charlottesville, Va., 4–5 Oct. 1996). See also Andrew Burstein, *The Inner Jefferson: Portrait of a Grieving Optimist* (Charlottesville: University Press of Virginia, 1993), 223; and David S. Shields and Fredrika J. Teute, "Jefferson in Washington: Domesticating Manners in the Republican Court" (paper presented at the Institute of Early American History and Culture, Williamsburg, Va., 1997).

9. Samuel Latham Mitchill to Catharine Akerly Mitchill, 13 Feb. 1807, in "Dr. Mitchill's Letters from Washington, 1801–1813," *Harper's New Monthly Magazine* (Apr. 1879): 752; Carl Anthony, *First Ladies,* 80–81.

10. Margaret Brown Klapthor, *The First Ladies Cookbook* (New York: Parents' Magazine Press, 1969), 44; Margaret Bayard Smith to Susan B. Smith, Mar. 1809, in Margaret Bayard Smith Papers, Library of Congress. The season lasted from the first Wednesday in December until the middle of February. See Kathryn Allamong Jacob, *Capital Elites: High Society in Washington, DC, after the Civil War* (Washington, D.C.: Smithsonian Institution Press, 1995), 18.

11. Maud Wilder Goodwin, *Dolly Madison* (New York: Charles Scribner's Sons, 1896), 93.

12. Klapthor, *First Ladies Cookbook,* 45; Carl Anthony, *First Ladies,* 82; James S. Rosebush, *First Lady, Public Wife: A Behind-the-Scenes History of the Evolving Role of First Ladies in American Political Life* (Lanham, Md.: Madison Books, 1987), 72; Katharine Anthony, *Dolly Madison: Her Life and Times* (Garden City, N.J.: Doubleday, 1949), 197; Sarah Gales Seaton, "Diary," 12 Nov. 1812, in *William Winston Seaton and the National Intelligencer,* ed. Josephine Seaton, 85 (Boston: James R. Osgood, 1871).

13. Boller, *Presidential Wives,* 38; Seaton, "Diary," 85; Carl Anthony, *First Ladies,* 82.

14. Shulman, "Dolley," 56.

15. Richard L. Bushman, *The Refinement of America: Persons, Houses, Cities* (New York: Alfred A. Knopf, 1992), 96–97.

16. Ibid., 40.

17. For a detailed examination of this process, see Conover Hunt-Jones, *Dolley and the "Great Little Madison"* (Washington, D.C.: American Institute of Architects Press, 1977).

18. Shulman, "Dolley," 54.

19. Elizabeth Ellet, *Court Circles of the Republic* (Hartford, Conn.: Hartford Publishing Co., 1869), 83.

20. Frances Trollope, *Domestic Manners of the Americans* (Barre, Pa.: Imprint Society, 1969), 194–95.

21. Catharine Akerly Mitchill to Margaretta Akerly Miller, 8 Apr. 1806, in Catharine Akerly Mitchill Papers, Library of Congress.

22. Catharine Akerly Mitchill to Margaretta Akerly Miller, 11 Jan. 1809, 2 Jan. 1811, in Catharine Akerly Mitchill Papers, Library of Congress.

23. Margaret Bayard Smith to Jane Bayard Kirkpatrick, 13 Mar. 1814, in Margaret Bayard Smith Papers, Library of Congress.

24. Abijah Bigelow to Hannah Gardner Bigelow, 29 Dec. 1810, in "Letters of Abijah Bigelow, Member of Congress to His Wife, 1810–1815," *Proceedings of the American Antiquarian Society* 40 (Oct. 1930): 312; "Exiled in Yankeeland: The Journal of Mary Bagot, 1816–1819," in *Records of the Columbia Historical Society of Washington, D.C.,* ed. David Hosford (Washington, D.C.: Columbia Historical Society, 1984), 51:35.

25. David Truman, *The Governmental Process: Political Interests and Public Opinion* (New York: Alfred A. Knopf, 1971), 322, 324.

26. Betty Boyd Caroli, "The First Lady's Changing Role," in *The White House: The First Two Hundred Years,* ed. Frank Freidel and William Pencak (Boston: Northeastern University Press, 1994), 180.

27. Irving Brant, *James Madison: The President, 1809–1812* (Indianapolis, Ind.: Bobbs-Merrill, 1959), 99, 260, 435.

28. Sophia May, "Diary," 23 Apr. 1812, in Sophia May Papers, Library of Congress.

29. Dolley Payne Todd Madison to Anna Payne Cutts, 27 Mar. 1812, in *Life and Letters of Dolly Madison,* ed. Allen C. Clark (Washington, D.C.: W. F. Roberts, 1914), 130.

30. James Madison to Thomas Jefferson, 23 Apr. 1810, in *Papers of James Madison*, ed. Ellen J. Barber, David B. Mattern, J. C. A. Stagg, and Anne Mandeville Colony (Charlottesville: University Press of Virginia, 1992), 321.

31. Young, *Washington Community,* 150–57.

32. Dolley Payne Todd Madison to Anna Payne Cutts, 27 Mar. 1812, in Clark, *Life,* 130.

33. John A. Harper to William Plumer, 13 Apr. 1812, in Plumer Papers, Library of Congress.

34. The *National Intelligencer* on 4 Mar. 1809 called Dolley the "Presidentress" on inauguration day. Sen. Samuel Latham Mitchill referred to Dolley as both

prospective "Presidentress" and "Lady President" in his letters to his wife, Catharine Akerly Mitchill; see Samuel Latham Mitchill to Catharine Akerly Mitchill, 25 Jan. 1808, 23 Nov. 1807, in Catharine Akerly Mitchill Papers, Library of Congress.

35. Geraldine Brooks, *Dames and Daughters of the Young Republic* (New York: Thomas Y. Crowell and Co., 1901), 31; Margaret Truman, *First Ladies: An Intimate Group Portrait of White House Wives* (New York: Random House, 1995), 21; Marshall Smelser, *The Democratic Republic, 1810–1815* (New York: Harper & Row, 1968), 318.

36. Carl Anthony, *First Ladies,* 86–88; Katharine Anthony, *Dolly Madison,* 212; Arnett, *Mrs. James Madison,* 111; Boller, *Presidential Wives,* 46; Brant, *James Madison,* 452–59; Betty Boyd Caroli, *First Ladies* (New York: Oxford University Press, 1987), 15–16; Bess Furman, *White House Profile* (New York: Bobbs-Merrill, 1951), 61, 68; Goodwin, *Dolly Madison,* 93, 142; Marianne Means, *The Woman in the White House: The Lives, Time and Influence of Twelve Notable First Ladies* (New York: Random House, 1963), 70.

37. Jonathan Roberts, cited in Linda Grant DePauw and Conover Hunt, *"Remember the Ladies": Women in America, 1750–1815* (New York: Viking Press, 1976), 140.

38. Joanne B. Freeman, "Dueling as Politics: Reinterpreting the Burr-Hamilton Duel," *William and Mary Quarterly* 53 (Apr. 1996): 289–318.

39. Sarah Gales Seaton describes a drawing room in early November the year the war was declared; see Seaton, "Diary," 84.

40. Arnett, *Mrs. James Madison,* 194; Furman, *White House Profile,* 72; Goodwin, *Dolly Madison,* 188; Charles Hurd, *Washington Cavalcade* (New York: E. P. Dutton, 1948), 50; Rosebush, *First Lady,* 54; Truman, *First Ladies,* 27.

41. For more on the female political culture of the early capital, see Catherine Allgor, *Parlor Politics: In Which the Ladies of Washington City Help Build a City and a Government* (Charlottesville: University Press of Virginia, 2000).

THREE

Betty Ford and the Transformation
of the Role of First Lady

MARY LINEHAN

INTRODUCTION

It was not easy to be a political wife in the 1970s. The assistant to one woman explained, "When the candidate can't be there, she is expected to give the speech and know the issue. When he is there, she is expected to cross her legs at the ankles and listen adoringly."[1] Subjected to intense public scrutiny, often ignored by ambitious husbands, and forced to tread the thin line between subservient helpmate and shrewd political operative, many political wives cracked under pressure. In 1973, after years of neglect, Angelina Alioto, wife of the San Francisco mayor, disappeared for seventeen days without telling anyone where she was going. Joan Kennedy's personal problems with depression and alcohol helped drive the leading Democratic contender out of the 1976 presidential race. The same year Margaret Trudeau, wife of the Canadian prime minister, was hospitalized under psychiatric care for emotional stress.

First ladies faced particular strains. One writer described the pressures inflicted upon presidential spouses, "forcing them into the mold of superwife and supermother, which always seems to mean keeping their mouths shut, their arms open, and their personal opinions carefully hidden."[2] Yet Betty Ford, the accidental first lady who served this nation at a time of unprecedented crisis (August 1974 to January 1977), managed to resist this pressure. She made the personal political, creating new options for women and for political wives. In so doing, she transformed the role of first lady.

Betty Ford brought about this transformation in three stages. First, through her courageous response to personal misfortune she realized the untapped potential of the office of first lady. Second, through her willingness to speak candidly and express opinions that resonated with American women she brought their private concerns onto the national stage. Finally, through her own political activism on behalf of controversial issues she challenged the traditional boundaries of what a first lady should do and what she could accomplish.

BACKGROUND

Born Elizabeth Bloomer in Chicago on 8 April 1918, she was two when her salesman father moved the family to Grand Rapids, Michigan. A young athlete, Betty used her fists to defend herself against boys who teased "Betty Pants." At age eight she enrolled in the Calla Travis School of Dance. Her natural talent soon emerged, and by age fourteen she was a teacher at the school.

After she graduated from Central High School, Betty spent summers studying dance at Bennington College in Vermont. The new school differed from traditional colleges of the 1930s in encouraging women to have careers. At twenty, Betty moved to New York to dance with famed choreographer Martha Graham. Supporting herself as a fashion model, she earned a place in Graham's Concert Group and performed at Carnegie Hall.

Betty's mother continued to pressure her to return home and marry. After two years in New York the dancer relented and returned to Michigan. Betty took a position as fashion coordinator at Herpolsheimer's department store. After work she taught dance to the deaf and to disadvantaged children. She caused a small scandal by staging a liturgical dance in a Baptist church. Also controversial in the conservative city was the fact that Betty joined the local branch of the National Association for the Advancement of Colored People. More in keeping with convention, in 1942 she married furniture salesman William Warren. The marriage quickly disintegrated, and the independent Betty Bloomer accepted only a token alimony of one dollar.

Shortly thereafter she met Gerald Ford, an up-and-coming attorney who had a brilliant record as a college athlete and navy officer. He was thirty-five and she thirty when they married on 15 October 1948. Ford had already broken into politics by winning an upset in the Republican congressional primary, and Betty instantly found herself in the role of political wife. The candidate even arrived late for the wedding ceremony because he was stumping for votes. The Fords' two-day honeymoon included campaigning at a University of Michigan football game and greeting supporters at a reception for Republican presidential nominee Thomas Dewey.

With Gerald Ford's election to Congress, the Fords moved to Alexandria, Virginia. During the 1950s, as he moved up the party ranks, she gave birth to three sons and a daughter. As a conventional suburban mother she served as a Boy Scout den mother, a fund-raiser for the Parent Teacher Association, and a Sunday school teacher. Betty Ford also supported her husband's career by working at his office, mailing campaign literature, hostessing, and standing by his side at innumerable official functions. She also participated in the Congressional Wives Club, volunteering at a children's hospital.

THE NATIONAL POLITICAL STAGE

In 1965 Betty Ford's husband became House minority leader and the demands on her increased. Gerald Ford wanted to be Speaker of the House. This ambition rested on electing a majority of Republicans. Thus, Ford began traveling two hundred days a year politicking for party candidates. Not only did this leave Betty to be both mother and father to four growing children, but it also required her to adapt to an increased political agenda. As she explained, "When Jerry became Minority Leader, I felt it was my duty to get the Republican wives out and make them active."[3]

Family and political obligations wore on, and in 1970 she sought psychiatric help to deal with the stress. Her therapist told her to express her feelings and get her frustrations out into the open. He taught her not to give up everything for her husband and children and to think about the things that mattered to her. The Fords discussed the situation and concluded that he would run for Congress one more time in 1974 and then retire. Gerald Ford later told reporters that he had taken an "oath in blood" to keep his promise to his wife.[4] Once again the obligations of public service interfered with Betty Ford's personal wishes. On 12 October 1973 President Richard Nixon nominated Gerald Ford to fill the unexpired term of vice president Spiro Agnew, who had been forced to resign amid allegations of corruption. Given the scandal, Ford believed that he owed it to his party and the nation to accept the appointment and restore dignity to the office.[5]

A new Betty Ford began to emerge as "second lady." Having benefited from therapy, and believing the vice presidency to be the last stage of her husband's political career, she felt freer to speak her own mind and make her own decisions. When Martin Luther King Jr. was murdered, the Nixon administration failed to respond. Outraged, Betty insisted that she be sent to the funeral as an official representative. She also gave over two hundred interviews in less than a year, establishing her reputation for candor. "I've been asked everything except how often I go to bed with my husband," she said, "and if they had asked me I would have told them."[6] As accusations of scandal in the Nixon administration mounted, Betty was often asked if she would like to be first lady. She always responded "no." Not only did she think impeachment or resignation bad for the nation, but she also had a personal reason; she admitted, "For a few years I wanted Jerry to myself."[7] However, once again politics disrupted Betty Ford's plan.

On 9 August 1974 Richard Nixon resigned, making Gerald Ford the first nonelected president of the United States. He was also the first president to mention the first lady in an inaugural address. Claiming, "I am indebted to no man and only to one woman—my dear wife Betty—as I begin the most difficult job in the world," Ford not only reassured a scandal-weary nation, but he also foreshadowed Betty Ford's groundbreaking role in his administration.[8] As she said, "I really felt like I was taking that oath too."[9] In the next 895 days Betty Ford transformed the role of the first lady by recognizing the office's potential power and using that power to help others. She made women's personal concerns public issues and publicly advocated the issues she believed in.

PUBLIC AND PERSONAL SPACE

From the start of her tenure as first lady, Betty Ford needed to respond in a public way to a series of personal misfortunes. This experience introduced her to the possibilities of a first lady's power. The Washington press corps, invigorated by the Watergate investigation and looking for scandal, accorded her less privacy than first ladies customarily received.[10] News of her divorce (she was only the second divorcee in the White House) caused a small sensation. Ford responded calmly and directly, dismissing her first marriage as "something I could have easily skipped" except that it helped her appreciate a good husband when she found one.[11] Likewise, she diffused the furor over her past psychiatric treatment by admitting, "I'd just sit and talk and it seemed to help. After all, if you have an abscessed tooth, you go to the dentist, don't you?"[12] Betty's honesty shocked reporters and Americans used to evasion from public officials. As the clamor over her divorce and therapy rapidly dissipated, Betty Ford recognized the power of her candor and her position. She would soon use this power to change lives.

On Thursday, 26 September 1974 the first lady saw her physician for a routine gynecological exam. He discovered a lump in her right breast and wanted to perform an immediate biopsy. Even though she suspected malignancy, Betty insisted on keeping her official commitments before undergoing treatment. Friday she presided over a Salvation Army luncheon, joined the president in dedicating a memorial to Lyndon Johnson, and entertained the Johnson family in the private quarters of the White House before entering the hospital. In a three-hour procedure Saturday morning, the doctor determined that the lump was cancerous and removed the entire right breast, its underlying pectoral muscle, and the lymphoid tissue in the adjacent armpit.

At the time cancer—particularly cancer of the sexual or reproductive organs—was not widely discussed. Cancer patients bore the stigma of victims of a poorly understood, possibly lethal disease. Female maladies were also shrouded in secrecy.[13] Yet Betty Ford honestly spoke out about her illness and mastectomy. News reports of Ford's operation indicated the horrific perceptions of breast cancer. *Time* claimed, "Of the hundreds of malignancies that affect the human race, cancer of the female breast is perhaps the most widely feared."[14] *Newsweek* charged that the first lady was "living every woman's worst nightmare." They questioned how she would cope with "the universal depression felt by mastectomy patients because of the damage to their sense of themselves . . . [and] the disfigurement."[15] Statistics bore out the gravity of the situation. Ninety thousand new cases of breast cancer were diagnosed in 1974, and more than one-third of those women died from the disease. Indeed, at the time the mortality rate for breast cancer had not dropped in thirty-five years.

Betty Ford did not surrender to the grim prognosis. Rather, she viewed her illness as a "blessing in disguise."[16] She already knew that her public honesty had quieted the uproar over her divorce and therapy, so she now determined to use that public honesty to reduce the stigma and shame associated with breast cancer and encourage women to get medical care. The first lady later reflected, "Lying in the hospital . . . I'd come to recognize more clearly the power of the woman in the White House. Not my power, but the power of the position, a power which could be used to help."[17] Accordingly, every step of the first lady's treatment and recovery was opened to public scrutiny. While she was still on the operating table the White House assembled a team of doctors for a thorough and technical briefing. Not twenty years earlier the Eisenhower administration had refused to use the word *hysterectomy* in describing the first lady's surgery, but Betty Ford made *mastectomy* a household word.[18]

As she recovered, Betty took an increasingly active role in promoting women's health and advocating awareness for cancer patients. She explained, "I realized there must be many women across the country who had the same thing I had and were either ignoring it or were oblivious to it. I thought if I spoke out, I might be able to help those women."[19] In 1975 she served as honorary chair of the American Cancer Society campaign.

Betty also gave a lengthy and unusual interview to *McCall's* in which she addressed women's fears about breast cancer. She answered women's most personal concerns, providing a public forum for information women could not find—or were too bashful to seek—elsewhere. Betty acknowledged the stigma but insisted that she did not feel "ashamed or dirty" because of her experience. She told women exactly what a mastectomy meant, what the options were, how a self-exam and regular medical care led to early detection, and what chemotherapy involved. Ford assured women that prostheses were available—"all you need is a little foam rubber"—and looked natural. She discussed her "typical" postoperative depression and empathized with women's need to be strong for their families. She explained that husbands would be "adult" enough to cope and that women did not need to feel mutilated or ugly because of their scars. Above all, she told women not to blame themselves, stating, "I accept it as one of those things that can happen to women in the course of . . . life."[20]

Betty Ford's courageous revelations encouraged increased numbers of women to go to clinics and doctors for cancer screens. The American Cancer Society reported a 400 percent increase in requests for checkups. Happy Rockefeller, wife of the vice president, was one of the thousands whose life was saved by Betty's decision to go public with her experience. A woman from Little Rock, Arkansas, wrote to the first lady: "Your going into the hospital and being so brave about having breast surgery has prompted me to do what I should have done long ago. I have a lump in my left breast and have put it off for too long. . . . Until now I have been too afraid."[21] So many women rushed to get mammograms that the cancer rate surged, indicating a higher incidence of early detection. Cancer researchers dubbed this the Betty Ford Phenomenon.

Through her personal misfortunes Betty Ford learned how a first lady's power could be used in the service of others. This was the key first step in changing the role of the president's spouse and opening new options for political wives. In the second step, Ford used her office as a forum to express the needs and concerns of American women and to bring those personal issues into the political discourse. While not all women shared the first lady's opinions, they appreciated her honesty and her ability to bring public attention to women's interests.

PUBLIC FORUM, PUBLIC VOICE

On 4 September 1974 Betty Ford held her first press conference. Nearly 150 reporters, women and men, attended the candid briefing. In a manner unusual for first ladies, she fielded controversial questions. Betty reaffirmed her commitment to reproductive rights, even for teenagers. When pressed,

Betty admitted that this was a "risky" answer but added, "I couldn't lie. That's the way I feel."[22] She also claimed that she would be happy to be a part of any campaign to achieve ratification of the Equal Rights Amendment (ERA) and encouraged women's political activism as a way to prevent future wars. Finally, reflecting the concern of mothers everywhere, Betty explained how she managed her family budget in inflationary times.

The following year the first lady solidified her reputation as a genuinely honest public figure and as an American mother concerned about the issues of the day. On 21 August 1975 Betty Ford appeared on the television program *60 Minutes*. She repeated her support of abortion rights, calling the recent *Roe v. Wade* ruling a "great, great decision." When reporter Morley Safer asked about marijuana, Betty admitted that she assumed her children had tried it and that she probably would have tried it herself if it had been around when she was young. Asked about the increasing tendency for couples to live together without marriage, she replied, "It's a disappointment to me, but I have to realize this is a different generation. Maybe they're smarter than we were." Finally, Safer inquired as to what her reaction would be if her eighteen-year-old daughter confided that she was having an affair. The first lady responded honestly, "I wouldn't be surprised. I think she's a perfectly normal human being. . . . I would certainly counsel and advise her . . . [but] she's a big girl."[23]

The immediate reaction to the *60 Minutes* interview was condemnation of the first lady and her progressive views. Criticism came from the Women's Christian Temperance Union, the Los Angeles Police Department, and the *Manchester (New Hampshire) Union-Leader,* among others. Conservative commentator William F. Buckley charged that Betty had abused her husband's power. A widely circulated cartoon showed a chagrined president with his hand on her mouth silencing the first lady. A Chicago man asked, "If Jerry Ford can't control his wife, how can he run the country?" Officials of the Mormon, Quaker, and Catholic religions voiced opposition, and the pastor of the largest Southern Baptist congregation declared himself "aghast." He added: "I cannot think that the first lady of this land would descend to such a gutter type mentality. For her to offer her own daughter in this kind of illicit sexual relationship with a man is unthinkable. Her own daughter!"[24]

Betty seemed slightly disconcerted by the criticism, but she did not back away from her comments. She explained that it was not in her nature to dodge questions or give an evasive answer. She was troubled, though, that some people did not understand that she was discussing her daughter's sex life in hypothetical terms.[25] Her husband, she reported, threw a pillow at her during the telecast but otherwise applauded her candor and "encourage[d] me to do my own thing."[26] This involved providing a public voice for the private problems of American mothers.

Overall, Betty Ford expressed satisfaction with the interview. She thoughtfully tried to answer the questions as a mother who loved her children and understood the not-so-simple times in which they were growing up.[27] She had used the power of her position to bring attention to the changing social behaviors and norms that concerned women. Many women, surveys indicated, felt trapped between the morality of their mothers and the very different standards of their daughters. In her *60 Minutes* interview the first lady focused attention on the conflicts—abortion, drugs, premarital sex—that mothers were forced to confront in the wake of the 1960s youth revolution. She made these private concerns national issues and comforted women by assuring them that even the first family faced the same intergenerational strife their families did.

But Betty Ford went even further in promoting the cause of American mothers. She argued that homemakers did not receive proper respect or appreciation for what they did, a conclusion drawn in her years as a suburban mother. The first lady advocated improving the lives of mothers to strengthen the families. She called for government-regulated day-care centers to give mothers respite from their children. Valuing a housewife's contribution to the family at thirty thousand dollars, she argued that women should be entitled to Social Security benefits. Above all, she argued against women's groups ignoring or discounting the choices made by homemakers. The first lady, who had been both a career woman and a homemaker, insisted: "A liberated woman is one who feels confident in herself and is happy in what she is doing. A woman who is satisfied with her life at home is just as liberated as a woman with a career outside the home."[28]

The mothers of America enthusiastically supported Betty's willingness to speak out on their issues and on their behalf. "AT LAST, A REAL FIRST LADY!" exclaimed one telegram to the White House, where mail ran about evenly for and against Betty's *60 Minutes* remarks. Feminist leader Betty Friedan wrote to the first lady, "Your sensitivity and strength are going to be a wonderful boost for millions of mothers and daughters and American women generally."[29]

Indeed, a *Ladies' Home Journal* poll of mothers in eight American cities —including conservative Grand Rapids, Michigan—found that more than two-thirds of mothers approved of the first lady's interview comments. Advice and household hints columnist Heloise offered an explanation for this spirited response: "The girls love the way she comes out and says what she thinks. They feel as if she's their next-door neighbor, just one of the bunch. She doesn't seem a bit stuck up." *Good Housekeeping* ranked Betty Ford the most admired woman in America, and *People* chose her as one of the country's "Three Most Intriguing People." While a Harris poll gauged the president's approval rating at only 36 percent, it concluded, "Betty Ford has now become one of the most popular wives of a President." Sixty-seven percent of respondents endorsed her outspokenness on controversial issues. Another indication of Ford's growing popularity were the blue-and-white "Betty's Husband for President in '76" buttons, which appeared a full year before the election.[30]

Time chose Betty Ford as one of eleven women selected as "Man of the Year" in 1975.[31] *Newsweek* also took note of the first lady's accomplishments. In honoring her as Woman of the Year in 1975, the *Newsweek* cited Betty's sixteen-month saga of courage, candor, and exuberance for changing the way many Americans thought about their first ladies. The editors claimed: "Not since Eleanor Roosevelt championed civil rights and organized labor in the 1930s has a First Lady spoken out more freely—or aroused more controversy. In a year when women are continuing their climb into public visibility, Betty Ford seems to be the symbolic Woman of the Year."[32]

POLITICAL ACTIVIST

Betty Ford is credited with politicizing members of the administration, including the president, to support women's rights.[33] Before becoming president, Mr. Ford scored zero on women's issues two years in a row in a congressional tally compiled by the *Woman Activist,* a respected feminist publication.[34] These votes were attributed to his conservative home district. But during his first month in office he showed that his presidential record would be different. Pledging his commitment to women's rights, Ford told an audience of federal appointees that his wife was a tough "taskmaster" who would see that he followed through.[35]

On 25 August 1974 the president declared "Women's Equity Day" and urged passage of the Equal Rights Amendment. The following week he appointed Mary Louise Smith to replace George Bush as chair of the Republican National Committee and held a special meeting with thirteen congresswomen who were supporting the Equal Rights Amendment.[36] During his short presidency Gerald Ford nominated twenty-one women to posts requiring Senate approval. These included several commission heads, federal judges in important districts, and secretary of housing and urban development Carla

Anderson Hills. Even though she did not always get her way, Betty Ford took credit for her husband's new commitment to women and their issues. She explained, "If he doesn't get it in the office during the day, he gets it in the ribs at night."[37]

Betty Ford did not limit her activism to the pillow talk traditionally employed by political wives. She spoke out and publicly campaigned on behalf of the causes she believed in. She addressed the National Council of Negro Women in 1974, promising "to take to the stump" against racism and sexism, "even if I have to build my own."[38] The following year the first lady championed the progressive National Black Women's Agenda. She also became the first first lady, and one of the first public figures, to support gay rights. She claimed: "I do think lesbians are entitled to free speech, the same as anyone else. God put us all here for his own purposes; it's not my business to try and second-guess Him, and I think Anita Bryant's taking action against the gay population was ill-considered. I don't think people should lose their jobs because of sexual preference."[39] The first lady also supported gun control—"I never thought guns were something people should have casually around"—a public issue made personal after two assassination attempts on her husband's life.[40]

Betty Ford's most energetic, and controversial, campaign was on behalf of the Equal Rights Amendment. Introduced in Congress for the first time in 1923, the version approved in 1972 stated: "Equality of rights under the Constitution shall not be denied or abridged by the United States or by any State on account of sex." When the Fords entered the White House, the amendment had been ratified by thirty-four states, four short of the necessary three-fourths majority required for ratification. The first lady focused her efforts on rallying support for the ERA in those states where the amendment had not yet been ratified.

In September 1974 Betty attended a fund-raising luncheon in Illinois for fourteen women running for statewide office. She told a large and enthusiastic audience, "I like what I see of women-power Illinois style. . . . We have all come a long way, and we have a long way to go, too. . . . It's important to elect qualified women to represent us in office." Although the sole purpose of her trip was to draw attention to the women candidates, she spoke on behalf of the ERA both in her speech and when interviewed by the local media. The amendment strongly divided Republicans in Illinois, but the state was considered critical by ERA advocates and targeted for ratification in 1975. One of the women candidates noted the importance of the first lady's efforts in the state: "I think Mrs. Ford's support will have a definite impact. Until

she spoke out, many women in Illinois thought the ERA was a bad thing.
... Women's rights have been viewed here as a little un-Republican, slightly
radical. I think Mrs. Ford's backing lends it credibility."[41]

The positive reception in Illinois touched the first lady in a personal way.
As she said, "This does a lot for the ego. It gives me an independence after
years of just coping."[42] After years of depression and neglect as a political
wife, first lady Betty Ford found a satisfying political role for herself. It
became her mission to speed up passage of the Equal Rights Amendment,
and she did so with a zest for public action not seen in the first ladyship since
Eleanor Roosevelt.

Betty Ford's activism became controversial as soon as she began to
approach elected officials on behalf of the ERA. In January 1975 she wrote
to William Kretschmar thanking him for leading the fight for ratification in
the North Dakota House of Representatives. Kretschmar used this letter to
bring off a victory. Pleased by this success, she placed calls to state legislators
in Illinois, where the ERA finally got out of committee; to Nevada, where it
was subsequently passed by the assembly but defeated in the senate; and
to Missouri, where the amendment passed in the house. Using "a very soft
sell," she promoted ratification in Arizona and Georgia. Betty explained her
approach: "I merely asked that the amendment be allowed to get to the floor
and to let the people vote their conscience."[43]

In spite of her subtle approach, Betty's lobbying caused a conservative
uproar. Watching television one night, the Fords saw a funereal procession of
black-clad women chanting "Betty Ford will be remembered as the unelected
First Lady who pressured a second-rate manhood on American women."
The Fords claimed that they laughed at the display. Women also picketed
the White House with placards reading "BETTY FORD, GET OFF THE
PHONE." The Fords proudly noted that this was the first protest march
organized against a first lady.[44]

Criticism also came from Phyllis Schlafly, a conservative Republican and
leader of the Stop-ERA forces. She accused Betty of not understanding that
the amendment would lead to coed bathrooms and the military draft for
teenage girls. The First Lady offered a light-hearted response to Schlafly's
(erroneous) charges: "They've had coed facilities in Asia for years and if men
have to serve in the military, I don't see why women shouldn't too, the way
they do in Israel. Why, if this had been an issue in my own time, I'd probably have been the first to enlist."[45]

One might speculate that Betty's breezy response to her critics came from
her growing pleasure in the political power she now wielded. A reporter

who interviewed the first lady in the fall of 1975 noted, "She mentions the word 'power' more than once and speaks with pride, for example, of the clout her name now brings." Betty offered a simple defense of her politicking: There was no reason why the first lady could not promote causes, "like any other woman," and she was proud of the good she accomplished.[46]

In her support of the ERA and in her advocacy of women's issues, she took satisfaction in creating expanded options for political wives, freeing others from the anomie she once experienced. She was touched by one letter from a congressional wife, who wrote, "No American has the right to ask another to silence her opinions—even if that person is her husband and a politician. I have fought for this right with my husband. . . . You are setting an example for me to continue that fight."[47] Once again Betty Ford made the personal political and used her power as first lady to help and inspire women.

Nonetheless, the battle to ratify the ERA dragged on into 1976. Betty remained committed to the cause and to bridging the divide that was believed to exist between employed women and homemakers. She championed equal pay for equal work and publicized the fact that Congress had discriminatory pay scales for women staffers. At the same time, however, she refused to surrender homemakers to the stop-ERA faction. Betty stated, "Phyllis Schlafly has her great motherhood thing. I've been through motherhood. I think it's marvelous. But I'm not so sure mothers shouldn't have *rights*. Equal acceptance of women is so important. And there is no better time than our two-hundredth anniversary."[48]

Betty tried to link her bicentennial-year appearances to the ERA issue. On 29 June 1976 she opened a museum exhibit entitled "Remember the Ladies: Women in America, 1750–1815," the title of which was taken from Abigail Adams's famous letter to her husband. The first lady told the crowd, "I look forward to the day when the wish of Abigail Adams is answered . . . this exhibit is dedicated to those neglected Americans . . . those forgotten ladies . . . who gave us the strength and courage . . . to seek equal rights for women today." When asked to name the most "meaningful" American to her, Betty chose woman suffrage pioneer Susan B. Anthony for her convictions, conscience, and courage.[49]

The first lady's strong advocacy of the ERA during the bicentennial year alarmed presidential advisers who hoped to get Gerald Ford elected president in 1976. Notwithstanding her strong showing in popularity polls, her political value was questionable. Would she attract voters as a symbol of new attitudes toward women or would she repel them as a first lady who overstepped traditional boundaries?[50]

For several reasons, the advisers' initial response was to consider the outspoken first lady a liability.[51] First, they recalled allegations that Gerald Ford could not "control" his wife, and they worried that this would cost the president votes among conservative voters. Second, because the Fords disagreed on several key issues—reproductive rights, the Vietnam War, and a financial bailout of New York City—they were afraid the first lady could not get her husband's message across. This was particularly true after she admitted to splitting her ticket on occasion to vote for Democrats. Third, Nancy Reagan and Helen Jackson—the wives of two leading primary contenders—quickly went on record stating that presidential spouses should not play a political role.[52] Thus, even as Betty Ford told *Newsweek* that she was eager to campaign independently, the president's advisers were hoping to restrict her appearances.

THE CAMPAIGNER

The vigor with which Betty Ford supported her causes and her resentment at Ronald Reagan's challenge to Gerald Ford for the Republican nomination compelled the first lady to make a commanding place for herself in the campaign. She announced that if her husband were elected, she would "amplify" her role. Betty identified her own platform and promised to work for the ERA, social security for homemakers, civil rights, a salary for future first ladies, and such traditional causes as senior citizens, mental retardation, and the arts.[53]

Betty took offense at the Reagans' divisive campaign for the nomination, which forced the president and his supporters to spend ten months and large sums of money on a bitter interparty contest. She believed that this could only hurt the Republicans in the general election. Nancy Reagan, moreover, represented the old-style political wife. Mrs. Reagan opposed the ERA, campaigned only at her husband's side, and insisted that her own political beliefs did not matter. Once again Betty Ford's political views intersected with her personal opinions, and she lashed out at her opponent with customary candor: "I just think when Nancy met Ronnie, that was it as far as her own life was concerned. She just fell apart at the seams."[54]

Because of the strong Reagan challenge, Gerald Ford's advisers were forced to send the first lady on independent campaign trips in order to cover as many primary states as possible. The first test of her effectiveness came in New Hampshire, where although she stirred interest among voters, she confined her efforts to such "safe" activities as a visit to a workshop for the mentally retarded and a meeting with senior citizens. When the president won the primary, one adviser was forced to concede, "She was a great asset to him. She got him votes from a lot of people who empathized with her but aren't favorable to some of the President's stands."[55]

Betty carried her strong convictions into Florida, where she addressed a patriotic rally, visited an elementary school, appeared at a cultural center, and attended a university dinner. Though she appeared before traditional Republican audiences and spoke primarily about her husband, the first lady also managed to work in advocacy of her causes. The president's advisers came to see this as a definite asset to the campaign, believing that the voters enjoyed her willingness to discuss issues that many people faced. Supporting this belief was the increased popularity of "I LOVE BETTY," "KEEP BETTY IN THE HOUSE," and "BETTY'S HUSBAND FOR PRESIDENT" buttons.[56]

Together, Betty and Gerald Ford beat back the Reagan challenge and captured the Republican nomination. They moved on to contest Jimmy and Rosalynn Carter in the presidential election. Pollsters predicted a close race, and *U.S. News and World Report* claimed, "In a tight race it could be the wives who will swing the election one way or another."[57] Although it amazed Betty when Rosalynn Carter signed her name "Mrs. Jimmy Carter," the wife of the Democratic candidate also supported the ERA. The Carter campaign was sufficiently confident of Mrs. Carter's effectiveness to charter, from their limited funds, two six-seater jets so as to keep the potential first lady on the road campaigning virtually all the time.

The less-organized Ford campaign repeated its early primary strategy and began the general election race by downplaying the independence of the first lady. It was announced that she would campaign only at her husband's side. A flurry of interviews attempted to portray a softer, gentler first lady. In 1975 Betty Ford had been selected Woman of the Year. In 1976 voters saw a more traditional Betty Ford who loved her mother, decorated with seasonal fruits and vegetables, dieted on celery and cottage cheese, and made "sensational" fashion choices. *McCall's* even attributed a very uncharacteristic quote —"the role of the politician's wife, in my mind, is to be a very understanding woman who stands behind her husband and supports him in every way she possibly can"—to the newly traditional First Lady.[58]

It was not long, however, before Betty rebelled and reverted to her candid and independent self. She accompanied her husband on some campaign jaunts but also took off on her own. In Pittsburgh, for example, she paid a surprise visit to a working-class neighborhood on the city's south side to participate in a Republican voter registration drive in one heavily Democratic precinct. In the rain she went door-to-door canvassing homemakers. She received a huge welcome from women, who responded to her unpretentious greeting, "Hi, I'm Betty Ford." Taking advantage of the popularity of citizen band radios, she adopted the handle "First Mama" and electioneered among truckers. When the American ambassador in Lebanon was assassinated, the first lady stepped in for the president and gave a major address to a rally in Des Moines, Iowa. As the election neared, she was almost continuously on the road. During the week of 10 October 1976, for example, there was a fund-raiser in Los Angeles on Thursday, a "People for Ford" rally on the steps of the state capitol in Seattle on Friday, and a reception in Denver on Friday night. Wherever she went Betty met with the local press to answer questions about her husband's agenda as well as her own.[59]

Ever outspoken, the first lady did not hesitate to speak her mind about the conduct of the Ford campaign. She publicly acknowledged that she disagreed with the president's choice of Robert Dole for vice president. Ford would have preferred Ambassador Anne Armstrong. The president later admitted that he came "very close" to choosing Armstrong as the first woman on a major party ticket.[60] Betty Ford was equally blunt about the flaws in the campaign. She told *Time* that while she did not know who was to blame— "maybe the President himself"—the campaign was poorly organized and the staff "not good enough."[61] The first lady found it frustrating to go into states to campaign and learn that "zilch" had been done to prepare for her visit. For instance, six days before she was to arrive for a four-day campaign trip in Texas, only one event had been scheduled. Only a quarter of the seats were filled for a "Stand Up for America" rally in Florida.[62] As a result of such gaffes, American voters received the erroneous impression that the president lacked popular approval. Gerald Ford took his wife's advice when she encouraged him to shake up his staff, and he gave her credit for the amazing comeback that nearly won him the election.[63]

Conclusion

The final public memory of Betty Ford as first lady came the day after the election when she stood in the White House briefing room and gave the concession speech for her husband, who had lost his voice in the exhausting last days of the campaign. "The President," she said with grace and composure, "wants to thank all those thousands of people who worked so hard on his behalf.... The President urges all Americans to join him in giving your united support to President-Elect Carter."[64] Thus, a thirty-month administration that began with the first tribute to a first lady in an inaugural address ended with the first concession speech delivered by a presidential spouse.

In that short time Betty Ford transformed the role of first lady. Immediately her candor was a balm to a nation weary of governmental lies and cover-ups. In the long term her honesty and willingness to take a public stand on important issues paved the way for her successors to assert their own opinions, to influence policy, and to express their own identities in the nation's most public marriages.

The women who immediately preceded Betty Ford as first lady—Jacqueline Kennedy, Lady Bird Johnson, and Pat Nixon—took on issues of personal interest. Yet restoration of the White House, highway beautification, and volunteerism were hardly the burning questions of the day. They remained silent on issues such as Vietnam, civil rights, and the women's movement. Moreover, through insensitivity or chauvinism, some earlier presidents kept their wives isolated from the critical activities of the West Wing of the White House.

The Ford years, by contrast, were ones of transition. The first lady took on controversial issues, and the president proudly admitted taking her advice on controversial matters. This partnership model was emulated by their successors. Rosalynn Carter's support of the Equal Rights Amendment followed Betty Ford's example. Her fact-finding mission to South America and her advocacy of mental health issues also expanded that example. Nancy Reagan used private moments to lobby her husband on public issues; she publicly challenged the loyalty of the presidential staff; and with her husband, she brought new intensity to the Fords' partnership model. Though she never expressed views that were at odds with her husband's, Barbara Bush's willingness to be herself—mature, gray-haired, normal-sized—recalled Betty Ford's desire to be "just me." Certainly the Clintons' "two-for-one" presidency draws from the Fords' partnership model, and Hillary's forceful stand on public issues echoes Betty Ford's understanding of the first lady's political responsibilities.

Through her courageous response to breast cancer—and later triumph over alcohol and drug addiction—she realized the untapped potential of the Office of the First Lady. Through her willingness to speak candidly about reproductive rights, recreational drugs, premarital sex, the demeaning of the housewife, and other issues that resounded with American women, Betty Ford brought their private concerns onto the national stage. Through her advocacy of the Equal Rights Amendment and her active campaigning on behalf of her husband, Betty Ford challenged the conventional wisdom of what a political wife should do and could accomplish. In so doing, Betty Ford transformed the office in a way that gave greater autonomy, influence, and power to first ladies.

NOTES

1. "The Relentless Ordeal of Political Wives," *Time* 104 (7 Oct. 1974): 16.

2. James T. Baker, "To the Former Miss Betty Bloomer of Grand Rapids," *Christian Century* 93 (13 Oct. 1976): 864.

3. Nick Thimmesch, "Ten-Four First Mama," *Saturday Evening Post* 248 (Sept. 1976): 120.

4. Ibid.

5. Gerald Ford, *A Time to Heal* (New York: Harper and Row, 1974), 104–5.

6. "Betty: The New First Lady," *Newsweek* 84 (19 Aug. 1974): 30.

7. Trude B. Feldman, "The New First Lady," *McCall's* 102 (Oct. 1974): 88.

8. Marjorie Hunter, "Ford Takes Office as 38th President," *Louisville Courier-Journal,* 10 Aug. 1974, A14.

9. "Betty: The New First Lady," 30.

10. Sheila Rabb Weidenfeld, *First Lady's Lady: With the Fords at the White House* (New York: G. P. Putnam, 1979).

11. "Betty: The New First Lady," 30.

12. Jane Howard, "Forward Day by Day," *New York Times Magazine*, 8 Dec. 1974, 86.

13. For an account of the public response to cancer in the 1970s, see Susan Sontag, *Illness as Metaphor* (New York: Farrar, Straus, and Giroux, 1978).

14. "Betty Ford: Facing Cancer," *Time* 104 (7 Oct. 1974): 14.

15. "Betty Ford's Operation," *Newsweek* 84 (7 Oct. 1974): 30–33.

16. Howard, "Forward," 64.

17. Betty Ford, *The Times of My Life* (New York: Harper and Row, 1978), 194.

18. Betty Boyd Caroli, *First Ladies* (New York: Oxford University Press, 1987), 301.

19. Isabelle Shelton, "I Feel Like I've Been Reborn," *McCall's* 102 (Feb. 1975): 142.

20. Ibid., 143.

21. "Dear Mrs. Ford," *McCall's* 102 (Dec. 1974): 66.

22. Donnie Radcliffe, "First Lady Holds News Conference, Takes Stand Favoring Abortion, ERA," *Louisville Courier-Journal*, 5 Sept. 1974, A3.

23. "On Being Normal," *Time* 106 (25 Aug. 1975): 15.

24. The Ford Presidential Library in Ann Arbor, Michigan, has collected and makes available to researchers the letters sent to Mrs. Ford after her interview, including the critical ones mentioned in this essay. William F. Buckley Jr., "Pity

Mrs. Ford," *National Review* 27 (12 Sept. 1975): 1008–9; Martin E. Marty, "Our Moral Arbiters," *Christian Century* 92 (17 Sept. 1975): 807; "Woman of the Year," *Newsweek* 86 (29 Dec. 1975): 19.

25. Weidenfeld, *First Lady's Lady,* 174.

26. "Woman of the Year," 21.

27. Weidenfeld, *First Lady's Lady,* 178.

28. Winzola McLendon, "Betty Ford Talks about Homemaking," *Good Housekeeping* 183 (Aug. 1976): 24.

29. As discussed and quoted in "On Being Normal," 15.

30. "Mrs. Ford and the Affair of the Daughter," *Ladies' Home Journal* 92 (Nov. 1975): 118.

31. Howard, "Forward," 88; "There's No Gilded Cage for Betty," *Time* 106 (1 Dec. 1975): 22; "On to the Showdown in Florida," *Time* 107 (8 Mar. 1076): 11; Weidenfeld, *First Lady's Lady,* 246.

32. "Woman of the Year," 19.

33. Weidenfeld, *First Lady's Lady,* 246.

34. While this is the view taken by historians, some who served in the administration disagree. The first lady's press secretary claimed that neither the president nor his advisers appreciated or understood Betty Ford's feminist commitment and regularly downplayed East Wing operations. This interpretation was given unintentional credence in Gerald Ford's autobiography, where ERA is only mentioned once and Betty Ford's role is generally described as standing at the president's side. See Weidenfeld, *First Lady's Lady,* 47–48, 71, 101, 143.

35. *Louisville Courier-Journal,* 2 Sept. 1974, B15.

36. Ibid.

37. Myra MacPherson, "The Blooming of Betty Ford," *McCall's* 102 (Sept. 1975): 134. President Ford cited the first lady's influence in the appointment of women officials. However, in spite of Betty Ford's advocacy, the president failed to appoint a woman to the Supreme Court and chose a man as his running mate in 1976. See Gerald Ford, *A Time to Heal,* 240.

38. "Betty Ford's Operation," p. 33.

39. Gerald Ford, *A Time to Heal,* 205.

40. Carl Sferrazza Anthony, *First Ladies: The Saga of the First Ladies and Their Power* (New York: William Morrow/Quill, 1991), 2:251–52.

41. "Betty Ford's Role on the Election Circuit," *U.S. News and World Report* (7 Oct. 1974).

42. "Relentless Ordeal of Political Wives," 20.

43. "A Fighting First Lady," *Time* 105 (3 Mar. 1975): 20; MacPherson, "Blooming of Betty Ford," 124; Weidenfeld, *First Lady's Lady,* 84–90, 121–22.

44. "Fighting First Lady," 20.

45. Howard, "Forward," 90.

46. MacPherson, "Blooming of Betty Ford," 122.

47. "Fighting First Lady," 20.

48. MacPherson, "Blooming of Betty Ford," 124.

49. Anthony, *First Ladies,* 261–65.

50. In his autobiography, Gerald Ford cited the *60 Minutes* interview as one of several factors that led to conservative Ronald Reagan challenging him for the Republican nomination.

51. "There's No Gilded Cage for Betty," 22; Howard, "Forward," 64; "Political Wives with Different Styles," *U.S. News and World Report* 80 (8 Mar. 1976): 16.

52. "Contest of the Queens," *Time* 108 (30 Aug. 1976): 31; "Betty vs. Rosalynn: Life on the Campaign Trail," *U.S. News and World Report* 81 (18 Oct. 1976): 24.

53. Betty Ford, *Times of My Life,* 255–56; "Contest of the Queens," 31.

54. "Political Wives with Different Styles," 16.

55. Betty Ford, *Times of My Life,* 257–58.

56. "Betty vs. Rosalynn," 22.

57. "The First Lady Talks," *Good Housekeeping* 182 (Mar. 1976): 70–72; Lynn Minton, "Betty Ford Talks about Her Mother," *McCall's* 103 (May 1976): 74; McLendon, "Betty Ford Talks about Homemaking," 24.

58. Minton, "Betty Ford Talks about Her Mother," 104.

59. Weidenfeld, *First Lady's Lady,* 365.

60. Thimmesch, "Ten-Four," 62; "Betty vs. Rosalynn," 22; Gerald Ford, *Time to Heal,* 403; Weidenfeld, *First Lady's Lady,* 370.

61. Thimmesch, "Ten-Four," 62; "Betty vs. Rosalynn," 390; Weidenfeld, *First Lady's Lady,* 370.

62. Trude B. Feldman, "Gerald and Betty Ford: 'It's Not the End of the World,'" *McCall's* 104 (Jan. 1977): 30; "Contest of the Queens," 31.

63. Feldman, "New First Lady," 30; Gerald Ford, *Time to Heal,* 431.

64. Myra MacPherson, "Keeping Up with Betty Ford," *McCall's* 105 (Nov. 1977): 207.

Ida McKinley reviewing a parade with President McKinley, Plattsburgh, New York, 1899. Reproduced from the collections of the Library of Congress.

Frances Cleveland poses for a photograph with the wives of her husband's cabinet members, 1897. Reproduced from the collections of the Library of Congress.

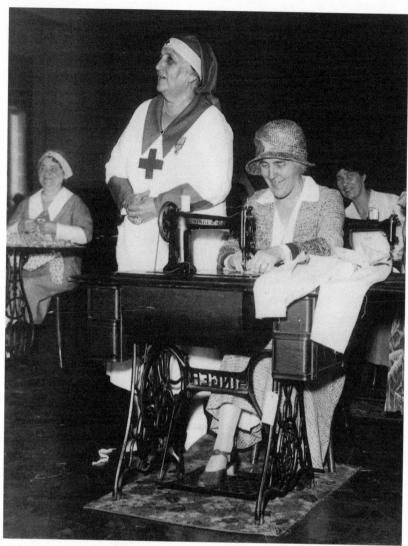

Lou Hoover, wife of President Herbert Hoover, visits Red Cross workers, 1932. Reproduced from the collections of the Library of Congress.

Eleanor Roosevelt testifies before the Senate Foreign Relations Committee, 1955.
Reproduced from the collections of the Library of Congress.

Florence Harding demonstrates support for U.S. troops, Walter Reed Hospital,
Washington, D.C., 1921. Reproduced from the collections of the Library of
Congress.

Edith Wilson rides beside President Wilson at inaugural festivities, 1917. Reproduced from the collections of the Library of Congress.

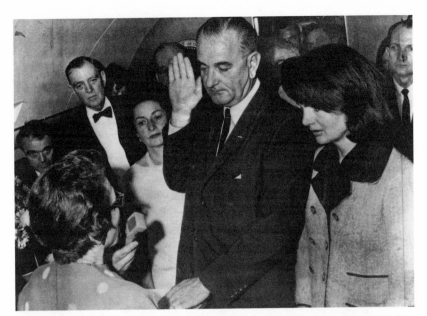

Jacqueline Kennedy and Lady Bird Johnson at the side of Lyndon Johnson as he takes the oath of office of the president, shortly after the assassination of President Kennedy, 1963. Reproduced from the collections of the Library of Congress.

Grace Coolidge at the "Bucket Signing Ceremony," in support of her husband's 1924 reelection campaign, August 19, 1924, Plymouth, Vermont. Seated, from left, are Harvey Firestone, President Calvin Coolidge, Henry Ford, Thomas Edison, Grace Coolidge, and the president's father, Col. John Coolidge. Russell Firestone is standing. Reproduced from the Calvin Coolidge Memorial Foundation.

Lady Bird Johnson leads her beautification program, 1966. The program involved an array of conservation and beautification initiatives around the nation. Courtesy of the Lyndon Baines Johnson Library.

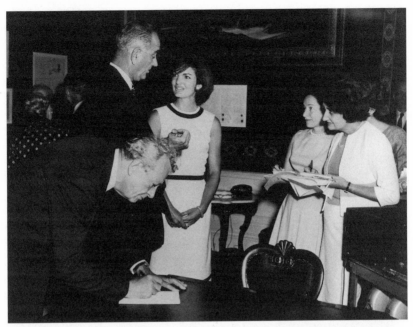

Jacqueline Kennedy with Vice President Lyndon Johnson and Senator Everett Dirksen at the opening of the Treaty Room in the White House, 1962. Mrs. Kennedy's renovation of the White House was one of the most comprehensive and well-known of such efforts. Courtesy of the John F. Kennedy Library.

Barbara Bush reading to children as part of the first lady's family literacy project, 1991. Courtesy of the George Bush Presidential Library and Museum.

As the president's personal envoy, Rosalynn Carter visited with heads of state during her visit to South America in June of 1977. Courtesy of the Jimmy Carter Library.

PART THREE

Social and Behind-the-Scenes
Influence

Overview

Strict gender roles have, historically, limited women's ability to participate fully in the political process. Women did not, for instance, even enjoy the basic constitutional right to vote until the passage of the Nineteenth Amendment in 1920. Yet such restrictions did not mean that women did not play a role in the nation's political development and history; nor did it mean that women's voices were completely without influence. Perhaps the only avenue to political power women had in an earlier day and age was spousehood. As the persons closest to the presidents, first ladies have exercised influence and power from behind the scenes. Among the few roles within the purview of women—indeed, dominated by women—was that of domesticity and the social role of hostess. It should not be surprising, then, that a long history of accomplishments in the first ladyship can be traced to the social arena, where first ladies have served as the nation's hostesses and White House managers—presiding over state affairs, renovating the White House, and making their presence known in the official residence. Although more difficult to assess, the potential for influence stemming from the first lady's relationship to the president, as his spouse, is the most profound source of influence and power associated with the office.

Even as women gained basic rights and enjoyed increasing success in the political, economic, and commercial facets of society, the nature of the first ladyship as unelected and unappointed—and thereby lacking any official portfolio and formal powers—has led first ladies to continue to wield influence through the social realm. Each first lady's role as loyal supporter of her spouse and her contributions of creating a sense of home and family in the White House are not to be minimized. Beyond these contributions, through their role as social hostesses, first ladies have courted important contacts, entertained eminent guests, and promoted American culture and arts while serving as the idealized image of American womanhood. Part 3 of the book considers this important component of the first ladyship, one often forgotten by contemporary scholars interested in assessing political participation, policy activism, and special charitable projects by first ladies.

First-lady scholar Elizabeth Lorelei Thacker-Estrada begins this section of the book by examining the spouses who served during the antebellum period in U.S. history. Together the first ladies of this era have often been ignored or dismissed by scholars as unimportant individuals and without influence on their spouses. Indeed, not much is known about them; in fact, their husbands are equally remote figures, unknown to most students of history and politics. Yet, as Thacker-Estrada reveals, each of the four women fulfilled unique roles, reflected the image of women during the period, and made many contributions to their husbands' careers and the presidency. Owing to the time period and corresponding status of women, these antebellum first ladies were forced to exercise any influence in a behind-the-scenes manner or through family and social forums considered acceptable—and even glorified—by the social mores of the time.

Dr. James McCallops, in the second essay of this section, considers the fascinating first ladyship, or "regency," of one of the most controversial first ladies: Edith Bolling Galt Wilson, second wife of President Woodrow Wilson. Edith's role during the president's serious illness and long convalescence has long been questioned. Historians have debated whether or not she overstepped her role as first lady—although it would be impossible to determine that she improperly discharged her "role" as spouse—and the extent that Mrs. Wilson made political and policy decisions either on her own or on behalf of her husband. Edith Wilson's story brings new meaning to the notion of behind-the-scenes influence, and McCallops's essay offers a detailed look at the momentous events surrounding her first ladyship.

The last essay in part 3, by Raymond Frey, concerns the first first lady of the post–World War II era, Bess Truman. Mrs. Truman remains relatively unknown and largely misunderstood in spite of—or perhaps because of— her husband's enduring popularity. She did not try to disguise her disinterest in politics or even her outright hostility to the presidency, the capital city, and the White House. She remains to some the epitome of reluctant first lady; yet, beyond her image as apolitical, Bess was influential in a behind-the-scenes manner through her close relationship with her husband. That Harry Truman nicknamed his wife "The Boss" and admitted that he never made an important decision without consulting her are factors that make consideration of Bess Truman's first ladyship compelling.

FOUR

True Women

The Roles and Lives of Antebellum Presidential Wives
Sarah Polk, Margaret Taylor, Abigail Fillmore, and Jane Pierce

ELIZABETH LORELEI THACKER-ESTRADA

With the burgeoning interest in First Lady studies . . . more information on the less renowned nineteenth-century presidential wives is likely to come to light.

> Lewis L. Gould, *American First Ladies:*
> *Their Lives and Their Legacy*

INTRODUCTION

Although they lived in the era of "fabled antebellum ladies," the wives of presidents who served in the decade and a half prior to the Civil War have largely been overlooked by history.[1] Sarah Childress Polk (1803–91), Margaret Mackall Smith Taylor (1788–1852), Abigail Powers Fillmore (1798–1853), and Jane Means Appleton Pierce (1806–63) served as first lady in succession from 1845 through 1857 against a dramatic backdrop of territorial expansion and conflicts over slavery. With the exception of Sarah Polk, the most politically active and therefore the most "modern" of the four, the actions and contributions of these first ladies have usually been dismissed, denied, or ignored. Margaret Taylor, Abigail Fillmore, and Jane Pierce were reluctant first ladies who did not want to serve publicly as the presidents' spouses—an attitude they shared with the first first lady, Martha Washington. Yet they helped to establish a "traditional" approach to the office, that of the publicly passive and seemingly nonpolitical first lady. Studying these relatively forgotten women contributes to an understanding of the often hidden history and development of the office of first lady and to the discovery that even the most obscure and seemingly inactive first lady performed—privately and behind the scenes—several roles during her husband's presidency. Placing them in the context of their time also reveals how each woman reflected the restricted social expectations for women of the era yet also managed to design for herself a place in the White House and emphasize certain established roles according to her personal preferences.

ARCHETYPES AND STEREOTYPES

Very much women of their time, these first ladies could readily be portrayed solely as conventional types of early-nineteenth-century women. Indomitable Sarah Polk, southern lady and plantation mistress, is viewed as having been ladylike yet strong, strict, and independent. Languishing Margaret Taylor most closely recalls the image of the tough, careworn pioneer woman and peripatetic military wife transplanted from her cultured eastern roots. Resourceful Abigail Fillmore was a schoolmarm with a bookish reputation as a woman of intellectual, cultural, and literary interests. The tragic Jane Pierce personifies the sweet Victorian flower; the fragile, fainting female; and the mournful, sentimental mother.

While these images are accurate in many ways, the lives of these first ladies have been heavily embroidered, reflecting assumptions and prejudices of both their time and ours regarding nineteenth-century women. Often the facts about them run counter to the prevailing—and limited—popular beliefs about them. Pious and straitlaced "Sahara Sarah" did ban hard liquor and dancing from the White House, yet served wine at dinners and entertained guests with music.[2] Margaret Taylor was supposedly hidden in shame by her embarrassed family for such uncouth, frontier behavior as smoking a long-stemmed western corncob pipe and murmuring incoherently, when in reality she was of a genteel and ladylike disposition and became physically ill around tobacco, according to a grandson who lived with the Taylors.[3] Varina Davis, the wife of Jefferson Davis and the future first lady of the Confederacy, asserted that Mrs. Taylor was never heard to moan or murmur.[4] A decade later Mary Todd Lincoln of Kentucky and later Illinois would similarly suffer from being depicted in Washington as a coarse and unrefined westerner. Portrayed primarily as absent first ladies, Abigail Fillmore and Jane Pierce actually fulfilled far more social obligations than has usually been acknowledged, and they were more politically aware than women of the age were expected to be. Reports implying that the reclusive Margaret Taylor and the retiring Jane Pierce were practically insane are greatly exaggerated.[5]

When these first ladies have been credited with significant accomplishments, it has been for activities associated with what have since become traditional female occupations. Sarah Polk worked alongside her husband in his White House office, but she was not his official private secretary. That title was held by a man, in this case a Polk nephew. Abigail Fillmore designed and established the permanent White House library, but the Fillmores employed a librarian, then a masculine occupation, to obtain most of the books. Since the positions of secretary and librarian are now assumed to be primarily female occupations, the unique contributions of Mrs. Polk and Mrs. Fillmore in expanding the first-lady role in the antebellum era are made more readily understandable, but they are also more easily minimized.

Obscurity

Several factors contribute to the lack of information about these women, who are not as well known as earlier presidential wives of the federal period, including Martha Washington, Abigail Adams, and Dolley Madison. The office of first lady declined in relation to the status of the presidency, as this was the "era of common man presidents."[6] In addition, the administrations of James Knox Polk (1845–49), Zachary Taylor (1849–50), Millard Fillmore (1850–53), and Franklin Pierce (1853–57) lasted one term or less. Historically these men have been eclipsed by the Founding Fathers and the heroic Andrew Jackson, who preceded them in office; by the mythical Abraham Lincoln, who followed; and even by their contemporaries who never became president, including senatorial luminaries Daniel Webster, Henry Clay, John C. Calhoun, and Stephen A. Douglas. The wives of these lesser known presidents have been similarly overshadowed.

Another factor in the minimal historical memory regarding these women is the lack of documentation about them. Unlike the present day, when the life and activities of the first lady receive enormous and often intrusive media coverage, the wives of presidents in the antebellum era were seldom mentioned in official or public records and rarely discussed in newspapers. The notable exception to this dearth of information, Sarah Polk, lived until 1891 and preserved much of the correspondence and papers from her life and her husband's administration long before the government adopted the practice of retaining presidential papers. Fortunately, her husband kept a detailed diary, and she was the subject of two memorial publications soon after her death. The relatively extensive amount of information about her partially contributes to the perception of her as a much more activist first lady than the other three women, much of whose correspondence was apparently lost or destroyed. We are left to rely on the recollections of long-lived acquaintances of these women to provide much of what we know about them. Still, enough information exists to allow us to piece together a basic profile of these women, their presidential years, and their times.

The Roles of Antebellum First Ladies

The roles they fulfilled in the White House reflected the social expectations for upper- and middle-class white women, which consigned them to a private and domestic sphere that has been referred to since as a "cult of domesticity" or "cult of true womanhood."[7] This "cult" pertains to an increasingly ubiquitous acceptance of and devotion to a set of attributes women were ideally expected to possess. While early-nineteenth-century women were being increasingly restricted to certain domestic roles, middle-class white men, in contrast, experienced greater occupational and political opportunities away from the home. Since women, including the presidents' wives, lacked the vote and other legal rights, they were expected neither to play as public a role nor to be as politically active as are modern first ladies.

Perhaps not surprisingly then, the first ladies' roles as wives, White House managers, and the nation's hostesses correspond to those of other wives and homemakers. Women, educated for the purpose of carrying out their domestic duties more gracefully and effectively, were encouraged to transmit positive cultural and moral influences to their families, including their husbands, to whom they were thought to be morally superior yet subservient. During an era of religious revivalism, the church became one of the few institutions in which women could be respectably active outside of the home. These cultural and religious aspirations were personified in the role of patroness of culture. Considered more spiritual than men, women often led elaborate mourning rituals in an age preoccupied with illness and death, and a first lady's role as chief mourner demonstrated this responsibility. As performed by Sarah Polk, the role of political partner and adviser to the president took the socially acceptable form of being a helpmate to her husband.[8]

Although separate spheres for men and women were commonly accepted —the public, political, and official world of men and the private, social, and unofficial realm of women—this does not mean that these women were inactive in or indifferent to their husbands' administrations. In this era of the "common man" these "true women" shared an uncommon experience: acting within the power circles in Washington, particularly the White House.[9] The more fortunate women could find influence and power in the private sphere, since "the woman who had been so firmly put in her place, the home, often showed unusual power within that restricted domain."[10] Although the public sphere of men and the private sphere of women were supposedly sharply delineated, they strongly influenced each other in the executive mansion, both the office and the home of the president. Although a woman's place was considered to be in the home, that sphere became all the more powerful when that home was the White House. The roles these first ladies played in the White House home include those of wife, manager, hostess, patroness, mourner, and political partner and adviser.

Wife

In the age of the "cult of domesticity," the fundamental but often overlooked role of wife could be quite influential and powerful, as "marriage was seen not only in terms of service but as an increase in authority for woman."[11] Since these four first ladies primarily exerted behind-the-scenes influence, their real although private influence as wives was that much more important. Sarah Polk, Margaret Taylor, and Abigail Fillmore particularly fulfilled the role of lifelong, loyal partner and companion. They worried, often justifiably, about the health of their husbands and fashioned a comfortable home for them and other family members, despite the challenges of living in the executive mansion. The following, written upon the death of Sarah Polk in 1891, acknowledges both woman's sphere and her domain over the home, sentiments that seem sexist and limiting in the twenty-first century but which were considered highly complimentary in the nineteenth century: "One is impressed with her thorough womanliness. She recognized the sphere in which God had placed her—the social sphere of which a true woman is the heart. With no vague ambitions for some different place, she did what she could to make life pure and sweet. While she was a woman of strong mind and of broad culture, yet these were used to minister help, and comfort and blessing in the domain of home."[12] Sarah Polk fulfilled much of her natural ambition when the executive mansion became her home.

White House Manager

The White House has correctly been referred to as the "First Lady's House," and Dolley Madison, the wife of the fourth president, James Madison, established "in the public mind the idea that the president's wife had a responsibility for the upkeep of the President's House."[13] Usually it is the first lady who oversees the renovation and refurbishing of the executive mansion. While the president concentrated on public duties, his wife was generally responsible for supervising the staff of the White House.[14] An example of this role was demonstrated during the Polk administration. On the first reception night after gas had been installed in the White House, the gas jets disappeared, leaving all the rooms dark except for the reception room in which Mrs. Polk had wisely insisted on retaining the elegant chandeliers with wax candles; she was complimented for her foresight.[15]

Nation's Hostess

One of the best-known roles of the first lady, probably because it involves one of her most public and glamorous duties, is that of hostess at the White House. This role was initiated by Martha Washington and perfected by Dolley Madison, to whom the more private and reserved first ladies discussed here suffer in comparison. In political Washington hostessing was a primary means of gaining access to those in power and affected the public image of the president and his administration.[16] In the nineteenth century it was considered improper for a woman to attend social gatherings where no hostess was present; thus the presence of the first lady or other White House hostess, usually another family member, was essential in permitting other women to visit the executive mansion.

The three first ladies who followed the generally healthy Mrs. Polk frequently suffered from illness, a common complaint for women in an era when robust female vitality seemed "crude" and fragility displayed a "genteel sensibility," views that contrast sharply to the present emphasis on female fitness.[17] These first ladies often relied upon the then-common practice of having surrogate or proxy hostesses, the first surrogate White House hostess being Dolley Madison for the widowed Thomas Jefferson. From the late 1820s through the early 1840s young female relatives had served as hostess for widowers Andrew Jackson and Martin Van Buren and, for a portion of his administration during the illness of his first wife and following her death, John Tyler.

Margaret Taylor and Abigail Fillmore, the two first ladies in this study fortunate to have daughters, often relinquished hostessing duties to them. Jane Pierce frequently depended upon her widowed aunt, Abby Kent Means, to serve as White House hostess. Margaret's youngest daughter, Betty Taylor Bliss, attended in her mother's stead the dinner hosted by the Polks in honor of Zachary Taylor and the inaugural balls. Margaret Taylor, like Jane Pierce, was more comfortable serving as hostess at private dinners rather than public receptions. When Abigail Fillmore missed a social event, it was often due to a "permanently broken ankle" from a severe injury she had sustained that had never healed properly. Mrs. Fillmore would stay in bed all day in order to rest the ankle sufficiently to be able to stand at receptions during the evening, but sometimes daughter Mary Abigail, known as Abbie, would literally need to stand in for her mother as hostess.[18]

Although both Mrs. Fillmore and Mrs. Pierce have often been portrayed as turning over almost all of their minimal hostessing duties to their daughter and aunt, respectively, several of their contemporaries stated that the first ladies carried out many hostessing duties so as not to disappoint the public.

A friend observed that "Mrs. Fillmore was proud of her husband's success in life, and desirous that no reasonable expectations of the public should be disappointed. She never absented herself from the public receptions, dinners, or levees when it was possible for her to be present."[19] As the years of the Pierce administration wore on, Jane appears to have taken an increasingly active role as White House hostess.[20]

The mode of receiving guests symbolized the state of each president's and first lady's marriage, their mutual approach to the presidency, and even their conception of the proper spheres of men and women. Abbie Fillmore's friend Julia Miller noted that at the last New Year's reception in the Fillmore White House in 1853, "The President and his wife and family stood together . . . [and] received in the Blue Room . . . [which] was full of these richly dressed men and women."[21] In contrast, Franklin and Jane Pierce separately received their guests, who were segregated by sex. In 1856 the "guests passed through the 'Crimson Parlor' to the oval blue room where the President received the gentlemen . . . and Mrs. Pierce welcomed the ladies."[22]

Patroness of Culture

All four presidential wives were well educated for women of their time. Their educational backgrounds ranged from Sarah Polk's five-hundred-mile trek from Tennessee to North Carolina to live and study at the Moravian Female Academy, to Abigail Fillmore's self-education in her father's ample library. At least three of the women—Sarah Polk, Abigail Fillmore, and Jane Pierce—were well read and enjoyed the company of writers in the executive mansion, much as modern first ladies invite celebrities and entertainers to the White House. Nathaniel Hawthorne, author of *The Scarlet Letter* and an old college friend of Franklin Pierce, visited Jane upstairs at the White House and took her sailing. Together they visited Mount Vernon, the former home of George and Martha Washington.[23]

All four antebellum wives shared another cultural characteristic: their Protestant piety. All were deeply religious during this era of religious revivalism. Mirroring the social expectations of their time, they faithfully attended church and influenced their husbands in matters of religion and morality. James Polk and Zachary Taylor, although they did not become members, worshiped at their wives' churches.[24] These presidential couples also avoided conducting business on Sundays.[25]

Chief Mourner

In an age preoccupied with illness and death—the result of shorter life spans, higher child mortality, and greater religious fervor—women in mourning wore distinctive clothing and jewelry, often for set periods of time (normally two and a half years following the death of a husband and one and a half years upon the death of a son or a daughter).[26] In the twentieth century grieving tended to be much less formal; a prominent recent example of this increasingly rare role for a first lady is that of Jacqueline Kennedy following her husband's assassination in 1963. All four antebellum first ladies experienced the deaths of loved ones during or in close proximity to their White House years. Mrs. Polk and Mrs. Taylor suffered the deaths of their husbands. In February 1851 Mrs. Fillmore suffered a severe personal loss upon the death of her only sister, Mary, during the first year of her husband's unexpected term. Although Abigail performed many social duties as first lady, occasionally her absences were attributed to her mourning for her late sister. Mrs. Pierce grieved the death of her son, Benjamin, throughout her White House years.

Political Partner and Adviser

Abigail Adams, wife of the second U.S. president, John Adams, initiated the role of political partner to the president, although nineteenth-century presidents' wives normally were not supposed to be interested in controversial issues, as dictated by prevailing social custom.[27] Women in Washington had long been routinely involved in patronage decisions, and these antebellum first ladies were no exception as they witnessed office seekers besieging their husbands, directly received appeals, and promoted family interests.

All four antebellum presidential couples were affected by the Mexican War of 1846–48. The subsequent expansion of United States territory threatened the balance of power between the North and the South over which new states carved from this territory would be slave or free, and the issue carried over into the realm of the first ladies. Sarah Polk supported the expansionist actions of her husband in this age of "Manifest Destiny," observing in an 1880s newspaper interview that "the results following the Mexican war, that is, the adding of California and New Mexico to the territory of the United States, [are] among the most important events in the history of this country."[28]

Sarah Polk and Margaret Taylor were, along with their husbands, southern slaveholders who referred to those in bondage as "servants." The first ladies' views on slavery appear to have been partly related to their religious beliefs. Mrs. Polk believed in a "Presbyterian predestination."[29] Much as women were believed to inhabit a restricted sphere ordained by God, a view now held to be sexist, slavery was also thought to be divinely predetermined, a belief now considered painfully racist. In the White House, Sarah commented to her husband that slaves "did not choose such a lot in life, neither did we ask for ours; we were created for these places."[30]

In contrast, evidence indicates that northerners Abigail Fillmore and Jane Pierce opposed slavery. Abigail Fillmore might have held antislavery beliefs as a result of her Baptist upbringing, since abolitionism was strong among northern Baptists.[31] Although the Compromise of 1850, which admitted California as a free state and abolished the slave trade in the District of Columbia, was popular because it averted civil war at the time, Mrs. Fillmore reportedly advised her husband not to sign one of the measures, the Fugitive Slave Bill, and warned him that it would ruin his political career. Although Millard Fillmore believed that slavery was evil, he signed all of the Compromise of 1850 legislation because he wanted to preserve the Union.[32]

Fillmore's successor, Franklin Pierce, also wanted to save the Union. Since the controversial Compromise of 1850 did not settle the slavery question as politicians had hoped, on 30 May 1854 the Kansas-Nebraska Act was enacted, which left the question of slavery up to "popular sovereignty" in those two territories. Jane Pierce, a relative of Amos Lawrence, for whom Lawrence, Kansas, an antislavery stronghold, had been named, reportedly and unsuccessfully advised her husband not to sign this bill, an action reminiscent of Mrs. Fillmore's warning against the Fugitive Slave Act.[33] Both acts eventually stirred conflict between the North and the South, and neither Fillmore nor Pierce would be nominated by his party for a second term of office.

Each of the antebellum first ladies fulfilled a dominant role that influenced the other roles she played. The theme of politics runs throughout the life of the proud and ambitious Sarah Polk. Margaret Taylor, the only one of the four to become a grandmother, comes closest to representing the ideal woman of the "cult of domesticity," as her life revolved around her husband and family and she kept to her sphere; she was so private that no authenticated likeness of her exists, and no letters written by her are known to have survived.[34] Abigail Fillmore raised herself from a backwoods background to become an arbiter of culture, creating a salon and enjoying literature and music. Jane Pierce was afflicted by so much tragedy that she seems to personify the role of chief mourner.

SARAH POLK: POLITICAL PARTNER

Sarah Polk was born on 4 September 1803 near Murfreesboro, Tennessee, to the merchant and planter Joel Childress and Elizabeth Whitsitt Childress. Sarah's proximity to politics and politicians began early in life since Murfreesboro was the state capital from 1819 to 1825 and her family knew leading public figures, including future president Andrew Jackson.[35] Prior to their marriage in the Childress home on 1 January 1824, Sarah encouraged James to run for the state legislature in 1823.[36] He was soon elected to the U.S. House of Representatives, where he eventually became the Speaker. In 1826 Sarah joined him in Washington, where they lived in a boardinghouse, or "mess," with other legislators, as was the custom of the time. The wives of politicians, freed from most housekeeping responsibilities, observed and even participated in politicking.[37] Sarah thrived in the center of the political and social life of the nation's capital. Franklin Pierce, a protégé of Mrs. Polk's husband, "was one of her most cordial and constant friends," who at one time lived in a boardinghouse next to the Polks and appreciated Sarah's interest in politics, which his own wife did not share.[38]

The only childless first lady of the four discussed in this essay, Sarah Polk was able to devote herself wholeheartedly to her husband's political career. An acquaintance, Judge Catron, told her, "You are not the one, Madame, to have the charge of a little child; you, who have always been absorbed in political and social affairs."[39] When James successfully ran for governor of Tennessee in 1837, Sarah orchestrated his campaign, helping to arrange "picnic-type" political gatherings, although her role was not publicly acknowledged.[40] In letters during the 1841 gubernatorial campaign, Sarah kept James informed of political news culled from newspapers and "women's gossip."[41]

She was one of the few first ladies during this time to expand the role of president's wife, thus prefiguring the more activist first ladies of the current era.[42] Sarah Polk effectively merged her domestic sphere with the political world of her husband by acting as his unofficial secretary, confidante, and full partner. Sarah was careful to preface her opinions with "Mr. Polk thinks that . . ." or "Mr. Polk believes that. . . ."[43] However, she used her considerable talents to advance her husband's political career and administration, and she was recognized in her own time as a powerful presence. Vice President George Dallas acknowledged her influence on the president, stating to his wife, "I go for the new lady. . . . She is certainly mistress of herself, and, I suspect, of somebody else also."[44] Both in their forties, the Polks were a young and active presidential couple who waged the Mexican War and instituted an "Imperial Presidency," which accentuated the majesty of the office.[45]

White House historian William Seale credits Sarah Polk with modernizing the management of the executive mansion.[46] During the 1844 campaign for the presidency, when Sarah Polk had learned that another lady hoped Henry Clay "would be elected to the presidency, because his wife was a good housekeeper, and made fine butter," Mrs. Polk had replied, "If I should be so fortunate as to reach the White House, I expect to live on twenty-five thousand dollars a year, and I will neither keep house nor make butter."[47] Sarah was apparently as good as her word, since the Polks were the first occupants of the White House in many years to make a concerted effort to live within the presidential salary.[48] Unfortunately, one of the cost-cutting measures Sarah instituted included replacing ten salaried White House staff members with the Polks' own slaves.[49] Due partly to the expenses entailed by the first family for bearing the cost of entertaining enormous numbers of people, Sarah did not serve refreshments at public receptions. She deemed this practice as beneath the dignity of the executive mansion, and many subsequent first families followed her example.[50]

Ironically, Henry Clay, to whose wife Mrs. Polk had been unfavorably compared, paid Sarah a compliment that could refer both to her White House management and her political power in the Polk administration. Mr. Clay told Mrs. Polk, "All agree in commending in the highest terms your excellent administration of the domestic affairs of the White House"; Sarah replied, "I am glad to hear that my administration is popular."[51] Many of the White House guests during the Polk administration embodied links with both the country's political past and its future. Dolley Madison, as a regular guest of the Polks, adorned hostess Sarah's receptions.[52] On one occasion the widow of Alexander Hamilton was a dinner guest, and future White House hostesses Harriet Lane, niece of Polk's secretary of state James Buchanan, and Martha Johnson, the daughter of fellow Tennessean and congressman Andrew Johnson, also visited the Polks.[53]

Making the most of her domain outside the White House and ensuring that her "workaholic" husband was regularly seen in public, Mrs. Polk, accompanied by the president, would sweep into the First Presbyterian Church gorgeously gowned, fashionably late, and highly visible.[54] James Polk's most frequent references to Sarah in his presidential diary refer to attending church with her. By far the most actively political of the four women, Sarah Polk "was always in the parlor" with her husband and directly assisted him in his work as president, editing his speeches at her desk.[55] In addition she performed other tasks requiring political acumen: "The President's duties left him little time for even a cursory scanning of the numerous newspapers. There were frequent allusions to his administration, and it was necessary for him to know the drift of public feeling and opinion. He would send the papers to his wife, requesting her to examine them and mark such articles as it was desirable for him to read. This task, requiring judgment and knowledge of public affairs, she gladly performed. Carefully folding the papers with the marked pieces outside, where a glance might detect them, she would place the pile beside his chair, so that whenever a few moments of leisure came, he could find and read without loss of time."[56]

Sarah's femininity and respectability deflected controversy regarding her political interests and activities. "Well informed, thoughtful, vivacious, her conversation had a charm for all, while she kept strictly within the sphere of a true and noble womanhood."[57] Writing in 1870, while Mrs. Polk was still alive, historian Laura Holloway noted: "Women were then as now, supposed to be too weak to understand the mighty problem of Government, and they evidenced their acquiescence in such a supposition by remaining entirely unacquainted with the politics of the country. Not so Mrs. Polk, who however was no politician, for her visitors were not aware of the depth of her understanding, nor were they offended by the recurrence to a subject deemed out of her sphere."[58]

James Polk died less than four months after leaving the presidency, and his widow wore mourning attire for the remainder of her forty-three years.[59] Sarah, ever the former first lady of the entire nation, maintained neutrality during the Civil War. From 1849 to the end of her life she refused to give letters of recommendation for political office, reasoning that it "would be heralded over the country that she was now meddling with politics . . . and render her liable to the loss of whatever influence she might possess."[60]

Margaret Taylor: Wife

In contrast to her predecessor, Margaret Taylor eschewed politics and wished that her husband, Zachary Taylor, would as well. Born on 21 September 1788 at Saint Leonard's, Maryland, she was the daughter of Maj. Walter Smith and Ann Mackall Smith. Margaret married career soldier Zachary Taylor on 21 June 1810 in a double log house close to the Taylor estate.[61] Both Margaret and Zachary, despite their subsequent frontier reputations, were of aristocratic backgrounds, Zachary being a cousin of President James Madison and Margaret a cousin of Nellie Parke Custis Washington, granddaughter of Martha Washington.[62]

Margaret became the mother of five daughters, two of whom died young, and one son. Mrs. Taylor accompanied her husband to numerous frontier outposts as far afield as Indiana, Wisconsin, Louisiana, and Minnesota. A homemaker in rough circumstances, Margaret went about her "domestic concerns—down in the cellar skimming milk or going to feed the chickens," according to her daughter Sarah.[63] Reflective of the "cult of true womanhood," Margaret not only performed domestic chores but focused her activities in the church. She converted a room in a Baton Rouge, Louisiana, garrison into a chapel and persuaded a rector to offer occasional services. Later she was instrumental in establishing the parish and church of Saint James, which "formed the beginning of a church still active in Baton Rouge."[64]

During the Mexican War of 1846–48 Mrs. Taylor, wife of the commanding U.S. general, "still always calm and cheerful[,] was a constant source of comfort, and shed around her an atmosphere of hope, an inspiration of true courage."[65] Zachary Taylor said to Jefferson Davis, the widower of the Taylors' middle daughter, "You know my wife was as much of a soldier as I was."[66] Zachary, known as "Old Rough and Ready," gained fame as the hero of the battle of Buena Vista, and in 1848 the Whig Party nominated him as president, even though the general had shown no interest in elections and had never before voted.[67] Margaret "stated that she prayed nightly that someone other than Zachary Taylor would succeed James K. Polk."[68] An amusing incident recounted in newspapers reveals Margaret's feelings regarding her husband's ascension to the presidency. General Taylor was approached by someone who did not know who he was. The stranger asked "the General if he was a Taylor man, to which the General replied, 'Not much of one'—that is, he did not vote for him—partly because of family reasons, and partly because his wife was . . . opposed to sending 'Old Zack' to Washington, where she would be obliged to go with him!"[69] Margaret believed that the presidential candidacy "was a plot to deprive her of his society, and shorten his life by unnecessary care and responsibility."[70]

Opposed to her husband's nomination for president, Margaret Taylor differed completely from Sarah Polk in her unwillingness to carry out the public duties of the wife of a president. Rather than enjoying a quiet, private retirement with her husband in their Louisiana cottage, as was her wish, Margaret reluctantly moved to the White House to be with Zachary. Margaret Taylor, at sixty the oldest of the four first ladies to enter the White House, lived a reclusive life there in poor health. Daughter Betty Taylor Bliss revealed that her mother was "seldom well."[71] Although she was frail and avoided the public eye, she created a pleasant home in the White House for her husband, as she had done at all of his postings. "Once established in her new home, she selected such rooms as suited her ideas of housekeeping, and, as far as was possible, resumed the routine that characterized her life at Baton Rouge. As was her merit, she attended personally to so much of it as affected the personal comforts of the General, and it was not long before the 'opposition' found fault with her simple habits, and attempted, but without effect, to lessen the public esteem felt for General Taylor, by indulging in offensive personalities."[72]

As White House manager, Margaret created a sitting room on the second floor.[73] In this room the women of an extended family congregated, creating a feminine realm in the soldier's house. Varina Davis, the second wife of Jefferson Davis, noted, "I always found the most pleasant part of my visit to the White House to be passed in Mrs. Taylor's bright pretty room where the invalid, full of interest in the passing show in which she had not the strength to take her part, talked most agreeably and kindly to the many friends admitted to her presence."[74] Ever actively domestic, she reportedly spent her days knitting, an activity then thought to promote "serenity and economy" in women.[75] Upstairs Mrs. Taylor "was the center of attention. She loved having her family around her. In-laws came from near and far. . . . Toddlers, infants and babes-in-arms arrived with mamas, papas and nursemaids—and with all the baggage of babyhood—for those lengthy, old-fashioned, Southern visits which the President enjoyed."[76]

Margaret worshiped at Saint John's Episcopal Church—"The Church of the Presidents"—across Lafayette Square from the White House. Two of the rare public events in which Margaret Taylor participated had religious associations. In 1849 Margaret, along with her husband, "listened to Baptist Sunday-school children treble a patriotic hymn" on the Fourth of July and became a life member of the American Sunday School Union.[77] As adherents to the "cult of domesticity," large "numbers of women joined Christian benevolent associations, to reform the world by the propagation of the faith."[78]

The only one of the four antebellum first ladies who had not been exposed to the political lessons of Washington boardinghouse life, Mrs. Taylor nonetheless occasionally attempted to play the political game on behalf of her husband. She received special guests in the upstairs rooms of the White House and "took every opportunity to drop a good word in company that might help her husband."[79] Along with Zachary, she received ubiquitous office seekers and, as political adviser, apparently influenced her husband's decision to appoint Reverdy Johnson as attorney general since his wife was one of her relatives.[80]

Her predictions that the presidency would be the undoing of her husband proved correct. Only a year following President Polk's death, as Congress vociferously debated slavery measures during a long, hot congressional session, Zachary Taylor fell ill and died of cholera morbus on 9 July 1850, just weeks following the Taylors' fortieth wedding anniversary. Margaret Taylor became the first first lady to be present when a president died in office. (William Henry Harrison, another Whig general, died in 1841 after only a month in office, but his wife, Anna Symmes Harrison, had not yet moved into the White House.) Romantic engravers depicted Mrs. Taylor, the chief mourner, beside her husband's deathbed with her face covered by a large handkerchief since "nobody knew what she looked like."[81] These inexpensive and mass-produced memorial prints were often hung on parlor walls.[82] Heartbroken, Margaret moved out of the White House on the evening of her husband's funeral despite the invitation of the new president, Millard Fillmore, to stay on as long as she needed.[83] She died only two years later, reportedly without ever mentioning the White House again.

ABIGAIL FILLMORE: PATRONESS OF CULTURE

Abigail was born on 13 March 1798 in Stillwater, New York, the youngest daughter of the Reverend Lemuel Powers, a Baptist clergyman, and Abigail Newland Powers. Her father passed away in 1800, leaving a widow with seven children. Raised in what was then the frontier of western New York, she became a schoolteacher, one of the few paid occupations open to women of the time and the most common profession of future first ladies.[84] Abigail has been credited with helping to create a circulating library in Sempronius, New York, to which the young Millard Fillmore purchased a subscription.[85] Abigail and Millard, the first presidential couple to rise from poverty, were married on 5 February 1826 in Moravia, New York. Abigail took what was then the unusual action of continuing to work for wages after marriage, and she became the first first lady to earn a living before and after marriage.[86] Eventually a son and a daughter were born to the Fillmores.

Like the Polks and the Taylors, the Fillmores enjoyed a long, supportive marriage. Not only was Millard Fillmore the classic self-made man, he was, according to biographer William Elliot Griffis, a "wife-made man" who owed much of his rise from a log cabin to the White House to "the ever-shaping personality" of his intelligent, supportive spouse.[87] When Millard was a U.S. congressman, Abigail lived with him in Washington from 1836 to 1842, where she, like Sarah Polk and Jane Pierce, experienced the boardinghouse life.[88] In Buffalo, New York, where the Fillmores made their home, they contributed to the founding of the local public library.[89] While Abigail inhabited the domestic sphere and Millard the world of politics, during his political career and presidential administration these spheres complemented each other. Together, Millard and Abigail established the permanent White House library in the second-floor oval room, which served both the president in his official capacity and his wife as the center of her duties and activities as first lady. But the Fillmores first had to obtain funding for the library from a Congress wary of strengthening the executive branch of government. Although initial legislation to fund the library was defeated, it passed on a second attempt following an effective appeal in the Senate that noted, during an era of evangelical fervor, that the executive mansion lacked even a Bible.[90]

The library reflected elements of the "cult of domesticity," and its design and use illustrate several of the roles performed by the president's wife. As White House manager and patroness of culture, Abigail converted the space into a library, music room, and sitting room. According to family friend Harriet Haven, "Here Miss Fillmore had her own piano and harp, and here Mrs. Fillmore, surrounded by her books, spent the greater part of her time, and in this room the family received their informal visitors."[91] Practicing the accomplishments of singing and playing a musical instrument so admired in "true women," daughter Abbie played and sang duets with both her mother and her brother Powers, with Millard sometimes joining in on a new Stephen Foster song.[92] In the library Abigail served as hostess to important and powerful politicians, including Secretary of State Daniel Webster.[93] The president found an ideal refuge in the library designed and maintained by his wife. "The President had but little time to give to this library, but he usually succeeded in leaving the executive chamber at 10:30 at night, and spending a pleasant hour in the library with his family."[94] In her choice of the second-floor location and the mahogany furniture, Abigail reflected the tastes of the typical American of that time.[95]

Abigail Fillmore evidenced both an appreciation for poetry and a consciousness of her role as patroness of culture in encouraging the literary accomplishments of American women. In one of the few surviving letters written while she was first lady, she expressed a particular interest in the popular book *Female Poets of America,* writing, "It was with great pride and pleasure that I saw these samples of the genius of my fellow-countrywomen."[96] The Fillmores played host and hostess to musical and literary guests. On 16 December 1850 the celebrated performer Jenny Lind, known as "the Swedish Nightingale," and her famous manager, P. T. Barnum, visited the White House at the invitation of the entertainment-loving Fillmores.[97] In contrast to the prim and proper Polks, who never stepped into a theater during their administration, the Fillmores enjoyed entertainment and attended both of Jenny Lind's Washington, D.C., concerts.[98] In February 1853 the Fillmores, president-elect Franklin Pierce, and *The Legend of Sleepy Hollow* author Washington Irving, almost as old and venerable as his character Rip Van Winkle, attended a lecture by William Makepeace Thackeray, the noted English author of *Vanity Fair.*[99] Both Irving and Thackeray attended a dinner held by the president and Mrs. Fillmore in honor of the incoming president on 28 February 1853.

Like Margaret Taylor, Abigail Fillmore was a strong woman who might have achieved more if not for declining health and a short White House tenure.[100] Less than a month after leaving the executive mansion, Abigail died at the Willard Hotel in Washington on 30 March 1853. President Pierce, who had recently suffered a tragic bereavement himself, addressed a heartfelt letter to his predecessor, suspended a cabinet meeting, ordered public offices closed, and sent his private secretary to notify the Senate, which promptly adjourned.[101] Ironically, the precedent for congressional adjournment upon the death of a first lady had been established during Abigail's tenure in 1852 when Louisa Adams, widow of John Quincy Adams, died in Washington, the first first lady to die in the capital while Congress was in session.[102]

JANE PIERCE: CHIEF MOURNER

Born 12 March 1806 in Hampton, New Hampshire, Jane was the daughter of the Reverend Jesse Appleton, who became the president of Bowdoin College in Maine, and Elizabeth Means Appleton. Coming from a family of teachers and ministers, she was both well educated for her day and religious.[103] Like Abigail Fillmore, Jane was the daughter of a minister who died when she was young, leaving her mother with six children and facing relative poverty. Jane's upbringing could be considered more "genteel" than Abigail's, as her family went to live with her mother's wealthy relatives.[104] Shy, reserved Jane finally married the gregarious congressman and attorney Franklin Pierce on 19 November 1834 in Amherst, New Hampshire.

As Margaret Taylor had, Jane Pierce disliked political life. Jane was whisked away from the shelter of rich relations to what must have been the shocking roughness of Washington. Although the "mess" life could be empowering for hardier women like Sarah Polk and a younger Abigail Fillmore, it challenged frail Jane because living conditions were often crude and uncomfortable and there "was nothing to do but talk, think, and act politics."[105] Illness was common in the city built on a disease-ridden swamp, and in the miserably hot summer months in Washington, "Mrs. Pierce wilted and took to her bed."[106] Jane Pierce suffered a lifetime of bad health and was often melancholy even before a series of tragedies beset her and her husband.

Whereas Sarah Polk had ambitiously promoted her husband's political career and administration, Jane Pierce opposed Franklin's political pursuits. The heavy drinking of other politicians, she felt, aggravated her husband's problems with alcohol.[107] Jane observed, "Oh, how I wish he was out of political life! How much better it would be for him on every account!"[108] In 1842 Jane persuaded Franklin to resign from the Senate, although he was a rising star, and come home to New Hampshire where he would be close to his family and away from bad influences. However, not all of Franklin's career moves can be solely ascribed to Jane's concerns about him. At the time of his resignation he and Jane had two sons, their first son having died a few days after birth. According to the campaign biography written by Nathaniel Hawthorne, Franklin left the Senate because he thought he could make a better living for his family as an attorney.[109] Sadly, the Pierces' second son died the following year.

In 1846 President Polk asked Franklin to join his cabinet as attorney general, but Franklin declined, stating, "Besides you know that Mrs. Pierce's health while at Washington, was very delicate."[110] Jane was even opposed to Franklin running for governor of New Hampshire, an office his father had held and in which he could have gained the executive ability he lacked before becoming president. When the Pierces learned that Franklin had been nominated for president, "Mrs. Pierce fainted away," and their last son, Bennie, wrote his mother, "I hope [Father] won't be elected for I should not like to be at Washington and I know you would not either."[111] Franklin Pierce was elected to the presidency in November 1852, but his happiness was short-lived.

Franklin and Jane saw their last surviving son killed in a railroad accident in Massachusetts on 6 January 1853, just two months before Franklin became president. Their car hurtled down a ledge, separating in the middle and breaking into "many thousand fragments." The Reverend Mr. Fuller, a passenger on the doomed train, gave this account to the *Manchester Mirror:*

> I saw the most appalling scene of all. There was [a] mother, whose agony passes beyond any description. She could shed no tears, but, overcome with grief, uttered such affecting words as I can never forget. It was Mrs. Pierce, the wife of the President-elect; and near her in the ruin of shivered glass and iron, lay a more terrible ruin—her only son, one minute before so beautiful, so full of life and hope . . . she was conveyed to a house near, and there she gave vent to the grief that rent her heart, while he [Franklin Pierce] consoled and comforted. . . . The blow by which he was killed instantly struck his forehead, and was so violent as to remove the upper portion of the head, leaving a part of the brain exposed. The face, with the exception of a bruise above the right eye, still remained uninjured, but bathed in blood.[112]

Jane was in mourning throughout her husband's administration, and much disagreement centers on how many of her duties as president's wife she performed. Generally it has been assumed that Mrs. Pierce, who never wanted to be first lady, became "the shadow in the White House" by sequestering herself to upstairs rooms and carrying out virtually no social and public duties. However, some of her contemporaries insist that she bravely discharged her duties at receptions and dinners, even though her heart was not in the public requirements of her position.

The Pierces' troubled marriage following the shock of Bennie's death represents a separation of the spheres, with Franklin immersing himself in his public and political duties and Jane retreating to her private domain. Jane felt betrayed when she learned that Franklin had actively sought the nomination despite his avowals to her that he had no interest in the presidency, and historians have usually placed the responsibility for the Pierce estrangement on Jane.[113] In the words of Pierce biographer Roy Nichols, "In two short months, she had lost her boy and her faith in her husband's integrity. Hereafter, she could look accusingly at him; his presidential ambitions were the cause of the boy's death . . . Mrs. Pierce chose her own apartments and retired to them."[114] Even as a devastated victim Jane Pierce has been attributed with negative power, as modern critics have blamed her for Franklin's subsequent failure as president and even for contributing to the "start of the Civil War by adversely affecting her husband's performance in office."[115]

However, in a letter to her sister Mary, Jane Pierce indicated that her husband's presidential duties kept them apart, as she decried the lack of closeness with him. "My husband is occupied every moment . . . if I sometimes have my hopes raised of having him with me for ten, twenty, or thirty minutes, I am generally disappointed—and often much disheartened and saddened for the want of communion in our sorrow, and thoughts and feelings connected with it."[116] Varina Davis, the wife of Pierce's secretary of war, Jefferson Davis, confirmed that Mr. Pierce's "society was the one thing necessary to her, and he was too overworked to give her much of his time."[117]

Sad, ethereal Jane perfectly embodied the conception of chief mourner. Like Sarah Polk, Jane wore mourning clothes for the rest of her life, and she carried with her locks of hair from her dearly departed sons.[118] Mrs. Davis would find Mrs. Pierce in the White House library "bent over the blinding fine print of Thornton's *Family Prayers,* which always was in evidence on a center table in the oval library."[119] Jane also read her Bible and wrote letters, including notes to her dead son. This minister's daughter urged staff to attend religious services, and Pierce's private secretary later admitted, "Many a time have I gone from respect to her, when left to my own choice, I should have remained in the house."[120]

In the state rooms Jane, as manager of the White House, "ordered mourning bunting placed indefinitely."[121] A journalist of the time evoked a desolate, gothic vision: "The President's house had assumed a somber, melancholy aspect. . . . Everything seemed to partake of her own serious melancholy and mournful feelings, and every echo of the merry laugh had died from the walls."[122] Jane linked the death of her predecessor, Abigail Fillmore, to the presidency and the White House, writing, "Fatality seems connected with the occupants of this office and Mansion."[123] Adding to the gloom, Pierce's vice president, William Rufus Devane King, died on 19 April, just a few weeks after Abigail Fillmore's death.

Jane Pierce, as a political adviser during the conflict over slavery in "Bleeding Kansas," played a role in preventing another death: She interceded with her husband to free from imprisonment Charles Robinson, who as leader of the antislavery, free-state settlers in Lawrence, had been indicted in 1856 for treason by proslavery courts.[124] Dr. Robinson's wife, Sara Tappan Doolittle Lawrence, was a distant relation of the Lawrence family of Massachusetts and therefore kin to Jane Pierce. Mrs. Pierce received letters from Mrs. Robinson and Nancy Means Lawrence, Jane's aunt, pleading for the release of Dr. Robinson. According to one letter, the proslavery Kansas governor had threatened that Robinson was "certain to be tried, and if tried he will be convicted, and if convicted he will be hung."[125] Jane showed Franklin the letters and President Pierce telegraphed orders satisfactory to the wishes of his wife's aunt, "whose good opinion he declared he valued 'more than that of all the politicians,'" and as a consequence, Dr. Robinson was eventually released.[126]

Jane never recovered from the deaths of her children, particularly the violent death of Bennie. After leaving the White House, Jane wrote that "the deep scars on the heart chafe & bleed afresh."[127]

Conclusion

In an era in which women were expected to remain in the private domain, these four proper ladies contributed to their husbands' administrations in varying degrees as loyal wives, homemakers, hostesses, cultural arbiters, intercessors, helpmates, and advisers. All four first ladies established their own places in both the White House and in their husbands' administrations. Indeed, the Fillmore and Pierce administrations might be looked upon more favorably had those men listened more to their wives.

Although she had to achieve her political ambitions through her husband, Sarah Polk set precedents and was actively political; yet she still managed to remain respected and socially accepted. Margaret Taylor avoided publicity but managed to remain with her husband and support him in the White House. Abigail Fillmore made the executive mansion more habitable for herself, her family, and future first families by establishing a library and presenting the presidency as a magnet of culture. Jane Pierce carried out required duties yet maintained room for her great grief. In a time quite different from our twenty-first century, these first ladies were "true women" faithful to the conventions of their era yet true to themselves.

NOTES

1. The quote is from Anne Firor Scott, *The Southern Lady: From Pedestal to Politics, 1830–1930* (Chicago: University of Chicago Press, 1970), ix.

2. Carl Sferrazza Anthony, *First Ladies: The Saga of the Presidents' Wives and Their Power, 1789–1961* (New York: Quill/William Morrow, 1990), 138–39; William Seale, *The President's House: A History* (Washington, D.C.: White House Historical Association, 1986), 261.

3. Edna M. Colman, *Seventy-Five Years of White House Gossip from Washington to Lincoln* (Garden City, N.J.: Doubleday, Page, 1925), 223; Holman Hamilton, *Zachary Taylor: Soldier of the Republic* (Indianapolis, Ind.: Bobbs-Merrill, 1941), 1, 117, 278.

4. "A Pipe-Dream Story," *Literary Digest* 86 (1 August 1925): 40.

5. Ibid.; Michael Minor and Larry F. Vrzalik, "A Study in Tragedy: Jane Means Pierce First Lady, 1853–1857," *Manuscripts* 40 (summer 1988): 178, 184–85.

6. Robert P. Watson, *The Presidents' Wives: Reassessing the Office of First Lady* (Boulder, Colo.: Lynne Rienner Publishers, 2000), 51.

7. Aileen S. Kraditor, *Up from the Pedestal: Selected Writings in the History of American Feminism* (Chicago, Ill.: Triangle Books, 1968), 11; Barbara Welter, "The Cult of True Womanhood: 1820–1860," *American Quarterly* 18 (summer 1966): 151.

8. The roles adapted for this essay were identified in the Smithsonian exhibit "First Ladies: Political Role and Public Image" and by Watson in *Presidents' Wives*.

9. Catherine Allgor, "Political Parties: Society and Politics in Washington, D.C.: 1800–1832" (Ph.D. diss., Yale University, 1998), 5; *Parlor Politics: In Which the Ladies of Washington Help Build a City and a Government* (Charlottesville: University Press of Virginia, 2000): 1–2, 83, 100–101, 118–19.

10. Scott, *Southern Lady,* 19.

11. Welter, "Cult of True Womanhood," 170–71.

12. *In Memoriam: Mrs. Jas. K. Polk* (Nashville, Tenn.: S. N., 1891), 12.

13. Watson, *Presidents' Wives,* 45; Betty Boyd Caroli, "The First Lady's Changing Role," in *The White House: The First Two Hundred Years,* ed. Frank Freidel and William Pencak (Boston: Northeastern University Press, 1994), 180.

14. Watson, *Presidents' Wives,* 80–81.

15. Anson Nelson and Fanny Nelson, *Memorials of Sarah Childress Polk* (New York: Anson D. F. Randolph & Co., 1892), 118.

16. Allgor, "Political Parties," 137; Allgor, *Parlor Politics,* 78–79; Watson, *Presidents' Wives,* 76.

17. Ann Douglas Wood, "The Fashionable Diseases: Women's Complaints and Their Treatment in Nineteenth Century America," *Journal of Interdisciplinary History* 4 (summer 1973): 26–25.

18. Bess Furman, *White House Profile* (Indianapolis, Ind.: Bobbs-Merrill, 1951), 156–57.

19. Laura Carpenter Holloway, *The Ladies of the White House* (New York: U.S. Publishing, 1870), 505.

20. Ibid, 526–28; Elizabeth F. Ellet, *Court Circles of the Republic or the Beauties and Celebrities of the Nation* (Hartford, Conn.: Hartford Publishing, 1871), 460.

21. Anne Hollingsworth Wharton, *Social Life in the Early Republic* (Philadelphia, Pa.: J. B. Lippincott, 1902), 312–13.

22. Roy Franklin Nichols, *Franklin Pierce: Young Hickory of the Granite Hills* (Philadelphia: University of Pennsylvania Press, 1958), 439–40.

23. Furman, *White House Profile,* 159.

24. Carole Chandler Waldrup, *Presidents' Wives: The Lives of 44 American Women of Strength* (Jefferson, N.C.: McFarland & Co., 1989), 98.

25. Sol Barzman, *The First Ladies* (New York: Cowles Book Co., 1970), 124; Mary Ormsbee Whitton, *First First Ladies, 1789–1865: A Study of the Wives of the Early Presidents* (1948; reprint, Freeport, N.Y.: Books for Libraries Press, 1969), 207–8.

26. Deborah Kent, *Jane Means Appleton Pierce, 1806–1863* (New York: Children's Press, 1998), 55.

27. Watson, *Presidents' Wives,* 34.

28. Nelson, *Memorials,* 198–99.

29. Seale, *President's House,* 273.

30. Nelson, *Memorials,* 99.

31. Whitton, *First First Ladies,* 248.

32. William Elliot Griffis, "Millard Fillmore's Forgotten Achievements," *Harper's Monthly Magazine* 122 (May 1911): 70; Griffis, *Millard Fillmore: Constructive Statesman, Defender of the Constitution, President of the United States* (Ithaca, N.Y.: Andrus and Church, 1915), 70.

33. Anthony, *First Ladies,* 159.

34. Thomas H. Appleton, "Margaret (Mackall Smith) Taylor," in *American First Ladies: Their Lives and Their Legacy,* ed. Lewis L. Gould (New York: Garland, 1996), 152.

35. Jayne Crumpler DeFiore, "Sarah (Childress) Polk," in *American First Ladies: Their Lives and Their Legacy,* ed. Lewis L. Gould (New York: Garland, 1996), 131.

36. Waldrup, *Presidents' Wives,* 97.

37. Allgor, "Political Parties," 227; Allgor, *Parlor Politics,* 111, 118–19.

38. Nelson, *Memorials,* 52.

39. Ibid., 162.

40. Waldrup, *Presidents' Wives,* 98.

41. Sarah Agnes Wallace, "Letters of Mrs. James K. Polk to Her Husband," *Tennessee Historical Quarterly* 11 (June 1952): 187–88.

42. Watson, *Presidents' Wives,* 52.

43. Edith P. Mayo, *Smithsonian Book of the First Ladies: Their Lives, Times, and Issues* (New York: Henry Holt and Co., 1996), 70.

44. George Dallas to Mrs. Dallas, 16, 18 Feb. 1845, Dallas Papers, Historical Society of Pennsylvania, Philadelphia.

45. Seale, *President's House,* 249–77.

46. Ibid., 256–57.

47. Nelson, *Memorials,* 80.

48. Margaret Brown Klapthor, *The First Ladies Cook Book* (New York: Parents Magazine Enterprises, 1982), 85.

49. Seale, *President's House,* 257.

50. Jessie Benton Fremont, *Souvenirs of My Time* (Boston: D. Lothrop & Co., 1887), 93; Whitton, *First First Ladies,* 208.

51. Nelson, *Memorials,* 114.

52. Anthony, *First Ladies,* 139.

53. Nelson, *Memorials,* 110–11; Waldrup, *Presidents' Wives,* 100.

54. William R. Polk, *Polk's Folly* (New York: Doubleday, 2000), 187; Seale, *President's House,* 265.

55. Nelson, *Memorials,* 94; Mayo, *Smithsonian Book,* 70.

56. Nelson, *Memorials,* 94.

57. *In Memoriam,* 4.

58. Holloway, *Ladies,* 441.

59. Waldrup, *Presidents' Wives,* 101.

60. Nelson, *Memorials,* 261–62.

61. Appleton, "Margaret Taylor," 145.

62. Klapthor, *First Ladies Cook Book,* 89.

63. Ibid., 87.

64. Waldrup, *Presidents' Wives,* 106; Appleton, "Margaret Taylor," 149.

65. Holloway, *Ladies,* 478–79.

66. Ishbel Ross, *First Lady of the South: The Life of Mrs. Jefferson Davis* (New York: Harper & Brothers, 1958), 58.

67. Colman, *Seventy-Five Years,* 218.

68. Holman Hamilton, *Zachary Taylor: Soldier in the White House* (Indianapolis, Ind.: Bobbs-Merrill, 1951), 25.

69. Ibid., 135.

70. Holloway, *Ladies,* 484.

71. Hamilton, *Zachary Taylor: Soldier in the White House,* 396.

72. Holloway, *Ladies,* 487.

73. Hamilton, *Zachary Taylor: Soldier in the White House,* 221.

74. Ross, *First Lady,* 58.

75. Colman, *Seventy-Five Years,* 223; Welter, "Cult of True Womanhood," 165.

76. Hamilton, *Zachary Taylor: Soldier in the White House,* 171.

77. Ibid., 223, 241.

78. Nancy F. Cott, *The Bonds of Womanhood: "Woman's Sphere" in New England, 1780–1835* (New Haven, Conn.: Yale University Press, 1977), 7.

79. Seale, *President's House,* 281.

80. Hamilton, *Zachary Taylor: Soldier in the White House,* 220, 165–66.

81. Anthony, *First Ladies,* 151.

82. Harvey Green, *The Light of the Home: An Intimate View of the Lives of Women in Victorian America* (New York: Pantheon Books, 1983), 171.

83. Hamilton, *Zachary Taylor: Soldier in the White House,* 398.

84. Cott, *Bonds,* 6; Karen O'Connor, Bernadette Nye, and Laura Van Assendelft, "Wives in the White House: The Political Influence of First Ladies," *Presidential Studies Quarterly* 26 (summer 1996): 838.

85. Kristin Hoganson, "Abigail (Powers) Fillmore," in *American First Ladies: Their Lives and Their Legacy,* ed. Lewis L. Gould (New York: Garland, 1996), 155.

86. O'Connor, Nye, Van Assendelft, "Wives in the White House," 838.

87. William Elliot Griffis, "Millard Fillmore's Forgotten Achievements," *Harper's Monthly Magazine* 122 (May 1911): 943.

88. Hoganson, *Abigail Fillmore,* 157.

89. John J. Farrell, *Zachary Taylor, 1784–1850; Millard Fillmore, 1800–1874: Chronology, Documents, Bibliographical Aids* (Dobbs Ferry, N.Y.: Oceana Publications, 1971), 51.

90. John C. Rives, *The Congressional Globe: New Series, Containing Sketches of the Debates and Proceedings of the First Session of the Thirty-First Congress,* vol. 22, pt. 2 (Washington, D.C.: Blair & Rives, 1850), 1926.

91. Furman, *White House Profile,* 156.

92. Welter, "Cult of True Womanhood," 165; Wharton, *Social Life,* 311; Elise Kuhl Kirk, *Music at the White House: A History of the American Spirit* (Urbana: University of Illinois Press, 1986), 70.

93. Holloway, *Ladies,* 506–7.

94. Furman, *White House Profile,* 156.

95. Elisabeth Donaghy Garrett, *At Home: The American Family, 1750–1870* (New York: Harry N. Abrams, 1990), 64–65.

96. Abigail Fillmore to Mrs. John Bryant, 26 Jan. 1851, Millard Fillmore Papers, State University of New York, Oswego.

97. P. T. Barnum, *Struggles and Triumphs: or, Forty Years' Recollections* (Hartford, Conn.: J. B. Burr & Co., 1869), 310–11.

98. Whitton, *First First Ladies,* 208; Kirk, *Music,* 69.

99. Ann Monsarrat, *An Uneasy Victorian: Thackeray The Man, 1811–1863* (New York: Dodd, Mead, 1980), 313.

100. Watson, *Presidents' Wives,* 51.

101. Seale, *President's House,* 304; Hoganson, "Abigail Fillmore," 164.

102. Public tour and conversation at Adams National Historic Site, Quincy, Mass., 18 Oct. 1998.

103. Minor and Vrzalik, "Study in Tragedy," 178.

104. Lloyd C. Taylor, "A Wife for Mr. Pierce," *The New England Quarterly* 28 (Sept. 1955): 339; Waldrup, *Presidents' Wives,* 120.

105. Roy Franklin Nichols, "The Causes of the Civil War," in *Interpreting American History: Conversations with Historians,* ed. John Arthur Garraty (New York: Macmillan, 1970), 282.

106. Nichols, *Franklin Pierce,* 104.

107. Nichols, "Causes," 286.

108. Nichols, *Franklin Pierce,* 104.

109. Nathaniel Hawthorne, *The Life of Franklin Pierce* (Boston: Ticknor, Reed, and Fields, 1852), 46.

110. Whitton, *First First Ladies,* 255.

111. Nichols, *Franklin Pierce,* 203, 205.

112. Whitton, *First First Ladies,* 260–61.

113. Nichols, "Causes," 286–87.

114. Nichols, *Franklin Pierce,* 536.

115. Nichols, "Causes," 286–87; Minor and Vrzalik, "Study in Tragedy," 185.

116. Jane Pierce to Mary Aiken, 1853, James S. Copley Library, University of San Diego, La Jolla, Calif.

117. Varina Davis, *Jefferson Davis: Ex-President of the Confederate States of America, A Memoir by His Wife,* vol. 1 (New York: Belford Co., 1890), 540.

118. Minor and Vrzalik, "Study in Tragedy," 182; Mayo, *Smithsonian,* 83; Anthony, *First Ladies,* 159.

119. Hudson Strode, *Jefferson Davis: American Patriot, 1808–1861* (New York: Harcourt, Brace, 1955), 257.

120. Whitton, *First First Ladies,* 262.

121. Anthony, *First Ladies,* 157.

122. Klapthor, *First Ladies Cook Book,* 100.

123. Jane Pierce to Mary Aiken, 1853, James S. Copley Library, University of San Diego, La Jolla, Calif.

124. Nichols, *Franklin Pierce,* 478, 483.

125. Frank W. Blackman, *The Life of Charles Robinson, the First State Governor of Kansas* (Topeka, Kans: Crane & Company, 1902), 433.

126. Nichols, *Franklin Pierce,* 483, 478.

127. Norman F. Boas, *Jane M. Pierce (1806–1863): The Pierce-Aiken Papers: Letters of Jane M. Pierce, her Sister Mary M. Aiken, their Family, and President Franklin Pierce, with Biographies of Jane Pierce, Other Members of her Family, and Genealogical Tables* (Stonington, Conn.: Seaport Autographs, 1983), 74.

Five

Edith Bolling Galt Wilson

The Protective Steward

James S. McCallops

Introduction

"Turn a corner and meet your fate" was the expression Edith Bolling Galt Wilson used to describe her first meeting with her future husband, Woodrow Wilson, in March 1915.[1] According to this story, she and Wilson's cousin Helen Woodrow Bones had just returned from an outing at Rock Creek Park looking quite disheveled and splattered with mud. Helen Bones, who had served as White House hostess since the death of the president's first wife, Ellen, in 1914, assured Edith that Wilson was out golfing and that they would not be seen in their present condition. However, as they exited the White House elevator on the second floor and rounded the corner, Edith and Helen came face-to-face with the president and his doctor, Adm. Cary Grayson, fresh from their golf game and looking quite dirty themselves. Years later Edith would remember this fateful meeting as the beginning of her presidential romance that would culminate with her role as first lady and confidante to the president.[2]

The closeness of the Wilson marriage served to change the dynamics of Woodrow Wilson's presidency, as old friends and key advisers were pushed out of favor and replaced by Edith, although she denied any influence over her husband, claiming that her role was only as a devoted wife. Her devotion to Wilson also fostered a protectiveness that was readily apparent during the Paris Peace Conference and after Wilson's subsequent stroke in the fall of 1919, when she became an unofficial regent. While Edith's true role during that period remains unclear, it can be said that her fame and power were unexpected achievements for this southern woman who previously had been disinterested in politics.

Background on Edith

Born in Virginia on 15 October 1872, Edith was one of nine surviving children in the Bolling family. Her father, whom she idolized, was a lawyer and circuit court judge. He had fought in the Civil War for the Confederacy, only to witness the loss of the family plantation near Lynchburg at the war's conclusion. He then moved his family to Wytheville, Virginia, where Edith was born. The Bollings were well respected and traced their lineage back to revolutionary times. In fact, they were descendants of Pocahontas, a point touted in press releases announcing Edith's engagement to Woodrow Wilson.

Growing up, Edith received an informal education from her father and paternal grandmother, but when she was fifteen Judge Bolling sent Edith away to Martha Washington College in Abingdon, Virginia. Edith recalled that the school lacked adequate food or heat and that she returned quite thin.[3] The next year Edith was sent to the Powell School in Richmond, Virginia. She seemed to enjoy her time there, but the tuition was expensive and the Bollings also had three sons to educate. Although pleased with Edith's intelligence, the judge believed that it was more important that his sons, rather than Edith, received quality educations. Thus Edith's formal education ended after less than three years, and consequently she traveled to Washington, D.C., to spend time with her newly married sister, Gertrude.

As a carefree eighteen-year-old in 1890, Edith was fascinated by the nation's capital. She enjoyed the opera and theater and was also exposed to high fashion, which would later become her trademark. One night at supper during her stay Edith, through her sister, met Norman Galt, the senior partner in a family silversmith firm and a cousin of Edith's brother-in-law. Norman was immediately struck by Edith's charm and beauty. It was months of flowers, candies, and dinners before his intentions became clear to Edith, but she was in no hurry to marry and settle down. Their courtship lasted four years until, on 30 April 1896, the twenty-three-year-old Edith married Norman, who was eight years her senior. She claimed that, although she cared for him, she was not in love.[4]

For the next twelve years Edith remained Norman's devoted wife, supporting her husband but not involving herself in his business affairs. Edith ran the household and enjoyed the financial resources her husband's business provided. She was always fashionably dressed, loved to attend the theater, and could be seen around town motoring in her new electric car. But the Galts were in "the trades," which meant that Washington, D.C., society was closed to them. The "Cliff Dwellers," as the social upper class was called, scorned shop owners and businessmen. The fact that Edith was never part of the higher social clique did not seem to bother her. She claimed that her marriage was fulfilling enough,[5] although her desire to have children was never realized after complications from an early miscarriage. Instead, Edith devoted her time, energy, and Norman's money to helping her rather large extended family.

Life changed in 1908 when Norman, diagnosed with a rare liver ailment, died suddenly. Edith was now a widow and sole owner of Galt's store. She elected not to sell the business and continued to run it through a manager. She was involved in daily operations, garnering praise from workers and associates for her astute business acumen. Things went well until her trusted manager died and she found it difficult to replace him. The business began to suffer. Finally, faced with mounting financial problems, Edith decided to sell the business to its employees. That decision allowed her a level of financial independence that middle-class women in the early twentieth century could rarely find outside of marriage.

She made one trip to Europe with her sister following the sale of the business. In 1911 she met seventeen-year-old Alice "Altrude" Gertrude Gordon, whose friendship would ultimately bring the paths of Edith and Woodrow Wilson together. Altrude was the only child of James Gordon, an engineer from Scotland who had made a fortune in Texas. Gordon's deceased wife had been a beauty from Virginia who was an acquaintance of the Bolling family. When James Gordon was diagnosed with cancer in 1911, Altrude found herself relying more and more on her new friend Edith for advice and companionship, and the two became close friends. Edith suggested that the two of them travel to Europe, which they did for five months and then took another trip to Europe in 1913, having even more fun than they had on their first voyage.

Ultimately a new romance in Altrude's life came to affect Edith. In late 1913 Altrude attended a barracks dance and caught the eye of Adm. Cary Grayson, who had been the personal physician to Presidents Theodore Roosevelt and William Howard Taft and who was currently assigned to President Wilson. Grayson was a distinguished gentleman, considered quite a catch by Washington society women. Because of his interest in Altrude and her growing interest in him, Edith served as a chaperon on many occasions. Grayson grew to respect Edith and found her to be charming and lively. It was Grayson who recommended that Edith meet Helen Woodrow Bones, the president's cousin and White House hostess, through whom Edith would be introduced to the president.[6]

Woodrow and Edith

Since Edith had no interest in politics, she knew little of President Wilson or his family. Woodrow Wilson and his first wife, Ellen, were married for more than twenty-five years and had three daughters. Two, Jessie and Eleanor, were married in the White House in 1913 and 1914 respectively, while

Margaret was too interested in music and art to spend much time in the White House, preferring New York City instead. Ellen Wilson championed the cause of slum clearance and lobbied politicians to clean up the Washington, D.C., area. In June 1914 she made national headlines for fainting during an official receiving line. Soon after the first lady was diagnosed with Bright's disease. Her health continued to fail until she finally passed away in August 1914. The president was grief-stricken, and the outbreak of war in Europe served only to exacerbate his feelings of sorrow, as he threw himself into his work in an attempt to push aside his grief. According to White House insiders such as Grayson, the pall within the executive mansion was stifling.[7]

As their friendship grew, Grayson kept Edith informed of the first family's plight. She never admitted to asking specific questions about Woodrow Wilson or his daughters and instead indicated that Grayson, unsolicited, provided those details. Her meeting and friendship with Helen Bones, however, without doubt resulted from Grayson's introduction. The two new friends motored around town in Edith's automobile and took extended walks in Rock Creek Park. It was after one of those excursions that Edith found herself face-to-face with President Wilson on that March afternoon. Following an agreement that all parties at that fateful meeting would freshen up and reassemble, the four gathered in the Oval Room for tea. The president loved good conversation and found a suitable companion in Edith. He enjoyed her quick wit and the stories she told, since he was quite a storyteller too. Although she was invited to stay for dinner, Edith declined, as she did not wish to impose herself too much after a first meeting.[8] Woodrow Wilson was captivated.

Wilson attempted to spend as much time with Edith as she would allow. They went for drives (he loved to be driven around in his Pierce Arrow, claiming that the fresh air allowed him to think), had dinner at the White House, and corresponded frequently beginning in April 1915. Wilson was in love and ready to propose. He discussed the matter with his daughters, who liked Edith and supported their father's decision. But Edith requested time to consider his sudden proposal.[9] First, if she married Wilson, she would become a stepmother to three adult daughters who might resent the new woman in their father's life. Second, she would be marrying a man who not only carried the burden of governing the country but was also struggling to keep the United States out of the raging war in Europe. Would her presence help Woodrow or add more stress to his already complex life?

Following the sinking of the *Lusitania,* Wilson confided in Edith that Secretary of State William Jennings Bryan had submitted his resignation in protest over the president's handling of the situation. Wilson asked Edith what she thought. Her response was, "Good; for I hope you can replace him with someone who is able and who in himself commands respect for the office both at home and abroad."[10] When he suggested Robert Lansing for the post, she dismissed the man as too young and inexperienced to handle the job. Although the president disregarded her opinion this time, his willingness to discuss governmental issues with her illustrated the trust and respect they shared.

Ultimately, after time and constant assurances of his love for her, Edith agreed to Wilson's marriage proposal.[11] Their engagement was publicly announced on 6 October 1915, and Edith immediately became the subject of intense scrutiny. The couple attended a World Series baseball game and the Army-Navy football game as a way of introducing her to the public. Edith recalled that it felt as if all eyes were on her, but she was comforted by the fact that she was well attired in fashionable outfits and hats. The scrutiny continued. Leading Democratic women attempted to "catch up" with Edith, but she avoided them and eluded the press whenever possible. Never one of the Washington, D.C., "insiders," Edith felt no need to hobnob with them now that she was the president's fiancée. Although she planned to pursue no personal causes, she stated that her time was limited so as to be "on call" whenever the president needed her.[12] Wilson's growing dependence on Edith concerned his advisers, who complained that he never had time for them and was increasingly turning to his fiancée for advice or consultation. Col. Edward House, a longtime Wilson supporter and political heavyweight who helped orchestrate Wilson's presidential victory, quickly recognized Edith's power over the president and chose to gauge her willingness to take advice from him as her soon-to-be husband had always done. He warned her about the burdens she was about to take on and cautioned her about discretion. Although she listened politely, Edith was unimpressed by House and, in fact, thought him rather meddlesome. Her disdain for him was immediate, evidenced by his failure to receive a wedding invitation, and grew during the Paris Peace Conference.[13]

On 18 December 1915 forty-three-year-old Edith Bolling Galt married fifty-nine-year-old (he would be sixty on 28 December) Woodrow Wilson in a quiet ceremony at Edith's home. Only fifty family members and intimate friends were invited to witness the event as Edith and Woodrow exchanged vows, he in a cutaway coat, white waistcoat, and gray-stripped pants and she in black velvet gown and hat, feather plume, and diamond brooch. Following the ceremony and a sit-down dinner, Edith and Woodrow departed for their honeymoon.

First Lady: Making Her Presence Felt

Upon returning to Washington, D.C., Edith entered the whirlwind of presidential politics in her role as first lady. Her wish was not to upset the pattern already established at the White House; she fired no staff and made no major rearrangements. She did, however, become recognized as a dignified and considerate hostess. While some people may not have liked her personally, they could not find fault with her control over White House events. After her first party for participants in the Pan-American Conference on 9 January 1916 Edith had decided to assume a larger role in official planning. Because of a mixup in invitation lists, over three thousand people attended. Although Edith and the president shook everyone's hand and remained cheerful and good-natured throughout the event, Edith was displeased.[14] A new order was issued that all invitation lists for such parties had to pass through the White House first. The same was true for lists of invitees compiled by the Senate and House of Representatives. Edith and her staff would now control those events.

Within their private quarters the Wilsons settled into their own routine. First, she set up a bedroom for him (bringing down the Lincoln bed) and fixed up her own bedroom with furniture from the house she inhabited before their marriage. Second, Edith knew that her husband often liked to work late into the night, only to awaken early and resume work again. To accommodate his schedule she had his breakfast ready by 6:00 A.M. The White House servants, who liked both Woodrow and Edith, readily complied with the first lady's request. Following breakfast Wilson played a round of golf (a form of exercise Dr. Grayson prescribed for the president), then commenced governmental business for a number of hours before breaking for lunch, followed by more work. In the late afternoon he enjoyed a car ride with his wife to clear his head and relax, followed by dinner and often more work.

Edith made it her priority to anticipate her husband's needs. For example, she understood that he had a temperamental stomach that often rebelled at food, so she kept snacks around for those times when he was hungry but the kitchen was closed. She also guarded his rest. She was known to reprimand a servant for making noise when the president was resting, but that was one of the few times she became angry with the staff. This guarding of his time and rest also translated into keeping advisers and cabinet officials from dropping in on the president. They quickly discovered that, without an appointment and with a gatekeeping first lady, it was difficult to see

Woodrow. Edith would claim that he was busy and ask that they visit another time.

For the new Mrs. Wilson, the first year of her marriage was stressful because of the limelight of the first ladyship and the presidential campaign in which she had to participate. Once Wilson received his party's nomination in June 1916, supporters of the president began arriving at the White House to discuss the campaign. She had to be charming and personable even when she was less than thrilled with those in attendance. This was the case with the suffragists who were attempting to get Wilson and the Democratic Party to back the woman suffrage amendment. Edith found the women pushy and aggressive in their determination to win their point, and although she smiled, inwardly she wished that they would all leave.[15] Having to hide her feelings and portray a smiling facade was even more difficult at public events, where she was under constant scrutiny. Edith joined her husband for rallies and speeches to throngs of supporters across the country.

The Wilsons traveled to Princeton, where the president voted, but since New Jersey did not yet allow women the right to vote, Edith waited in the car. Her hopes for a victory were small. She truly felt that Wilson had done some wonderful things for the country, but she believed that the Republican candidate, Charles Evans Hughes, had a large amount of money that would turn the tide in his favor. In addition Edith still wondered if her marriage to the president had hurt his chances with some voters. Personally she was conflicted.[16] On the one hand, she would have been happy to retire from the spotlight and spend her time with Wilson. But on the other hand, she knew that her husband desperately wanted another term. Consequently she put aside her wants to support her husband. The early returns looked dismal; most papers were expecting a Hughes victory and had run stories highlighting his personal and professional life. The vote tally stretched into a third day before it became clear that Wilson had pulled out a victory by over five hundred thousand votes. He was jubilant.

WARTIME PARTNER

The election was but one of Wilson's concerns. The European war, a constant threat during the previous three years, built during the fall of 1916. While the president had been holding off those militants, such as Theodore Roosevelt, who had been pushing for United States involvement, he was secretly offering his mediation services to the warring parties in hopes of settling the conflict. By December 1916 it became clear that this was not working. This allowed Wilson to draft a speech calling for "Peace Without Victory," which laid out some of the issues that would eventually make up his Fourteen Points in 1918. Edith listened to early drafts and made suggestions that Wilson incorporated into the final version.

Although the speech was well received, the Germans answered his call for peace with a declaration of unrestricted submarine warfare around the British Isles, set to begin on 1 February 1917. Immediately Wilson recalled the United States ambassador to Germany and severed all diplomatic ties. As the situation with Germany heated up, Edith faced her own personal crisis when on 25 February her favorite sister, Annie Lee, died suddenly. Although stricken with grief, she appeared cheerful and positive largely to bolster the spirits of her husband,[17] who was weighted down with the looming prospect of war. In March, when Wilson took the oath of office for his second term, it was a solemn event. The parties and socializing that normally accompanied an inauguration were missing as the nation readied for war. Wilson caught a bad head cold and was ordered to bed, where he read all the reports available on the current war situation. Edith guarded his privacy, keeping people away for a week. After his recovery and faced with a disintegrating diplomatic situation, Wilson ultimately approached Congress on 2 April 1917 and asked for a declaration of war against Germany, which was granted after four days of debate.

U.S. entry into the war meant that the nation had to sacrifice and unify around the cause. The White House typified this move by ceasing all receptions and parties except those for visiting allies. This was not an unwelcome burden, as Edith much preferred time alone with Woodrow to large, formal receptions. Carriages were used instead of cars to preserve fuel, and Edith even arranged to have sheep brought onto the White House lawn to manage the growing grass so that men could be released for war service. People complained that the use of sheep was ridiculous and cheapened the appearance of the executive mansion, but those critics were quickly silenced when those same sheep produced ninety-eight pounds of wool that was used for the soldiers. Edith went to work for the war, volunteering with the Red Cross by serving coffee and sandwiches in the afternoon and bringing out her sewing machine to work on clothes for the soldiers. During meetings she would knit items for the soldiers too. The Shipping Board often asked the first lady to name and christen the new ships that came off the assembly line, and she was pleased that she could help in this manner, although she found it difficult to come up with hundreds of names.[18]

The war served to disrupt the personal routine that the Wilsons had established. For Edith, the war years took a toll on her love of high fashion.

She commented that she had not bought any new clothes during the war except a riding outfit.[19] More substantively, Edith witnessed the constant strain around her husband's eyes and also was aware of the newspaper articles that were highly critical of the president and his handling of the war effort. In an attempt to counter the effects of the criticism on her husband, Edith tried to create family gatherings that were lighthearted. While such diversions helped him, the war burdens continued to mount, threatening his precarious health. To avoid this, Edith doubled her efforts to get her husband to relax. Because they both loved sailing, they sometimes sneaked off to the presidential yacht, *Mayflower*, to sail out into the Chesapeake. But Wilson found happiness and contentment just having Edith close by, either listening to his stories, doing her knitting, or decoding his messages.[20] He also liked to have her around when important allies visited or cabinet officials came to discuss the domestic war issues. Most officials were unsure what role Edith actually played in the president's ultimate decisions and were uncomfortable with her presence.[21] It seems clear from what Edith and others have reported that her role was that of Wilson's sounding board and confidante.

As 1917 ended, the outcome of the war was far from certain. Romania had fallen, the Italians were in retreat, and Russia had been taken over by the Bolsheviks. As the Wilsons celebrated Christmas that year, they were well aware that the United States' involvement in the war had not reached its peak and more sacrifices were coming. Yet Wilson looked with hope on the future. He worked through the fall and into 1918 to compose his blueprint for world peace. Taking cues from earlier peace organizations along with his own personal sentiments, Wilson drafted his Fourteen Points and released the document in January 1918.[22] He envisioned it as the basis for ending war in Europe, so copies were distributed to the warring nations (though none was willing at that point to accept his terms). It was Woodrow's way of putting himself forward again as the mediator he had tried so hard to be in the early years of the war. For Edith this seemed like a natural position for her husband, as she felt he was so gifted and knowledgeable that it would be ludicrous for foreign leaders to ignore his talents. Her blind devotion to his abilities and her constant reinforcement of him served only to make him intransigent to other opinions, a failure that emerged both in Paris and later during his battle with the United States Senate.

With the end of war in November 1918, controversy erupted over who should represent the United States at the Paris Peace Conference. Wilson felt that he was the only man who could effectively champion the Fourteen Points proposal, and Edith naturally agreed. She began to undertake her own preparations for the trip as if it were a foregone conclusion that she would accompany the president. But Colonel House was concerned, as was Secretary of State Lansing, who argued that Congress was against Wilson going.[23] France and England were sending tough, street-smart politicians in Georges Clemenceau and David Lloyd George, who both claimed that they would not welcome Wilson's participation. Faced with all these opponents, Wilson became more convinced that he should attend, fearing that true peace would fail if left to others. While Wilson did take along advisers to help with the conference, no representative from the U.S. Senate or House of Representatives was included. This point came back to hurt him later, especially since off-year elections in November 1918 gave the Republicans a majority in both houses.[24]

In December the United States delegation departed for Paris. Edith had arranged the packing with much care to her own wardrobe. She commented that, faced with constant scrutiny, it was her obligation to dress well as a representative of the United States people. She turned to her favorite designer, Worth, whose American representative had workers traveling back and forth between New York City and Washington, D.C., for fittings and discussions with Edith. Some still felt Edith overspent on clothes, a lingering sentiment from her thirteen-hundred-dollar Worth wedding dress, but she ignored such criticisms. Her primary focus was on her husband, who was facing much greater pressure than even during the war. His goal was to create lasting world peace, which meant an international stage with many competing players. She worried over his health and was determined to be even more vigilant in protecting him.

During the voyage Edith shielded him from the press whenever possible and stressed the need for him to rest and eat well. Unfortunately his sensitive digestive tract was acting up, making it hard for him to eat. Edith also attended meetings that the president held with other conference participants. Thanks in part to his wife's efforts, the president arrived in France fit and ready to undertake the enormous task ahead of him. As the United States delegation reached Paris, they were greeted with cheers and applause from Parisians who turned out to thank the U.S. president for his country's help. Edith wrote that she had never before witnessed such a display of gratitude and love.[25] It was a pleasant beginning to a most arduous process.

Since the conference did not begin until January 1919, the first weeks of the Wilsons' trip to France were filled with ceremonies and official functions. They accepted gifts from the French, traveled to spend Christmas with U.S. troops stationed in the countryside, and sailed to England to meet the king and queen. In Paris they were housed in the Murat Palace, which Edith described as beautiful, although a bit pretentious.[26] A huge block wall protected it from the street, and two guard posts were the only ways into or out of the palace, providing a sense of security. Edith immediately began to create an environment within the palace where the president would feel comfortable and where she could see to his care.

The conference was immensely draining on Wilson. The political bickering among conference participants caused Wilson to put in eighteen-hour days in meetings with various parties as well as in his own research and writing. Although all nations involved in the conflict were invited to attend and participate in the conference, it quickly became a gathering controlled by France, England, Italy, and the United States. The competing and contradicting pleas from individuals and nations for spoils presented another challenge to the participants. However, unlike the French (Clemenceau), English (Lloyd George) and Italian (Vittorio Orlando) participants, whose entourages were involved in sharing the workload for the conference, Wilson preferred to do all his work himself. The U.S. delegation was rarely involved.

Following intense work and constant negotiations, Wilson submitted a draft of his League of Nations to the conference participants for their approval. This international body would serve as a meeting place where member nations could solve future disputes, and it was the cornerstone of the president's plan for lasting peace and of the Treaty of Versailles. He wanted to return with a draft document for the Senate Foreign Relations Committee, which would ultimately have to approve it before it could reach the full Senate for a vote. Wilson felt that, although the conference was not near completion, the U.S. Senate and the American public should have time to mull over the League of Nations in preparation for its formation. Leaving Colonel House in charge of the U.S. position (even though Secretary of State Lansing was technically second in command), the Wilsons departed in early March for home. Both were pleased with the conference participants' approval of the League of Nations document and were excited to see family and friends again after almost four months away.

Upon arrival they immediately became aware of the postwar issues facing the nation in their absence. Unemployment, poverty, and inflation were causing hardships that needed to be addressed. Some newspapers criticized the president for "abandoning" his country during the difficult time.[27] They made much of the official gatherings in which the Wilsons participated in Europe and eluded to extravagant gifts received from foreign heads of state.

Attempting to quash such criticisms, the president quickly moved to unveil his League of Nations for the public's approval and to illustrate the important work that had taken place in Paris. His first step was to present it to Congress. Hoping to do that in an informal manner, Wilson welcomed members of the Senate Foreign Relations Committee to the White House for dinner. Edith purposefully sat next to Henry Cabot Lodge, a key Republican and critic of her husband, so that she could engage him in conversation and attempt to understand him better. After two hours of discussion and questions Wilson apparently believed that the senators would support the League of Nations document (with some minor changes). He claimed that Senator Lodge, when asked if the Senate would approve it, replied that if the Foreign Relations Committee approved it, then he believed the full Senate would ratify it. To Wilson that meant support. However, Lodge was deeply concerned with the document. He did not voice the full extent of his concerns with the president, which was the beginning of some confusion, but he was more than willing to voice his opposition to the current document two days later in front of the Senate. According to Edith, Wilson was completely shocked and angered. He felt that he had been deceived, and Edith was even angrier to see her husband and his dreams being attacked. Woodrow believed that the lack of support at home would make his job that much more difficult in Paris. With these developments still fresh, the Wilsons returned to Paris.

Bad news heralded their arrival at the conference. According to Edith, in Woodrow's absence Colonel House had compromised the League of Nations plan. House defended himself by arguing that criticisms in the United States had weakened the president's hand in Paris and House could not hold out against the other participants' demands. Wilson accepted this explanation and prepared to double his efforts to defend the League of Nations. Edith, however, blamed House for sabotaging the plan. His actions supported Edith's earlier mistrust of him, and after this crisis House was quickly pushed out of the president's inner circle by the first lady, who had gained enormous power over the president's personal relationships.

The Wilsons were now housed at 22, place des Etats-Unis, a more modest dwelling that pleased both Woodrow and Edith. Yet they had little time to enjoy their surroundings. April and May were tumultuous months for the conference as tempers flared and antagonisms grew among participants. Edith did her best to humor and divert Wilson from the constant demands on his time and the pressure to create a lasting world peace. Those around her claimed that she never let Wilson see her fatigued or concerned about what this was doing to his health.[28] His chronic digestive problems worsened, and he had to give up the exercise regime that Dr. Grayson believed was so crucial to his health. In spite of Edith's efforts, the conference demands were too staggering and ultimately took their toll. On 3 April 1919 Woodrow suffered a thrombosis (an often temporary closing of an artery to the brain). He had suffered minor strokes and thromboses before, but this one came in the midst of crucial negotiations. The official word was that president Wilson had influenza, but gossip spread. Critics, believing that Wilson had crumbled under the pressure, portrayed him as a weak academic incapable of dealing with tough political issues.[29] After a few days of bed rest the blockage cleared, but Wilson to all observers looked older and frailer. Realizing that in his brief absence more chaos had ensued at the conference, Woodrow ordered the *George Washington* (his ship of travel) to set sail; the United States delegation was going home. This announcement shocked Parisians and conference participants. While some argued that it was a bluff, the rest seemed to realize the sincerity of the decision and buckled down to complete the conference work. Intimates of the president commented that after his "illness" he was a different man—more unyielding, rigid, and determined. Those traits seemed to coalesce as Wilson steered the conference to a conclusion.

On 28 June 1919 the treaty with Germany was signed. Edith described a chaotic scene as thousands turned out to witness the historic occasion. Planning to escape Paris soon after the signing, Edith had the staff pack up their belongings and prepare for an early departure. But official invitations from the French leadership to a post-treaty celebration could not be ignored, so their departure was delayed. Edith's praise of her husband for the world peace she believed he had accomplished and the voyage home seemed to rejuvenate the weary president, but the Wilsons could not escape criticism that circulated accusing him of yielding everything for the sake of the League of Nations. Edith was angry, and Wilson was dismayed. They clearly believed that his work had been successful and he had accomplished his goals without compromise. Regardless of his performance in Paris, he was aware that his real battle would take place at home.

Edith Wilson's "Stewardship"

Woodrow Wilson decided that, faced with stiff opposition from the Senate, he would take his case for the League of Nations to the American people. He believed that once his position was made clear, the people would recognize the merits of the plan and force their senators to support it as well. Edith was concerned about how the trip would affect her husband's precarious health, but he was adamant that this trip was vital and could not be delayed. At one point he even stated that his own life was unimportant as long as the treaty was approved. Therefore, on 6 September 1919 the presidential train, carrying reporters along with Edith and Dr. Grayson, embarked on an eight-thousand-mile journey through the Midwest and West to drive home the need to ratify the Treaty of Versailles and support the League of Nations. Edith remembered the trip as a nightmare whereby the president sacrificed himself for the cause of peace.[30] He pushed himself mercilessly by delivering thirty-two speeches in twenty-two days. With each day his physical condition worsened. Edith was ever vigilant, and only those close to her could see the worry hidden behind her smile. Those who came out to hear the president witnessed a well-dressed, smiling first lady physically supporting the president's back with her hand to stabilize him against the moving train. After a few days, however, her hand also served to keep Wilson standing so that he could deliver his speeches. His condition became visible to the public through his thin and grayish appearance and the lack of enthusiasm he put into many of his speeches. Privately, Wilson could not eat and was battling blinding headaches that prevented him from sleeping.[31] The anxiety in Edith's face grew accordingly, yet she tried to stay lively and good-humored around her husband.

By the end of September as they neared Wichita, Kansas, Wilson's condition grew worse. Along with Dr. Grayson, Edith was able to convince her husband to cancel the rest of the speaking tour. He was initially resistant because he felt that without his campaign the treaty and the league would fail. But his condition was so grave that he was unable to hold out against those around him. Telegrams were sent to his daughters simply saying that the Wilsons were returning to Washington, D.C., but not to be alarmed. Knowing that their father would not cancel the trip unless something serious was happening, his daughters headed to Washington. The press was told only that the president was suffering from digestive problems and exhaustion.[32] Except for a stop to change engines, the president's train raced home, covering seventeen hundred miles in two days. Upon arrival at the station Wilson was whisked off to the White House, where he remained unable to sleep or to concentrate. Edith tried to keep him occupied and denied herself much sleep in the process. To dispel rumors she invited the press to tea and impressed upon them the regret of the president that he could not attend because he was not feeling well. To all gathered, Edith seemed calm and unconcerned, convincing reporters that rumors of a serious illness befalling the president were exaggerated. But no one, Edith included, foresaw a worsening of his condition.

On the morning of 2 October 1919 Edith entered Wilson's bedroom and discovered him sitting on his bed unable to move his left arm or leg. He appeared to have suffered a stroke. Immediately Edith called Dr. Grayson and barred servants from the family quarters. Specialists who were called in verified the stroke and offered opinions as to the president's prognosis. As the press, political leaders at home and abroad, and the general public waited for word on the president's condition, Dr. Grayson simply issued statements that the president needed rest without explaining what had happened. Edith, who did not want the public to know the extent of her husband's affliction, was also caught up in her own fears about his health. She hovered nearby to hold Woodrow's hand and reassure him with a smile.

Edith was advised that Wilson should avoid worry and disturbances, which meant that he could not perform his governmental duties. So she simply stepped into that role. It is unclear what her actual role in policy and decision making was, as Edith disavowed any part in running the nation and called what she did a "stewardship."[33] But she commented later that she felt uniquely qualified to deal with matters since she was her husband's confidante and knew his feelings on most issues. Politicians who knew the strong and steady signature of Woodrow Wilson were concerned when three weeks after the announcement of his illness four bills came out of the executive mansion, supposedly signed by the president, with odd signatures. Edith had simply put the pen in Wilson's hand and guided it, claiming that was what Woodrow wanted and she was just helping him.[34] Over the next few months his signature gradually improved. Later she contended that she "never made a decision regarding the disposition of public affairs. The only decision that was mine was what was important and what was not, and the very important decision of when to present matters to my husband."[35]

That statement belied the power she wielded. Although insisting that the important matters were discussed with her husband and that he made the ultimate decisions, Edith prioritized matters for him. She determined what was important and what information he should receive. That illustrated power. As to how well Wilson understood things in the first few weeks after the stroke, we will never know. Edith refused to spend much time discussing matters of state, and her memoirs focus on Wilson's health and the progress he made physically.[36] Some domestic issues were handled by cabinet officials who had been given such latitude early in Wilson's presidency. Most, however, were ignored even after repeated letters to Edith by administrative staff requesting the president's attention. If she replied to such requests, she merely stated that the president did not feel that the issue was serious, deflecting any contention that she was making those decisions. Yet the first lady's role and the president's absence from the public eye created rumors that spread across the country.[37]

Some claimed that Wilson was insane or had contracted a venereal disease in France. Others believed that his condition had reduced him to blabbering like a child.[38] Edith was called "Lady President" and the "Regent," and Senator Albert Fall called her the head of a "Petticoat Government."[39] But Edith largely ignored the rumors and criticisms lodged against her. Keeping her husband safe and quiet were her main concerns, even though she worried over how his illness might play into calls for an early retirement. Edith felt that if Wilson were forced to leave office, the League of Nations would die and so would he.[40]

By December, Wilson was devoting more time to affairs of state, although Edith was always there to read and discuss matters with him. Often reports would come out of the White House with Edith's comments on the margins. This furthered rumors that Wilson was incapable of running the nation and that Edith was doing it. She argued that she was only writing what Wilson had told her to write, but this did not satisfy the Republican-led Congress, which was increasingly anxious over the president's health. The Senate demanded to see the president to ascertain whether he should continue to serve in his present capacity or whether Vice President Thomas R. Marshall should step in as chief executive. Edith carefully arranged a meeting for two senators (Republican senator Albert Fall and Democratic senator Gilbert Hitchcock). She had Wilson positioned in the bed with his paralyzed face in shadow. A blanket was placed to his neck covering his left arm, while his right arm was free to gesture. Edith stayed in the room and took notes to make sure no misunderstandings occurred. The president was quite animated, and except for a slight heaviness in his speech due to the stroke, he seemed much like the Woodrow Wilson of old. As the senators were leaving, Edith overheard a comment that she enjoyed repeating. Senator Fall, a strong supporter of Henry Cabot Lodge and critic of her husband, bent over Wilson and said, "I am praying for you." To this President Wilson was heard to say, "Which way, Senator?"[41] The meeting proved successful. Both senators met with the news-hungry press and reported that the president seemed fine and able to carry out the business of running the country. For Edith a large hurdle was cleared.

The Wilsons settled into a new routine for the remainder of his presidency. They had breakfast around 8:00 A.M., after which Wilson would engage in some official business. After lunch he would take a four-hour nap, followed by dinner and a movie. Edith's only time alone was during Wilson's naps, when she would take walks. Yet she walked outside his windows in case he awoke and called for her (which he often did). The staff, now aware of the improving condition of the president, rolled up all the carpets in the private quarters, and Ike Hoover, head usher, designed a type of wheelchair that the president could use. But Wilson never returned to his old self. He rarely spoke and would often begin crying without warning. He seemed to like the newly developing movie industry, and Edith and the staff worked to bring in a new movie almost every day. He especially liked the westerns, but extremely violent scenes upset him. Sensing this, the ever-protective Edith would wheel him to bed.[42]

During his illness—and he would argue because of it—the Treaty of Versailles failed to pass the U.S. Senate. It came up for a vote in November 1919 and again in March 1920. Senator Lodge suggested some compromises that would limit U.S. military involvement in the League of Nations, and some original league and treaty supporters were inclined to support those measures in order to get the treaty passed. Wilson was encouraged to accept Lodge's resolutions by cabinet members and even Edith. According to her, he looked up and said, "Don't you desert me," and she felt as if she had betrayed him. Wilson argued that the document could not be changed unless every signatory who had signed in Paris were consulted.[43] She stated that from that point on she never wavered in her support of his position, blaming her action on momentary weakness.

As 1920 progressed, Wilson again held monthly cabinet meetings. For Edith they were torturous, as she was unsure of how the president would react. At times he was keenly interested in matters, while on other occasions his stare held no hint of recognition. Cabinet members, solicitous of Wilson and willing to overlook his lapses, conducted business as usual. One prominent issue discussed was the upcoming Democratic National Convention. Since he was incapacitated, Wilson made it clear that he wanted his cabinet members to attend. The president's son-in-law and cabinet member, William McAdoo, was a rising star who had presidential aspirations. He hoped for the president's endorsement, believing, as many political insiders did, that an endorsement from Wilson could garner McAdoo the nomination. However Wilson refused to nominate anyone to replace him, and those around him recognized that he had hopes of being the party's nominee again. Edith and Dr. Grayson were opposed to this, and cabinet members were told to make sure that Wilson was not considered as a potential candidate. Instead, the convention chose James Cox of Ohio. Wilson, though disappointed at not being renominated, believed that Cox would win even when those around him predicted a Republican landslide. In retrospect, it is clear that Wilson felt that if the nation's people turned away from the Democratic Party they would, in essence, be turning away from all he (Woodrow) had accomplished. So too would any hope of resurrecting the League of Nations die. It was a hard pill to swallow as Warren Harding won easily in November.

Woodrow Wilson's last official function was to escort newly elected President Harding to his swearing-in ceremony. It was a tradition that, regardless of his own disability, Wilson intended to follow. Edith was worried over whether he could withstand the strain of a public ride and exhaustion of meeting so many people. She was also easily offended and found the Hardings' lack of appreciation for Wilson's condition appalling. For example, since the president could not mount the steps to the Capitol, as was the custom, arrangements were made for both the Wilsons and the Hardings to enter a side door and take an elevator to the ceremony site. But when the car arrived outside the Capitol, the Hardings exited out front and climbed the steps to cheering crowds. This left Wilson to be driven around to a side door and brought up in virtual isolation. To Edith this was a slap in her husband's face. Later she would not be surprised to hear of scandal in the Harding White House, since she felt that they were ungracious people.[44]

Retirement

When the Wilsons left the ceremony, it was as private citizens. Edith had spent weeks locating what she believed would be the perfect house for them. Although this was their third choice, the Wilsons found great comfort in the house, and Edith continued to live there until her own death. The former president's new bedroom was an exact replica of the room to which he had grown accustomed in the White House. Edith realized his comfort with the bedroom and also that in his present state Wilson would not adjust well to change. Thus she wanted to make his transition to private citizen as easy as possible. Unfortunately, his worsening health prohibited Wilson from academic or political projects. Edith and her brother Randolph (hired as their secretary) even censored all mail and news stories so as not to upset him. Her husband's illness took its toll on Edith. Acquaintances began to comment on how tired and strained she appeared, but she did not want to leave Wilson alone in case he needed her. In 1923 he convinced her to take a short vacation (since she had not left him except for a few days since 1919) and then lamented the fact that she was gone. His moods continued to swing back and forth between anger, frustration, loneliness, and depression as his condition worsened. Edith reported that there were times when his eyes cleared from the confusion and he seemed almost like his old self.[45] Yet those times were rare. The arteriosclerosis that had caused his stroke was affecting other portions of his body, including his eyesight.

To the public Woodrow Wilson remained the respected war president who had defended the ideas of world peace. Foreign dignitaries and national politicians still called on the Wilsons, and many hoped they could convince him to endorse certain policies or candidates publicly. But for Woodrow only information about the League of Nations held much interest.

The public did get rare glimpses of Wilson, once for the dedication of the tomb of the unknown soldier at Arlington National Cemetery in November 1921 and again at President Harding's funeral in August 1923. On each occasion old acquaintances who had not seen the former president in a while were startled by his appearance. Some began to comment that he wore a mask of death. Wilson had begun to recognize his own fading condition and after the Harding funeral told Edith that he wanted a simple, private funeral when his time came. To her it was clear that Wilson was thinking about his own death. As his health continued to decline in the fall of 1923, Edith realized that it would probably be their last Christmas together.[46] Therefore, she tried to make the occasion extra bright and cheerful.

When Edith entered Wilson's room on 29 December, he supposedly said, "It won't be very much longer."[47] His condition worsened considerably, and Dr. Grayson was summoned. It was clear that the former president's kidneys were failing and that the end was near. Edith held a constant vigil, carrying trays and holding Woodrow's hand. She was outwardly calm but unaware of anything going on around her. Those in attendance remarked how strong she was, but she later explained that she had to be strong for Wilson and the family.[48] On Friday, 1 February 1924, news was released that Woodrow Wilson was dying. Messages poured in from around the globe, and well-known personages came calling to pay their respects. The public gathered outside to await news and pray for the war president. But Woodrow's condition continued to worsen, and he lost consciousness on Sunday morning. At 11:55 A.M. on Sunday, 3 February 1924, sixty-seven-year-old Woodrow Wilson died in his sleep.

Through it all Edith remained in control, planning the private funeral her husband had wanted. The largest issue centered around where to bury the former president. His birthplace was considered, but no one else in the family was buried there. His parents and sister were buried in South Carolina, but there was no room left in the family plot for him. Wilson had instructed

Edith that he did not wish to be buried in Arlington National Cemetery. Edith ultimately chose to bury her husband in the crypt of Saint Peter and Saint Paul at the new national cathedral being built in Washington, D.C. Thus, following a private ceremony in the Wilson home and a cathedral service that was attended by a large gathering and broadcast by radio throughout the country, Woodrow Wilson was laid to rest.

A new chapter began in Edith Wilson's life. After a year of mourning in which she stayed out of sight and made frequent trips to the cathedral, she began to emerge once more into the public light. Her dislike of newspaper reporters and speech making remained unchanged, but she could now be seen traveling around Washington again, visiting friends and attending events to honor her husband. In fact, for the rest of her life Edith strove to maintain control over all images of her late husband in order to protect him and his legacy. This protectiveness of Wilson was apparent throughout their marriage, but it became more pronounced after Wilson's death, especially when books discussing the former president began to be published. Many people who had worked for or served in the cabinet of Woodrow Wilson penned accounts of the war years or the peace conference. To Edith, most contained inaccuracies that painted the president in an unflattering light. She was especially angered by Colonel House's book and that of Robert Lansing. She was angered if accounts misinterpreted some event or were not as praiseworthy of Wilson as Edith felt they should be. It was because of this that she compiled Wilson's papers and appointed someone to write a "true" account of the Wilson presidency.

Edith chose Ray Stannard Baker, whom the Wilsons knew from his service as press liaison in Paris. Immediately Edith contacted everyone who might be in possession of letters from Wilson and asked that they send them for the project. The process was tedious, and Baker pored through the hundreds of boxes of correspondence that arrived. Edith was in constant contact with him, suggested people to interview (which he did), and read over everything he wrote. Baker was often frustrated by Edith's inability to be objective regarding her husband or his decisions and her attempt to remove anything negative from the book.[49] Because of his own poor health and the massive scope of the project, it was not until 1939 that Baker's book was completed and all the papers were sent to the Library of Congress for public scrutiny (although under strict guidelines from Edith, which ensured that she controlled what was said about her husband until her own death in 1961). The biography won Baker a Pulitzer Prize, and he was quick to thank Edith for her hard work and perfectionism.

Edith was convinced to write her own recollections of life with Woodrow Wilson. Entitled *My Memoir,* her book contains unflattering descriptions of some notable people. Originally friends thought that she should tone down some of her dislike for people—for example, Edward House—but she refused. Thus the book caused quite a stir when it was published in 1939. While some people disputed what Edith said, no one could dispute her clear devotion to the late president. In her eyes he was the sage of his generation whose goals of world peace were ruined by near-sighted politicians. He never made a wrong decision, but sometimes external factors served to paint him as less than successful. For example, his refusal to compromise on the League of Nations was explained by Edith as the fault of Henry Cabot Lodge and his followers, who wanted the president to breach the document signed by the warring parties. They were only interested in scoring political points, while her husband stayed ethical and honorable.

Edith traveled quite a bit in her later life, making frequent trips to Europe and even around the world. She remained aware of the political scene through the 1920s, although she was kept out of the spotlight while Republican leadership was in place. The election of Democrat Franklin Roosevelt in 1932 brought Edith back into public view when she was invited to state dinners and events. She liked Roosevelt because he spoke so highly of Wilson and his ideals of peace. The coming war and FDR's handling of it, however, brought back old memories. While feeling vindicated that what Woodrow had predicted had come true, Edith was equally sad that another war had to be fought. As with the last one, she volunteered at the Red Cross and brought out her old sewing machine. She kept busy but was forced to give up her volunteerism when diagnosed with extremely high blood pressure.

Throughout the 1950s Edith remained active, spending time with her family, playing bridge, going to the theater, and dressing in high fashion. Her last public appearance was in October 1961, when at the age of eighty-nine she witnessed President John Kennedy sign into law a commission, approved by Congress, to establish a memorial for her husband. On 28 December 1961 she planned to attend the opening of the Woodrow Wilson Bridge across the Potomac River, but her heart gave out. Ironically it would have been Woodrow Wilson's 105th birthday.

Conclusion

Edith Bolling Galt Wilson led a fascinating life. She never intended to ascend to the White House or to become involved in international issues, yet ultimately she wielded enormous power as first lady. While she denied ever influencing her husband on matters of state, her autobiography and the accounts of others dispute that statement. But the depth of her influence is debatable. Most, including Edith, argued that Wilson was often inflexible and determined when his mind was set and that no one could get him to change it. His love and respect for her, however, allowed Edith to become his closest confidante and adviser, a position that clearly contained power even if she refused to acknowledge it. As to her running the country during the president's illness, she remained the protective wife. She stated that she only followed orders and that Woodrow Wilson made the decisions and she conveyed them to the right people. Edith refused to take credit for anything she did, claiming that her husband deserved the credit since she was only his wife, a title she cherished and protected until her own death over thirty-seven years after Woodrow Wilson's.

NOTES

1. Edith Bolling Wilson, *My Memoir* (1939; reprint, New York: Arno Press, 1981), 56.

2. This meeting has been disputed, however, by the Wilson Papers and some historians who claim that it never occurred.

3. Wilson, *Memoir,* 14.

4. Wilson, *Memoir,* 18.

5. Ishbel Ross, *Power with Grace: The Life Story of Mrs. Woodrow Wilson* (1958; reprint, New York: G.P. Puntam's Sons, 1975), 22.

6. Ibid., 32.

7. Ibid.

8. Wilson, *Memoir,* 56.

9. Ross, *Power,* 36; Wilson, *Memoir,* 61.

10. Wilson, *Memoir,* 61.

11. Many of Wilson's closest advisers, such as House and Joseph Tumulty, a secretary, friend, and public relations man, worried about the suddenness of the engagement and the political damage it would do to Woodrow's reelection campaign. They voiced their opposition and, according to some insiders, concocted a story that an "old flame" of Woodrow's was still in the picture, but this failed to dissuade Edith Bolling Galt.

12. Ross, *Power,* 64.

13. Ibid., 51.

14. Ibid., 51, 62.

15. Ibid., 308.

16. Wilson, *Memoir,* 117–19.

17. Ibid., 129.

18. Ibid., 129, 140.

19. The president was urged to give up golf, which the public might perceive as frivolous, and gain exercise by riding instead. Edith joined him once she had purchased new riding clothes.

20. The White House had a code office, but Woodrow had his own code that was used with people such as Colonel House. Edith knew the code and was adept at both decoding and encoding messages for Woodrow.

21. Ross, *Power,* 103.

22. The Fourteen Points called for "open covenants of peace openly arrived at," with freedom of the seas, open diplomacy, removal of trade barriers, armament reduction, self-determination of all peoples, and a League of Nations as noteworthy examples.

23. Ross, *Power,* 124.

24. Much has been made of Wilson's failure to include Republicans in the conference. While it is true that animosity existed both over Wilson's open endorsement of Democrats in the off-year elections and in his refusal to take ranking Republicans to Paris, the dispute over the Treaty of Versailles was more complex. Republicans and some Democrats were genuinely concerned about possible U.S. troop involvement as called for by the League of Nations.

25. Wilson, *Memoir,* 177–78.

26. Ibid., 178–79.

27. Ross, *Power,* 167.

28. Joseph Tumulty, *Woodrow Wilson as I Know Him* (Garden City, N.J.: Doubleday, Pages & Co., 1921), 436.

29. Ross, *Power,* 169. Edith interestingly does not mention it.

30. John Milton Cooper Jr., in his essay "Disability in the White House: The Case of Woodrow Wilson," in *The White House—The First Two Hundred Years,* ed. Frank Freidel and William Pencak (Boston, Mass.: Northeastern University Press, 1994), argues that the thrombosis Wilson suffered altered his personality by exaggerating certain traits. According to Cooper, "In Wilson, tenacity and self-reliance metamorphosed into stubbornness and self-righteousness" after Wilson consulted neurologists (Wilson, *Memoir,* 274).

31. Edwin A. Weinstein, in his book *Woodrow Wilson: A Medical and Psychological Biography* (Princeton, N.J.: Princeton University Press, 1981), notes that Woodrow almost surely suffered from high blood pressure, which would explain the headaches and, ultimately, the stroke.

32. Ross, *Power,* 194.

33. Wilson, *Memoir,* 289.

34. Ross, *Power,* 203–4.

35. Wilson, *Memoir,* 289.

36. Ibid., 292–300.

37. Ibid., 298.

38. Ibid.

39. Ross, *Power,* 201.

40. Wilson, *Memoir,* 290.

41. Ibid., 299.

42. Ross, *Power,* 207.

43. Wilson, *Memoir,* 297. This is another example of the intransigence Wilson would exercise after a stroke.

44. Ross, *Power,* 243.

45. Weinstein, *Wilson,* 373.

46. Ross, *Power,* 251.

47. Wilson, *Memoir,* 359.

48. Ross, *Power,* 258.

49. Ibid., 269–70.

Six

Bess W. Truman

The Reluctant First Lady

Raymond Frey

Introduction

On the night of 12 April 1945, almost eighty years to the day after the death of President Abraham Lincoln, Harry S. Truman took the oath of office as the thirty-third president of the United States. Franklin D. Roosevelt, who had been president longer than any other man, had died a little more than two hours previously. Truman had been Roosevelt's vice president a mere eighty-two days, and now the tremendous burden of leading the country through the final months of world war and the dawn of the atomic age was his to bear. Standing next to Truman as he solemnly took the oath of office were his wife Bess and his daughter Margaret.

Unlike Eleanor Roosevelt, who preceded her, the new first lady would be uncomfortable with the public role she was required to play. The evening of Roosevelt's death Bess recounted that she spent most of the night thinking about how their lives would be changed. "I was very apprehensive," she admitted. "The country was used to Eleanor Roosevelt. I couldn't possibly be anything like her. I wasn't going down in any coal mines."[1]

Throughout Harry Truman's political career Bess supported her husband but would rarely speak in public. During Truman's 1934 campaign for the U.S. Senate, for instance, they bought a secondhand Dodge roadster and crisscrossed the seven townships of Jackson County, Missouri, attending dozens of picnics and square dances. Bess was frequently invited to speak but would graciously refuse. "A woman's place in public," she said, "is to sit beside her husband, be silent and be sure her hat is on straight."[2]

Young Bess Wallace

Elizabeth Virginia Wallace was born on 13 February 1885 in Independence, Missouri, the oldest child of Margaret "Madge" Gates Wallace and David Wallace. She first met Harry Truman at Sunday school when he was six years old and she was five. "I saw a beautiful curly haired girl there" he later wrote. "I thought she was the most beautiful girl I ever saw. She had tanned skin, blond hair, golden as sunshine, and the most beautiful blue eyes I've ever seen, or ever will see."[3] From the moment he saw her, he later remembered, he thought of no one else but that blue-eyed, golden-haired girl. He would remain in awe of her for the rest of his life.

As a young girl Bess chose sports as the way to assert herself. She played third base on her brothers' sandlot baseball team and was their best hitter. In high school, besides being an outstanding student, she was considered to be the best tennis player in Independence—male or female—as well as an excellent ice skater and horseback rider.

Throughout grammar and high school she and Harry were just friends. In spite of his infatuation with her, they saw little of each other during their school days. Harry was busy working at the local drugstore and spending time with his piano lessons—he dreamed of someday becoming a concert pianist. When he was six years old he received his first pair of eyeglasses to correct his farsightedness, and this kept him from participating in many of the sports and outdoor activities enjoyed by Bess. Instead, he spent most of his free time reading books in the public library.

After graduation from high school in 1901, Bess would not see Harry for five years. He had hoped to attend college, but his parents could not afford to send him, so he stayed to help his father run the family farm. Meanwhile, Bess's life was shattered by the violent death of her father. David Wallace was one of the most well-known and popular men in town, but in reality he was a profoundly unhappy person. He held a succession of minor political patronage positions that provided a steady income, but not enough to support his extravagant wife and five children. He could not afford to send Bess to college, even though her mother continued to employ several servants.[4] Becoming increasingly frustrated and depressed, Bess's father began drinking heavily.

On the morning of 17 June 1903 David Wallace rose at dawn, dressed, and quietly took a blue-steel revolver from his writing desk drawer in the bedroom. He walked softly to the bathroom at the rear of the house. Standing in the middle of the floor, he placed the muzzle of the gun behind his left ear and pulled the trigger. He was forty-three years old; Bess was eighteen. David Wallace's violent death by his own hand would profoundly influence Bess for the rest of her life. Up to that time she was a charming, athletic girl, popular and witty, with many boyfriends. After her father's death she became much more reserved, private, and pessimistic. She resolved that if she ever married, the union would be a partnership.[5]

THE TRUMAN MARRIAGE

In 1906 Bess and Harry renewed their acquaintance. He would frequently travel to Independence to see her, and they wrote to each other almost every day. Mother Wallace strongly disapproved of the blossoming relationship, but Harry was determined to win Bess's hand in marriage. In June 1911 he finally summoned up the courage to propose, but Bess refused. She knew that her mother was almost totally dependent upon her only daughter, which had discouraged other suitors but not Harry. Afraid that Truman would take Bess away from her, Mrs. Wallace told her daughter, "You don't want to marry that farmer boy, he's not going to make it anywhere."[6] Two years later, in spite of her mother's warning, twenty-eight-year-old Bess Wallace decided to make her intentions known. On the first Sunday of November in 1913 Harry sat speechless as she told him that if she ever married anyone, it would be him. Finally, in 1917, after seven years of courtship and just before Truman joined the army and was to be shipped overseas, Bess accepted his proposal and wanted to get married at once. Harry, however, said no. He told her that she must not tie herself to a man who might come home from war a cripple or not at all.[7]

Truman returned safely from World War I, and on 28 June 1919 he and Bess were married. They moved in with Bess's mother at 219 North Delaware Street in Independence, Missouri. Harry and a war buddy, Eddie Jacobson, opened a men's furnishings store in Kansas City, but it went bankrupt in 1921. Unemployed and in debt, he decided to try his hand at politics. He accepted the support of the powerful Pendergast family, a Kansas City political machine, much to Bess's dismay. She always believed that her father's lack of success in politics had much to do with his depression, alcoholism, and suicide, and she remembered the scathing publicity and public humiliation to which the press had subjected her family following his death. In addition she felt that Harry was being supported by a corrupt and unrefined lot of political cronies. Bess had no desire to be a politician's wife.

THE RELUCTANT POLITICIAN'S WIFE

Truman was elected county judge of the eastern district of Jackson County, in 1922. It was not a judicial post under the Missouri system but rather an administrative one, equivalent to a county commissioner in most states. He was defeated for reelection two years later; it would be the only election defeat he would suffer in his long political career. In 1926 the Pendergast machine agreed to support Truman for presiding judge of the county court.

After talking it over with Bess, he accepted the offer. The salary was modest —six thousand dollars a year—but this was an important decision, and they both knew it. Truman was now forty-two years old and getting past the time to be thinking of starting a new career.

He took Bess along to political meetings and speaking engagements, possibly in an effort to interest her in his work, but she seemed aloof. However, quietly and behind the scenes Bess was both aiding and protecting her husband's reputation. Her handling of a small political crisis during the campaign illustrates her political astuteness. Truman was the unopposed Democratic Party nominee for presiding judge in the upcoming primary. A local attorney, J. Allen Prewitt, a political outsider, wanted Truman to join a committee he was putting together for the visit of a Saint Louis candidate for the U.S. Senate, Henry B. Hawes. Truman, however, was away on army reserve duty, so Bess took charge. "I'm afraid Mr. Hawes won't get very far under his (Harry's) patronage," Bess told Prewitt. When word of Bess's remarks reached Tom Pendergast, the patriarch of the Kansas City political machine, she was warned that "Mr. Pendergast considered it best for you to keep out of all fights." Bess coolly telephoned Prewitt and told him that her husband could be of no help to his committee."[8]

Truman easily won the August 1926 primary and the subsequent general election in November. Bess was now a professional politician's wife. She considered herself to be an equal partner in the venture, becoming her husband's eyes and ears when he was away on reserve duty. During his summer tour of duty in 1927 completed at Fort Leavenworth, Kansas, she kept him informed of the political situation in Jackson County, sending him clippings of the *Kansas City Star,* regularly visiting his office, and fielding phone calls. Her public persona, however, was more subdued. She belonged to a bridge club and served as secretary of the Needlework Guild, a group of women who collected clothing for the needy. For Bess, that was quite enough. Her family was her life, and beyond assisting her husband in his job she had no desire for public attention or acclaim.[9]

Harry Truman had much success as a county judge. His greatest triumphs were the creation and construction of a modern road system for Jackson County, which changed forever the lives of its rural residents, and the construction of a new county courthouse. He had gained a reputation for honesty and integrity as well, despite his ties to Pendergast. He handily won reelection as presiding judge in 1930, but since the job was limited to two terms, Harry would soon have to seek another political office. There was talk of Truman as a candidate for governor of Missouri—"You may yet be the first lady of Missouri," he told Bess.[10] Although Truman wanted more than anything to be governor, "Boss" Tom Pendergast had another candidate in mind, and Harry was passed over for the nomination. He had come to love politics but was now certain that his political career was over. Pendergast did have plans for Truman, but Truman had to make a choice. He could become county collector at a salary of ten thousand dollars a year or run for the U.S. Congress, which paid seventy-five hundred dollars a year. For Harry Truman the choice was clear. He considered the collector's job, in spite of its higher pay and security, to be a minor county office and a do-nothing position. As a U.S. congressman he would be a player on the national scene during one of the greatest and most exciting times of political change in American history.

Bess did not approve. Concerned about her ailing mother, she was not eager to leave Independence, Missouri, for Washington, D.C. In the meantime Tom Pendergast had changed his mind and picked another congressional candidate. Truman was dejected and nearly out of money, but a few weeks later he would receive some astonishing news: Pendergast had chosen Truman to run for the U.S. Senate.

Bess Truman supported her husband's decision to accept the nomination, but her heart was troubled. She did not want to live in Washington if he were elected. She was not certain that she could endure the personal and political attacks that were sure to come their way. For example, Truman was called "Pendergast's office boy," and one of his opponents said that Truman would get "calluses on his ears listening on the long distance telephone to his boss."[11] Bess was quickly discovering that enduring the smear tactics, lies, and innuendo published in the press was the hardest part of being a politician's wife.

Truman waged a relentless campaign across the state, often speaking as much as sixteen times in a single day. Bess would frequently appear with him on the platform but never said a word on his behalf. Political speeches, she told her husband, were not her style.

Truman won the August primary and went on to enjoy an overwhelming victory in the November 1934 election. The day after the election Bess went to her usual weekly meeting of her bridge club. Members were amazed at her absolute calm. The text of an interview the following day in the *Kansas City Star,* however, hints that Bess was not at all pleased with the prospect of being a senator's wife. "Of course I'm thrilled to be going to Washington," she said. "But I have spent all my life here on Delaware Street and it will be a change. I was born on Delaware Street and was married to Harry sixteen years ago when he came back from the World War. We never have had or desired another home."[12] *Collier's* magazine reported: "The wife of the junior senator from Missouri explained that everyone is away from home in Washington. Unquestionably she still regards herself as away from home when she is in the capital, or any place except Independence."[13] She said nothing to her husband about her true feelings.

In early January 1935 the Trumans, along with their ten-year-old daughter, Margaret, drove to Saint Louis and boarded a train for Washington, D.C. They stayed in the Hamilton Hotel while Bess hunted for a suitable apartment. A senator's salary at that time did not go far—Truman's salary in 1935 was only $10,000 a year. They finally settled on a four-room apartment on Connecticut Avenue at $150 a month, a rent they could ill afford.

Bess, Margaret, and Mother Wallace, who also lived with the Trumans, were not at all happy about moving to Washington. They had little money and were still in debt from the campaign. Their small-town, mid-American values and lifestyle did not mesh well with Washington high society, and they had little money to keep up with the pace of Washington social life.[14] Bess intended for her and Margaret to spend only six months a year in Washington. She enrolled her daughter in Gunston Hall, a private school for young girls. Margaret would spend the school months there and return home with her mother for the summers.

Harry Truman summed up the years he spent in the U.S. Senate as "filled with hard work but which were also to be the happiest 10 years of my life."[15] During those years he would grow in political stature and gain the experience that would later help him shoulder the enormous responsibilities of the presidency.

Truman's greatest accomplishment came during the second half of his first term, when he was appointed to chair a special committee, dubbed by the press the "Truman Committee," to investigate the national defense program. His probing investigations saved billions in taxpayer dollars by helping to eliminate waste and fraud in defense contracts with private industries and made Truman a national figure. Bess and Margaret spent only a few months of each year in Washington. The Trumans moved from one small apartment to another—at one point they moved four times in four years—but whenever they could, Bess and Margaret stayed in Independence. Harry hated this arrangement and missed having Bess by his side, but he understood her homesickness. Bess missed him too and would occasionally adjust her schedule when his pleas became frantic. She usually tried to stay as long as possible in Independence, but the fact was that he was relying on her more and more.

Senator Truman called his wife a genius at handling reporters, and she became his favorite speech writer. When she was away, he constantly kept her informed of events in the Senate, and she was his eyes and ears at home. He often used his letters to her as an opportunity to clarify his thoughts, although he rarely asked her for advice.

Truman faced a tough primary reelection for his Senate seat against Missouri governor Lloyd Stark in 1940. During this brutal battle Bess urged Harry to keep the fight clean, fed him one-liners, and tried to tone down his sometimes salty language. But publicly she remained silent.[16]

By Truman's second term, because Bess had become such an important partner and because their finances were so low, he put her on the Senate payroll as his secretary. As his work on the Truman Committee required frequent travel to visit arms factories and military installations, Bess became more involved in the daily operation of the office. He was quick to give her credit for his emergence as a "senator's senator" in Washington. In 1942, reflecting back on their twenty-three years of marriage, he told her: "Thanks to the right kind of a life partner for me we've come out reasonably well. A failure as a farmer, a miner, an oil promoter, and a merchant but finally hit the groove as a public servant—and that due mostly to you and lady luck. . . . When a man gets the right kind of wife, his career is made—and I got just that."[17]

Truman was quite content being a senator. He had found a home in the Senate, rising above his past connections with the Pendergast machine to become one of the most powerful and respected men in Washington. By the summer of 1943 rumors about Truman as a possible vice-presidential candidate began to circulate. As far as he was concerned, they were just rumors, and one year later in 1944, on the eve of the summer Democratic Convention in Chicago, Truman was preparing to attend to nominate another man. "I don't want to be the vice-president," he said. "The Vice President simply presides over the Senate and sits around hoping for a funeral," he explained to a friend. "It is a very high office which consists entirely of honor and I don't have any ambition to hold an office like that." And besides, he added, "The Madam (Bess) doesn't want me to do it."[18] Behind closed doors the Democratic Party bosses were searching for a "safe" candidate to satisfy both the conservative and liberal wings of the party. Roosevelt's current vice president, Henry Wallace, was considered by many to be too liberal; Jimmy Byrnes of South Carolina, a popular southern senator, was too conservative and had strong segregationist leanings. Truman's name had emerged as a compromise candidate. He had established a reputation as an honest, hardworking senator and a loyal supporter of Roosevelt's New Deal; he was also popular with labor unions. The president, however, simply saw him as a running mate who would do the ticket the least amount of harm. Preoccupied with the war and in declining health, Roosevelt did not much care who the vice-presidential candidate would be. But privately many of the Democratic Party bosses knew that the president was dying and that their choice would likely be FDR's successor.

Truman knew perfectly well that Roosevelt's days were numbered. He knew what his nomination meant. A reporter remarked to him that as vice president he might "succeed to the throne." Truman replied, "Hell, I don't want to be president."[19] He had worked hard to build a good name in the Senate, and surely, if nominated, his past connections with the Pendergast political machine would surface. Moreover, Truman was concerned about his family's privacy and worried that Bess's position on his Senate office payroll would create a scandal. Bess, too, had no desire to see her husband become president and absolutely no desire to become the first lady. She feared that her father's suicide—that terrible and, in her eyes, disgraceful event that had so profoundly affected her as a young girl—would become public.

But on the convention floor momentum was building for a Truman vice-presidential nomination, although he insisted that he was not interested. On the afternoon of 19 July he was summoned to a hotel room where the party bosses were waiting. On the phone they had Roosevelt, who stated, "You tell the Senator that if he wants to break up the Democratic party in the middle of the war, that's his responsibility." A stunned Truman replied, "Well, if that's the situation, I'll have to say yes."[20]

Bess was unhappy about the sudden turn of events but would have to stand aside. After Harry delivered his brief acceptance speech, the Trumans made their way through a crush of reporters and photographers to a waiting car. As they got into the car, Bess glared straight at Harry. "Are we going to have to go through this for the rest of our lives?" she asked. It was not a good beginning.[21]

Truman campaigned tirelessly for Roosevelt in 1944, traveling thousands of miles around the country. Throughout most of the campaign Bess Truman had remained so obscure as the potential vice president's wife that reporters knew virtually nothing about her. She was briefly thrown into the spotlight when the Republicans began probing into his family life. As Harry had feared, Bess's job in his Senate office and her yearly salary quickly became an issue. Republicans charged that Bess had been "secretly" employed in Truman's office at a salary of forty-five hundred dollars a year. Republican congresswoman Clare Booth Luce, the glamorous wife of wealthy publisher Henry Luce, infuriated Harry by calling her "Payroll Bess." Truman was accustomed to the usual criticism that a candidate must endure during the heat of a campaign, but nothing aroused his anger more than attacks directed at his family. In a statement that reveals much about their political partnership, Truman vigorously defended his wife, telling the Associated Press that it was no secret that Bess was on the Senate payroll. "She's a clerk in my office and does much of my clerical work," he said. "I need her here and that's the reason I've got her there. I never make a report or deliver a speech without her editing it. . . . There's nothing secret about it."[22] The issue was defused when one of Truman's fiercest political opponents, arch-Republican Roy Roberts, managing editor of the *Kansas City Star,* came to Mrs. Truman's defense. "She earned every penny of it," he wrote.[23] Truman's Senate colleagues knew how much clerical work she did. She was routinely in the office early and often stayed late. This would be the only time as the vice president's wife that Bess would be scrutinized by the press. To the Trumans' immense relief, nothing was said about the death of her father.

The First Lady

On 12 April 1945 Franklin Roosevelt died of a massive brain hemorrhage at Warm Springs, Georgia. On the return trip to Washington after the president was laid to rest, Bess spoke candidly with Frances Perkins, Roosevelt's secretary of labor. According to Perkins,

> She [Bess] said to me, "I don't know what I'm going to do . . . I'm not used to this awful public life. Mrs. Roosevelt is on the way to Washington now and is going to pack up. She suggested to me that on Tuesday next I hold a press conference. . . . She will sit with me and sort of introduce the girls and get me familiar with the procedure. Do you think I ought to see the press?"
>
> I had to think quickly, and I said, "No, Mrs. Truman, I don't think you ought to feel the slightest obligation to do it. Mrs. Roosevelt is an unusual person. She had a special talent for publicity. She does it well. She enjoys it . . . I don't think any of the other First Ladies did it."
>
> "Do you really think so?" she said. "You relieve me greatly, because I just thought I was going to be forced into this."
>
> Harry agreed with Perkins's advice. "Well, I think she's right," he told Bess. "There's no reason why you should do it."[24]

A few days later the new first lady held her first press conference, which, she announced, would also be her last. A reporter asked her, "Mrs. Truman, how are we ever going to get to know you?" She quickly replied, "You don't need to know me. I'm only the President's wife and the mother of his daughter."[25]

During Harry's first years as president, Bess held no press conference, made few public appearances, and expressed few personal opinions. "People don't warm up to her easily," one article said. "Her inability to unbend before strangers and her resolute silences do not win friends. She rarely gets a hand when she makes a public appearance. . . . Mrs. Truman's mien suggests to many that she is digging her heels in and saying to people, 'I dare you to like me.' People, in turn, respect her integrity and recognize her determination to measure up to the requirements of her position, but they do not enthuse about her."[26]

In private, Bess was a completely different person. Her Washington friends, most of them senators' wives she had befriended during Harry's Senate years, were extremely fond of her. They said that she was kind, considerate of others, a gracious hostess, and an entertaining conversationalist, although she almost never discussed public affairs.[27] Old friends from Independence or members of the White House staff who saw her on an almost daily basis would speak warmly of her kindness.[28]

The newspaperwomen who had the run of the White House during Mrs. Roosevelt's regime were incredulous and enraged at Bess's public silence. They protested, they objected, they tried to bring pressure, and some swore privately to wear her down. But all of their words and wrath failed to lift the veil Mrs. Truman had lowered. She flatly refused to be interviewed.[29] Finally, after months of trying, Washington women reporters got Mrs. Truman to answer a series of written questions in 1947. Her written, penciled replies were read aloud by two White House secretaries and are listed below.

Bess Truman's Interview with the Press

Q. What is your conception of the role of First Lady?

A. No comment.

Q. What qualities innate or acquired do you think would be the greatest asset for the wife of a President?

A. Good health and a well-developed sense of humor.

Q. If such a thing were possible, what special training would you recommend to prepare a woman for the role of First Lady?

A. No comment.

Q. Any special professional background?

A. Skill in public speaking would be very helpful.

Q. Do you think there will ever be a woman President of the United States?

A. No.

Q. Would you want to be President?

A. No.

Q. Do you keep a scrapbook of your husband's activities?

A. Yes.

Q. Of your activities?

A. No.

Q. Of Margaret's activities?

A. Yes.

Q. Do you keep a diary?

A. No.

Q. Do you follow domestic and international events closely?

A. Yes, I do. Both.

Q. If so, how?

A. Newspapers, largely.

Q. Does unfavorable criticism of the president disturb you?

A. After 25 years in politics I have learned to accept it to a certain extent.

Q. How about unfavorable criticism of you?

A. No, I always learn something about myself.

Q. How about unfavorable criticism of Margaret?

A. No comment.

Q. What is your reaction to musical criticism of Margaret's singing?

A. No comment.

Q. Have you discovered any ways of sparing yourself during such tasks as receiving hundreds of guests?

A. So far, I have not felt it a task.

Q. Would you want Margaret ever to be First Lady?

A. No.

Q. Would you prefer that Margaret be a wife and mother or a career girl, or both?

A. Entirely up to Margaret.

Q. Do any of the demands of your role as First Lady give you stage fright?

A. No comment.

Q. Did you ever think or dream before Mr. Truman's nomination as Vice Presidential candidate of being First Lady?

A. No comment.

Q. What would you like to do and have your husband do when he is no longer President?

A. Return to Independence.

Q. Would you please describe some of your feelings of pride of your husband as President?

A. No comment.

Q. Years ago did you worry with him before he made a speech? And did he rehearse it before you?

A. Yes, to both questions.

Q. Do you worry about the President's safety when he is away on trips to distant points?

A. Yes, of course.

Q. What was your father's business?

A. Government position in Kansas City, Office of Collector of Customs.

Q. What experience since you have been in the White House do you consider most worthwhile?

A. No comment.

Q. What experience do you consider most amusing?

A. No comment.

Q. How does supervising the White House compare with supervising your own home in Independence, Missouri?

A. On a very much broader scale, but with a housekeeper there is not the personal responsibility.

Q. Are you interested in White House history?

A. Yes.

Q. What period of White House history, aside from the present, is most interesting to you?

A. Around the Monroe Administration.

Q. Have you ever traveled on a campaign train?

A. Yes, briefly.

Q. Would you enjoy this experience?

A. I did enjoy the first trip I made.

Q. Will you go along in 1948 if the travel is by train, if by plane?

A. Will answer this one in July 1948.

Q. Will you make any speeches?

A. No comment.

Q. Has living in the White House changed any of your views on politics and people? If so, how?

A. No comment.

Q. What extracurricular activities do you enjoy most? The H Street USO? The Spanish class?

A. The H Street USO has folded up, but I did thoroughly enjoy the work there. No comment on Spanish class.

Q. How would you add up what being First Lady has meant to you?

A. No comment.

Q. Will you go to the Democratic National Convention in 1948?

A. Expect to—wouldn't miss a Democratic convention if I could help it.

Q. If you had a son, would you try to bring him up to be President of the United States?

A. No.[30]

Private Life, Private Influence

Longtime White House servant J. B. West, who wrote a book about his service in the Truman White House, commented that "Bess guarded her privacy like a precious jewel, yet within that privacy played a prominent role far exceeding what any but a few suspected. She did advise Truman on decisions. And he *listened* to her."[31]

Early in his presidency one of Truman's most difficult decisions was whether to use the atomic bomb on Japan. To what extent he actually consulted Bess is uncertain. When questioned specifically about it, he said he had. Margaret Truman later wrote that although Bess may have known about the atomic bomb, Harry did not discuss it with her. The first lady later defended his decision by saying, "Harry always placed high value on the life of a single American boy. If the war with Japan had been allowed to continue, it would have claimed the lives of perhaps a quarter-million American soldiers, and twice the number would have been maimed for life." Presidential counsel and close confidant Clark Clifford believed that Bess "wouldn't pretend to make a final approval of such a decision. . . . She left that to experts."[32]

When the first bomb exploded over Hiroshima on 6 August 1945, Bess was in Missouri, but she had returned to Washington before the second bomb was dropped on Nagasaki three days later. It appears that Truman did seek her advice on the use of the second atomic bomb. White House butler Charles Ficklin reported that the night before the president issued the order, the Trumans were in their nightly meeting in the president's office longer than usual. When they emerged, Ficklin said, they "both looked real serious. Usually, they'd joke or kid around before going to bed. Now they didn't say a word, just looked straight ahead."[33]

To the American public Bess remained a mystery. The *New York Times Magazine* wrote of her in June 1946: "Because she has not yielded by one iota the Bess Truman of pre–White House days, she remains remote. . . . It is impossible for Bess Truman to be anything but Bess Truman, who didn't give a hoot for the whole goldfish-bowl business. . . . She is so much the individual that she would be stepping clear out of character if she tried to be like any other woman who ever lived in the White House."[34]

Harry Truman commented on his wife's perception of her role as first lady: "She was entirely conscious of the importance and dignity of White House life. She was not especially interested, however, in the formalities and pomp or artificiality which inevitably surround the family of a president."[35]

It took Bess some time to warm up to the press and the public. She attended hundreds of dinners, teas, and receptions and hosted dozens more for various associations. She found hosting, greeting scores of people and shaking thousands of hands, to be exhausting work. Soon she came to dread what she called "one of those dismal teas."[36]

The Trumans' private life during the presidency was simple. In the evenings Harry, Bess, and Margaret would chat, play the piano, and enjoy each others' company. Mrs. Truman was a baseball fan and liked to listen to the broadcasts of the Washington Senators' night games. Sometimes Bess and Margaret would play ping-pong. Many evenings the president would work in his study, assisted by Bess.[37]

Every first lady is always on trial, and the press watched Mrs. Truman constantly, looking for any faux pas to fill the gossip pages. During her first autumn in the White House, Bess uncharacteristically became entangled in controversy. On 12 October 1945 the Daughters of the American Revolution (DAR) wanted to give a tea in her honor in Constitution Hall. Seeing no reason not to participate, Bess accepted the invitation. It then came to light that Hazel Scott, one of the leading nightclub entertainers of the time and wife of New York congressman Adam Clayton Powell Jr., a leading Democrat and minister of the Abyssinian Baptist Church in Harlem, wanted to give a concert in Constitution Hall but was turned down by the DAR because she was an African American. On 1 October 1945 Powell fired off a telegram to Truman: "REQUEST IMMEDIATE ACTION ON YOUR PART IN THE SITUATION OF MY WIFE HAZEL SCOTT PIANIST BEING BARRED FROM CONSTITUTION HALL BECAUSE SHE IS A NEGRO."

Eleanor Roosevelt had resigned from the DAR in 1939 when Marian Anderson, the great African American opera singer, was barred. The day before Mrs. Truman was to attend the tea, Powell sent her a telegram urging her not to attend. "I can assure you," Powell told her, "that no good will be accomplished by attending and much harm will be done. If you believe in 100 percent Americanism, you will publicly denounce the DAR's action."[38]

Mrs. Truman wired back: "May I call your attention to the fact that the invitation was extended and accepted prior to the unfortunate controversy which has arisen. Personally I regret that a conflict has arisen for which I am in no way responsible. In my opinion my acceptance of the hospitality is not related to the merits of the issue which has since arisen. I deplore any action which denies artistic talent an opportunity to express itself because of prejudice against race or origin."[39] Bess attended the tea; Powell began calling her the "last lady." From that day until Truman left office, Congressman Powell was never invited to the White House, even for the annual receptions for members of Congress.

Bess's part in the hard-fought presidential campaign of 1948 was considerable. Harry called her his "chief adviser," and she was. Every decision he made was her personal concern. *Newsweek* reported that she "was a one-woman Gallup poll and audience-reaction tester, keeping a sharp watch on the crowds which listened to her husband's oratory. She was also the careful censor of the President's occasional lapses into humorous over-exuberance."[40] Frequently the president would use rather caustic language, and the first lady, fearful that reporters would write negative stories, would remind him to be careful with his words. On one occasion a well-known Democratic woman pleaded with Bess to make her husband clean up his language. "It seemed that he'd called somebody's statements 'a bunch of horse manure.' Unfazed, Bess is said to have replied, 'You have no idea how long it took to tone it down to that.'"[41] Harry Truman's most famous outburst—a scathing letter sent to Paul Hume, music critic for the *Washington Post,* who wrote a devastating review of daughter Margaret's singing debut at Constitution Hall—appeared in print only because the president wrote it and mailed it himself rather than running it by Bess, as was his custom.

Bess accompanied her husband on the famous "whistle stop" campaign across the country; they traveled over twenty-one thousand miles by train in just thirty-five days, during which Truman gave 475 speeches. At every stop the routine was the same: They would appear together on the rear platform of their private car; Harry would deliver a few words and introduce Bess as "the boss" and then Margaret as "the boss's boss." This homespun display of family solidarity (although Bess eventually came to detest being referred to as "the boss") helped to portray Truman as a simple, decent, and devoted family man to the small-town crowds of the American heartland.

Behind the scenes Bess was her husband's toughest critic. Newsmen told of seeing her sitting at a window of the train busily blue-penciling his speeches. She scolded him when he told a mother-in-law joke or acted undignified. She met with reporters and politicians' wives. Visiting former vice president John Nance Garner in Texas, Bess even gave a rare but characteristically brief speech. "Good morning, and thank you for this wonderful greeting," she said and then sat down.[42]

Truman went on to win an amazing upset victory in 1948, but the second term, especially the last two years, would be the most difficult of his entire presidency. His New Deal programs for domestic reform and his groundbreaking civil rights initiatives were crushed by an uncooperative Congress, and the war in Korea would grind to a stalemate. His approval ratings in the polls had reached all-time lows, especially after his firing of Gen. Douglas MacArthur, the popular supreme commander of the United Nations forces in Korea. In 1952 Truman's rating numbers were even lower than President Richard Nixon's on the day Nixon resigned.

Physically, Truman was beginning to feel the stress. And yet early in 1952 he was still toying with the idea of running for another term. Bess told him that she feared he would not survive another term, and she did not think that she could either. He was sixty-eight years old; he would be seventy-three at the end of another term. Truman biographer David McCullough believes that Bess would have left him if he had chosen to run again in 1952.[43]

On 29 March 1952 Truman announced to the American people what most had already suspected: He would not be a candidate for president. Bess was both happy and relieved. In most of the photographs of the first lady there is no hint of a smile, but on that day she looked, as one of Harry Truman's aides told the president, "like you do when you draw four aces."[44]

Conclusion

In January 1953, after the inauguration of President Dwight Eisenhower, Bess and Harry Truman returned to their home on 219 North Delaware

Street in Independence, Missouri. There they lived much as they had before they had left for Washington: as just ordinary citizens. Harry S. Truman died on 26 December 1972 at the age of eighty-eight. Bess continued to live in the Independence house for another ten years, still doing her own shopping at Milgram's Supermarket and keeping her weekly appointments at Miller's Beauty Shop. She died on 18 October 1982 at age ninety-seven, the longest-lived first lady.

Unlike Eleanor Roosevelt, who preceded her, Bess Truman preferred to remain in the background. As first lady, Eleanor would pursue a prominent public agenda, while Bess, in contrast, would see her most important role as being the president's sounding board and confidante. There is no doubt that she was the most important person in Harry Truman's life, and she was his trusted adviser in private.

Being first lady of the United States did not change Bess Truman one bit. As well-known historian and Truman biographer David McCullough describes her:

> Five foot four and stout, Bess Truman stood as straight as a drum major, head up, shoulders squared. She dressed simply and conservatively. There was nothing ever in any way mannered or pretentious about her. She was exactly as she had always been and saw no reason to change because she had become First Lady.
>
> Some guests at the White House found her so natural and unprepossessing they had to remind themselves to whom they were speaking. *Time* said somewhat condescendingly that with her neatly waved gray hair and unobtrusive clothes she would have blended perfectly with the crowd at an A&P.[45]

No doubt Bess would have wanted it that way.

Notes

1. Jahn Robbins, *Bess and Harry: An American Love Story* (New York: G. P. Putnam's Sons, 1980), 82.

2. Ibid., 38.

3. William E. Pemberton, *Harry S. Truman: Fair Dealer and Cold Warrior* (Boston: Twayne, 1989), 13.

4. Ibid., 12–13.

5. Ibid., 13.

6. David McCullough, *Truman* (New York: Simon and Schuster, 1992), 92.

7. Ibid., 103.

8. Margaret Truman, *Bess W. Truman* (New York: Macmillan, 1986), 100–101.

9. McCullough, *Truman,* 188.

10. Margaret Truman, *Bess W. Truman*, 117.

11. Ibid., 130.

12. Ibid., 133.

13. "Meet Harry's Boss, Bess," *Collier's* 12 Feb. 1949, 14.

14. Robert H. Ferrell, *Truman: A Centenary Remembrance* (New York: Viking Press, 1984), 85.

15. John W. McDonald, "Ten of Truman's Happiest Years Spent in Senate," *Independent Examiner,* Truman Centennial Edition, May 1984.

16. Gil Troy, *Affairs of State: The Rise and Rejection of the Presidential Couple Since World War II* (New York: Free Press, 1997), 30.

17. Ferrell, *Dear Bess: The Letters from Harry to Bess Truman* (New York: W. W. Norton, 1983), 479, 480.

18. McCullough, *Truman,* 289–99.

19. J. T. Salter, ed. *Public Men in and out of Office* (Chapel Hill: University of North Carolina Press, 1946), 4–5.

20. Harry S. Truman, *Memoirs, Vol. 1: Year of Decisions* (Garden City, N.Y.: Doubleday, 1956), 12.

21. Margaret Truman, *Bess W. Truman,* 231.

22. "'No Secret,' Truman Says of Wife's Job in Senate," *New York Times,* 27 July1944, 11.

23. "Meet Harry's Boss, Bess," 14.

24. Robbins, *Bess and Harry,* 80–81.

25. Ibid., p. 78.

26. Helen Worden Erskine, "The Riddle of Mrs. Truman," *Collier's*, 9 Feb. 1952, 12.

27. "First Lady," *Newsweek* (7 Jan. 1946): 26.

28. McCullough, *Truman,* 573–74.

29. "Meet Harry's Boss, Bess,"14.

30. "Behind Mrs. Truman's Social Curtain: No Comment," *Newsweek,* 10 Nov. 1947, 16.

31. McCullough, *Truman,* 578.

32. Carl Sferrazza Anthony, *First Ladies: The Saga of Their Power and Legacy* (New York: William Morrow, 1990), 524.

33. Ibid.

34. Bess Furman, "Independent Lady from Independence," *New York Times Magazine,* 9 June 1946, 19.

35. Harry S. Truman, *Memoirs* (New York: Doubleday, 1955), 45.

36. Troy, *Affairs of State,* 34–35.

37. Robert J. Donovan, *Conflict and Crisis: The Presidency of Harry S. Truman, 1949–1953* (New York: Norton, 1977), 146.

38. Ibid., 147–48.

39. "Tea for Fifty Ladies," *Newsweek,* 8 Nov. 1945, 36.

40. "Truman Ladies: Part of His Appeal," *Newsweek,* 8 Nov. 1948, 13.

41. J. B. West, *Upstairs at the White House* (New York: Warner Books, 1974), 72.

42. Troy, *Affairs of State,* 43.

43. *Truman,* videotape produced by David Grubin, PBS Home Video, 1997.

44. Alonzo Hamby, *Man of the People: A Life of Harry S. Truman* (New York: Oxford University Press, 1995), 605.

45. McCullough, *Truman,* 575.

Part Four

Political and Policy Influence

Overview

The entrance facade to the modern first ladyship was built by Eleanor Roosevelt. More than any other modern post-world-war first lady, Mrs. Roosevelt established professional, political, and behavioral patterns that her successors would strive to emulate. As Susan Roth Breitzer's essay indicates, Eleanor Roosevelt's activities as first lady and beyond were varied, controversial, groundbreaking, and compassionate. Shortly after her marriage to Franklin, on a trip to England, Mrs. Roosevelt was embarrassed that she could not explain the different levels of government in our constitutional structure. Her activities from that point illustrate her desire to master the political process in order to advance her agenda.

Even before she became first lady, Mrs. Roosevelt was involved in volunteer work for the Red Cross and was a champion on behalf of mental health issues. Breitzer credits Franklin Roosevelt's chief political strategist, Louis Howe, for helping to develop Mrs. Roosevelt's political skills. As Governor Roosevelt's wife she offered advice concerning appointments and was well schooled in "politics at its roughest."

As first lady Mrs. Roosevelt held her own press conferences covered largely by women reporters. These encouraged and aided female journalists. She wrote a daily newspaper column and virtually transformed the Office of the First Lady from a ceremonial post to a bully pulpit. She was involved in various issues, such as the plight of mine workers, youth problems, and civil and women's rights. She raised eyebrows with her controversial membership in the National Association for the Advancement of Colored People (NAACP).

Breitzer provides valuable insight into Eleanor and Franklin's marriage and the debilitating psychological effect of President Roosevelt's affair with Lucy Mercer. While this affair put distance between the president and the first lady, Mrs. Roosevelt maintained her activities in support of various social causes and became more independent of her husband over time.

Mrs. Roosevelt's activities did not end upon leaving the White House. She continued to be an activist for social causes and served as a delegate to the United Nations. Her contributions to the first ladyship helped move the position toward greater professionalism and eventual integration with the White House Office.

One groundbreaking development ushered in by Eleanor Roosevelt was her testimony before Congress. Colton C. Campbell and Sean E. McCluskie explore the congressional testimony and influence of first ladies on Capitol Hill. First ladies have often been used by presidents as influential lobbyists for the presidents' agendas. However, Campbell and McCluskie note that the more active a first lady becomes, the more controversial she is perceived. Lawmakers tend to scrutinize active first ladies because of their unelected and unconfirmed status. The authors describe the activities of Lady Bird Johnson, Eleanor Roosevelt, Rosalynn Carter, and Hillary Clinton. They explain why both Eleanor Roosevelt and Hillary Clinton were heavily criticized for their activities, while Rosalynn Carter escaped such criticism. Mrs. Roosevelt was the first to testify before Congress, and not only did Mrs. Clinton testify on behalf of her husband's health care plan, but she was the prime architect of the plan. In a interesting parallel, the authors compare the criticisms of first ladies Roosevelt and Clinton to that of Mary Todd Lincoln.

Most important, Campbell and McCluskie trace the development of the Office of the First Lady and document its increasing professionalization and integration with the White House Office. They provide useful information on the various types of congressional testimony by first ladies and the various committees involved in such testimony.

Because first ladies have acquired a modern office with a highly professional staff integrated with the White House Office, they have expanded their circle of influence. As Glenn Hastedt notes, first ladies are now heavily involved in foreign policy issues. Just as the social reforms concerning civil and women's rights had an impact upon first ladies and their office, these changes along with increasing interdependency and globalism have impacted the role of first ladies in the foreign policy area. Hastedt examines a series of analytical frameworks useful for studying first ladies, such as images and roles of first ladies, types of presidential partnerships, international relations conceptions of power, individual influence upon foreign policy, and the five stages of the policy process. He ultimately settles upon utilizing the five stages of the policy process framework to analyze the foreign policy efforts of Rosalynn Carter and Hillary Clinton. He concludes that both first ladies were important in the agenda-building stage of the policy process.

Anthony J. Eksterowicz and Kristin Paynter, in "The Evolution of the Role and Office of the First Lady: The Movement toward Integration with the White House Office,"[1] trace the evolution of the Office of the First Lady. They note the impact of modern activist first ladies upon the office. Two trends are evident. First, modern first ladies have contributed to the professionalization of the office. The Office of the First Lady is now highly structured and staffed by well-paid professionals skilled not only in public relations but public policy as well. Second, this trend has contributed to the increasing integration of the first lady's staff with the White House Office staff. Eksterowicz and Paynter propose a new independent/integrative model for the study of first ladies.

Throughout this section the reader can trace the development of the modern first lady. While Eleanor Roosevelt set the stage, other activist first ladies quickly followed and exerted their influence in both domestic and foreign policy.

SEVEN

Eleanor Roosevelt

An Unlikely Path to Political Activist

SUSAN ROTH BREITZER

INTRODUCTION

When Franklin Delano Roosevelt (FDR), two-term governor of New York, first received the Democratic presidential nomination in 1932, most people in his immediate circle were visibly rejoicing. However, when one of the women reporters present asked the first lady of New York, Eleanor Roosevelt, if she was "thrilled" at the idea of living in the White House, "Mrs. Roosevelt did not answer. She merely looked at the girl. And the expression on her face, almost angry, stopped all questioning along that line." Associate Press (AP) reporter Lorena Hickok, who was puzzled by this unexpected response, initially concluded that Eleanor had "merely thought it was a stupid question."[2]

Lorena Hickok (known to close friends simply as "Hick") would become one of Eleanor Roosevelt's closest friends and companions. Hickok gave up her hard-earned AP job as a result of the friendship, for fear of compromising her objectivity as a reporter. She was the first person to whom Eleanor would talk concerning her ambivalence about the idea of being first lady following FDR's election. To Hickok, Eleanor admitted, "If I wanted to be selfish, I could wish Franklin had not been elected."[3] This public ambivalence displayed by Eleanor Roosevelt even before FDR's election as president was reflective of her life prior to becoming first lady of New York.

After all the years it had taken her to build a life and identity apart from that of upper-class wife and mother, Eleanor Roosevelt, though she had campaigned for her husband, did not welcome the possibility of being restricted to the largely social and ceremonial role of first lady. In a conversation shortly after FDR's election, in which Hickok remarked awkwardly, "Well, anyway, you'll be first lady," Eleanor grudgingly admitted that people would call her that. But, wrote Hickok, "she added emphatically: 'There isn't going to be any First Lady. There is just going to be plain, ordinary Mrs. Roosevelt. And that's all.'"[4] Yet "plain, ordinary Mrs. Roosevelt" would end up being much more, and in the process she would forever reshape the role and office of first lady.

At first glance, Eleanor Roosevelt's background made her seem well suited to being a traditional first lady, one whose primary function was serving as national hostess. Yet there were also signs from early on that she could, if she so chose, remake the role of first lady as something other than "first hostess," even while expertly filling (and in many cases redefining) the traditional hostess role. This paradox can be explained by examining her previous roles as Mrs. (and earlier Miss) Roosevelt.

Miss Roosevelt

Anna Eleanor Roosevelt was born on 11 October 1884 to one of the most aristocratic families in the United States during this period. As the niece of Theodore Roosevelt, she was from an early age familiarized with both the privileges and the obligations of her social class. Yet from the beginning her aristocratic roots did not guarantee her an easy life or an ingrained sense of security.[5]

Her mother, Anna Hall Roosevelt, an extraordinarily beautiful woman who believed that feminine beauty counted more than anything else, judged her only daughter to be deficient not only in terms of looks but in terms of personality as well. Because little Eleanor was a shy, solemn child, her mother mocked her by calling her "Granny." By contrast her father, Elliot Roosevelt, the brother of Theodore, showered his "Little Nell" with loving acceptance and told her often of the happy life they would have together someday.[6] But that day was never to come. Elliot Roosevelt suffered from a serious drinking problem that would result in his separation from his family and an early death. When Eleanor was a young girl, her mother died of diphtheria at the age of twenty-nine. At the age of eight young Eleanor had no tears to shed for her mother's death, and on hearing the news she could only think about how she would soon get to see her father again. That was not to be, however, because after her mother's death Eleanor was placed in the custody of her strict maternal grandmother. Elliot Roosevelt went away to Abingdon, Virginia, to dry out and rarely saw his daughter. After his death from a fall while in a drunken stupor, Eleanor consoled herself with fantasies of what life with him might have been.[7]

The first time Eleanor Roosevelt received encouragement that she could be something other than a conventional society matron was during her years at Allenswood, an exclusive boarding school for girls located on the outskirts of London, where she was sent at the age of fifteen. Although the school included the strict schedule and behavioral expectations of the finest finishing school of the era, Allenswood was far from a mere finishing school. Its head-mistress, the iconoclastic Frenchwoman Mademoiselle Souvestre, included a fairly rigorous course of study in history and literature in her curriculum and encouraged her young charges to think for themselves and not merely parrot what anyone had taught them. During Eleanor's years at Allenswood, Made-moiselle Souvestre took a special interest in her promising pupil, inviting young Eleanor to her select after-dinner salons and taking her to the Euro-pean continent during one of the school breaks.[8]

Eleanor Roosevelt studied at Allenswood from 1899 to 1902 before hav-ing to return to the United States to take her place in high society. The most important ritual for a young woman of her class was to make a formal debut at some point between the ages of sixteen and eighteen, which signified that she was now eligible for marriage to a suitable young man. The formal debut, which for her took place at the Assembly Ball at New York's famous Waldorf-Astoria Hotel, was for her a dreaded coming-of-age ritual because it was in many ways a popularity contest, measured in terms of how full a young debutante's dance card became. Years later she recalled that she felt "deeply ashamed" of not being the belle of the ball as her mother and grandmother had been.[9]

Following her debut Eleanor Roosevelt continued her participation (albeit as little as she could get away with) in the social whirl of New York high soci-ety. She found far greater satisfaction volunteering at the Rivington Street Settlement House on the Lower East Side of the city, fearlessly riding the streetcar back and forth and teaching dance and calisthenics to poor immi-grant children. It was her first serious brush with "how the other half lived." During this time she also came to know her fifth cousin, Franklin, more than any of her many other cousins.[10]

It should be noted that during this period Eleanor Roosevelt was living between two worlds—the comfortable upper-class world into which she had been born and the world of service and usefulness to which Mademoiselle Souvestre had introduced her.[11] Souvestre, with whom Eleanor Roosevelt kept in contact until the former's death, sensed the "contradictory" nature of this period in Eleanor's life and predicted to her that it could "take you and drag you into its turmoil." In a letter following Eleanor's return to the United States, Souvestre warned her recent pupil: "Protect yourself to some extent against it—above all from the standpoint of your health which is not strong enough—to sustain the strain of this worldly rush. Give some of your energy, but not all, to worldly pleasures which are going to beckon to you. And even when success comes, as I'm sure it will, bear in mind that there are more quiet and enviable joys than to be among the most sought-after women at the ball or the woman best liked by your neighbor at the table, at luncheons and the various fashionable affairs."[12]

Eleanor's courtship with Franklin was not an easy one. Although fairly soon into their relationship the two were sure that they wanted to marry, Franklin's mother, the formidable widow Sara Delano Roosevelt, was most reluctant to let go of her only son. Only when she had failed to sidetrack Franklin from marrying at what she believed was too young an age did she consent to the match, nonetheless requiring the young couple to keep their engagement secret for a time. At their 17 March 1905 wedding President Theodore Roosevelt gave away his orphaned niece, congratulated the young couple on "keeping the name in the family," and then proceeded to draw the assembled crowd after him into the next room, leaving the bride and groom momentarily alone and forgotten. As Alice Roosevelt Longworth explained years later, this behavior was Teddy Roosevelt's way of being "the bride at every wedding, the baby at every christening, and the corpse at every funeral."[13]

Immediately following the wedding the Roosevelts had what amounted to a mini-honeymoon at Hyde Park, and once Franklin had completed law school at Columbia University, they scheduled a formal honeymoon in Europe, as was expected of newlyweds of their class. Although the three-month honeymoon was pleasant overall, it was far from free of discomfort for the bride. At a stop in the Dolomite Mountains in Italy, Franklin wanted to go climbing, while Eleanor, unsure of her ability, declined. Her husband thereupon found a woman tourist to climb with him instead, leaving his bride "jealous beyond description."[14] At another stop in England to visit some friends of the family, the new bride, when queried, was to her embarrassment unable to explain the differences between the federal and state levels of American government.[15]

Shortly before her marriage Eleanor Roosevelt's active volunteer work ceased under the influence of her mother-in-law, who successfully argued that she could be bringing germs home to infect her own children. Eleanor resigned herself to more genteel and indirect participation, serving on charitable boards and making modest donations.[16] Family matters also increasingly took up her time and energy. For most of the next ten years, she recalled, "I was always just getting over having a baby or about to have one."[17] Taking care of them, however, was something of a different story, since Eleanor had had no previous experience with small children and had little confidence in her maternal capabilities. She protested little when her mother-in-law stepped in to take on the major child-rearing responsibilities (and subsequently claimed that her grandchildren were really "her children," telling them, "Your mother only bore you"), including the hiring and firing of a series of baby nurses and nannies.[18]

During this period Eleanor's role in her husband's advancing public career was that of conventional wife. She believed that a woman's place was in the home and that government and politics were a male province but that it was a wife's duty to share and support her husband's interests "whether it was politics, books, or a particular dish for dinner."[19] This paradox was especially evident in her views on woman suffrage. Though she never went as far as to speak out in any way against the issue, neither did she favor it until she learned that her husband, by then a New York state assemblyman, publicly supported it.[20] She did not get directly involved in the political process until somewhat later, well after she had resumed volunteer activism during their early Washington years, when Franklin D. Roosevelt was appointed as assistant secretary of the navy by President Woodrow Wilson.[21]

EARLY POLITICAL CAREER

When they first arrived in Washington, Eleanor adhered rigidly to the demands of family and of the social duties expected of a subcabinet member's wife. This meant, among other things, filling most of her daylight hours making social calls on the wives of various Washington officials and then often either hosting or attending a social function that same evening. Tedious as calling duties were, Eleanor performed them not merely out of a rote sense of duty but with an understanding of the potentially valuable contacts they could create to help advance her husband's career.[22] In an effort to better keep on top of the myriad of social obligations thrust upon her, she hired a social secretary for three afternoons a week. Her social secretary, a young woman named Lucy Page Mercer, also had an aristocratic lineage but no longer possessed the money that went with it.

Lucy was, in many ways, ideally suited to the job, given her inside knowledge of Washington society, diligent nature, and pleasant, charming demeanor. However, her striking physical attractiveness and charm soon became a problem, as Eleanor began to notice Franklin's interest in Lucy and how he seemed to be a bit too eager to send Eleanor off with the children to the family's summer home in Campobello, Maine, while he stayed on the job in Washington.[23] When she expressed suspicions, Franklin brushed her off as "a goosy girl to think or even pretend to think that I don't want you here all the summer, because you know I do!" He assured her, "Honestly you ought to have six weeks straight at Campo, just as I ought to, only you can and I cant!"[24]

While Eleanor was away, however, Franklin spent more and more time with Lucy, even taking her to cousin Alice Roosevelt Longworth's lavish dinner parties. Alice justified her aiding and abetting of Franklin's affair with the argument that "he deserved a good time, he was married to Eleanor." However, more recent scholarship has suggested that Alice, who was never noted for her gentleness of spirit and whose own marriage to Ohio congressman (and eventually Speaker of the House) Nicholas Longworth was by this time visibly on the rocks, was also trying to soothe herself by making the cousin she disliked suffer.[25]

Before Eleanor could purse her suspicions far, however, the United States entered World War I. She was happy to curtail the practice of social calling and threw herself into volunteer work for the Red Cross, setting up a canteen for the soldiers who passed through Washington's Union Station. Eleanor often worked there from early morning until evening, not even stopping when she seriously cut her finger in a bread-slicing machine. She also supervised a navy knitting project for the servicemen and similar Red Cross knitting operations. Her devotion to wartime volunteerism resulted in an invitation by the Red Cross to organize a Red Cross canteen in England. Yet, she confessed later, she did not seize upon this opportunity for public service because she was not yet independent enough and felt a responsibility to her children.[26]

Even before the United States' entry into the war, Eleanor religiously practiced food-saving guidelines, following the call of Herbert Hoover, then head of the wartime Food Administration. In doing so, she experienced her first brush with public relations as well as her first public relations gaffe.[27] In the summer of 1917 she was selected by the Food Administration as the model for food saving for large families. The story was carried by the *New York Times*. Although undoubtably the intention was to show her as a model of frugality and efficiency, when the article quoted her proclaiming that "making the ten servants help me do my saving has not only been possible but highly profitable," it conveyed quite a different impression![28] Franklin Roosevelt's response to her public blunder was one of as much amusement as consternation. He wrote to her that her "latest newspaper campaign" was "a corker" and remarked, "I am proud to be the husband of the Originator, Discoverer, and Inventor of the New Household Economy for Millionaires! Please have a photo taken showing the family, the ten cooperating servants, the scraps . . . saved from the table and the handbook. I will have it published in the Sunday Times. Honestly, you have leaped into public fame, all Washington is talking of the Roosevelt plan."[29] Eleanor was visibly mortified, writing back, "I do think it was horrid of that woman to use my name in that way . . . because so much of it is not true and yet some of it I did say," adding, "I never will be caught again, that's sure."[30]

Even when merely the wife of a public figure, Eleanor Roosevelt had already become a public person. Also during the war her activities extended beyond simple meliorative activity to activism on behalf of the mentally wounded at Saint Elizabeth's Hospital, the federal mental hospital. After viewing the horrible conditions under which the mentally ill veterans were housed and their substandard treatment, she persuaded Interior Secretary Franklin K. Lane to consider the problem. Her work resulted in increased congressional appropriations for the facility. Eleanor enjoyed her first efforts as an advocate.[31]

In 1918 Franklin desired to play a more active role in the war, so he went on an inspection trip to Europe. He returned home with influenza and pneumonia and was carried on a stretcher. While he was bedridden, Eleanor dutifully unpacked his suitcase, and there she uncovered unmistakable evidence of her husband's dalliance: a bundle of love letters from Lucy Mercer. What type of confrontation took place between them will probably never be known, but Eleanor's recorded initial response was to offer Franklin "his freedom." Divorce, however, was strongly discouraged by Franklin's mother, who even threatened him with disinheritance, and by his chief political adviser, Louis McHenry Howe, who made it known that should Roosevelt leave his wife for this other woman, it would mark the end of his political career.[32]

Eleanor and Franklin's marriage remained intact but would never be the same again. The arrangement Eleanor demanded of her husband was that he never see Lucy again. She also insisted on ending their sexual relationship. Recovering herself from this almost unbearable blow took time, and she increasingly felt distanced from Franklin, even as she maintained her part in keeping up outward appearances of a marriage.[33] As their eldest son, James, described it, his parents maintained "an armed truce . . . that endured until FDR's death."[34]

Eleanor's devotion to other marital duties remained undiminished when the next family crisis arose. FDR was stricken with polio and paralyzed from the waist down during the family's vacation at Campobello in the summer of 1921. Through the difficult initial period following the illness, Eleanor stoically stood by her husband, nursing him through the ordeal and struggling to keep the family spirits intact.[35] Most notably, she held firm in encouraging Franklin to keep his dreams and political career alive and, for the first time, stood up to her mother-in-law, who would have been perfectly happy to see her son retire back to Hyde Park and live the leisured life of a country squire.[36]

Although it is still popularly believed that Eleanor Roosevelt's early political activism was solely on her husband's behalf and in order to keep his name before the public while he attempted to rehabilitate himself from polio, her activism predated his illness. This was largely a result of the efforts of FDR's chief political strategist, Louis Howe. Although at first she barely tolerated this irascible, gnomelike little man who smoked heavily, he soon drew her out and encouraged her to take a more active role in politics. Howe also gave Eleanor a necessary crash course in public speaking.[37]

Before Eleanor could make serious use of her newfound political skills, however, she devoted most of her time and energy to holding the family together while her husband convalesced. Once Franklin had regained his strength to the point that he no longer needed the same level of care and was mostly supervising his own rehabilitation, Eleanor's political activities increased along with her awareness of the limitations on women's involvement in politics. She participated in social causes and political campaigns, even using mudslinging against her own cousin Theodore Roosevelt Jr. in the 1924 New York gubernatorial race by linking him to the Harding administration's embarrassing Teapot Dome scandal.[38] Having shown such a willingness to play politics at its roughest, she would conclude that "women must learn to play the game as men do" and not be repulsed by the power brokering necessary in politics.[39]

Her transition from private wife to a public figure in her own right was also aided by the friendships of two women: Nan Cook and Marion Dickerman. With the help of these two friends she undertook small business ventures and redefined her identity and independence. These new directions also grew out of Eleanor's desire for a place of her own, and under FDR's supervision a cottage was built for Eleanor. A factory was added to the site, named Val-Kill for a stream that ran nearby. Val-Kill Industries, co-owned by Eleanor, Cook, and Dickerman, would go on to employ women and the needy and successfully manufacture reproductions of early American furniture. None of Eleanor's social and political activities, however, gave her as much satisfaction as her teaching at the Todhunter school, a progressive school for girls located in New York City that was also run with the assistance of Cook and Dickerman.[40] Even though she would eventually have to curtail many of her activities and business ventures when her husband became governor, she continued her work with the Todhunter school, noting, "In my teaching I really had for the first time a job that I did not wish to give up."[41]

Eleanor spent part of every week commuting by train between New York City and the state capitol in Albany, grading papers and preparing lesson plans on the ride.

During FDR's years as governor Eleanor began her practice of bringing representatives of causes she believed to be worthy to meet her husband, explaining the act as part of her expected role as hostess. She also persuaded her husband not to retain Belle Moskowitz, the previous governor's most able assistant. In so doing, Eleanor displayed much political savvy, as Moskowitz was too loyal to her previous employer and his agenda. Eleanor also played a role in persuading her husband to name Frances Perkins his state commissioner of labor.[42] The precedent-breaking activism that was characteristic of Eleanor Roosevelt's long tenure as first lady grew out of her work as first lady of New York and her social activism with Cook and Dickerman.

A First Lady Like None Before

When FDR was elected president, the first thing on the soon-to-be first lady's mind was what she would (or could) do with herself. Already, she had encouraged Etty Garner, the wife of vice president–elect John Nance Garner, who had worked as her husband's secretary while he was senator, to continue as his secretary if she so chose. While it is doubtful that Eleanor would have chosen a publicly subservient role for herself in the White House, Etty Garner's dilemma, according to Eleanor's longtime friend and biographer Joseph P. Lash, "may have influenced her own thinking about what kind of useful role she could play—that would not provoke public criticism—and would enable her to be the counselor and confidante of her husband."[43] One of her first thoughts was to serve as an unpaid assistant to the president, helping answer his mail, a suggestion FDR swiftly vetoed on the grounds that it impinged on the territory of his devoted secretary, Marguerite "Missy" LeHand. The irony of this proposal was that Eleanor would end up requiring several assistants plus the tireless work of her own secretary, Malvina "Tommy" Thompson, to deal with her own mail as first lady.[44]

One of the earliest signs that Eleanor was departing from the traditional background role of first lady was her decision to hold her own press conferences, the first of which even preceded the president's first press conference. Her press conferences were most notable at first in that they were restricted to women reporters, in large part to keep (and get) many women journalists employed in a time when newspaper and wire services were cutting their staffs and women reporters were the most likely to be let go. In addition to keeping many women journalists employed, she took extra efforts to make them feel valued and, in return, assured herself of positive press coverage. Because the prestigious Gridiron Club's annual dinner for journalists was then closed to women, Eleanor made a practice of holding an annual "Gridiron Widows" party, which was open to women government officials and the wives of Gridiron Club members, the same night as the Gridiron dinner.[45]

By the end of FDR's first term, Eleanor Roosevelt was not only helping the careers of many women in journalism, but she was most decidedly building her own career. Among her many written endeavors, the most notable was starting up a daily syndicated column called "My Day" in 1936. Although, as the title suggests, it started out as a brief recounting of her daily activities as first lady, the column soon became much more. In addition to her various writing ventures, she embarked on a public speaking career, which was a source of controversy. The criticism was based on accusations that the first lady was profiting from her position, even though her earnings went to charity.[46]

Beyond her speaking and writing, however, she still struggled to carve out a role for herself and some semblance of a normal life. Here again she was helped by her friends, especially Hickok. Although there has been much recent speculation concerning the true nature of Eleanor Roosevelt's relationship with Lorena Hickok, particularly the possibility that they were lesbian lovers, what is known is that Hick provided Eleanor with vital emotional support and a source of much-needed companionship.[47] The two women took trips together—along the East Coast, to the West Coast, to the Caribbean— always attempting to travel as just a regular pair of tourists, but they met with less success with this on each trip.[48]

As she accepted the reality of her growing status as a public figure, Eleanor also began, haltingly at first, to transform the "office" of first lady from a merely ceremonial post to a "bully pulpit" from which she would speak out and act on a variety of issues. In contrast to the expectations that affected the first ladies who followed her, Eleanor Roosevelt never chose a "pet cause." Rather, she gave her time and attention in various forms to a number of issues as they came up, most of which followed along the lines of her previous voluntary interests in social reform. They also grew out of her previously well-developed role as FDR's "eyes and ears" (and legs), going where her husband could not to inspect closely public institutions and situations of official concern. The thorough inspections for which she became so famous had been carefully perfected when she was first lady of New York. During FDR's governorship she would accompany him on his inspection trips of institutions around the state, during which FDR would ride around the grounds with the head of the particular institution to gain "a personal knowledge of the exterior," while his more mobile wife went inside to "get a real idea of how it was being run from the point of view of overcrowding, staff, food, and medical care." While at first she admitted, "My reports were highly unsat-isfactory," she soon "learned to look into the cooking pots on the stove and to find out if the contents corresponded to the menu—to notice whether the beds were too close together," and even "to watch the patients' attitude towards the staff." As first lady of the United States she continued this thoroughness.[49] Although she always treaded a narrow line concerning an acceptable level of influence on governmental policy, her areas of activism frequently inter-sected with New Deal policy and programs.

THE FIRST LADY'S ACTIVITIES

One of the earliest well-known examples of Eleanor's social activism was the Arthurdale Housing Project. Following on Hickok's investigation of the wretched living conditions of the long-out-of-work miners at Scott's Run, West Virginia, Eleanor made her own inspection of the situation, and from the horrors she saw there the idea of Arthurdale was born. Arthurdale, founded in Reedsville, West Virginia, was intended to become a self-sustaining sub-sistence farming community.[50] While the experimental community ended up falling short of its goals, Eleanor nonetheless argued that it helped the unem-ployed residents. To members of Congress she suggested that they "had never seen for themselves the plight of the miners or what we were trying to do for them."[51]

Among her other more controversial activities was to address the special problems of American youth, which during the Depression became a trou-bling presence in American society. The problems of young people became especially apparent in the late 1930s with the rise of the American Youth Congress (AYC), an umbrella organization that officially represented a vari-ety of youth organizations but became increasingly dominated by youthful leftists. Even before the AYC and/or its leaders arrived in Washington for what became a series of confrontational encounters with the federal govern-ment, Eleanor Roosevelt had urged FDR and his advisers to do more for young Americans who were leaving high school and college and finding no jobs available for them. When the AYC delegates were in the capital city, Eleanor even helped them find places to sleep and invited some to the White House.[52]

On matters regarding essential public policy, much of Eleanor Roosevelt's work took place in the background at the behest of President Roosevelt, who freely used his first lady as a sounding board on a variety of issues. Whether working openly or in the background, on few issues did the first lady take a more risky stand than those concerning African Americans. Although she had only limited familiarity with the concerns of African Americans at the time she became first lady, the more she personally viewed the effects of the Great Depression, the more she saw how it often disproportionally affected African Americans. Eleanor joined the National Association for the Advancement of Colored Persons (NAACP) and became an important ally to the group's leader, Walter White. Together they worked to support the Costigan-Wagner Bill, which intended to make lynching a federal crime. Eleanor spoke out on behalf of the initiative and earned public criticism from the South.[53] She also worked to improve employment and equal rights for African Americans and has been credited with bringing African Americans to the Democratic Party. In matters of race Eleanor Roosevelt took her most visible—and risky—public stands, whether in speech, writing, or action.

Although it was a comparatively small part of her efforts on behalf of race relations, in the public mind and in the history books no single event equaled the significance of Eleanor Roosevelt's actions on behalf of Marian Anderson. Anderson, an African-American contralto, overcame both poverty and racial discrimination to become one of the foremost classical singers of her day. In early 1939 Anderson's manager attempted to book her for a concert on Easter Sunday of that year. In the days before the Kennedy Center, Washington's premier performance venue was Constitution Hall, owned and run by the Daughters of the American Revolution (DAR), to which Eleanor Roosevelt had belonged since 1933 (DAR's long-standing custom was to offer lifetime membership to all incoming first ladies). When an attempt was made to book a performance date for the singer, however, it was discovered that all black performers were prohibited from the stage of Constitution Hall.[54] Anderson's exclusion became a subject of national controversy. Amid the furor Eleanor's famous response must be considered as decidedly subtle, for she never mentioned the DAR by name or described the actual situation.[55] Instead she remarked, almost casually and in the middle of her regular "My Day" newspaper column, about "a question which I have had to debate with myself only once or twice before in my life." The question was, "If you belong to an organization and disapprove of an action which is typical of a policy, should you resign or is it better to work for a changed point of view within the organization?" She then explained, "In the past, when I was able to work actively in any organization to which I belonged, I have usually stayed until I had at least made a fight and had been defeated." Under those circumstances, she felt, "I have, as a rule, accepted my defeat and decided I was wrong, or perhaps, a little too far ahead of the thinking for the majority at that time." But now, she stated, "I belong to an organization in which I can do no active work." This unnamed organization had "taken an action which has been widely talked of in the press," and she had decided that "to remain a member implies approval of that action." Therefore, she publicly announced her resignation from the DAR.[56]

Eleanor Roosevelt's activism and breaking of precedent not only continued but took new twists and turns as the nation emerged from the Great Depression just in time for a new world war to break out. At first it seemed, ironically, that the war returned her to a more traditional first-lady role; wartime restrictions on travel curtailed her speaking engagements, allowing her to fill more time in the traditional hostess role. She continued to welcome an unprecedented diversity of people to the White House, yet she soon found new opportunities to expand the boundaries of the first lady's role further.

Franklin Roosevelt at that point was already breaking a long-established American tradition by seeking a third term as president of the United States. Although Eleanor was, for a number of reasons, opposed to her husband seeking a third term, her innate sense of duty overcame personal convictions enough for her not only to fall in line behind FDR but to endure the hostility of Republicans seeking to make her an issue. The Republican opposition even distributed buttons that proclaimed, "We Don't Want Eleanor Either."[57]

Eleanor's bold service and her devotion to public duty are evident in her participation in the Democratic National Convention of 1940. The convention, having accepted FDR as their candidate for an unprecedented third term as president of the United States, was threatening to split over his choice of running mate: the left-leaning secretary of agriculture, Henry Wallace. Eleanor, who had been summoned to the convention in hopes of calming the fractious delegates on behalf of her husband, succeeded in exhorting the party to support the nomination in light of the international crisis.[58]

When the United States entered World War II, Eleanor continued to find new outlets for her public activism. One of the first upon which she embarked was taking a government position (unpaid) as the codirector of the Office of Civilian Defense. This not only proved to be her most controversial role but clearly demarcated the acceptable limits for a first lady's public role. The position was abandoned amid the ensuing controversy. Eleanor found success during the war as a goodwill ambassador to U.S. servicemen, especially when she traveled to the South Pacific in 1943.[59]

During the war years, through her columns, speeches, and writings, Eleanor increasingly began to shape her vision for the postwar world, a vision that would become more clearly and forcefully articulated in her post–White House years. In this vision she would not only refer to but expand upon the president's publicly proclaimed "Four Freedoms." Although Eleanor's activism brought her widespread acclaim, this notoriety came with a price. Beyond the expected criticism and controversy concerning her "meddling" in political affairs, perhaps the largest price she paid was in her family relationships, both in terms of how she related to various family members and in the increasingly strained "truce" in her marriage. While she played the public role of first hostess with aristocratic aplomb when present at the White House, private and semiprivate socialization among the family and close friends became a notably different matter. The Roosevelts' separate social circles became quite pronounced during the war years, impacting their family, political partnership, and relations with presidential aides. The breakdown of the truce was further exacerbated by the deaths of two people who had been instrumental in making it work: Louis Howe, who on top of his political role served as vital link between Eleanor and Franklin; and Missy Le Hand, who had fulfilled the president's companionship needs.

There was no question then or now that leading his country through economic depression and then world war took a toll on President Roosevelt's health, although the extent to which it did was kept hidden not only from the public but from the president himself.[60] Eleanor Roosevelt, healthy and energetic, seemed increasingly blind to her husband's weakened state. This became especially apparent by 1944, when the first lady was fully justifying her Secret Service code name, "Rover." She had long and frequent absences from the White House, and her daughter, Anna, who had moved into the White House with her young son, assumed responsibility for the day-to-day running of the White House. In the process, according to Elliot Roosevelt, Anna became "chatelaine, confidante, and jealous protector" of her father, even at the expense of Eleanor.[61]

Eleanor did nothing to ameliorate the situation and continued to badger her husband about issues of importance to her, even during the president's designated periods of relaxation, such as the predinner cocktail hour. As Anna recalled, near the end of one such cocktail hour in 1944, Eleanor "came in and sat down across the desk from Father [with] a sheaf of papers this high and said, 'Now, Franklin, I want to talk to you about this.'" At that point the normally imperturbable president threw the whole pile of papers in the direction of his daughter and said, "Sis, you handle these tomorrow morning." At that, Eleanor, "the most controlled person in the world . . . stood there a half second and said 'I'm sorry,' and walked away."[62]

The estrangement between husband and wife and daughter Anna's growing role in the White House paved the way for Anna to assist in reintroducing Lucy Mercer Rutherfurd (by then widowed) back into FDR's life. Taking advantage of the first lady's frequent absences, Lucy was invited to many private White House events (where no record of attendance was required). FDR also spent time with Lucy while at and en route to Warm Springs, Georgia, and other presidential retreats. When he died of a cerebral hemorrhage on 12 April 1945, it was while sitting for a portrait with Lucy present. When FDR's aunt Laura "Polly" Delano, who had also been present, unsparingly informed Eleanor of the truth of her husband's last moments, the resulting confrontation within the family just before the funeral was ugly and painful.[63]

Although most unvarnished accounts of Eleanor Roosevelt's personal life suggest that she and her husband made a go of their working partnership and that their troubles were merely personal, recent scholarship suggests something a little different in terms of any public policy impact. Their differing approaches to the political issues of the day, once a source of effective policy making, became an increasingly wide gulf between them, as the concerns of the Depression gave way to concerns of the war in Europe. As the Roosevelt relationship deteriorated, so did Eleanor's access to and influence with the president.

CONCLUSION

Even in the wake of the final humiliation of Lucy Mercer's presence at FDR's death and the permanently closed-off possibility of reconciliation in the Roosevelt marriage, Eleanor presented a positive picture for public consumption after the president's death, as she had during their life together. When evaluating her role as FDR's wife and first lady, she wrote: "When I went to Washington I felt sure that I would be able to use the opportunities which came to me to help Franklin gain the objectives he cared about. . . . He might have been happier with a wife who was completely uncritical. That I was never able to be, and he had to find it in other people. Nevertheless, I think I sometimes acted as a spur, even though the spurring was not always wanted or welcome."[64]

When reporters tried to query a newly widowed Eleanor Roosevelt about her post–White House plans, she quickly brushed them off with the assertion that "the story is over."[65] Yet the story was far from over for her personally and in terms of her legacy. During the remaining decades of her life Eleanor firmly established herself as a public person in her own right, both as delegate to the United Nations and as the universally respected and beloved "First Lady to the World," as President Harry S. Truman first dubbed her.[66]

Eleanor Roosevelt served briefly in an appointed office and she helped pave the way for many other women in government and politics. The appointment of Frances Perkins to the cabinet as secretary of labor is the best-known example. Many other women held subcabinet governmental positions during the Roosevelt administration through her efforts in partnership with Molly Dewson, head of the Women's Democratic National Committee.[67]

Eleanor Roosevelt forever altered public expectations concerning the role of the first lady, to the point that her immediate successor, Bess Truman, was initially a source of disappointment to the public when she resolutely refused to follow Eleanor's example of public activism. Bess Truman and Mamie Eisenhower preferred to avoid politics and social activism. But the first ladies who followed Jacqueline Kennedy made deliberate public activism part of their role. By the time Pat Nixon and Betty Ford became first ladies, "the question was not whether she [the first lady] would have a project, but what the project would be."[68] Yet even as public activism by the first lady became generally acceptable, there still remained (and remains) limits on the specific kinds of public activities considered acceptable, as demonstrated by the criticism directed at Hillary Rodham Clinton, the first lady perhaps most identified with Eleanor Roosevelt.

As Eleanor Roosevelt wrote on the eve of the 1960 election, only two years before her death, "The job of the President's wife is in many ways quite an onerous one . . . turning her slightest act, her most trivial word, into a public action." She concluded, "It is also tremendously interesting."[69]

NOTES (FROM OVERVIEW)

1. Anthony J. Eksterowicz and Kristin Paynter, "The Evolution of the Role and Office of the First Lady: The Movement toward Integration with the White House Office," *The Social Science Journal* 37, no. 4 (2000): 547–62.

2. Lorena A. Hickok, *Eleanor Roosevelt: Reluctant First Lady* (New York: Dodd, Mead & Co., 1962), xi.

3. Ibid., 1.

4. Ibid.

5. J. William T. Youngs, *Eleanor Roosevelt: A Personal and Public Life* (Boston: Little, Brown, 1985), 13–14, 20–24, 30. A second edition of the book was published in 2000 as part of The Library of American Biography series by Longman Publishers.

6. Eleanor Roosevelt, *The Autobiography of Eleanor Roosevelt* (New York: Curtiss, 1958), 1–3, 9; Roosevelt, *This Is My Story* (New York: Harper & Bros., 1937), 8, 18–21, 24; Youngs, *Eleanor Roosevelt,* 36–50.

7. Joseph P. Lash, *Eleanor and Franklin: The Story of Their Relationship Based on Eleanor Roosevelt's Personal Papers* (New York: W. W. Norton, 1971), 74–77, 80–85.

8. Ibid., 88–93; Eleanor Roosevelt, *Autobiography,* 36–37.

9. Youngs, *Eleanor Roosevelt,* 68–72.

10. Ibid., 67–69.

11. Marie Souvestre to Eleanor Roosevelt, Geneva, Switzerland, 7 July 1902, quoted in Lash, *Love, Eleanor: Eleanor Roosevelt and Her Friends* (New York: Doubleday, 1982), 31.

12. Eleanor Roosevelt, *Autobiography,* 41–42; Lash, *Eleanor and Franklin,* 101, 109, 111–13, 132–33, 141.

13. Blanche Wiesen Cook, *Eleanor Roosevelt: 1884–1933* (New York: Penguin Books, 1992), 169–72; Eleanor Roosevelt, *My Story,* 130.

14. Eleanor Roosevelt, "Wives of Great Men," *Liberty* 9 (Oct. 1932): 216; Lash, *Eleanor and Franklin,* 150.

15. Lash, *Eleanor and Franklin,* 153.

16. Eleanor Roosevelt, *Autobiography,* 62.

17. Cook, *Eleanor Roosevelt,* 177–80, 203.

18. Eleanor Roosevelt, *My Story,* 173.

19. Youngs, *Eleanor Roosevelt,* 97.

20. Eleanor Roosevelt, *Autobiography,* 72.

21. Cook, *Eleanor Roosevelt,* 207–8.

22. Lash, *Eleanor and Franklin,* 221–23.

23. Franklin D. Roosevelt to Eleanor Roosevelt, Washington, D.C., 16 July 1917, in Elliot Roosevelt, *FDR: His Personal Letters (1905–1928)* (New York: Duell, Sloan and Pearce, 1948), 347.

24. Cook, *Eleanor Roosevelt,* 220–22; Carol Felsenthal, *Alice Roosevelt Longworth* (New York: G. P. Putnam's Sons, 1988), 135–38.

25. Lash, *Eleanor and Franklin,* 208–15; Eleanor Roosevelt, *My Story,* 254–55, 262.

26. Youngs, *Eleanor Roosevelt,* 112.

27. "How to Save in Big Homes: Food Administration Adopts Mrs. F. D. Roosevelt's Plan as Model," *New York Times,* 17 July 1917.

28. Franklin D. Roosevelt to Eleanor Roosevelt, Washington, D.C., 18 July 1917, in Elliot Roosevelt, *FDR,* 249.

29. ER to FDR, Washington, D.C., 24 July 1917, quoted in Lash, *Eleanor and Franklin,* 211.

30. Eleanor Roosevelt, *Autobiography,* 91–93.

31. Cook, *Eleanor Roosevelt,* 227–31.

32. Ibid., 230–36.

33. Ibid., 101.

34. Ibid., 114–15.

35. Ibid., 310–11; Lash, *Eleanor and Franklin,* 272–76.

36. Eleanor Roosevelt, *Autobiography,* 109–10.

37. Peter Collier, *The Roosevelts: An American Saga* (New York: Simon & Schuster, 1994), 297–98.

38. Eleanor Roosevelt, "Women Must Learn to Play the Game as Men Do," *The Red Book Magazine* 50 (Apr. 1928): 78–79, 141–42; reprinted in Allida Black, ed., *What I Hope to Leave Behind: The Essential Essays of Eleanor Roosevelt* (Brooklyn, N.Y.: Carlson, 1995), 195–200.

39. Kenneth S. Davis, *Invincible Summer: An Intimate Portrait of the Roosevelts, Based on the Recollections of Marian Dickerman* (New York: Atheneum, 1974), 34–35, 43–45.

40. Ibid., 52–55, 77–80.

41. Eleanor Roosevelt, *This I Remember* (New York: Harper & Row, 1949), 54.

42. Lash, *Eleanor and Franklin,* 321–28.

43. Ibid., 357.

44. Ruth K. McLure, *Eleanor Roosevelt, An Eager Spirit: The Letters of Dorothy Dow, 1933–1945* (New York: W. W. Norton, 1984), 21–22; Mollie Somerville, *Eleanor Roosevelt As I Knew Her* (McLean, Va.: EPM Publications, 1996), 59–62.

45. Ruby Black, *Eleanor Roosevelt: A Biography* (New York: Duell, Sloan and Pearce, 1940), 93, 157–58.

46. Jess Flemion and Colleen M. O'Connor, *Eleanor Roosevelt: An American Journey* (San Diego, Calif.: San Diego State University Press, 1987), 101–2.

47. Faber, *Lorena Hickok,* 238–39.

48. Hickok, *Eleanor Roosevelt,* 119–31, 157–67.

49. Eleanor Roosevelt, *This I Remember,* 56.

50. James R. Kearney, *Anna Eleanor Roosevelt: The Evolution of a Reformer* (Boston, Mass.: Houghton Mifflin, 1968), 157–67. Congress generally ignored or was somewhat skeptical of Mrs. Roosevelt's efforts in Arthurdale. The first lady's plans had been rather utopian from the outset, and the Arthurdale experiment was not a success. However, Mrs. Roosevelt's efforts did produce a few of her goals, and her suggestion that Congress should have demonstrated more financial and moral support for the miners was probably accurate.

51. Eleanor Roosevelt, *Autobiography,* 179.

52. "Address to the American Youth Congress," 10 Feb. 1940, in *The Public Papers and Addresses of Franklin D. Roosevelt,* vol. 9, *War and Aid to Democracies* (New York: Russell and Russell, 1969), 86–93.

53. Eleanor Roosevelt, *This I Remember,* 201–5.

54. Tamara K. Haraven, *Eleanor Roosevelt: An American Conscience* (Chicago: Quadrangle Books, 1968), 119–23.

55. Doris Kearns Goodwin, *No Ordinary Time: Franklin and Eleanor Roosevelt: The Home Front in World War II* (New York: Simon & Schuster, 1994), 330–31.

57. Somerville, *Eleanor Roosevelt,* 143–48.

58. Ibid., 145.

56. Eleanor Roosevelt, "My Day" (27 Feb. 1939), in *Eleanor Roosevelt's* "My Day": *Her Acclaimed Columns, 1936–1945,* ed. Rochelle Chadakoff (New York: Pharos Books, 1989), 113.

57. Lash, *A Friend's Memoir,* 614–19, 628–30.

58. Eleanor Roosevelt, "Address to the 1940 Democratic Convention," *New York Times,* 19 July 1940.

59. Youngs, *Eleanor Roosevelt,* 1–11, 193–97.

60. Jim Bishop, *FDR's Last Years: April 1944–1945* (New York: Pocket Books, 1975), 2–15.

61. Elliot Roosevelt and James Brough, *A Rendezvous with Destiny: The Roosevelts of the White House* (New York: G. P. Putnam's Sons, 1975), 372–73.

62. Bernard Asbell, *Mother and Daughter: The Letters of Eleanor and Anna Roosevelt* (New York: Coward, McCann, and Geoghegan, 1988), 176–77.

63. Goodwin, *No Ordinary Time,* 611–14.

64. Ibid., 611–14, 632; Eleanor Roosevelt, "My Day" (24 July 1944), in Chadakoff, *My Day,* 349.

65. Richard S. Kirkendall, "ER and the Issue of FDR's Successor," in *Without Precedent: The Life and Career of Eleanor Roosevelt,* ed. Joan Hoff-Wilson and Marjorie Lightman (Bloomington: Indiana University Press, 1984), 176, 190, 197.

66. Eleanor Roosevelt, *Autobiography,* 279.

67. Susan Ware, *Beyond Suffrage: Women in the New Deal* (Cambridge: Harvard University Press, 1981), 43–50; Susan Ware, *Partner and I: Molly Dewson, Feminism, and New Deal Politics* (New Haven, Conn.: Yale University Press, 1987), 192–94, 233–37.

68. Abigail Q. McCarthy, "ER as First Lady," in *Without Precedent: The Life and Career of Eleanor Roosevelt,* ed. Joan Hoff-Wilson and Marjorie Lightman (Bloomington: Indiana University Press, 1984), 220–21.

69. Eleanor Roosevelt, "My Advice to the Next First Lady," *Redbook* 116 (Nov. 1960): 95–96, 118–21; reprinted in Allida Black, *What I Hope,* 281–85.

Eight

Policy Experts

Congressional Testimony and Influence of First Ladies

Colton C. Campbell and Sean E. McCluskie

Introduction

The ties between lawmakers and the president are complex and interdependent. The Constitution deliberately engenders institutional competition and cooperation between Congress and the presidency. But does this relationship encompass the first lady, who holds no official position and earns no salary? Although the Constitution is silent regarding her, she is a prominent public figure who can, and often does, use her close proximity and indirect power to influence the president's political decisions.[1] In addition the first lady has the power to shape lawmakers' perceptions of her husband's administration.[2] From the ceremonial role played by presidents' wives in the early days of the republic, the job of the first lady has grown to one of considerable clout, involving campaigning, speaking out on issues, heading projects or causes that complement the president's legislative agenda, developing and crafting strategy to rally a winning coalition of members, and serving as a catalyst for policy debates of perhaps lasting import.[3] Like any elected official sent to Washington, to succeed she must appear articulate, well informed, and self-assured.[4]

This chapter is an exploratory study of the congressional testimony and influence of modern first ladies on Capitol Hill. Since the first lady's duties and responsibilities have never been fully defined, each woman experiments with the job's potential.[5] Contemporary first ladies have expanded their activities beyond pet projects and stately and social functions to encompass substantive policy issues. They are increasingly engaged in more "inside" lobbying, channeling their efforts through formal decision-making processes within Congress.[6] Specifically, this includes testifying before committees or subcommittees to place their positions on the record and communicating directly with lawmakers or their personal staffs to promote points of view. Explanations for the extent and effect of interaction with Congress and its members are numerous and complex; some of them are entwined with the willingness of the first lady to shoulder a public role, and some lie with the wide latitude left to the chief executive to choose his advisers freely.

The policy role of first ladies and their influence as policy experts working with Congress can be traced to the advent of a public role for first ladies. For much of the eighteenth and nineteenth centuries presidential wives followed the pattern set by Martha Washington, accepting their husbands' elections as a propellant into public life that included entertaining at receptions and dinners, calling on other women in Washington, and overseeing the White House domestic staff. These tasks were accomplished without entangling themselves in partisan disputes or taking sides in debates on public policy.[7] The job of the first lady has gradually come to include direction of a project or cause complementary to the president's agenda but separate from it. Part of the public role for first ladies has developed out of their association with the executive mansion, where they have functioned to maintain the residence as a public monument and schedule entertainment. As the public relations aspect of the presidency has increased, presidents have turned to their spouses to augment their effectiveness. Today the Office of the First Lady is an institutionalized segment of the presidency.[8] The office is served by a sizable staff and a significant budget.[9] It mirrors the organization of the president's West Wing operation, with its own chief of staff, press secretary, speech writers, project directors, and various other aides who carry out specialized tasks.

There have been several instances in which first ladies have testified before congressional committees, beginning with the first wife of a president to do so, Eleanor Roosevelt. It is important to examine such committee appearances because these legislative workshops perform a broad range of functions for Congress as a whole—preparing groundwork for legislation, bringing public issues into the spotlight, and whipping legislation into shape—and offer Congress the potential of increased efficiency and expertise. There lawmakers make their most effective personal contributions to public policy; pursue constituency interests; develop strong relationships with political advocates, executive officials, and other participants in the political arena; and produce measures that can stand up on the floor of each chamber.[10] Given this capacity to enable a legislature to engage actively in a nation's governance, testifying before these bodies, at least anecdotally, provides more access points and potential influence for first ladies to contribute to the presidency.

There is also the question of first ladies' effectiveness at persuading congressional action. In an age when husbands and wives, at least in the professional classes, are increasingly likely to share professional interests, the president's spouse's role will increasingly become an issue. But do lawmakers prefer a more traditional role for the first lady, one that entails exercising influence behind the scenes rather than in public? A notable paradox about first ladies is that the greater their perceived political and policy influence, the more they are scrutinized by legislators because of their unelected and unconfirmed (by the Senate) status.[11]

FROM CEREMONIAL HOSTESS TO FIRST PARTNER

Early White House wives principally entertained at receptions and dinners, called on other women in the nation's capital, and oversaw the White House domestic staff. In a move rare for a first lady, Dolley Madison acted as her husband's "secretary" for a few days while he was ill, forestalling a congressional committee requesting to see him.[12] In private, however, first ladies such as Helen Taft often attended House and Senate debates and discussed them with their husbands.[13] First ladies Mary Todd Lincoln and Ida McKinley advised their spouses on presidential appointments. Hints of modern development, however, did not appear until the nineteenth century when Edith Roosevelt, second wife of Theodore Roosevelt, began to hire her own staff to answer mail and reporters' questions instead of relying on the president's staff.

It was not until the twentieth century that first ladies began to emerge as "activist political partners," selecting their own undertakings rather than simply responding to public pressure to champion their husbands' causes.[14] Before her death Ellen Wilson lent her name to slum-clearance projects and invited reformers to meet members of Congress at the White House. Using official vehicles to transport observers around Washington, D.C., she showed them the decrepit and inadequate housing located near Capitol Hill. Wilson quietly lobbied legislators for the Alley Dwelling bill of 1914 to demolish slums and build new housing with federal money. Her association with this cause became so popular that on the day she died the Senate passed a housing bill in her honor.

Historians have questioned to what extent President Woodrow Wilson's second wife, Edith Bolling Wilson, ran the government after he suffered a stroke that left him partially paralyzed and incapable of conducting national business for six months. Edith Bolling Wilson did not make many important political decisions during her husband's illness, but she alone decided who could see the president (see the essay on Edith Bolling Galt Wilson by McCallops in this book). Early on, she took a deep interest in Wilson's work and the president willingly involved her in it. "Much as I love your delicious letters," she wrote in a letter to Wilson, "I believe I enjoy even more the ones in which you tell me . . . of what you are working on . . . the things that fill your thoughts and demand your best effort, for then I feel I am sharing your work and being taken into partnership as it were."[15] When the two were apart, President Wilson sent Edith envelopes of state papers dealing with national and international affairs, writing his comments in the margins and asking for her feedback. President Wilson's relationship with Congress was never close, but it became more aloof after Edith became first lady. One senator noted that it was impossible to speak with President Wilson at dinners because the president sat next to the first lady and virtually ignored their guests across the table, devoting his full attention to his wife.[16]

Contemporary first ladies are clearly brought more formally into the process of governing and policy making than earlier presidents' wives were, and at times they actually developed public policy or legislation. This gradual evolution from ceremonial hostess to symbol surrogate, issue highlighter, campaign worker, and political adviser reflects the impact of certain activist presidential wives, the changing role of women in society, increased power in the executive branch, and the increased public and press attention focused on the presidency's politics and personalities.

Eleanor Roosevelt was the first presidential wife to testify before a congressional committee, the first to hold a government office (as assistant director of the Office of Civilian Defense), the first nominated to a post requiring Senate confirmation (as a U.S. representative to the United Nations General Assembly), and the first to promote or oppose legislation through newspaper columns and radio addresses (see the essay on Eleanor Roosevelt by Breitzer in this book). Citing her husband's partial paralysis, she became the president's eyes and ears, traveling to almost every state and congressional district.

Despite her disinterest in politics and crowds, Jacqueline Kennedy was a valuable partner with her husband along the campaign trail and took an active, albeit subtle, interest in carrying out the social and honorary role of first lady.[17] Shortly after Mrs. Kennedy left the White House, Claudia Taylor "Lady Bird" Johnson tackled the legislative side of beautification. She and her staff sponsored and partly wrote a law that President Lyndon B. Johnson submitted to Congress. The initiative sought to eliminate the proliferation of junkyards and billboards along the nation's highways. Lady Bird personally oversaw the White House lobbying for the bill, making numerous calls, and despite criticism from such opponents as then-representative Robert J. Dole (R-Kans.), she was successful in passing the Highway Beautification Act of 1967, known as "Lady Bird's Bill," and advancing a proposal to landscape Capitol Hill.[18] As a result of her efforts, President Johnson advocated beautification and conservation in his 1965 State of the Union address and submitted a host of proposals to Congress pertaining to beautification and conservation. Lady Bird's work initiated or at least supported a variety of important natural and environmental policies enacted in the late 1960s, including the National Historic Preservation Act, the Clean Rivers Restoration Act, the Air Quality Act, the National Trail Systems Act, and the Wild and Scenic Rivers Act.[19]

Rosalynn Carter was an active adviser to her husband, meeting with him regularly to discuss policy, sitting in on cabinet meetings, and occasionally representing him on trips abroad. Mrs. Carter also spoke to and lobbied members of Congress on behalf of her own interests, which included mental health education, the Equal Rights Amendment for women, and the plight of refugees. After persuading her husband to appoint a National Commission on Mental Health, she worked closely as honorary chairperson with professionals on the commission, gathering data, making recommendations, and devising legislation to improve mental-health programs at the local, state, and national levels. On 7 February 1979 she went before the Senate Resources Subcommittee to testify in favor of increased federal spending for mental health programs, tangling with then-chair Edward Kennedy (D-Mass.) over what constituted a satisfactory federal health budget. Mrs. Carter also championed legislation to reform Social Security, extend the mandatory retirement age for federal workers, and improve medical services for the elderly in rural areas.

Hillary Rodham Clinton openly wielded influence as one of her husband's closest political advisers. Not attuned with the traditional role of first lady, Rodham Clinton spearheaded the Clinton administration's health care reform efforts on Capitol Hill in 1993 and 1994. In that role she traveled around the country meeting with health care professionals, interest groups, and ordinary people to hear their views on the nation's health care system. She regularly attended policy strategy meetings, consulted with members of Congress, and testified before congressional committees on the president's health care plan.[20] Then-representative and cochair of the Congressional Caucus for Women's Issues, Patricia Schroeder (D-Colo.) attributed the "Hillary factor" with pushing through thirty bills affecting women and children in the latter days of the 103rd Congress (1993–94); "First Lady Hillary Rodham Clinton's influence and popularity has given women more clout," she declared.[21] This, in turn, increased sensitivity in Congress to listening to women and their concerns. Such political influence is not, by historical standards, unusual, but the openness about it was.

In recognition of the political role of Hillary Rodham Clinton, a 1993 U.S. Court of Appeals decision, *Association of American Physicians and Surgeons v. Hillary Rodham Clinton,* addressed the question of whether the role of first lady constitutes an "Office under the United States." That issue arose in response to the Clinton administration's health reform task force that Mrs. Clinton chaired in 1993. A group of physicians contended that the task force was a federal advisory committee and therefore subject to the sunshine provisions that apply to such advisory entities. The Clinton administration countered that the advisory committee law did not apply because of an exception for groups composed solely of "full-time officers or employees" of government.[22] It argued that, as first lady, Mrs. Clinton was the functional equivalent of a government officer or employee. The court eventually accepted this position, concluding that Congress itself had recognized that a presidential spouse acts as the fundamental equivalent of assistant to the president when it established, by statute, the Office of the First Lady, to include a full-time staff paid for with public funds.

CONGRESSIONAL REACTION TO FIRST-LADY ACTIVISM

Of the three first ladies to testify while their husbands were in office, two of them suffered heavy criticism from members of Congress. Hillary Rodham Clinton and Eleanor Roosevelt received increased congressional scrutiny, while Rosalynn Carter did not. As Daniel Diller and Stephen Robertson point out, Hillary Rodham Clinton pushed her office's power to the limits of the time.[23] Mrs. Clinton's public activism in developing President Clinton's national health care reform encouraged Republican members of Congress to increase their scrutiny of her actions. The Republican-controlled Congress investigated the Clintons' Whitewater real-estate venture dating from the late 1970s and her role in the 1993 firings in the White House Travel Office. Many Republican lawmakers pushed hard for these investigations because they believed that the president and, especially, Hillary Clinton acted illegally in both cases.

This criticism of the first lady was not unique to the activism of Hillary Clinton. Eleanor Roosevelt provoked congressional scrutiny by speaking out on matters that many on Capitol Hill preferred to avoid; she agitated their constituents, challenged their assumptions about a "woman's place," and ran a "parallel administration" alongside her husband.[24] Mrs. Roosevelt was capable of charming and exasperating many lawmakers by her unconventional behavior (e.g., northern liberals applauded her as an ally, while southern conservatives objected to her civil rights advocacy). Republicans often suspected her motives, some calling her "Lenin in skirts," while Democrats sometimes regarded her as a cross to bear.[25] As first lady, Eleanor Roosevelt made a special effort to aid women members of Congress, inviting Republicans and Democrats alike to the White House. Rep. (later Sen.) Margaret Chase Smith (R-Maine) "respected and admired Mrs. Roosevelt for her intelligence and active leadership and also because, in whatever circumstances, she was a lady."[26] Eleanor Roosevelt encouraged Helen Gahagan Douglas (D-Calif.) to run for office and bolstered other women's congressional careers.[27] During her last years in the White House, Eleanor Roosevelt's support for civil rights legislation triggered acerbic attacks from segregationist Senator Theodore Bilbo (D-Miss.). He concluded one Senate speech by asserting, "If I can succeed eventually in resettling the great majority of the Negroes in West Africa —and I propose to do it—I might entertain the proposition of crowning Eleanor queen of Greater Liberia."[28] The galleries, however, hissed these remarks.

First ladies Clinton and Roosevelt both suffered personal insults from political commentators. For instance, there were often comments in the press about them acting the male roles in their relationships, and accusations were made that they were homosexual. Unlike these two first ladies, Rosalynn Carter did not suffer excessive attacks from the opposing party. It is difficult to make any broad, sweeping conclusions about why this was so, since there are only three cases of first ladies testifying before Congress. However, Eleanor Roosevelt's and Hillary Rodham Clinton's testimonies before Congress were substantial deviations from the roles played by previous first ladies. Roosevelt was the first in her position to testify before Congress. By the time Rosalynn Carter testified before Congress, the liberalization of women's rights had progressed greatly from the 1940s. Because of the change in the country's social environment, society was more accepting of a first lady being the country's leading voice on an issue. Additionally, Carter's testimony was similar to Eleanor Roosevelt's in that her role was to discuss an issue and bring attention to its importance. Therefore, it is possible that Rosalynn Carter escaped the criticism of Eleanor Roosevelt because her type of testimony had been given by Mrs. Roosevelt first.

In contrast, Hillary Clinton broke new ground when she not only testified before Congress but put forth a proposal on health care of which she was the principal architect. Although well treated during the hearing process, Hillary Clinton is still heavily criticized for her role in the health care reform process. If the experience of Eleanor Roosevelt's testimony is any indicator, it may be some three decades before another first lady ascends to such a central role in a policy debate. In any case, future first ladies will likely act in the role of traditional ceremonial figures rather than activists.

To examine further the position that first ladies Roosevelt and Clinton were excessively criticized for their activism, it is worth comparing them to other first ladies who have not testified before Congress but who also have been heavily chastised. The most severely criticized first lady in comparison to Mrs. Roosevelt and Mrs. Clinton was Mary Todd Lincoln.[29] Republican lawmakers viewed Mrs. Lincoln as high-handed, untruthful, and untrustworthy. Some thought that she had covered up financial irregularities in both her personal and White House accounts. Others doubted her loyalty to the nation, since she was a Kentucky native whose family members were largely Confederate sympathizers and her brothers had served in the Confederate army.[30] In this contentious atmosphere President Lincoln's State of the Union address was obtained before the speech was given and under mysterious circumstances, while it was still in draft form. It was apparently removed from his desk and printed by a New York newspaper reporter who was known to be a close friend of the first lady. Questioning her patriotism and mindful of what later generations would regard as national security leaks, the House Judiciary Committee pondered issuing a subpoena for Mary Todd Lincoln, the suspected source of the leaked address. A popular dramatic anecdote that first appeared in print in 1905 told the touching story of President Abraham Lincoln, hat in hand, appearing before a congressional committee to defend his wife.[31] In light of the fact that Mary Todd Lincoln had such close ties to the Confederacy during the most divisive time in the country's history, the Civil War, it is not surprising that she came under criticism. While first ladies Roosevelt and Clinton were criticized because of their unique activism, this unique time and event seemed to be the cause of the extensive criticism of Mary Todd Lincoln.

Scarcely a year into the first term of President Ulysses S. Grant, his wife, Julia Grant, was besieged with questions of political impropriety and ill-gotten profits in the "Black Friday" attempt to corner the gold market. To determine just what Julia Grant knew, House Democrats wanted to hear from her and the president's sister, to whom Julia had written about gold speculation.[32] For a month in 1870 the House Committee on Banking and Currency, headed by future president James A. Garfield, conducted the "Gold Panic Investigation." Its purpose was to investigate the causes that led to the unusual and inordinate fluctuations of gold in New York City during the latter months of 1869. But House Republicans—of the same party as President Grant—deftly prevented the first lady from having to testify by protesting that such a request was unseemly and undignified.

The Grant administration suffered from many scandals among its cabinet members. Therefore, it is not surprising that the Democrats in Congress scrutinized his administration so closely. More important, Democrats, who were known as the "Party of the South" because members of the Republican Party were seen as the instigators of the Civil War, had a strong motivation to embarrass the president, who had been the general of the army that defeated them.

OFFICE OF THE FIRST LADY

Until the late 1970s Congress allocated provisions for staff and space for the first lady's office on an ad hoc basis. Historically, the president's wife paid out of her own funds for one or more social secretaries and relied on friends to assist her in answering letters, greeting well-wishers, arranging parties, promoting causes, improving the White House's appearance, and keeping a record of its furnishings and of the guests invited to each official event.[33] In January 1946 Congress briefly discussed the merits of institutionalizing funding for the first lady. Standing on the House floor, Rep. James Grove Fulton (R-Pa.) offered a pro forma amendment to provide the wife of the president a salary of ten thousand dollars per year to cover her services for maintaining the White House establishment, "not to be expended as the President may determine." Representative Fulton stated on the House floor: "She is known as the First Lady of the land. She has that status, whether she has been elected to it or not. She is the only case of involuntary servitude in the United States of America. She serves completely without pay, completely without expenses, [and] could not resign from the position if she wanted to."[34]

Speaking further to her responsibilities, Representative Fulton continued:

> She has to travel to conventions of many lodges. She has to receive women from all parts of the country. She has to hold press conferences either directly or through her assistants. Those are duties that must be recognized. In addition to that, she has the duty of supervising the expending of all the money for the maintenance of the household in the White House. She supervises the servants. She supervises the purchases. She has secretaries who work for her and who are paid, but she herself is paid not one red cent by the people of the United States. . . . May I add also that she even has the burden of entertaining Congress from time to time, because we Members are

invited up there both from the upper House and the lower House; and, believe me, that is some burden, too.[35]

Rep. Joseph Edward Hendricks (D-Fla.) countered: "While I concede there is some merit to the proposal, I make the point of order against the amendment that it is an appropriation not authorized by law."[36] The point of order was sustained and by unanimous consent withdrawn.

Lawmakers eventually cleared up the issue of White House staff in the last days of the 95th Congress (1977–78). By voice vote the House approved a conference report (H Rept 95–1639) on a bill (HR 11003) granting legal authority for the establishment of funds to manage the White House— authorizing salary levels for, and setting limits on the number of, top White House staffers. The Senate had passed the conference report a month earlier, also by voice vote. Explicit authorization also was provided for assistance and services for the presidents' and vice presidents' spouses in connection with the discharge of their duties.

The bill was lauded by its sponsors as a needed and rational way of putting an end to confused White House staffing procedures. Supporters also noted that the reporting provisions allowed Congress some oversight ability for White House staffing for the first time.[37] Opponents attacked the bill as an expansion of White House staffing, noting that the number of high-level staffers authorized would be nearly double the current actual number; they also criticized the reporting requirements as inadequate.[38]

Today coordination and lines of authority between the Office of the First Lady and those of the president are frequently entwined as each administration develops its own rules of operation, and personnel designations shift with each incumbent. Whether or not this happens is often determined by how each presidential wife arranges her own office. Rosalynn Carter, for example, maintained headquarters in the East Wing, making a point of announcing that she went there regularly to work. Betty Ford kept an office in the residence on the second floor, installing her own telephone for lobbying and partisan pursuits. Nancy Reagan and Barbara Bush also worked out of the presidential residence, but both downplayed the "office" aspect of being first lady. In an unprecedented move, Hillary Rodham Clinton moved her office to the West Wing, near the president's Oval Office.

The organization and duties of the staff vary with each first lady. Like the president, the first lady uses staff as she sees fits.[39] Most staff, however, are divided into social, press, and policy sections. The press secretary manages media inquiries; the social office organizes events; and policy advisers address policy questions that interest the first lady. The increasing activism of first ladies—as seen when three presidential spouses testified to Congress while their husbands were in office and two testified after their husbands left office—marks a new policy role for first ladies. This activism caused the office to become more institutionalized as well as more scrutinized.

TESTIFYING BEFORE THE LEGISLATIVE WORKSHOPS

Political scientist and U.S. president Woodrow Wilson observed over a century ago that the committee system is the very heart of the lawmaking process in the United States. "Congress in session," commented Wilson, "is Congress on public exhibition, whilst Congress in its committee rooms is Congress at work."[40] This maxim continues to describe much of the business of Capitol Hill. Though the procedure is absent from the Constitution, Congress has long organized itself into standing (more or less permanent) committees in order to shape policy, to create parliamentary strategy, to disentangle complexity, and most important, to pare down the institution's workload into more manageable portions. Fashioned gradually, congressional committees are institutionalized mechanisms that reflect change on Capitol Hill. In many instances committees evolved in connection with historical events and shifting perceptions of public problems.[41] As novel political problems arose, new committees were added. Committees are decision-making agencies of crucial importance that inevitably determine the fait of legislation. They provide a point of departure for the political process.

Scholars have long realized the importance of committees and their hearings.[42] However, they have differed as to the role such committees and hearings play in the legislative process.[43] In his case study Ralph K. Huitt makes the potent assertion that committees are "miniature legislatures" or "microcosms" of their parent bodies.[44] It has since been argued that not only are particular committees subject to the "same influences" as the chambers as wholes, but the parent chambers are significant environments for their committees.[45] Today the intents of committees and their hearings can often be seen from three perspectives: to arrive at the common good of the larger society; to further the interest of individual legislators; or to grapple with complexity. The truth of these conceptual portraits has varied over time and across committees because they differ in their policy-making environments, mix of members, decision-making objectives, and ability to fulfill individual members' goals.[46]

The "common good" model emphasizes that committees are tools used by the larger chamber to arrive at the common good, with the committee acting as the guardian of the general public interest after hearing from special-interest advocates who appear before it.[47] From this perspective, committee hearings take on features of a legislative court where members verify the need for legislation in a particular policy area based upon the evidence of law and fact brought before them by interested parties. Concurrently, these hearings serve as a public forum where the public interest will emerge from the clamor of competing special interests.

By fulfilling such functions as managing growing workloads and congressional interaction with executive departments, holding hearings on important issues, conducting investigations, writing reports, and offering advice to colleagues, committee members could meet the needs of all members who would like their chamber to be responsive to national problems and who needed information on which to base their votes.[48] From this perspective, committee members use their committee position not to satisfy parochial interests, but mainly to help fulfill the chamber's need for accurate information on policy choices.[49] Hearings take on features of a legislative court where members decide what to do based upon the evidence of law and fact brought before them by the interested parties. They furnish information with which members can educate themselves on the issues involved in a bill, and they serve as a clearinghouse for information needed by all the contestants in the legislative process.

By a second view, the legislative process is but a struggle between competing, self-interested groups, none of whom is concerned with a guiding abstraction such as the common good.[50] Popularized by Harry Truman, this "competing groups" perspective suggests that public policy emerges from the push and pull of competing groups, each seeking its own interests; the demands and concerns of diverse interests and perspectives partially shape policy outcomes.[51] In this process committee members act as advocates of important clientele and not as neutral judges seeking the general good. Committee hearings, therefore, are not neutral fact-finding tribunals but vehicles to advance the interests of committee members in one of three ways: to allow for the transmission of information from the various interest groups to the committee; to be used as a propaganda platform by the interest groups, with little thought to a meaningful debate; or to be a safety valve whereby group conflicts can be adjusted before they become explosive.

Although the format and ground rules for congressional hearings vary with the committee and the circumstances, most are conducted with little fanfare. In general, witnesses give testimony from prepared statements while committee or subcommittee members occasionally follow along. More often than not members utilize this time to review their correspondence or consult with staff. When the testimony ends, a rotating cast of committee members ask questions in order of seniority, beginning with the chair, then the ranking minority member, and so on, alternating back and forth between the parties. Ordinarily time is restricted, making it unusual for very junior members—especially those in the House—on either side to question witnesses. Committee interrogation, like cross-examination in a courtroom, is an art in itself. Effective interrogation is based upon clear understanding of the objectives to be achieved and a grasp of the basic facts involved in the matter at hand. Conversely, unfriendly interrogation begins with questions that demonstrate the incompetence or unreliability of the witness.

One commonality to every hearing is that the president's name rarely appears on any witness list. Such presidential testimony before a congressional committee would be too time-consuming, and it would be beneath a president's dignity to subject himself to committee interrogation. Nor do members of Congress seriously entertain the idea that a president should come to Capitol Hill and testify before a committee. If compelling reasons for a meeting between a committee and the president do present themselves, then it is, as one scholar suggests, "Mahomet who will go to the mountain."[52] A question therefore arises: Who should appear before a congressional committee to explain the president's position on specific matters?

A few spouses of presidents and vice presidents have been so identified with policy issues and recognized as authorities on those issues that they have been called to testify formally before congressional committees. The testimonies of first ladies generally involve friendly interrogation with questions that build up their character and competence. In most cases first ladies offer their comments on policies initiated by others. As the nation's "No 1 migrant,"[53] Eleanor Roosevelt was invited to address select, more or less temporary committees in 1940 and 1942 on nonpivotal issues such as discrimination against migrant workers, against women, against African Americans, and in employment and training practices. Calling for improving the living and working conditions of migrant labor, Mrs. Roosevelt noted to committee members: "If you are living under conditions which are poor, sleeping conditions that are bad, if you have overcrowding, medical health conditions that are very poor, you are not going to do your job as well nor are you going to produce as much."[54] "Well, Mrs. Roosevelt, you speak my language," committee chair John Tolan (D-Calif.) commented.[55] In the 1950s Mrs. Roosevelt scorned the anti-Communist investigations of Sen. Joseph R. McCarthy (R-Wis.). She testified before other, more congenial committees, lending her stature to House and Senate hearings on strengthening the United Nations (1955), raising the minimum wage (1959), improving conditions for migrant labor (1959), regulating the price of hearing aids (1962), and ensuring equal pay for equal work (1962).

At the start of her husband's administration Hillary Rodham Clinton made a series of unprecedented treks to Capitol Hill to testify before key committees that were considering the Health Security Act of 1993, the Clinton administration's proposal to provide for comprehensive reform of the health care system. Mrs. Clinton was the first spouse of a president to testify before congressional committees as the architect of a social policy or plan. And although Mrs. Clinton was appearing publicly before Congress for the first time, her responses to members' questions made it clear that she knew many of the lawmakers well.

Hillary Clinton's appearances involved testifying before five committee hearings, each scheduled to last about two hours, although several ran on for nearly three. In the House she appeared before the Ways and Means, Energy and Commerce, and Education and Labor Committees. In the Senate she testified before the Finance Committee and the Labor and Human Resources Committee. Many members seemed unsure about how to treat the first lady. Many of those who disliked the Clinton plan seemed to separate the plan from Mrs. Clinton, praising her work but disparaging the president's proposal, as if she had had little to do with it.[56] The words of commendation by Rep. Pat Williams (D-Mont.), chair of the subcommittee that carried the lion's share of hearings, were typical:

> Mrs. Clinton, welcome. You are, as you know, the Nation's 38th First Lady. It was May 27, 1789 when our first First Lady, Martha Washington, joined her husband, the Nation's new and first President, in New York following an arduous coach ride from their home in Mount Vernon. At that time, it was written, and I quote, "If Providence itself had divinely intervened, a woman who better looked and played the part could not have been found." Well, since that first First Lady, America has celebrated its President's wife: Abigail, and Bess, and Mary Todd, and Jackie, and Nancy. But none, Mrs. Clinton, have had in their husband's first year the effect that you have had on a crucial major domestic issue. Americans have been lucky more than a few times in their choices of Presidents. We could not have been more fortunate in our current President's choice of a wife, if Providence had divinely intervened. I think we could say of you what people at

the time said of that First Lady so many years ago: we are delighted you are here.[57]

On the other side of Capitol Hill senators expressed similar accolades for Mrs. Clinton. In his opening remarks before the Senate Committee on Labor and Human Resources, Sen. Edward M. Kennedy (D-Mass.) commented: "No individual has contributed more to the development of the President's plan than our witness this morning, the First Lady, Hillary Rodham Clinton, and she has worked tirelessly with great skill to shape this plan. In doing so, she has reached out to a large number of citizens, to experts on all sides of the debate, and to all of us in Congress. Her leadership has been extraordinary, and we are honored by her presence here this morning."[58]

Sen. James M. Jeffords (R-Vt.) noted, "I am sure managing your task force of 500 was a tough job, but I suspect it was nothing compared to the task of 535 that are here on Capitol Hill that you now have to deal with."[59] Sen. Howard M. Metzenbaum (D-Ohio) added: "Mrs. Clinton, as I sat here, I was thinking to myself that you and your husband are truly unique because both you and your husband are knowledgeable about the specifics of this program. I have served here with five different Presidents, but I remember the record of many other Presidents as well, and I don't remember any other President, and certainly no other Presidential spouse, that was as fully involved and fully knowledgeable about a legislative program as the two of you are."[60]

In the absence of any frame of reference, lawmakers fell back on the ceremonial idiom of formal congressional occasions, in which members customarily praise each other's work before tearing it to shreds.[61] "Just before Mrs. Clinton answers," then-senator Claiborne Pell (D-R.I.) noted before his opening remarks, "over in the House they restricted Mrs. Clinton to 2 minutes, for both the question and the answer. . . . We have developed marvelous skills here. We want to give you the assurance that you take whatever time you want to respond to the cumulative questions of our colleagues."[62] Following the opening remarks of ninety-two-year-old senator Strom Thurmond (R-S.C.), First Lady Clinton stated: "Thank you, Senator, and could I just say amen to your opening statement. I thought especially the emphasis on primary and preventive health care is absolutely on target. You are a living example of that and I hope everybody will pay attention to you. [Laughter.]"[63]

Mrs. Clinton exhibited a generous tone in speaking to members, except in one instance. During the Education and Labor Committee hearing, Rep. Richard K. "Dick" Armey (R-Tex.), a sharp-tongued conservative, assured Mrs. Clinton that he did not want a government-run health care system.

Earlier he had compared the plan to Dr. Jack Kevorkian, a Michigan doctor known for assisting patients in suicide. Armey said that the plan would kill jobs. At the hearing he promised to make the debate "as exciting as possible." Mrs. Clinton replied, "I am sure you will . . . you and Dr. Kevorkian."[64] Not missing a beat, Representative Armey replied, "I have been told about your charm and wit and, let me say, the reports on your charm are overstated. The reports on your wit are understated."[65] Following her skillful and sharp-witted answers to Representative Armey, Rep. Harris W. Fawell (R-Ill.) noted before his inquiry: "After seeing how you impaled my comrade-in-arms . . . I will proceed most cautiously and with great respect."[66]

Beneath the polite comments, the praise and the quips were an elaborate mating dance between Congress and Mrs. Clinton as White House emissary.[67] Each side signaled its needs to the others. Congressional attention varied. Those Democrats who supported the Clinton proposal lofted easy questions that enabled Mrs. Clinton to explain how the proposed plan worked to the scores of reporters in attendance. Sen. Max Baucus (D-Mont.) asked about rural health care, providing Mrs. Clinton the opportunity to explain that the plan aimed to tie rural Americans into urban medical centers. Other members simply sought clarification or information. Rep. Richard E. Neal (D-Mass.), for example, wanted to know whether the Shriners hospital in his hometown would be affected by all regulations.

From the small number of cases that exist (see tables 1 and 2), it is clear that presidents have had first ladies testify on issues that were pressing in society and those that were priorities to their administrations. Eleanor Roosevelt testified about migrant workers, which was a direct result of the Great Depression, while Rosalynn Carter testified about the energy crisis, one of the single most important factors contributing to the economic recession of the late 1970s. The issues of health care coverage and mental health coverage have been pressing in society since President Harry S. Truman attempted to nationalize health care. Although the topic is not immediately pressing for the whole of society, various polls suggest that the American public views health care coverage as an important issue.[68]

A central question, therefore, is whether the testimonies of first ladies serve the purposes of hearings expressed by congressional scholars (to arrive at the common good of the larger society, to further the interest of individual legislators, and to grapple with complexity). The testimony of all three first ladies could be characterized as trying to achieve policy goals that were for the common goal: improving working and health conditions of migrant workers, finding solutions to the energy crisis, increasing health coverage for mental health and for the uninsured. These issues were serious problems at the times of the first ladies' testimonies, and their testimonies brought increased attention to these issues. More important, these hearings served the agendas of the respective committee chairs. For example, when Ted Kennedy (D-Mass.) chaired the Senate Committee on Labor and Human Resources, he was known to be a strong supporter of increasing health coverage for mental health and for all Americans.

Hillary Clinton's testimony was fundamentally different than her predecessors' testimonies. Not only did she bring attention to the issue, but she articulated a plan to solve the problem. Prior to testifying, Mrs. Clinton consulted health advocates, medical groups, and business representatives in an effort to hammer out the complexity of the issue, dealing with the give-and-take of different powerful interests. Her approach to the problem eventually failed to muster a winning bloc of votes. The three committees in the House of Representatives responsible for reporting out a health plan had very different experiences: the Committee on Commerce did not report a bill; the Committee on Education and Workforce reported a bill more expensive

TABLE I First- and Second-Lady Appearances
before Congress, 1940–98

First Lady	Years in Office	Appearances before Congress	
		First Lady	As Former First Lady
Anna Eleanor Roosevelt	(1933–45)	2	5
Elizabeth "Bess" Wallace Truman	(1945–53)	0	0
Mary Geneva "Mamie" Doud Eisenhower	(1953–61)	0	0
Jacqueline "Jackie" Bouvier Kennedy	(1961–63)	0	0
Claudia "Lady Bird" Taylor Johnson	(1963–69)	0	0
Thelma "Pat" Ryan Nixon	(1969–74)	0	0
Elizabeth "Betty" Bloomer Ford	(1974–77)	0	2
Rosalynn Smith Carter	(1977–81)	2	2
Nancy Davis Reagan	(1981–89)	0	1
Barbara Pierce Bush	(1989–93)	0	0
Hillary Rodham Clinton	(1993–2000)	5	–

Note: Congressional testimony includes supplementary material: submitted statements, correspondence, and a first lady's written response to committee questions. Source: Data collected by authors.

TABLE 2 First and Second Ladies Who Have Testified before Congress

Spouse	Date	Committee	Subject
Eleanor Roosevelt	12/10/40	House Select Committee to Investigate the Interstate Migration of Destitute	Interstate migration
Eleanor Roosevelt	1/14/42	House Select Committee Investigating Defense Migration	National defense migration
Rosalynn Carter	2/7/79	Senate Labor & Human Relations Committee	Reappraisal of mental health
Rosalynn Carter	4/30/79	House Science & Technology Committee	Technology
Joan Mondale	6/26/79	Senate Labor & Human Relations Committee	Arts, humanities, & museum services
Joan Mondale	9/25/79	Senate Governmental Affairs Committee	Art, architecture
Joan Mondale	2/7/80	House Select Committee on Aging	Arts and sr. citizens
Joan Mondale	3/3/80	House Education & Labor Committee	Re-authorization of National Foundation for the Arts Act, Humanities Act, Museum Services Act
Marilyn Quayle	4/23/90	House Committee on Energy and Commerce	Women's health
Marilyn Quayle	5/16/90	House Select Committee on Aging	Breast cancer
Mary Elizabeth "Tipper" Gore	5/13/93	Senate Committee on Labor and Human Resources	Mental health
Hillary Clinton	9/28/93	House Ways & Means Committee	Health care reform
Hillary Clinton	9/28/93	House Committee on Energy and Commerce	Health care reform
Hillary Clinton	9/29/93	Senate Committee on Labor and Human Resources	Health care reform
Hillary Clinton	9/29/93	House Committee on Education and Labor	Health care reform
Hillary Clinton	9/30/93	Senate Committee on Finance	Health care reform
Testimony by Former First and Second Ladies			
Betty Ford	3/25/91	House Select Committee on Aging	Alcoholism treatment coverage under health care plans
Betty Ford	3/8/94	Senate Committee on Labor and Human Relations	Health Securities Act
Rosalynn Carter	5/14–16, 21/91	House Committee on Appropriations	Health and welfare
Rosalynn Carter	3/8/94	Senate Committee on Labor and Human Resources	Health Securities Act
Nancy Reagan	3/9/95	House Committee on Government Reform and Oversight	Drug control, drug abuse, drug trafficking

than the Clinton proposal; and the Ways and Means Committee reported a bill closely resembling the Clinton plan.

After the failure of the president's health care initiative in 1993, Hillary Clinton took a recognizably different role as first lady, returning to a more traditional ceremonial role. However, the special prosecutor and congressional investigations into the Clintons' role in the Whitewater land deal prevented her from being completely out of the press's eye. With this intense investigation, some may have thought that Mrs. Clinton would be called to testify in front of the congressional committees investigating the sour land deal. Even though President Gerald Ford testified before Congress concerning his pardon of President Richard Nixon, there is no precedent of a first lady being called to Capitol Hill for illegal activities. It seemed that although the congressional committees requested testimonies from most of the Clintons' associates, they either did not think that they had enough evidence or were not comfortable breaking precedent to call upon the first lady. If Mrs. Clinton had been called before the committee, President Clinton may have asked for executive privilege since the first lady had been so involved in policy meetings with the president. But this issue never came up because lawmakers opted not to call her to testify.

CONCLUSION

The position of first lady has evolved over the years in response to changing social attitudes and the efforts of a succession of women. This is, in part, because public expectations of the first lady have changed. Americans now anticipate that the first lady will take up some social problem as her own and work for its solution. Indeed, the consequences of having no program can be serious. Contemporary presidential spouses, therefore, are increasingly distinct political figures in their own right with their own special issues. In short, the modern first lady completes her husband's administration. As Diller and Robertson note, the wife of a president can largely shape the role of the first lady to her needs, but it is clear that a set of imprecise yet definite expectations about her role has emerged.[69] The first lady must satisfy them if she is to be successful and an asset to the president. Too much involvement, however, can raise suspicion and even congressional censure. For example, Rosalynn Carter's open assistance to her husband was so great that it aroused animosity in many lawmakers who felt that an unelected first lady had no business being as active in matters of the presidency as she was."[70]

Congress is inherently slow in responding to change. It is characterized by structure and routine, following established traditions. Not surprisingly, most members remain unsure of how to deal with a first lady when she testifies and are uncertain of the authoritative capacity with which she speaks. Time and familiarity should change this. Contemporary lawmakers appear more sympathetic to first ladies who take active roles than were their predecessors. At one time the idea of a first lady testifying before a congressional committee was inconceivable. Eleanor Roosevelt blazed the trail to Capitol Hill for first ladies, speaking to lawmakers twice in twelve years. Hillary Rodham Clinton has been described as "a transitional first lady, taking on a new, bolder role as woman, mother, and policy maker."[71] As more presidential spouses arrive at the White House fresh from careers in business or professions, they may be more prominent and more visibly political than their predecessors had been. Like Eleanor Roosevelt, Mrs. Clinton may be the first of a new generation that will expand the possibilities and responsibilities of the Office of the First Lady.

At least anecdotally, the more receptive contemporary congressional environment will continue to provide more access points and potential influence for first ladies. Whereas in the past first ladies could achieve influence on Capitol Hill by discreetly lobbying lawmakers with whom they enjoyed relationships, future first ladies might routinely and openly participate in the dance of legislation.

NOTES

1. Alice E. Anderson and Hadley V. Baxendale, *Behind Every Successful President: The Hidden Power and Influence of America's First Ladies* (New York: Shapolsky, 1992); Myra G. Gutin, *The President's Partner: The First Lady in the Twentieth Century* (Westport, Conn.: Greenwood Press, 1989); Edith P. Mayo, "The Influence and Power of First Ladies," *Chronicle of Higher Education* 40 (15 Sept. 1993): A52; Karen O'Connor, Bernadette Nye, and Laura Van Assendelft, "Wives in the White House: The Political Influence of First Ladies," *Presidential Studies Quarterly* 26 (1997): 835–53; Robert P. Watson, "The First Lady Reconsidered: Presidential Partner and Political Institution," *Presidential Studies Quarterly* 27 (1997): 805–18; Judy L. Weaver, "Edith Bolling Wilson as First Lady: A Study in the Power of Personality, 1919–1920," *Presidential Studies Quarterly* 15 (1985): 51–67.

2. Michael Nelson, *The Presidency: A to Z* (Washington, D.C.: CQ Press, 1998), 188–99.

3. Betty Boyd Caroli, *First Ladies* (1987; reprinted New York: Oxford University Press, 1994), 255–79; Virginia Sapiro and David T. Canon, "Race, Gender, and the Clinton Presidency," in *The Clinton Legacy*, ed. Colin Campbell and Bert A. Rockman (New York: Chatham House, 2000).

4. Nelson, *Presidency*, 189, 199.

5. Caroli, *First Ladies,* xvii–xix.

6. Alissa J. Rubin, "Mrs. Clinton Conquers Hill, Sets Debate in Motion," *Congressional Quarterly Weekly Report* (2 Oct. 1993): 2640–43.

7. Caroli, *First Ladies,* 631.

8. An example is the congressional committee system's division of labor. The committee system was initially intended to be an efficient device to organize the two chambers, shape the measures on which Congress acts, create parliamentary strategy, disentangle complexity, and most important, manage a growing workload. In many instances committees evolved in connection with historical events and shifting perceptions of public problems.

9. Thomas E. Cronin and Michael A. Genovese, *The Paradoxes of the American Presidency* (New York: Oxford University Press, 1998), 299–301.

10. Joseph Cooper, "Organization and Innovation in the House of Representatives," in *The House at Work,* ed. Joseph Cooper and G. Calvin Mackenzie (Austin: University of Texas Press, 1981); Richard F. Fenno, *Congressmen in Committees* (Boston: Little, Brown, 1973); Bertram M. Gross, *The Legislative Struggle: A Study in Social Combat* (Westport, Conn.: Greenwood Press, 1953); Nelson W. Polsby, *Congress and the Presidency* (Englewood Cliffs, N.J.: Prentice-Hall, 1981).

11. Cronin and Genovese, *Paradoxes,* 299; Robert P. Watson, *The Presidents' Wives: Reassessing the Office of First Lady* (Boulder, Colo.: Lynne Rienner Publishers, 1999).

12. Carl Sferrazza Anthony, *First Ladies: The Saga of the Presidents' Wives and Their Power* (New York: William Morrow, 1990).

13. Watson, *Presidents' Wives,* 95.

14. Anthony, *First Ladies,* 462–85; Mary C. Ryan and Nancy Kegan Smith, *Modern First Ladies: Their Documentary Legacy* (Washington, D.C.: National Archives and Records Administration, 1989); Watson, "First Lady Reconsidered," 137–39; Betty Houchin Winfield, "Madame President: Understanding a New Kind of First Lady," *Media Studies Journal* 8 (1994): 59–71.

15. Quoted in Weaver, "Edith Bolling Wilson," 52.

16. Anthony, *First Ladies,* 369.

17. Godfrey Sperling, "New First Ladies, in 1960 and Today," *Christian Science Monitor,* 8 Dec. 1992, 19.

18. Watson, *Presidents' Wives,* 88.

19. Ibid.

20. Cronin and Genovese, *Paradoxes,* 300.

21. "Record 30 Women's Bills Passed in '93 as Ranks in Congress Grow," *Star Tribune,* 3 Dec. 1993, A5.

22. James Blumstein, "A Land Mine on the Path from First Lady to Senator," *The Wall Street Journal,* 7 June 1999, A23.

23. Daniel C. Diller and Stephen L. Robertson, *Presidents, First Ladies, and Vice Presidents: White House Biographies, 1789–1997* (Washington, D.C.: CQ Press, 1997).

24. Susan B. Garland, "First Lady, and No Second Fiddle," *Business Week* (19 July 1999): 18.

25. Donald A. Ritchie, "Eleanor Roosevelt and Congress," in *The Eleanor Roosevelt Encyclopedia,* ed. Maurine H. Beasley, Holly C. Shulman, and Henry R. Beasley (Westport, Conn.: Greenwood Press, 2001), 103–5.

26. Margaret Chase Smith, *Declaration of Conscience* (New York: Doubleday, 1972), 203.

27. Ritchie, *Eleanor Roosevelt,* 103–5.

28. *Congressional Record,* 78th Cong., 2d sess., 1943, 89, pt. 6: 6253.

29. Watson, *Presidents' Wives,* 35–37.

30. Richard Pearson, "A Republican Congress, An Embattled First Lady; It Happened Before, with Mary Todd Lincoln," *Washington Post,* 27 Jan. 1996, A12.

31. Ibid.

32. Delia M. Rios, "Goldgate? Wife of an Earlier President Had Problems with Congress," *St. Louis Post-Dispatch,* 24 Jan. 1996, C5.

33. Caroli, *First Ladies,* 637.

34. *Congressional Record,* 79th Cong., 2d sess., 24 Jan. 1946, 97, pt. 1: 352.

35. Ibid.

36. Ibid.

37. *Congressional Quarterly Almanac* 34 (1978): 797.

38. Ibid.

39. Diller and Robertson, *Presidents,* 8.

40. Woodrow Wilson, *Congressional Government: A Study in American Politics* (1885; reprint, New York: Meridian Books, 1956), 79.

41. Joseph Cooper, "The Origins of the Standing Committees and the Development of the Modern House," *Rice University Studies* 56, no. 3 (1970): 1.

42. John F. Bibby and Roger H. Davidson, *On Capitol Hill: Studies in the Legislative Proc*ess (New York: Rinehart and Winston, 1967); Christopher J. Deering and Steven S. Smith, *Committees in Congress* (Washington, D.C.: CQ Press, 1997); Fenno, *Congressmen in Committees;* Ralph K. Huitt, "The Congressional Committee: A Case Study," *American Political Science Review* 48 (1954): 340–65; David B. Truman, *The Governmental Process: Political Interests and Public Opinion* (New York: Knopf, 1951).

43. Joseph K. Unekis, "Committee Hearings," in *Encyclopedia of the United States Congress,* ed. Donald C. Bacon, Roger H. Davidson, and Morton Keller (New York: Simon and Schuster, 1995), 423–26.

44. Huitt, "Congressional Committee," 340.

45. Heinz Eulau and Vera McCluggage, "Standing Committees in Legislatures: Three Decades of Research," *Legislative Studies Quarterly* 9 (1984): 195–270.

46. Roger H. Davidson and Walter J. Oleszek, *Congress and Its Members* (Washington, D.C.: CQ Press, 2000), 224.

47. Arthur Maass, *Congress and the Common Good* (New York: Basic Books, 1983); Unekis, "Committee Hearings," 424.

48. Cooper, "Origins," 1; Keith Krehbiel, *Information and Legislative Organization* (Ann Arbor: University of Michigan Press, 1991).

49. Maass, *Congress.*

50. Unekis, "Committee Hearings," 424.

51. Truman, *Governmental Process.*

52. Gross, *Legislative Struggle,* 295.

53. Beasley, Shulman, and Beasley, ed., *Encyclopedia,* 104.

54. *National Defense Migration Report* (Washington, D.C.: U.S. Government Printing Office, 1942), 9766.

55. Ibid., 9767.

56. Rubin, "Mrs. Clinton," 2640–43.

57. U.S. House of Representatives, House Committee on Education and Labor, *Health Care Reform,* 103d Cong., 1st sess., 29 Sept. 1993, 3.

58. U.S. Senate, Senate Committee on Labor and Human Resources, *Health Security Act of 1993,* 103d Cong., 1st sess., Sept. 29, 30, Oct. 5, 6, 15, 19, 1993, S. Hrg. 103–216, pt. 11.

59. Senate Committee on Labor and Human Resources, *Health Security Act of 1993,* 13.

60. Ibid., 15.

61. Rubin, "Mrs. Clinton," 2641.

62. Senate Committee on Labor and Human Resources, *Health Security Act of 1993,* 18.

63. Ibid., 19.

64. House Committee on Education and Labor, 24.

65. Ibid.

66. Ibid., 27.

67. Rubin, "Mrs. Clinton," 2643.

68. There have been many polls focusing on this issue. See, for example, a summary Gallup on-line (2000): gallup.com/poll/indicators/indhealth.asp

69. Diller and Robertson, *Presidents,* 22.

70. Lewis L. Gould, "First Ladies," *The American Scholar* 55 (autumn 1986): 534.

71. Bob Woodward, *The Agenda: Inside the Clinton White House* (New York: Simon and Schuster, 1994), 103.

Nine

First Ladies and U.S. Foreign Policy

Glenn Hastedt

Introduction

As the other essays in this volume demonstrate, the place of first ladies in the United States political process is a dynamic and evolving one. A most recent transformation is the active participation of first ladies in the policy process. Even more recent is their active participation in foreign policy matters. This chapter will employ a policy-making process perspective to examine the foreign policy activities of Rosalynn Carter and Hillary Clinton. In particular it will focus on the agenda-building actions of these two first ladies in order to highlight the points of similarity and the differences in their efforts to place human rights on the American foreign policy agenda.

Evidence from the Past

Prior to introducing frameworks that might be used to study the involvement of first ladies in the formulation and conduct of American foreign policy, it should be noted that antidotal and fragmented evidence exists concerning the involvement of first ladies in American foreign policy. Karen O'Connor, Bernadette Nye, and Laura Van Assendelft surveyed the policy activities of first ladies.[1] They conclude that while only five influenced policy and fifteen made their policy preferences known to their president-husbands, thirty-one discussed politics with them and twenty-six could be termed presidents' confidantes/advisers.

First ladies have been involved in American foreign policy. In 1799 Abigail Adams lobbied President John Adams on a treaty with the Netherlands. Edith Wilson served as President Woodrow Wilson's communication link with both foreign governments and others in the U.S. government while he was incapacitated by a stroke. As a general rule she acted in a neutral fashion, but she did try, and failed, to get Wilson to agree to accept Sen. Henry Cabot Lodge's reservations regarding the League of Nations when Lodge made it clear to her that Senate approval of the Treaty of Versailles hinged on their acceptance.

Eleanor Roosevelt was known to engage in spirited conversations and debates with President Franklin Roosevelt over a wide variety of policy issues during his presidency. They often disagreed. She remained a supporter of the League of Nations after Roosevelt abandoned it, and she unsuccessfully urged him to drop U.S. neutrality during the Spanish civil war. At Yalta she lamented Roosevelt's willingness to allow Lithuania, Latvia, and Estonia to be absorbed into the Soviet Union. Prior to U.S. involvement in World War II, Eleanor Roosevelt pushed the State Department to admit more Jewish refugees to the United States.

Bess Truman had frequent conversations with President Harry Truman on the Marshall Plan, although she was not, as a general rule, informed about American foreign policy initiatives. The most significant of these was the dropping of the atomic bomb on Hiroshima, something she opposed and only learned of through the newspapers. Both Pat Nixon and Jackie Kennedy undertook goodwill tours abroad for their husbands, often improving the overall state of U.S. relations with visited countries.

Robert McFarlane, President Reagan's national security adviser, asserts that White House options in responding to the Iran-Contra scandal were limited by what Nancy Reagan would allow. Nancy Reagan counseled President Reagan against laying a wreath at Bittburg cemetery in Germany, sided with foreign policy moderates in moving to tone down Reagan's harsh anti-Soviet rhetoric, urged him to reduce military spending, and favored a diplomatic solution for the Nicaragua conflict.

FRAMEWORKS FOR ANALYSIS

Today evidence reveals that some first ladies have become systematically involved in foreign policy matters. This raises the need to develop frameworks for studying their activity. However, as the above listing of examples makes clear, influence and involvement do not automatically translate into policy victories. Any framework for studying the involvement of first ladies in American foreign policy must permit the systematic study of successes and failures. Numerous possibilities exist. For purposes of discussion they can be grouped under four headings.

First Ladies Frameworks

The first of these includes frameworks developed to study first ladies systematically. Two have been forwarded by Robert Watson. The first framework is historical in focus and traces the evolution of the first lady's political role.[2] Six distinct roles are identified, beginning with a first period in which the image and role of the first lady began to take shape (1789–1817) through modern times when first ladies have come to be public presidential partners (1974–96). Watson's second framework categorizes first ladies by their relationships with their president-husbands.[3] The five possibilities identified by Watson are full partner, partial partner, behind-the-scenes partner, partner in marriage, and nonpartner. These partnership roles do not proceed in chronological fashion, and contemporary first ladies sometimes occupy several different categories. Rosalynn Carter and Hillary Clinton are full partners; Betty Ford and Lady Bird Johnson are partial partners; Nancy Reagan and Barbara Bush are behind-the-scenes partners; and Pat Nixon is a partner in marriage.

A third framework for studying first ladies is presented by O'Connor, Nye, and Van Assendelft.[4] Borrowing from the literature on vice presidents, they note that three distinct role orientations have emerged: the ceremonial first lady, the political first lady, and the policy first lady.

Foreign Policy Frameworks

A second set of frameworks for studying first ladies and American foreign policy has been developed by international relations scholars. Traditional international relations theorizing accords primary explanatory power to either power considerations (realism), the structure of the international system (neo-realism), or international law and organization (neo-liberalism). The ability of individuals to influence events and trends is not held in high regard, although neo-liberalism does cite the ability of individuals to cooperate with one another as an important prerequisite for law and organization to order international affairs.

There have always been important dissenting voices to this ordering of influence. James Rosenau has been among the most noteworthy. Writing in 1971, he hypothesized that the influence of individuals on foreign policy making should not be dismissed entirely but was contingent on the characteristics of the state.[5] Rosenau anticipated that in a large, economically developed, open political system such as the United States, role orientations would be the most significant explanatory factor in a study of foreign policy, followed in order of importance by societal, governmental, systemic, and individual variables. Rosenau ranked role and individual variables as first and second in importance in a large, economically developed, closed political system such as the former Soviet Union. Recently Rosenau and W. Michael Fagan raised the research question of whether or not individuals are becoming more equipped to play a central role in international affairs.[6] Their initial test was confined to elites in the United States, but the argument has applicability to the citizens around the world who are linked together by the Internet and other means of communication.

Concrete work concerning individuals' influence on world politics has taken two forms. The first stresses the central role of perceptions. Through the use of case studies John Stoessinger identifies four misperceptions that can lead to war.[7] Leaders misperceive their own power, the power of the enemy, the enemy's goals, or the enemy's intentions. Robert Jervis studies the manner in which decision makers process information and maintain and change their belief systems.[8] He also examines several common misperceptions such as those of centralization, overestimating one's importance, and wishful thinking.

The second research track in the international relations literature begins by trying to identify the circumstances under which individuals could be expected to be influential in determining foreign policy outcomes. Once this is established, determination can be made about whether the personality, perceptions, or roles of an individual mattered. A key distinction in this line of inquiry is between action indispensability and actor indispensability. The former refers to situations in which an individual's action made a difference for the outcome. The latter refers to situations in which, in addition, the identity of the actor made a difference. Work by Fred Greenstein provides the basis for identifying the following conditions under which a president's personality could be expected to matter on foreign policy issues:

when the issue is new on the agenda;

when the issue is addressed early in the administration;

when the president is deeply involved in the issue; and

when the issue is at a point of "precarious equilibrium" and multiple plausible policy options present themselves.[9]

The first ladies frameworks and the international relations theory frameworks provide a starting point for systematically analyzing first ladies and American foreign policy. Each, however, suffers from the handicap of being tightly focused at a point in time when first ladies' involvement in American foreign policy is not yet well established. There are relatively few existing cases that permit an in-depth evaluation. Moreover, there is no guarantee as to how many future first ladies will make American foreign policy a point of emphasis.

Feminist Frameworks

A third set of frameworks for studying first ladies and foreign policy comes from feminist writings on international relations. Christine Sylvester identified three different feminist frameworks that have been employed by feminist theorists.[10] The first seeks to highlight the role and activities of women in foreign policy. The goal is to bring into the open significant behavior that has gone unnoticed. The second framework, feminist empiricism, seeks to redirect and reformulate scientific inquiry into international relations by bringing gender to the forefront of these studies. Postmodernist feminist studies seek to problematize women in the study of international relations. They are unconvinced that simply focusing more directly on women will produce a full understanding of the role that women and gender play in world politics.

The most frequently employed feminist framework in the study of women and American foreign policy is the first, that which seeks to highlight the role of women. Two recent volumes on women and American foreign policy have this as a goal. Edward Crapol and his colleagues present accounts of eight women, from Lydia Maria Child to Jane Fonda and Jeanne Kirkpatrick, who have shaped the course of American foreign policy.[11] Rhodri Jeffreys-Jones explores the careers of notable women such as Eleanor Roosevelt as well as the activities of lesser known women with regard to specific issues such as tariffs in the 1930s.[12] They provide little by way of a conceptual starting point for studying women and foreign policy. Jeffreys-Jones notes that "the historiography of the field [of women and foreign policy] is immature."[13] He can only identify two broad schools of thought: the peace school, which stresses women as advocates of peace; and the belligerent school, which emphasizes their roles as heroines in combat. To the extent that they tell a story of women influencing foreign policy, these accounts are compatible with the policy process framework used in this study.

Policy Process Frameworks

More appropriate at this time for studying first ladies and American foreign policy are frameworks that allow examination of prolonged (rather than sporadic or episodic) activity so that comparisons can be made between different undertakings. A third set of analytical frameworks that focus on the structure and operation of the policy process is well suited for this purpose. American foreign policy is often analyzed through such frameworks. With the growing recognition that foreign policy and domestic policy need not be treated as two separate and distinct spheres of activity, these frameworks provide an opportunity for analyzing the growing policy-related activities of first ladies regardless of the content of those activities. Policy-process-focused models will allow empirical establishment of the ways in which the public policy activities of first ladies are alike and different, the factors that encourage and inhibit these undertakings, and the conditions that promote success.

Flexibility is an important characteristic to consider in choosing a conceptual framework to examine the public policy activity of first ladies, since such efforts are just now becoming prominent. A stages-oriented framework provides this flexibility because it allows concentration on a particular stage or the linkages between stages. Furthermore, it makes no assumptions about the appropriateness of policy-making activities engaged in by first ladies or the proper method for judging the ultimate success or failure of first ladies' policy-making efforts. Five stages generally are identified as comprising the policy-making process:

agenda setting

policy formulation

policy adoption

policy implementation

policy analysis and evaluation[14]

First Lady Rosalynn Carter

The most visible foreign policy undertaking by Mrs. Carter involved traveling abroad. She traveled to Latin America in June 1977.[15] Rather than having a singular focus, she was to emphasize the dominant themes of Jimmy Carter's foreign policy—an emphasis on human rights, nuclear arms control, and slowing down conventional arm sales—but not to engage in a defense of past policies, make promises regarding the future direction of American foreign policy, nor offer policy advice. The president wanted Latin American leaders to understand that his definition of human rights embraced promoting economic and social progress as well as furthering political freedoms. The first lady was also to recognize and stress the uniqueness of each state in her discussions with foreign leaders in an effort to overcome long-standing concerns over American paternalism.

Mrs. Carter's trip was not undertaken in the best of circumstances. A heated arms race was building up in the hemisphere as Latin American states sought to buy and sell arms on the international market. Shortly before she left, President Carter signed a treaty establishing a nuclear-weapons-free zone in Latin America, and while she was in Costa Rica he signed the American Convention on Human Rights. Both of these documents placed the United States squarely at odds with several of its southern neighbors, who saw these documents as unwarranted intrusions into their domestic affairs. Carter's interest in these areas marked a profound shift in the rhetoric of American foreign policy. Under Richard Nixon and Gerald Ford, American foreign policy had focused on U.S.-Soviet relations. Arms control and human rights were of concern only as they related to managing this relationship. Arms sales became a primary tool of American foreign policy as a method of supporting third-world allies. Carter's election signaled that these priorities had changed. Mrs. Carter was to urge each leader to sign the two agreements.

Her first stop was Jamaica, where she had discussions with Prime Minister Michael Manley that covered trade and development problems as well as Jamaica's relations with Cuba. Manley was a vocal supporter of Fidel Castro, a policy that had earned Jamaica the enmity of the Nixon and Ford administrations and many in Congress. The next stop was Costa Rica. Trade and human rights were major topics of conversation between Mrs. Carter and President Daniel Oduber. While these meetings had been quite cordial, her meetings with representatives of the Ecuadoran military regime were formal and stiff at the outset. They were resentful that the Carter administration had blocked a purchase of fighter planes from Israel. Concern was also expressed over Peru's recent purchase of tanks and fighters from the Soviet Union. Ecuador feared a Peruvian attack on its oil fields and wanted U.S. assistance in meeting this threat. Peru was ruled by a military government, and its leaders stressed the defensive nature of their military policy and downplayed its "supposed" military buildup.

Nuclear proliferation was a major topic of conversation with Brazilian leaders. Mrs. Carter described this as her most difficult stop. Not only was Brazilian foreign policy at odds with most aspects of American foreign policy, but an unscheduled meeting with two American missionaries who claimed to be the victims of human-rights violations further complicated the trip. The last two stops were Colombia and Venezuela. In Colombia drug trafficking was the major topic of conversation. Discussions in Venezuela were relatively brief because of an impending state visit by President Carlos Andres Perez to the United States.

First Lady Hillary Rodham Clinton

The foreign policy initiative that stands out as most important during Hillary Clinton's eight-year term as first lady was her promotion of women and children's rights. The centerpiece of her efforts was her September 1995 participation in the United Nations Fourth World Conference on Women held in Beijing. Representatives from more than 180 states attended the conference. The main issues addressed at the gathering were the need to stop violence against women, measures to empower women economically and politically, granting sexual rights to women, and ensuring that such programs were funded and implemented.

The Clinton administration announced that Mrs. Clinton would attend the September conference on 25 August, one day after Harry Wu, a Chinese-American human rights activist, was convicted of spying and expelled. Wu, who had served nineteen years in Chinese labor camps, fled to the United States in 1985. Since then he documented abuses in China's prison system and periodically made undercover trips to China. His arrest in June strained U.S.-Chinese relations. The Clinton administration reportedly had given serious consideration to not sending the first lady to the conference as a sign of its displeasure with China's policy, although in the official announcement that Mrs. Clinton would go, the administration denied that the two were linked.

The first lady's presence or absence was treated by the press as an important symbolic statement regarding the credibility of the conference. Several Republican members of Congress had urged the Clinton administration to boycott the conference because of China's human rights record and the likelihood that the conference would endorse a proabortion position. Among those who urged Mrs. Clinton not to attend were 1996 declared presidential candidates Robert Dole and Richard Lugar. In announcing the first lady's trip, the Clinton administration rejected charges that the conference was radical or antifamily in outlook. The goal, the administration asserted, was to find "common ground" to "advance the interests" of women around the world.[16]

At the conference Mrs. Clinton delivered a strongly worded speech that indirectly criticized China's treatment of women. She asserted that "it is time for us to say here in Beijing, and for the world to hear, that it is no longer acceptable to discuss women's rights as separate from human rights." She continued: "It is a violation of human rights when babies are denied food, or drowned, or suffocated, or their spines broken, simply because they are born girls. . . . It is a violation of human rights when women are doused with gasoline, set on fire and burned to death because their marriage dowries are deemed too small."[17]

Her remarks described conditions identified by human-rights observers as prevalent in China. They were far more stringent than the muted criticism of Chinese human-rights policies issued publicly by the Clinton adminis-tration. A senior Clinton administration official stated that nothing in her remarks signaled a turn to a more vocal and confrontational policy toward China. He stated that this was "a United Nations Conference and she was speaking out on a global problem."[18]

Mrs. Clinton had spoken out on women's rights earlier in the year. She delivered an address at the First United Nations World Summit on Social Development, which met in Copenhagen in March. Vice President Al Gore chaired the U.S. delegation. In attendance were 118 presidents, vice presidents, and prime ministers. The conference endorsed a nonbinding program of action designed to eliminate poverty worldwide and end social injustice.

The conference was held against a backdrop of declining foreign aid budgets. In her address Hillary Clinton stated that many states were wasting valuable resources on weapons of mass destruction and doing violence to basic human rights. She called upon leaders to revise their social policies in order "to protect their most vulnerable population in a time of shrinking resources and accelerated global competition."[19] Also at the conference Hillary Clinton announced that the Agency for International Development would begin a ten-year program to improve the lives of girls in Africa, Asia, and Latin America.

In his comments to the conference Vice President Gore gave reassurances that the Clinton administration would resist Republican pressures to cut social aid programs and continue to aid the poor both in the United States and abroad. He outlined the administration's New Partnership Initiative intended to empower small businesses, increase the role played by private organiza-tions in international development efforts, and promote local democracy.

One week after her address to the United Nations World Summit on Social Development, Hillary Clinton spoke at a conference on Women and the United Nations in New York, where she continued to defend the admin-istration against its Republican critics and pronounced her support for UN social and development efforts. She stated that "when full economic, social, and political opportunities for women too often remain an elusive goal, we should commend the United Nations for inviting serious discussion of the unique obstacles confronting women in every country, rich and poor."[20]

Still later in March she and her daughter, Chelsea, embarked on a five-state tour of South Asia. Stops included visits to hospitals, orphanages, and schools in India, Nepal, Sri Lanka, Pakistan, and Bangladesh. Press accounts reported that the tour was tightly scripted. Mrs. Clinton made only two sub-stantive speeches and gave no interviews. Her performance was criticized by the press for her failure to address the region's human-rights abuses more forcefully and for being "singularly insensate and solely decorative."[21] Her trip also provoked demonstrations. In Nepal demonstrators threw rocks and shoes at Mrs. Clinton's motorcade through the capital city in protest of the government's close ties to the West. In Bangladesh a reported two thousand protestors demonstrated against groups that promoted women's rights.

In defense of her trip Mrs. Clinton asserted that 'by talking about girls and women you're talking about human rights." Moreover, she said, "I believe we have to emphasize as much as possible that the denial of education, the denial of basic health care and the denial of choices to girls is a human rights issue."[22]

After the Beijing trip Mrs. Clinton continued to speak out on women's and children's issues. She made a four-country trip to Latin America in October with stops in Nicaragua, Brazil, Chile, and Paraguay. As with the trip to South Asia, during her visit to Latin America she shied away from controversial topics. The first lady's consistent message was the need to treat women's rights as human rights and the need to invest in people. She reaffirmed the Clinton administration's commitment to internationalism and defended its foreign aid programs. Her trip concluded with a speech at a conference of sixteen wives of Latin American leaders.

Agenda Setting

Rosalynn Carter's and Hillary Rodham Clinton's policy-making activities are best understood as taking place during the agenda-setting stage of the policy process. In this initial stage of the policy-making process problems are recognized and defined into existence. As John W. Kingdon observes, there is a difference between a condition we find troubling and a problem. Something must occur for a condition to become defined as a policy problem. Policy entrepreneurs often play a key role in this transformational process. They invest time and resources, "political capital," into convincing the political community not only that an existing condition is unacceptable but that politically and technically feasible solutions exist. Kingdon describes them as softening up the political system and serving as a broker between people and ideas.[23]

Policy entrepreneurs do not operate in a political vacuum. Central to their success is timing. Opportunities to get items onto the political agenda are limited. Policy windows are open only briefly. In some cases these openings occur at regular intervals, such as at the beginning of a legislative session or a new presidency. Other times they open unexpectedly or irregularly as international and domestic events unfold. In either case, the opening of a policy window onto the agenda brings about overcrowding as more conditions are put forward as demanding political action for scarce resources. Kingdon describes the resulting mix of competing calls for action as a policy stream in which many ideas float around but only a few actually reach the political agenda. The flow of the stream is heavily conditioned by the prevailing political climate and the strengths or weaknesses of the various participants. A skilled (or lucky) policy entrepreneur will be able to unite conditions, policies, and the politics of the moment into a successful call for action.

Failure is a constant possibility in the agenda-building process. Successfully navigating the policy stream once does not ensure a permanent place high on the political agenda. One's place can always be taken by another issue as conditions change. The distinctions drawn by Roger Cobb, Jennie-Keith Ross, and Marc Howard Ross are helpful here. They note the existence of three political agendas: 1) the public agenda that consists of issues which have achieved a high degree of public interest; 2) the formal agenda that consists of policy problems that policy makers have accepted for active consideration; and 3) the pseudo-agenda that receives little more than symbolic attention. Their formulation of the agenda-building process highlights the fact that there are several different resting places for conditions even after they are recognized by the political community as problems.[24]

Rosalynn Carter's entrepreneurial activity during the agenda-building stage of the policy process was not that of an independent catalyst seeking to move an item on to the formal agenda. Hers was that of an inside player signaling to others that the political terrain had changed and that a new policy stream had commenced. Human rights, controlling conventional arms transfers, and nuclear arms control were issues that had either populated the pseudo-agenda of the Nixon-Ford administrations or had become bogged down on the formal agenda. Jimmy Carter's presidential campaign had conveyed the need for a change to the American people. Now the need was to convey the message to other governments. Mrs. Carter's trip to Latin America was part of a strategy designed to accomplish this end.

Her trip followed a 14 April Pan American Day speech made by President Carter, in which he stated: "As nations of the New World we once believed that we could prosper in isolation from the Old World. But . . . all of us have taken such vital roles in the international community that isolation would now be harmful to our own best interests."[25] Carter's call for openness and a new relationship between developing and industrializing nations was met with skepticism by many Latin American leaders. He announced that he would place the American Convention on Human Rights before the Senate for its approval. Carter also invited several Latin American leaders to Washington in order to discuss an impending decision on sugar quotas. It was at this same time that he announced that Mrs. Carter would be visiting Latin America.

The countries she visited were selected by the president and representatives from the State Department and National Security Agency. Jamaica, Costa Rica, Ecuador, Peru, Brazil, Colombia, and Venezuela were chosen because they were democracies or leaning toward becoming democracies. Mrs. Carter was selected to make the visit for political reasons consistent with a concern for agenda building. The president was preoccupied with completing the Panama Canal Treaties, the Middle East peace process, and the SALT II negotiations; he had little time for foreign trips. The administration did feel, however, that it was necessary to show in some dramatic fashion that the United States was committed to human rights and democracy in the Western Hemisphere. The consensus among President Carter and his advisers was that someone other than State Department officials should convey this important message.

Mrs. Carter began preparing for her trip two months before it began. Briefings by scholars and officials from the Treasury Department, State Department, National Security Council, and Organization of American States provided her with information about past U.S. relations and current issues. She also studied speeches that Jimmy Carter had given on Latin America and the seven countries she would visit. During her trip Mrs. Carter was always accompanied by Robert Pastor, the national security adviser for Latin America, and Terry Todman, assistant secretary of state for Latin America. They provided her with supplementary speaking notes and questions for her meetings with foreign heads of state. The first lady also prepared speaking notes for each of her meetings.

In her memoirs Mrs. Carter observes that throughout the meetings she took notes and that at the conclusion of each session with a foreign leader she would write a long memo that was sent to the president and the State Department. The meetings went far beyond purely ceremonial encounters. For example, her session with Ecuador's military leaders was scheduled to last ninety minutes but went on for three hours, and her meeting with Peruvian president Morales Bermudez went several hours over its allocated time. She described her conversations with Brazilian president Ernesto Geisel as "interesting and intense—too intense, it seemed, for our ambassador to Brazil, John Crimmins," who passed word to her that she was pressing the president "too hard" and preferred that she make "polite dinner conversation."[26]

As a political force in the agenda-building process, Rosalynn Carter succeeded in her meetings with Latin American leaders because she brokered people and ideas. She was able to convey to the countries' leaders that the American foreign policy agenda had changed and that with it a change was envisioned in U.S.–Latin American relations. Success comes with spending political capital in the agenda-building process, and her preparation for the trip was a necessary investment in building that capital. Mrs. Carter notes that she "was prepared for the private debate" with Jamaican prime minister Manley. The payoff was also evident over time. The first lady notes that as her trip progressed, "the leaders of the countries were taking me seriously." She also observes that "they all knew that I would carry their concerns directly back to him [President Carter] rather than to a desk at the State Department. I did both."[27]

On her return from Latin America, Mrs. Carter briefed the president and Secretary of State Cyrus Vance. There quickly followed an Organization of American States General Assembly meeting that took up the question of human rights. The issue proved to be as divisive as it had been before and during Mrs. Carter's trip, with some states feeling that human rights was strictly an internal matter and others considering it to be a legitimate foreign policy question. Secretary of State Vance made the strongest statement to that date of the Carter administration's support for human rights and tied continued American economic aid to its observance.

Human rights was a visible and controversial issue throughout the Carter presidency. Mrs. Carter's trip to Latin America helped get this issue (and, especially, hemispheric human rights) onto the formal agenda of American foreign policy. It was not enough, however, to move this issue through the remainder of the policy process to a successful conclusion. Overly optimistic at the outset, the Carter administration moved ahead on several controversial fronts early in its term. Considerable political energy was expended in securing passage of the Panama Canal Treaties and seeking passage of the SALT II Treaty. These political costs became even greater as instability in the third world and concerns for Soviet-Cuban aggression placed cold war security issues back atop the foreign policy agenda. This changing international climate made it increasingly difficult for the administration to champion human rights, and though the rhetoric remained constant and the administration's good intentions were seldom questioned, progress was uneven.

Human rights issues did not again achieve prominence on the foreign policy agenda until the Clinton administration. Under Reagan it was first discarded and then transformed into a prodemocracy position that was a key component of his administration's tough anti-Soviet foreign policy. During the Bush administration the most notable opportunity to champion human rights came with the Tiananmen Square riots in Beijing. Here, rhetoric and action moved in different directions as Congress sought to punish China for the attacks on prodemocracy demonstrators while the Bush administration moved to temper this criticism with policies designed to maintain good relations with the Chinese government.

As was the case with Rosalynn Carter's advocacy of human rights, Hillary Clinton's agenda-building efforts involved collaboration and planning with other executive branch agencies. Preparations for her participation in the UN conference in Beijing lasted more than a year and involved representatives from her office, the State Department, the National Security Council, the office of the U.S. ambassador to the UN, and nongovernmental organizations. These discussions addressed the first lady's role, the people who would be part of the delegation, and the kinds of themes that would be stressed.

Similar consultations were held for her other overseas trips. These included discussions with representatives from the State Department and the National Security Council, who identified from the outset what Hillary Clinton would do on the trips and why she, rather than the president or a representative from the State Department, would represent the United States. The spirit of cooperation extended to all other areas of the first lady's involvement in foreign policy. As a representative from her office noted, "I don't move on a foreign policy issue without consulting the National Security Council. The expertise is in the National Security Council, but we will work hand and hand."[28]

ANALYSIS

The foreign policy activities of Rosalynn Carter and Hillary Clinton were not "lone ranger" actions. They were coordinated efforts undertaken with the approval and involvement of key foreign policy bureaucracies and the White House. The trips were deliberately undertaken to advance the interests of the respective administrations. An agenda-setting perspective permits a comparative analysis of Mrs. Carter's and Mrs. Clinton's participation in the formation of American foreign policy in ways that a simple narrative or other framework does not.

First, while Mrs. Carter served as a direct communication link between foreign leaders and the White House, this was not the case with Mrs. Clinton on her trips. Several factors interacted to produce Hillary Clinton's schedule. There was no mandate from the president to serve as a communication link between foreign leaders and the White House. Another factor was that Mrs. Clinton's personal interest was in the advancement of women and the importance of micro credit development programs. The very logic of promoting these activities pointed toward meetings with private sector groups and nonprofit initiatives, and not with government leaders. Yet another factor was that, according to political observers at the time, Mrs. Clinton's foreign trips were an attempt to redefine her image as first lady into more traditional terms (goodwill ambassador) following the political battles that surrounded the lead role she took in promoting the administration's health care proposal.

Second, in acting as policy entrepreneurs, Mrs. Carter and Mrs. Clinton were picking up issues that were at very different points in the policy stream. International human rights as an issue was far more "upstream" and closer to the policy agenda for Mrs. Carter than it was for Mrs. Clinton. Disclosures of CIA abuses abroad and disenchantment with the realpolitik of the Nixon administration had provided fertile ground for human rights activists and others to promote an alternative foreign policy agenda. The issue did not have to be created but was already "in the water" and ready to be seized. No such comparable disenchantment with foreign policy or groundswell of public opinion in favor of human rights was present in the 1990s. Promoting democracy was in vogue, but for most that meant promoting capitalism, not human rights. In fact, for many, with the advent of democracy human rights abuses became a less pressing foreign policy issue. And for all the talk of a new world order during the Bush administration, the focus of American foreign policy quickly returned to a focus on the traditional triad of Russia, Europe, and Asia. To the extent that the agenda of American foreign policy had expanded, it now gave more prominence to trade and investment issues.

Third, the two first ladies were placing human rights on different foreign policy agendas. Mrs. Carter was connecting with the formal agenda of American foreign policy. Not only was promoting human rights a highly visible foreign policy issue, but the Carter administration was committed verbally to promoting human rights and, at that point at least, to taking concrete actions in the name of human rights. A similar situation did not exist in the Clinton administration, which came into office largely uninterested in foreign affairs and gravitated toward it as events abroad unfolded and as domestic initiatives floundered. Enlarging the sphere of democracy was the rhetorical centerpiece of Clinton's foreign policy, but most of its attention was focused on a succession of hot spots such as Somalia, Iraq, Bosnia, and Kosovo as well as trade with China. With no formal agenda resting place available,

Mrs. Clinton's efforts largely were designed to place women and children's rights on the public agenda rather than on the formal agenda. Involved here was a consciousness-raising effort intended to move women's rights from a symbolic pseudo-agenda to one where real discussions were held but concrete policy initiatives were not yet likely to be forthcoming.

Fourth, neither Mrs. Carter nor Mrs. Clinton was completely successful in her efforts to place human rights issues on the American foreign policy agenda. The reasons for each's failure were similar. Political weakness at home plus an international system in which violent conflicts commanded the world's attention produced a dramatic narrowing of the policy stream. As each president's political standing fell, policy initiatives became increasingly expensive. Successful policy entrepreneurship under these conditions demands resources that neither first lady possessed. Their political capital was too tightly dependent upon and derivative of the presidents' to allow them to act as independent political brokers linking people, issues, and ideas.

CONCLUSION

It is not uncommon to see first ladies representing the United States abroad. Typically, their trips are characterized as goodwill journeys that produce photo opportunities and little else. An examination of the foreign travels of Rosalynn Carter and Hillary Rodham Clinton using a policy-making-process perspective reveals that much more may be involved. The foreign policy activities of first ladies can contribute directly to the formulation of American foreign policy by highlighting issues and steering those issues onto the policy agenda. Use of this framework points out meaningful distinctions between the actions of Mrs. Carter and those of Mrs. Clinton. The framework can also be used to compare their efforts with those of past and future first ladies in both domestic and foreign policy. There is no reason to suspect that in the future the foreign policy activities of first ladies will be restricted to the initial stages of the policy process. An understanding of the agenda-building process provides a mechanism for linking this type of policy-making activity by a first lady to other activities later in the policy process and to the broader policy-making undertakings of the administration.

NOTES

1. Karen O'Connor, Bernadette Nye, and Laura Van Assendelft, "Wives in the White House: The Political Influence of First Ladies," *Presidential Studies Quarterly* 26 (1996): 835–53.

2. Robert P. Watson, "The First Lady Reconsidered: Presidential Partner and Political Institution," *Presidential Studies Quarterly* 27 (1997): 805–17.

3. Robert P. Watson, *The Presidents' Wives: Reassessing the Office of First Lady* (Boulder, Colo.: Lynne Rienner, 2000), 140–41.

4. O'Connor, Nye, and Assendelft, "Wives in the White House," 835–53.

5. James Rosenau, "Pre-Theories and Theories of Foreign Policy," in *Approaches to Comparative and International Politics,* ed. R. Barry Farrell (Evanston: Northwestern University Press, 1966), 27–92.

6. James Rosenau and W. Michael Fagan, "A New Dynamism in World Politics: Increasingly Skillful Individuals?," *International Studies Quarterly* 41 (1997): 655–86.

7. John Stoessinger, *Why Nations Go to War,* 7th ed. (New York: St. Martin's Press, 1998).

8. Robert Jervis, *Perception and Misperception in International Relations* (Princeton, N.J.: Princeton University Press, 1976).

9. Glenn Hastedt, *American Foreign Policy: Past, Present, and Future,* 4th ed. (Upper Saddle River, N.J.: Prentice Hall, 2000), 186–87.

10. Christine Sylvester, *Feminist Theory and International Relations in a Postmodern Era* (Cambridge: Cambridge University Press, 1994).

11. Edward Crapol, ed., *Women and American Foreign Policy: Lobbyists, Critics, and Insiders* (New York: Greenwood Press, 1987).

12. Rhodri Jeffreys-Jones, *Changing Differences: Women and the Shaping of American foreign Policy, 1917–1994* (New Brunswick, N.J.: Rutgers University Press, 1995).

13. Ibid., 4.

14. For examples see Randall Ripley, *Policy Analysis in Political Science* (Chicago: Nelson-Hall, 1985), 48–55; and Harold Lasswell, *The Decision Process: Seven Categories of Functional Analysis* (College Park: University of Maryland Press, 1956).

15. Rosalynn Carter, *First Lady from Plains* (1984; reprint, Fayetteville: University of Arkansas Press, 1994), 195–226. All quotes in this essay regarding her trip to Latin America are from this chapter.

16. *Facts on File* (New York: Facts on File, Inc., 16 Mar. 1995), 182; Joyce Milton, *The First Partner: Hillary Rodham Clinton* (New York: William Morrow, 1999), 351–52.

17. Patrick Tyler, "Hilary Clinton in China, Details Abuse of Women," *New York Times,* 6 Sept. 1995, A1.

18. Ibid.

19. Milton, *First Partner,* 356.

20. Quoted in *Facts on File,* 183.

21. The statement is from the *Calcutta Times* as reported in *Facts on File* (New York: Facts on File, Inc., 6 Apr. 1995), 248.

22. Molly Moore, "First Lady 'Moved,' 'Overwhelmed' on Asian Journey of Self-discovery," *Washington Post,* 6 Apr. 1995, A25.

23. John W. Kingdon, *Agendas, Alternatives, and Public Policies* (New York: Little, Brown, 1984), 205–15.

24. Roger Cobb, Jennie-Keith Ross, and Marc Howard Ross, "Agenda Building as a Comparative Political Process," *American Political Science Review* 70 (1976): 126–38.

25. Dan Oberderfer, "Carter Addresses OAS, Stresses Human Rights," *Washington Post*, 15 Apr. 1977, A1.

26. Carter, *First Lady from Plains,* 218.

27. Ibid., 206.

28. Anthony J. Eksterowicz and Kristin Paynter, "The Evolution of the Role and Office of the First Lady: The Movement toward Integration with the White House Office," *The Social Science Journal* 37 (2000): 547–62.

Ten

The Evolution of the Role and Office of the First Lady

The Movement toward Integration with the White House Office

ANTHONY J. EKSTEROWICZ AND KRISTEN PAYNTER

The increasing influence and activism of first ladies is not without consequence. Two results have been the growth and professionalization of the first
lady's office and its integration with the office of the president. Indeed, it
benefits our understanding not only of the first ladyship but of the presidency
as well to develop approaches for assessing the first lady's many roles and
functions. This article proposes a model to understand and study these phe-
nomena.

As the twenty-first century opened, it did so with an unprecedented and
historic event pertaining to first ladies. Hillary Rodham Clinton became the
first presidential spouse to announce a candidacy for the United States Senate, and ultimately to succeed in election to that office. While it is true that
the New York political establishment once attempted to enlist Eleanor Roosevelt in a campaign for the Senate, they were not successful. Mrs. Clinton's
candidacy and election demonstrates the increasing influence of first ladies
throughout the political and policy processes. Indeed, there has been a slow
evolution toward this increasing influence in the modern era since Eleanor
Roosevelt occupied the Office of the First Lady. This influence attracted
attention in the 1996 presidential campaign when some observers suggested
that all potential first ladies announce their agendas before the election;
others suggested that a debate take place between Hillary Rodham Clinton
and Elizabeth Dole.[1]

This essay will trace the evolution of the roles and office of first ladies. It
is the hypothesis here that the Office of the First Lady has become more *pro-*
fessional in nature and has been moving in the direction of full integration with
the President's White House office. This movement has primarily occurred
through the efforts of a few activist first ladies, but even nonactivist occupants have moved the office marginally in this direction. This study will first

provide models pertaining to the influence of first ladies. The time frame for this study is the modern era, defined as post–Eleanor Roosevelt. Second, it will trace the historical evolution in the direction of full integration with the White House Office and document the contributions of various first ladies towards this end. Finally, it will categorize the various elements necessary, but not necessarily sufficient, for full integration with the White House office.

MODELS OF INFLUENCE

The study of first ladies is a new field. Historians have pioneered the field, but in recent years the disciplines of political science, psychology, and sociology have contributed to it. While each of these disciplines has been interested in the modern era of first ladies, working in the modern era presents some problems. Since Eleanor Roosevelt only ten first ladies have occupied the office, and the tenure of seven of them was less than two terms. Two, Jacqueline Kennedy and Betty Ford, served less than one term. Only Mamie Eisenhower, Nancy Reagan, and Hillary Clinton have served two terms. Only three can be classified as *strong activists:* Lady Bird Johnson, Rosalynn Carter, and Hillary Clinton. Only one of these, Hillary Clinton, served two full terms.

With such an uneven base concerning the tenure of the first lady, it becomes difficult to detect trends and assess the impact of reforms associated with the Office of the First Lady. One must also keep in mind the changing nature of society and political culture, especially concerning women's roles and issues during this era. These changes have also affected modern first ladies and their offices.

We can begin to view these changes by discussing a few models concerning first ladies. R. P. Watson has presented a useful typology. He categorizes first ladies as *full partners, partial partners, behind-the-scenes partners, partners in marriage,* and finally, *nonpartners.*[2] He views the first lady's role as conditioned by the type of partnership she has with her spouse and notes that only Eleanor Roosevelt, Rosalynn Carter, and Hillary Clinton achieved full partnership. This typology emphasizes the professional and personal relationship between the first lady and the president.

Gladys Engel Lang presents a model of women based upon different types of status. A *satellite status* implies that women are mere appendages of their spouses with no independent ideas. These women define themselves through their spouses and remain in the spouse's shadow. *Sponsored status* implies that women achieve recognition by their relationship with a prominent man; however, they use this relationship to find or earn their own way.

Sponsored status is obviously more influential than satellite status. Concerning first ladies, such a model would suggest that they could devote time and energy to programs and policies either with or eventually independent from their spouse's agendas. *Autonomous status* and recognition are conferred upon women who have their own ideas and act independently of their spouses. Their status resides within themselves and their accomplishments are manifestations of this type of status.[3]

If we merge Watson's notions of partnership, Lang's ideas of status, and add first ladies' concerns for policy along with considerations affecting the evolution of the Office of the First Lady we have a new model and useful way of viewing first ladies. This "independent/integrative model" assumes that a first lady can develop a public policy agenda independent of the president's and still rely on a partnership, either professional or personal, to help in the implementation of such an agenda. Furthermore, such a relationship is highly professionalized by the integration of the first lady's office with the various offices within the White House Office. In other words, the interests of the first lady and the president are tempered by their professional and personal relationship (which includes mutual respect and trust concerning professional advice among other elements) and furthered by the professional integration of their offices. This integration facilitates the passage of a public policy agenda that can be in the interest of both the president and the first lady or perhaps solely in the interest of the first lady. In this model a first lady draws influence from her professional reputation, work, and knowledge of the issues independent of the president, her political influence upon her husband due to the nature of their relationship, her complimentary public policy agenda, or from what Watson has termed her "pillow influence" as confidante, lover, and partner.[4] Theodore Sorensen observed long ago in his classic *Decision Making in the White House* that the "office affects the man as the man affects the office."[5] The same sentiment applies to the first lady and her office. It is this integration that the new model hopes to explain.

As with any model, it is probably best to view it along a continuum that exists from a strong independent/integrative manifestation to a weak manifestation of such a model. Partnerships are not perfect; they exist in degrees. When public policy variables are added to the mix, along with the various interests of presidents and first ladies and the inner workings of their offices, the strength of any model will be affected. We can view the movement toward this model by examining the various developments in the administrations of first ladies from Roosevelt to Clinton.

The Evolution of the Role and Office of the First Lady

Eleanor Roosevelt

Most historians credit Eleanor Roosevelt with changing the role of first ladies. She, more than any other occupant to her time, defined the role of a modern, activist first lady. Under Eleanor Roosevelt the East Wing of the White House became the focal point for first ladies. She became the first presidential spouse to speak at a national convention, author a column (it was titled "My Day"), serve as a radio commentator, and hold regular press conferences. She hired a personal secretary, Malvina Thompson, and a social secretary, Edith Helm, each of whom occupied stations on the second floor of the White House in a bedroom suite, then moved to the East Wing following its construction in 1942. Mrs. Roosevelt relied upon a network of friends and relatives to form committees rather than a professional and educated staff. Mrs. Roosevelt's social bureau also borrowed staff from various departments to respond to the unprecedented volume of mail that she received. In addition, her press conferences provided her with a de facto press office to promote her issues.[6]

Although Mrs. Roosevelt did not particularly like to campaign, she did become an active campaigner for her husband. Campaigning was just the tip of the iceberg. Mrs. Roosevelt delivered speeches not only for her husband but also for the many causes in which she was actively involved. She served as an informal presidential adviser and was not shy concerning her opinions. She also became the first first lady to testify before Congress.[7]

Mrs. Roosevelt was involved in a plethora of issues such as miners' rights, the plight of the unemployed, women's rights, youth issues, civil rights, and war relief. What was different about Mrs. Roosevelt was the independence she exercised apart from her husband on these issues. For example, on civil rights she argued throughout the war years that these issues should be at the top of the political agenda. This argument created tensions between her and the White House staff.[8] As D. Goodwin notes, Mrs. Roosevelt sought a certain amount of independence from her husband since discovering his extramarital affair with Lucy Mercer.[9] Thus, the partnership displayed by Eleanor and Franklin was more professional in nature. Although she had enormous influence over FDR's policies and appointments, she displayed independence on the issues. Media coverage reflected this fact.[10] One could argue that Mrs. Roosevelt appeared to occupy a position somewhere between sponsorship and autonomy. However, her office, given its nascent nature, was not highly integrated with the White House Office. As S. L. Robertson concludes:

When Eleanor Roosevelt left the White House in 1945, the role of the first lady had been changed drastically and permanently. She had established it as something separate from the presidency and with her outspokenness, activity, and visibility had made it independent from, although linked to, the Oval Office. She also changed forever the public's expectation of the first lady. After her, the public would begin to look for an active woman in the White House; the passive, retiring first lady was gone for good.[11]

Bess Truman and Mamie Eisenhower

Perhaps Robertson's appraisal was a bit premature, for Bess Truman did not seek to use the Office of the First Lady as had Mrs. Roosevelt. Although Mrs. Truman was not very active in Mr. Truman's Senate campaigns, she did occupy a position in his Senate office. However, as First Lady, Mrs. Truman refused to hold press conferences and never really developed a working relationship with the press.[12] Her responses to a set of questions posed by news reporters and published in a 1947 *Newsweek* issue concerning her conception of the role of first lady drew many "no comment" answers.[13] She had an aversion to publicity and to photographs.[14] Mrs. Truman once told President Roosevelt's Secretary of Labor, Frances Perkins, after President Roosevelt's funeral, "I don't know what I am going to do. I'm not used to this awful public life."[15] Mrs. Truman did little to further the professionalization of the Office of the First Lady. She even reduced her staff size to five.[16]

Yet Mrs. Truman may have achieved influence with her husband by the very nature of her role as spouse and trusted confidante. She fits nicely within the satellite status role, using her relationship to give advice to President Truman. Watson characterized her as a *behind-the-scenes partner*.[17] Upon her death, a 1982 *Washington Post* editorial noted:

> Surely she was not a political power in her own right, like Eleanor Roosevelt, or glamorous and exciting, like Jacqueline Kennedy. She had no causes of her own, no protégés, no press conferences. Her husband said she looked "just the way a woman who has been married 25 years should look," and she described the role of first lady as requiring that a spouse "sit beside her husband, be silent and be sure her hat is on straight."[18]

Despite these observations, professional innovations did occur within Mrs. Truman's staff. Mrs. Truman retained Edith Helm as her social secretary and expanded her job to include weekly press briefings although no questions were allowed. The social secretary also began providing reporters with a copy of the first lady's itinerary, making her the first presidential spouse to have such a record. In addition, during Mrs. Truman's term the White House was renovated again. To assist with the project, Congress enacted the Commission on the Renovation of the Executive Mansion. This group foresaw the need for other future committees to assist the first lady in personal projects.[19] Even a more traditional first lady like Mrs. Truman, with no specific policy agenda, moved the office forward professionally.

Like Mrs. Truman, Mrs. Eisenhower simply did not seek the glare of publicity. She was a behind-the-scenes player with no social causes of her own to advance, and she suffered from a chronic illness that contributed to her desire for privacy.[20] Watson categorized her as a *partner in marriage,* a label that implies a less active status than Mrs. Truman's *behind-the-scenes partner.*[21] In terms of public policy she attained satellite status, for there was minimal, if any, sponsorship of issues during her tenure. Mrs. Eisenhower seemed uninterested in politics and often worked from her bedroom on a small table tray.[22] On the other hand, she was responsible for expanding the staff attached to the Office of the First Lady to six secretaries and a staff director.[23] Traditional first ladies have had at least a marginal impact upon staffing. This is important because it slowly contributed to the professionalization of the office. However, during these tenures integration with the White House Office did not formally occur. The nature of these first ladies and their personalities and interests simply did not allow for such integration. They were in many respects manifestations of more traditional models of women and first ladies.

Jacqueline Kennedy

Mrs. Kennedy represents a transitional figure in first lady studies. She was, at most, a reluctant campaigner, never really exhibiting an interest in politics.[24] Her primary emphasis was on White House restoration and promoting the arts in America. Her relations with the press were difficult because she insisted on a certain amount of privacy for the sake of her young children.[25] Yet the emphasis upon White House restoration had an effect upon the Office of the First Lady. Under Mrs. Kennedy, the office grew enormously and was transformed into "a grand public stage."[26] Although Mrs. Eisenhower managed eight years without a social secretary, Mrs. Kennedy not only hired one but revolutionized the office by adding an assistant social secretary solely responsible for press relations. From the Treaty Room, she formed many committees to promote her causes.[27] The staff in the Office of the First Lady increased to approximately forty, but this growth created efficiency problems and resulted in tense relations with the White House staff.[28] Part of this expansion was on the social side, as Mrs. Kennedy sought to emphasize glamour, good taste, and high art.

Although Mrs. Kennedy's interests were safely feminine, this should not obscure her private political maneuvering for causes dear to her. It is no secret that she supported the president's agenda and monitored his legislation as it passed through the Congress. She was not shy about lobbying Congress for her initiatives. As C. S. Anthony notes:

> But behind the scenes, she enmeshed herself in politics as well, later admitting that she "convinced" President Kennedy "to ask Congress to give money to save the tombs at Abu Simbel which would have been inundated by the building of the Aswan Dam." Congress had previously treated it as a non issue. The president said he would support her, only on one condition that *she* "could convince [Congressman] John Rooney of the Appropriations Committee (who was always against giving money to foreigners)." West Wing aide Richard Godwin began compiling a report of cost estimates and techniques to move the temples, so that Congress would have an accountable basis upon which they could formally donate matching funds of about $10 million. Proudly, Jackie recalled how she and Godwin invited Congressman Rooney to the White House "and convinced him." Godwin said funding was due to Jackie's power. In gratitude, Egyptian president Nasser would give the Temple of Dendur to America.[29]

The quote is instructive, for it demonstrates that President Kennedy was willing to *sponsor* Mrs. Kennedy if she could convince Congressman Rooney. To do this, President Kennedy allowed for a close working relationship between Mrs. Kennedy and his West Wing aide Richard Godwin. Thus Mrs. Kennedy not only had an impact upon the formal structure of the office, she also forged a working relationship with the West Wing of the White House. This relationship was not an integration of their offices but a personal working relationship based upon presidential sponsorship of the issue along with the personality and reputation of Mrs. Kennedy.

Lady Bird Johnson

Mrs. Johnson was even more active in the policy process than her predecessor. She received an early education in presidential politics as the vice president's spouse when she often substituted for Mrs. Kennedy at functions.

While Mrs. Kennedy was not particularly interested in many aspects associated with the role of the first lady, Mrs. Johnson relished these opportunities. As a result, when she unexpectedly was thrust into the role of first lady she had significant experience.

Lady Bird Johnson's marriage to Lyndon Johnson was difficult due to his dominating nature and extramarital liaisons, but the two formed a professional partnership based upon mutual political respect. Mrs. Johnson gave her husband advice on his speeches, appointments, and campaigns and she served as his trusted political adviser. Mrs. Johnson was interested in the Head Start program, illiteracy, poverty, civil rights and, of course, beautification. Nowhere is the partnership between Mr. and Mrs. Johnson closer than on the issue of beautification. Mrs. Johnson reinforced the president's natural proclivities towards conservation. President Johnson, in turn, worked toward her goal of beautification.[30]

Mrs. Johnson was active and open about her policy preferences. She worked closely with Secretary of the Interior Morris K. Udall on beautification issues, received briefings from the White House staff on various issues, and assembled a network of influential women to help in her beautification campaign.[31] During her fight for highway beautification she participated in legislative and lobbying strategy sessions with the White House staff, becoming the first presidential spouse to do so.[32] Lady Bird became an active lobbyist for her programs with the consent and enthusiastic support of her husband. The Johnsons were true partners in these endeavors, and yet the issue of beautification was Mrs. Johnson's own.

The interaction of these issues and their partnership had a profound effect upon the Office of the First Lady. Mrs. Johnson made her ambitions known when she announced that Liz Carpenter would be her press secretary. Good press relations would be essential for the success of her programs, and the beautification initiative required Mrs. Johnson to hire a program director and borrow staff from other agencies such as the Interior Department. This fostered a team approach to problems and set the stage for future efforts toward full integration with the White House Office. Although Mrs. Johnson's predecessors maintained a staff director, she was the first to institutionalize the role.[33] By the end of her tenure, she employed a staff of thirty professionally trained specialists and organized her office to mirror the West Wing, thereby making major contributions to the organizational structure of the office.[34] Mrs. Johnson's tenure produced a press secretary under the direction of Liz Carpenter, a social secretary under the direction of Bess Abell, a special projects assistant (for beautification issues) under the direction of

Sharon Francis, and a correspondence office under the direction of Mrs. Johnson's personal secretary Ashton Gonella. Ms. Francis's position was an innovation in structure and it set the stage for future first ladies to obtain help with their projects. While the office was becoming more professional, the pay for these positions was quite low, the funding coming from the Office of the President.

The personal relationship between the Johnsons worked to the advantage of Mrs. Johnson's policy agenda which, in turn, resulted in greater professionalization of the Office of the First Lady. While Mrs. Johnson operated with *sponsorship status* she did exhibit traits of independence and autonomy.

Pat Nixon and Betty Ford

Pat Nixon served as first lady during the controversies of Vietnam and Watergate and her relationship with her husband appeared warm but traditional. Watson has characterized her relationship as a *partner in marriage*.[35] Mrs. Nixon did not like politics or campaigning, although she reluctantly participated in both. She tended to shun publicity yet she traveled widely and acted as an ambassador for the Nixon administration on her various travels abroad.[36]

Mrs. Nixon had no wide-ranging political agenda like her immediate predecessor's. Her main interest lay in increasing volunteerism throughout the nation that was sponsored by the president. She also expanded the fine arts and furniture collection in the White House. The First Lady served as an effective symbol for President Nixon's domestic agenda.[37] On balance, her actions as first lady were mainly in support of her husband's agenda. It seems as though Mrs. Nixon achieved a type of satellite status during her tenure. Thus, her marital relationship and her own reluctance to actively engage in a political agenda precluded the kind of activism practiced by Lady Bird Johnson. The absence of a true partnership between the first lady and president had an effect upon the relationship of her office with the White House Office. Tensions and mistrust existed between the two. As Anthony notes:

> Her first press secretary, reporter Gerry van der Heuvel, had been chosen by Mrs. Nixon, but within nine months, the president's chief of staff, H. R. Haldeman, ousted her. The First Lady acquiesced only after arranging another job for her at the State Department. Connie Stuart, an industrial film producer, was chosen as a replacement not only by the First Lady but also by Haldeman.[38]

This was just the beginning; over time both Haldeman and John Ehrlichman attempted to overrule many decisions that germinated from the Office of the First Lady.[39] A true integration of the Office of the First Lady with the White House Office never took place in the Nixon Administration. The marital relationship, Mrs. Nixon's personal proclivities, and her limited agenda all worked against such integration. While the Office of the First Lady may have been weakened during the Nixon administration, Mrs. Nixon did add a position for scheduling and advance to her staff.[40]

Mrs. Nixon's successor, Betty Ford, assumed the position of first lady during the end of the Watergate scandal, when her husband became the first unelected president. The marital relationship between the President and Mrs. Ford was a good one, with mutual respect between the two partners. There was a tendency toward activism in Mrs. Ford: she spoke on many subjects and adopted the ratification of the equal rights amendment as one of her causes.[41] She exercised her influence with President Ford on a variety of issues such as the pardon of President Nixon and the firing of Agricultural Secretary Earl Butz.[42] Watson characterized Mrs. Ford as a *partial partner*.[43] However, these efforts did not comprise an activist agenda such as that of Mrs. Johnson or Mrs. Roosevelt.

As a transitional figure she had an impact upon the office. She based her headquarters on the second floor of the East Wing of the White House and employed twenty-eight staffers. She was the first occupant of the office to have her own speechwriter, a deputy press secretary, and an appointments secretary.[44] One wonders what these developments would have meant with a longer tenure in office. In the short run they created tensions between the East and the West Wings of the White House and thus severely limited Mrs. Ford's impact upon such policies as the Equal Rights Amendment.[45]

The relationship between the president and his wife was simply not strong enough to overcome these tensions during such a brief tenure. While the office was upgraded, it was not used to its maximum potential. The marital relationship, Mrs. Ford's health problems, her brief tenure, and limited agenda all precluded efforts to integrate her office with that of the White House. On the other hand, the upgrades to the Office of the First Lady would serve future activist occupants well.

Rosalynn Carter

The relationship between President and Mrs. Carter was a personal and professional partnership. The Carters were best friends and business partners. When President Carter announced Mrs. Carter's Latin American trip, he noted that she had "long been his partner."[46] Even before she was first lady she was a full and essential partner in the Carter's peanut business.[47] The relationship was and is one of mutual respect and admiration. Mrs. Carter thrived in this type of relationship. As first lady she made sure that she was taken seriously by other policy-makers. She was active in President Carter's campaigns and served as an influential presidential adviser. Like the vice president, Mrs. Carter formally lunched with the president once a week. She gave her opinions on appointments and championed various women's issues and causes. She attended formal cabinet meetings and even took notes during the Camp David negotiations.[48] The personal relationship eased the professional relationship between the Carters and it moved beyond mere *sponsorship* toward limited *autonomy* for Mrs. Carter.

Mrs. Carter displayed a certain amount of independence from her husband on a few issues such as capital punishment, abortion, the firing of Health and Human Services Secretary Joseph Califano, and the timing of the Panama Canal Treaty.[49] Mrs. Carter had been concerned about the mentally ill long before her tenure at the White House and she used her influence to help pass the Mental Health Systems Act, where she functioned as honorary chair of the President's Commission on Mental Health. She worked with Health and Human Services and the White House staff, lobbied and testified before Congress, becoming the first presidential spouse to testify before Congress since Eleanor Roosevelt.[50] Her tireless work for passage of the Mental Health Systems Act included a certain amount of office integration with the White House. The full partnership Mrs. Carter shared with her husband facilitated such integration. Gould attributes Mrs. Carter's success to "her relationship with the president, her organization of her staff and their activities, her communication and political skills, her personality, and her commitment to focused goals."[51]

There were significant changes in the Office of the First Lady that in turn aided the integration of the president's office and the Office of the First Lady. While operating out of the East Wing of the White House, Mrs. Carter approached her duties professionally.[52] Her staff attended daily West Wing briefings and, while her staff numbers were smaller, due to the pressure on her husband to downsize the bureaucracy, she became the first to hire a management consultant to streamline her office.[53] Mrs. Carter also reorganized her office to include the following divisions: projects and community liaison, press and research, schedule and advance, and social and personal. She also created a new position of chief of staff to the first lady. Assistants to the first lady began to draw a more professional salary.[54] Under Mrs. Carter the Office of the First Lady became highly organized, professional, and integrated with the White House Office. Future first ladies would build upon these trends.

Mrs. Carter also relied upon the President's staff, such as the staff from the State Department and the National Security Council when she undertook her diplomatic trip to Latin America.[55]

The most significant development affecting the Office of the First Lady was the passage of Public Law 95-750 in 1978. This act legally established funds for the upkeep of the mansion and provided for "assistance and services" for first ladies in connection with the discharge of the president's duties. Before this act, first ladies obtained monies, as needed, from a general White House budget.[56] Now first ladies had a formal act of Congress recognizing their importance.

Nancy Reagan and Barbara Bush

Mrs. Reagan's relationship with her husband is difficult to characterize. The two were very close in office, with Mrs. Reagan acting mainly in defense and support of her husband. While other first ladies worked as active partners in both marriage and politics, Mrs. Reagan was active mainly in support of President Reagan the man. Watson characterized this relationship as a *behind-the-scenes partnership*.[57] Yet one must inquire as to partner in what—policy, personal relations, staffing matters, or politics? There is no doubt that Mrs. Reagan was committed to President Reagan and that their marriage was a strong one. There is also no doubt that Mrs. Reagan exercised influence over her husband and his staff. But what were her primary motivations?

Mrs. Reagan was extremely protective of her husband, and she exercised her influence behind the scenes. Her intervention on behalf of John Sears, President Reagan's campaign manager, is a testament to this fact. She was also very influential in controlling the president's appointments schedule, especially after the 1981 assassination attempt.[58] Another example is her role in the firing of White House chief of staff Donald Regan and the transfer of national security advisor William Clark to the Interior Department. Mrs. Reagan was also influential over policy, such as when she influenced President Reagan to pursue arms control and de-emphasize various divisive social issues.[59]

Although there can be no doubt about her influence, it was a type of influence exercised for the good and well being of the president. Mrs. Reagan did not seek to influence policy for the sake of policy alone like Lady Bird Johnson or Rosalynn Carter. She did it in relation to the plight of her husband. To the extent that integration occurred between her office and the White House Office it was with President Reagan's well being in mind, not Mrs. Reagan's specific policy agenda. In fact, Mrs. Reagan was criticized early in her tenure by the public and the press for not having a policy agenda. She did not want to attend cabinet meetings or play a role in a wide-ranging policy agenda. Her commitment to the "Just Say No" antidrug program was largely a reaction to the negative press concerning her lack of a cause. So, while the marriage was a strong and loving one, Mrs. Reagan did not seek influence beyond the interests of her husband. The relationship falls somewhere between *satellite* and *sponsorship status*. It does not approach an *independent/ integrative model* unless one considers issues concerning the president's personal and professional well-being.

Despite these observations, Mrs. Reagan did have an impact upon the Office of the First Lady. She had trouble keeping a chief of staff largely because she herself wanted to function in that capacity.[60] However, she did contribute to the professionalization of the office by attaching an Office of the First Lady letterhead to her press releases.[61] She added more positions to her staff and both her chief of staff and deputy chief of staff held presidential commissions or West Wing titles.[62] As Patterson notes, "Attending senior staff and Scheduling Committee meetings, joining the advance teams, her staff chief is the link between the two separate but interdependent White House universes."[63] This interrelationship between the two offices allowed for easier access to presidential resources. Mrs. Reagan also moved her office to a center room at the north side of the White House, which was equidistant between the two wings.[64] Mrs. Reagan used such integration primarily (but not exclusively) to further the well-being of her husband politically, socially, and professionally. Mrs. Reagan did have one consuming cause: her husband.

First Lady Barbara Bush approached both policy and politics more traditionally. She did not run a business like Rosalynn Carter, nor did she run a congressional office like Lady Bird Johnson. As first lady she was extremely supportive of President Bush's positions and policy agenda, campaigning vigorously not only for him but for Republican candidates in congressional races.[65] The relationship between Mrs. Bush and President Bush was very traditional, resembling that of Bess and Harry Truman. There was a mutual respect and trust between the Bushes. Watson has correctly characterized Mrs. Bush's relationship with her husband as a *behind-the-scenes partnership*.[66]

Mrs. Bush chose to highlight the issue of illiteracy during her tenure. While she became outspoken on other issues such as civil rights and abortion, her main focus was on illiteracy.[67] However, she did not formally testify before the Congress in favor of legislation, nor did she chair intergovernmental commissions. Mrs. Bush selected the illiteracy issue independently and she drew enthusiastic support from the president. Still, this effort represents *sponsorship* rather than demonstrable independence in setting and making policy.

Mrs. Bush's marital relationship and her personal proclivities do not fit within an *independent/integrative model.*

Mrs. Bush's approach to her office was indicative of this. She first used the White House sitting room next to her bedroom as her office and she later transferred her personal office to the north side of the White House in what was the beauty parlor. As Mrs. Bush explained:

> Neither during the vice presidential or White House years did I have an office in the Old Executive Office Building (part of the White House complex) or the East Wing, traditionally where the First Lady's staff works. . . . I always suspected my staff appreciated my staying out of their way.[68]

Such geographical distance hinders the integration of the Office of the First Lady with the White House Office. While Mrs. Bush did not expand the work of her predecessors regarding her formal office, she did ensure that her Chief of Staff secured a presidential commission as deputy assistant to the president.[69] Mrs. Bush's marital relationship and her own preferences influenced the traditional way she used her office.

Hillary Rodham Clinton

Mrs. Clinton shared a deep commitment to activism and social issues reminiscent of Eleanor Roosevelt's. She was an activist in her own right before and during her White House tenure. Many scholars and pundits have commented on the marriage of President and Mrs. Clinton, but there can be no real doubt about the nature of the partnership displayed in this relationship. The Clintons worked together in mock trials as law students at Yale; a political and personal relationship began there that would survive many obstacles and last through many political campaigns in Arkansas, Washington, and even New York. Watson characterized this relationship as a *full partnership,* a designation he applied otherwise only to Eleanor Roosevelt and Rosalynn Carter.[70] The media covered the Clintons as a team.[71] Here, President and Mrs. Clinton agreed on the issues, with the president supporting the issues near to Mrs. Clinton and vice versa. As with First Lady Carter, Mrs. Clinton served as her husband's closest adviser. The closeness of this relationship had an impact upon policy in Arkansas when Bill Clinton as governor asked his wife to chair the state's Education Standards Committee. Similarly, in Washington, President Clinton asked her to head a panel formulating a national health care plan. Mrs. Clinton also worked on campaigns, testified before Congress, and worked closely with congressional staff on many issues. In terms of status Mrs. Clinton achieved a certain measure of independence and *autonomy* (due to her background) mixed with *sponsorship*. She accepted the president's help on her issues but she was involved in many of them long before her White House years. As Mrs. Clinton's chief of staff, Melanne Verveer explained:

> Mrs. Clinton happens to have worked on issues relating to foster children and adoption for twenty plus years so she is preceded with a reputation on these issues that is not to be taken lightly. When she works with a group of experts in this issue area, she is also very knowledgeable.[72]

Mrs. Clinton even asked not to be judged solely upon her partnership with the president but rather on her performance.[73]

Mrs. Clinton's education, activism, political proclivities, and marital partnership all served to impact her office. Mrs. Clinton was the first presidential spouse to have an office in the West Wing of the White House.[74] In fact, Mrs. Clinton also had office space in the Old Executive Office Building, where her chief and deputy chief of staff were located.[75] Although this helped facilitate matters in an operational sense, Mrs. Clinton's chief of staff, Melanne Verveer, cautions that geographical proximity to the White House (by itself) is not very meaningful. More important are the types of people in the office and their working relations with the White House staff and the preferences of the president and Mrs. Clinton on the issues. Ms. Verveer stresses the practice of office integration, noting:

> Everything is integrated. We are not only integrated as the First Lady's staff but we are integrated into the president's staff. I go to senior staff meetings. My colleagues are involved in the domestic policy staff meetings, in economic meetings, in national security meetings depending on what is relevant with respect to any particular issue that the first lady is asked to undertake or has been engaged in. All of that is integrated largely into the wider operations of the White House.[76]
>
> . . . I don't move on international issues without consulting with the National Security Council. The expertise is in the National Security Council but we will work hand in hand.

Mrs. Clinton's office adopted a team approach to getting things done. Just as in the Johnson and Carter Administrations this type of operation had an impact upon the formal nature of the office. For example, Ms. Verveer noted that Mrs. Clinton's work as chair of the President's Task Force on Health Care was integrated with the White House staff.[77] While this work did not represent a separate project from the Office of the First Lady, the involvement of First Lady Clinton in this issue led to a federal court of appeals decision in *Association of American Physicians and Surgeons v. Hillary Rodham Clinton* that had ramifications for her office. The court sided with the Justice Department's argument suggesting that Mrs. Clinton was a government employee. This is the first ruling on the position of the first lady and it will serve to advance the Office of the First Lady as an institution.[78] It is also an example of how issue activism, partnership, and office integration can have a historical and institutional impact.

Due to Mrs. Clinton's influence her staff earned more respect and money than any previous first lady's staff. She has contributed to the increasing professionalization of the office and several members of her staff have received presidential commissions aiding the integration with the White House staff.[79] The nature of her staff also contributed to integration and a professional team approach in that many original members of the Office of the First Lady worked on the Clinton campaign. These relationships are important to an integrative, team-oriented approach.

Mrs. Clinton's activism and independence on the issues, her marital relationship and her highly integrated office all suggest that she operated out of the *independent/integrated model* of first ladies. Table 1 provides a flash picture of a few of the variables mentioned in this analysis for the various offices of first ladies. It visually depicts the movement toward the professionalization of the Office of the First Lady.

Conclusions

Social and cultural events, the proclivities of each occupant of the office, issue activism, staff personnel, the first couple's marital and professional relationship, and the integration of the first lady's office with that of the White House Office have all affected the first lady's office. This study has shown that there has been a historic evolution of the first lady's office in the direction of professionalization and integration. This movement requires a new model to aid in the understanding of this new environment. The *independent/integrated model* serves this purpose. It depends upon a number of variables including the personal nature of the first lady toward issue or policy activism, her marital relationship, and the nature of her office and staff.

Generally, we conclude that activist first ladies have had a profound impact upon the workings of their office. When one analyzes Eleanor Roosevelt,

TABLE 1. Analysis of Variables for Offices of First Ladies

First Lady	Office	Staff	Organization	Director	Press	Projects
E Roosevelt	2nd Floor	2	Social	No	No	New Deal
B Truman	Bedroom	5	Social	No	No	WH Restoration
M Eisenhower	Bedroom	7	Social	Yes	No	American Heart Association
J Kennedy	Treaty Room	40	Press; Social; Correspondence	Yes	Yes	WH Restoration; Humanities
L Johnson	Dressing Room	30	Press; Social; Correspondence; Projects; Errands; Committees	Yes	Yes	Beautification
P Nixon	Dressing Room	—	Press; Social; Correspondence; Scheduling and Advance	Yes	Yes	Volunteerism
B Ford	2nd Floor	28	Press; Social; Correspondence; Speech	Yes	Yes	ERA; Health; Disabled Children
R Carter	EW	24	Press; Social; Scheduling; Projects	Yes	Yes	ERA; Mental Health; Elderly
N Reagan	Northside	22	Press; Social; Correspondence; Scheduling; Projects; Liaison	Yes	Yes	Drugs; WH Staff Interactions
B Bush	Sitting Room; Beauty Parlor	14	Press; Social; Correspondence; Scheduling; Projects; Graphics	Yes	Yes	Literacy
H Clinton	EW; WW; Old Exec	18	Press; Social; Correspondence; Scheduling; Public Policy Issues	Yes	Yes	Health Care; Child Advocacy Int'l Social Rights and Social Development

Lady Bird Johnson, Rosalynn Carter, and Hillary Clinton the progressions toward professionalization and integration become quite apparent. As indicated earlier, the strength of this model has varied historically. For example, Mrs. Carter operated out of a weaker conception of the *independent/integrated model* than did Mrs. Clinton. However, actions taken by Mrs. Carter and circumstances that occurred under the Carter Administration all worked to benefit the Office of the First Lady under Mrs. Clinton. Future activist presidential spouses will undoubtedly benefit from the legacy of First Lady Hillary Rodham Clinton.

NOTES

1. Matthew Cooper, "First Ladies: Speak Up," *Washington Monthly* 28 (1996), 36; Robert P. Watson, *The President's Wives: Reassessing the Office of the First Lady* (Boulder, Colo.: Lynne Rienner Publishers, 1999), 5.

2. Watson, *The President's Wives,* 142–43.

3. Gayle Tuchman, Arlene Kaplan Daniels, and James Walker Benet, eds., *Hearth and Home: Images of Women in the Mass Media* (New York: Oxford University Press, 1978), 148.

4. Robert P. Watson, "The First Lady Reconsidered: Presidential Partner and Political Institution," *Presidential Studies Quarterly* 27 (1997), 805–18.

5. Theodore Sorensen, *Decision Making in the White House: The Olive Branch or the Arrows* (New York: Columbia University Press, 1963).

6. Betty Boyd Caroli, "The First Lady's Office," in *Encyclopedia of the American Presidency,* ed. Leonard Levy and Louis Fisher (New York: Simon and Schuster, 1994), 2:637; Doris Kearns Goodwin, "Eleanor Roosevelt," *Time* 151 (1998), 122; Frances M. Seeber, "Eleanor Roosevelt and the Women in the New Deal: A Network of Friends," *Presidential Studies Quarterly* 20 (1990), 707–17; Lewis L. Gould, "Modern First Ladies: An Institutional Perspective," *Prologue* 18–19 (1986–87), 71.

7. Carl Sferrazza Anthony, "The First Ladies: They've Come a Long Way, Martha," *Smithsonian* 23 (1992), 135–57; Watson, *The President's Wives,* 96.

8. Lewis L. Gould, *American First Ladies* (New York: Garland, 1996), 443.

9. Goodwin, "Eleanor Roosevelt," 122.

10. Betty Houchin Winfield, "Madame President: Understanding a New Kind of First Lady," *Media Studies* 8 (1994), 63.

11. Stephen L. Robertson, "The First Lady, The First Family, and the President's Friends," in *Guide to the Presidency*, vol. 2 (Washington, D.C.: CQ Press, 1996), 1012.

12. Gould, *American First Ladies*, 449–62.

13. "No Comment," *Newsweek*, November 10, 1947, 16.

14. Nina W. Burke, "Mrs. Truman: First Lady," *Western Farm Life*, October 1, 1945, 18–22.

15. Gerry Van der Heuvel, "Remembering Bess," *Washington Post,* October 19, 1982, D1.

16. Charles S. Clark, "First Ladies: What Is the Role for the President's Spouse?," *Congressional Quarterly Researcher* 6 (1996), 515.

17. Watson, *The President's Wives,* 143.

18. Editorial, *Washington Post,* October 20, 1982.

19. Gould, "Modern First Ladies," 87, 76.

20. Lewis L. Gould, "First Ladies," *The American Scholar* 55 (1986), 533.

21. Watson, *The President's Wives,* 143.

22. Carl Sferrazza Anthony, "Office Politics and the First Ladies," *Washington Post,* 25 January 1993, B1.

23. Martin M. Teasley, "Ike Was Her Career," *Prologue* 18–19 (1987), 109.

24. Gould, *American First Ladies,* 479.

25. Ibid, 486.

26. Robertson, "The First Lady, The First Family," 1012.

27. Gould, "Modern First Ladies," 77.

28. Robertson, "The First Lady, The First Family," 1018; "Office Politics and the First Ladies," p. B3.

29. Carl Sferrazza Anthony, *First Ladies,* vol. 2, *The Saga of the President's Wives and Their Power 1961–1990* (New York: William Morrow, 1991), 89.

30. Gould, *American First Ladies*, 36.

31. Ibid, 26, 38, 47.

32. Ibid, 96.

33. Gould, "Modern First Ladies," 87, 78.

34. Caroli, "The First Lady's Office," 637.

35. Watson, *The President's Wives,* 143.

36. Robertson, "The First Lady, The First Family," 1013.

37. Gould, *American First Ladies*, 528–29.

38. Anthony, *The Saga of the President's Wives*, 168.

39. Gould, *American First Ladies*, 533.

40. Caroli, "The First Lady's Office," 638.

41. Karen M. Roher, "'If There Was Anything You Forgot to Ask . . . ': The Papers of Betty Ford," *Prologue* 19 (1987), 145.

42. Lessa E. Tobin, "Betty Ford As First Lady: A Woman for Women," *Presidential Studies Quarterly* 20 (1990), 764.

43. Watson, *The President's Wives,* 143.

44. Gould, "Modern First Ladies," 87, 79.

45. Sheila Rabb Weidenfeld, *First Lady's Lady: With the Fords at the White House* (New York: Putnam, 1979), 26.

46. Rosalynn Carter, *First Lady From Plains* (Fayetteville: University of Arkansas Press, 1994),198.

47. Gould, *American First Ladies*, 560.

48. Carter, *First Lady From Plains*, 162, 311, 184, 265–66.

49. Ibid, 173.

50. Watson, *The President's Wives,* 96.

51. Gould, *American First Ladies*, 564–65.

52. "Office Politics and the First Ladies," p. B3.

53. Robertson, "The First Lady, The First Family," 1018.

54. "Being First Lady Isn't What It Used to Be," *U.S. News and World Report* 84 (1978): 74.

55. Bradley Hankes Patterson, *The Ring of Power* (New York: Basic Books, 1988), 281.

56. Watson, *The President's Wives,* 109.

57. Ibid, 143.

58. Paul Gray, "A First Lady of Priorities and Proprieties," *Time,* January 5, 1981, 25.

59. Patterson, *The Ring of Power*, 281; Gould, *American First Ladies*, 583–606.

60. Gould, *American First Ladies*, 598.

61. Gould, "Modern First Ladies," 79.

62. James S. Rosebush, *First Lady, Public Wife: A Behind-the-Scenes History of the Evolving Role of First Ladies in American Political Life* (Lanham, Md.: Madison Books, 1987), 7.

63. Patterson, *The Ring of Power*, 284.

64. "Office Politics and the First Ladies," p. B3.

65. Gould, *American First Ladies*, 624.

66. Watson, *The President's Wives,* 143.

67. Barbara Bush, *Barbara Bush: A Memoir* (New York: Charles Scribner's Sons, 1994), 272–74.

68. Ibid., 279.

69. Jessica Lee, "First Lady's Staff Members Carry Clout," *USA Today,* 20 January 1993, A4.

70. Watson, *The President's Wives,* 143.

71. Winfield, "Madame President."

72. Melanne Verveer, interview with Anthony Eksterowicz and Kristin Paynter, Old Executive Office Building, Washington, D.C., October 19, 1999.

73. Ann Devroy, "First Lady Defends Role She Calls a Partnership," *Washington Post,* 18 October 1995, p. A.

74. "Office Politics and the First Ladies," p. BE-2.

75. Verveer interview, October 19, 1999.

76. Ibid.

77. Ibid.

78. Gould, *American First Ladies*, 643; O'Connor et al., "Wives in the White House," 835–39.

79. Lee, "First Lady's Staff Members Carry Clout," A4.

PART FIVE

Modern First Ladyship

Overview

Modern first ladies confront enormous scrutiny of their public and private activities. The public wants a first lady to perform more traditional roles; yet cultural changes in women's social roles have contributed to increasing professional public expectations from modern first ladies. Kay Knickrehm and Robin Teske document the problems associated with any first lady as she attempts to cross the divide between her public life and her private life. They note the changes in women's roles that have produced paradoxes and conflicts in the job of first lady. They caution against assuming that attitudes toward the status of women have dramatically changed. Knickrehm and Teske refer to survey data suggesting that even among some who generally favor a more equal role for women, there is ambivalence when the effects of the women's movement on families are raised. All of this results in boundaries for any first lady and consequences if these boundaries are crossed.

Gil Troy continues this public/private exploration by noting that "the first lady . . . is given extraordinary opportunities but also suffers from great . . . restrictions." He discusses this paradox and illustrates its effect on first ladies from the Truman administration to Clinton's administration. Troy observes that "the personal has not only become political, . . . the political has become . . . personal." One can clearly see this as a result of the Lewinsky scandal. Troy wisely counsels that reporters and scholars should take note of the complexity in the lives of first ladies.

Myra G. Gutin concentrates on the complex and controversial first ladyship of Hillary Clinton. She traces the developments in the Office of the First Lady and notes the contributions of first ladies Eleanor Roosevelt, Jacqueline Kennedy, Lady Bird Johnson, Betty Ford, Rosalynn Carter, and Nancy Reagan. Gutin briefly discusses the early life and education of Mrs. Clinton and notes her politicization and commitment to various issues such as health care and child poverty. Echoing the themes developed in the previous essays, Gutin explores the various setbacks and successes that confronted Mrs. Clinton. She concludes that Hillary Clinton not only recovered from each setback but learned valuable lessons from them. As a result Mrs. Clinton helped remove some limitations placed on the first ladyship by pushing the boundaries of the role. She became the first first lady to run successfully for public office while she was still first lady. Gutin notes that this will be part of her enduring legacy.

In a poignant essay MaryAnne Borrelli documents first lady Betty Ford's battle with breast cancer. Perhaps this event best illustrates the problem of the public/private divide that all first ladies face. Borrelli painstakingly organizes the private correspondence that Mrs. Ford received during her illness. Letters were received from breast cancer survivors, religious witnesses, and well-wishers. Borrelli concludes that Mrs. Ford did share the bully pulpit by entering the public sector to share her private struggle with breast cancer. Mrs. Ford's decision was both proactive and responsive, and she advanced the cause of preventative health care. The letters to the first lady are a testament to this fact and part of Betty Ford's brief but significant legacy.

Eleven

First Ladies and Policy Making

Crossing the Public/Private Divide

KAY M. KNICKREHM
AND ROBIN TESKE

Twelve years after Jimmy lost, Rosalyn[n] remained baffled by America's ambivalence over the role of the First Lady. "Americans know that women are going to work," she said of the controversy Hillary touched off. "They don't mind if women work. They think it's nice for women to have leadership positions—I think they really do—but they think the First Lady ought to sit in the White House and take care of the president. I cannot understand that. I told Hillary, 'You're going to be criticized no matter what you do, so be criticized for what you think is best and right for the country.'"

Donnie Radcliffe, *Hillary Rodham Clinton: A First Lady for Our Time*

INTRODUCTION

Observers agree that the role of first lady is a difficult one. Robert Watson refers to it as an office under siege and notes that every first lady has attracted criticism.[1] Paradoxes concerning the position abound. She holds an office to which she has not been elected and that she is not paid to occupy. Yet clearly much is expected of her in the way of duties. She is expected to fill the traditional female roles. She should be attractive and well dressed, with every hair in place, but she should not appear extravagant or obsessed with her appearance. She must be the perfect wife and mother, endlessly supportive and sacrificing. She must be knowledgeable and intelligent about public affairs, but at the same time she should not be too obtrusive in her influence. She must be active in pursuit of social causes but should not be seen to be making policy. She must be the perfect hostess. The first lady walks a tightrope between being too aggressive and not doing enough. When Betty Ford expressed her own views on such issues as premarital sex, a Texan told her that she was "not an individual. You are, because of the position your husband has assumed, expected and officially required to be PERFECT!"[2]

Although there has always been confusion and controversy over the first lady's role, in previous eras acceptable behavior was consistent with conceptions of the proper role of women within the public and private spheres. In the twentieth century, however, a number of changes have occurred affecting views of women's social roles, beginning with their enfranchisement and continuing through the feminist movements of the 1960s and after. Cultural change concerning the expectations of women has made the role of the first lady even more ambiguous. First ladies during this transition find themselves in a more difficult situation than did their predecessors. Although all the more recent first ladies have retained considerable popularity with the general public, they also have been subjected to extensive criticism from both the media and from spokespeople on both sides of the political spectrum. This essay will examine the expectations concerning the proper role for recent first ladies in light of changing cultural values and popular perceptions. The argument will be made that first ladies are particularly subject to public ambivalence concerning the balancing of women's private and public roles. As Gil Troy notes, conservatives expect the first lady to mind her own business, while many feminists do not want women attaining power through their spouses.[3] For example, traditionalists saw Hillary Clinton as a threat to the family, while feminists criticized Clinton for abandoning a promising New York–Washington legal career to follow her husband to Arkansas.[4] Discussion is divided into three sections. Topics explored in the first section include the "public/private distinction," recent blurring of the boundaries between what is considered public and what is considered private, and what this has to do with the position and role of women. Today the meanings of "public" and "private" are "undergoing such rapid change that many people find it difficult to determine exactly what is expected of anyone in any realm, public or private."[5] This is especially true of first ladies, who find themselves in a public role as a result of their private position.[6] The second section includes discussion of changes that have occurred in American culture and the resulting ambivalence that surrounds women's roles. The final section will explore how this ambivalence affects first ladies and under what circumstances they are most likely to avoid criticism.

THE PUBLIC/PRIVATE DISTINCTION

As many people have described it, the public/private distinction, or dichotomy, is complicated, complex, and controversial.[7] Traditionally much of Western political thought has focused on "the public," to the exclusion of "the private." Liberalism sets up a barrier between the public and private spheres and establishes rights only within the public sphere. As Martin Köhler puts it, "The term 'public sphere' denotes not so much a theoretically coherent concept as an organizing principle for the legitimacy of political order. . . . Within this historical understanding, it is the function of the public sphere to articulate and aggregate social demands."[8]

The public was considered the life of politics and the marketplace; the private was the domestic life of the family. The sphere of the political public is seen as different from the sphere of the nonpolitical private.[9] Frances Olsen notes that two important private/public dichotomies are the state/civil society dichotomy and the family/market dichotomy.[10] The state/civil society dichotomy distinguishes the state from the remainder of society and public or state action from the actions of private individuals and nongovernmental actors. This means of delineating spheres of activity is not neutral. As Donna Sullivan points out: "The demarcation of public and private life within society is an inherently political process, that both reflects and reinforces power relations, especially the power relations of gender, race, and class. . . . Economic, social, and political power inheres in the public realm, to which women have limited access and over which they have limited control."[11] Obviously this distinction has implications beyond gender, but certainly one effect has been to exclude women from civil and political life. As Susan Moller Okin writes, "Anglo-American theories of justice were to a great extent about men with wives at home."[12]

The second dichotomy identified by Olsen, the family/market distinction, also is important to women. Productive life occurs in the marketplace. The home is the locus of private, affective life where marital relations and child rearing occur. Lesser value is assigned to activities occurring in the private sphere.[13] The family was idealized and was considered "the place of peace; the shelter, not only from all injury, but from all terror, doubt, and division."[14] Marriage and the family were assumed to be self-regulating, not subject to state regulation. Theorists either relied on "love, altruism and generosity" as the foundation of family relations or simply assumed that the institution of the family was just, without examining it further.[15] The state, the site of public decision making, was and is dominated by men. Liberalism views the law as a means of regulating state intervention in private life.[16] In mainstream political theory, family matters were relegated to the private sphere, and women's activities were either invisible or marginalized.

To give an example of just how marginalized women were, Carolyn Heilbrun quotes from an 1854 pamphlet by Barbara Leigh Smith Bodichon entitled *Married Women and the Law*:

A man and wife are one person in law; the wife loses all her rights as a single woman, and her existence is entirely absorbed in that of her husband. He is civilly responsible for her acts; she lives under his protection or cover, and her condition is called coverture.

A woman's body belongs to her husband; she is in his custody, and he can enforce his right by a writ of habeas corpus.

What was her personal property before marriage, such as money in hand, money at the bank, jewels, household goods, clothes, etc., becomes absolutely her husband's. And he may assign or dispose of them at his pleasure whether he and his wife live together or not.

A wife's chattels real (i.e., estates) become her husband's.

Neither the Courts of Common law nor Equity have any direct power to oblige a man to support his wife. . . .

The legal custody of children belongs to the father. During the life-time of a sane father, the mother has no rights over her children, except a limited power over infants, and the father may take them from her and dispose of them as he thinks fit.

A married woman cannot sue or be sued for contracts—nor can she enter into contracts except as the agent of her husband; that is to say, her word alone is not binding in law. . . .

A wife cannot bring actions unless the husband's name is joined.

A husband and wife cannot be found guilty of conspiracy, as that offence cannot be committed unless there are two persons.[17]

Heilbrun notes that for many years, for women, there was a certain similarity between marriage and death. "For the women before modern times marriage is, except in rare circumstances, a kind of death. It is the death of her individual identity, the death of her as a person under law."[18] Okin calls this "vulnerability by marriage"—women lose social and personal power simply by marrying.[19] Marriage was an acceptance of a life of marginality; "within the marriage plot women might only wait to be desired, to be wed, to be forgotten."[20]

However, while thinking in dichotomous terms (public or private) serves to simplify analysis, quite often theory and practice do not coincide. In liberal society, separating the public from the private and focusing only on the public has never described reality. As Hilary Charlesworth puts it, "The division into public and private spheres is not a simple, monolithic construct."[21] Indeed, one of the central questions addressed by feminist scholars is the relationship of the public to the private and the location of the boundary between them. The idea that "the personal is political" is one of the central tenets of feminism. But as Shelley Wright and other feminist scholars have pointed out, "the 'private' realm has never been free from 'public' regulation."[22] For example, there are laws regulating marriage, divorce, inheritance, social welfare, taxation, and the nature of deviance in such areas as, for example, sexual orientation, birth control, abortion, and pornography. As Okin writes, "To the extent that a more private, domestic sphere does exist, its very existence, the limits that define it, and the types of behavior that are acceptable and not acceptable within it all result from political decisions."[23] She continues that the issue is not whether but how the state intervenes: "The myth that state intervention in the family is an option allows those who support the status quo to call it 'nonintervention' and to label policies that would alter it—such as the provision of shelters for battered wives—'intervention.'"[24] As Shelley Wright puts it, "The 'private' is necessarily circumscribed by the 'public,' just as the 'public' realm is partially defined by those areas of 'private' rights which are excluded from it."[25] Karen Engle writes that focusing too much on public and private as a dichotomy excludes an important part of women's experiences. It ignores those parts of women's lives that figure into the "public," but it also assumes that the "private" is bad for women. "It fails to recognize that the private is a place where many have tried to be."[26] We all live in overlapping and multiple arenas; it is becoming increasingly difficult to make distinctions between public and private institutions, the state and civil society, domestic and international.

Mary Ann Tétreault's concept of metaspace might be helpful here. Tétreault writes that "the essence of meta-space is its character as a site of overlapping domains 'between' or 'beyond' spaces and places that we generally accept as unambiguously public or private. Meta-space refers not only to the concrete geographic—locations such as coffeehouses, mosques, classrooms, and shopping malls, each of which displays both public and private characteristics—but also to metaphors that describe similarly ambiguous social, political, and psychological milieu. Consequently meta-spaces sometimes are seen as part of the public sphere while at other times they are regarded as private."[27]

Tétreault writes that metaspace is the place where the boundaries between public and private shift to include or exclude specific activities that share the qualities of both; metaspace exists "in all areas of human interaction where dimensions of private and public space intersect or overlap, erasing actual though not ideological boundaries that separate life into public and private spheres."[28] She notes that the boundary moves according to what the individual intends to interpret as public or private at any particular time; metaspace is not a geographical analogy but a "process of contested interpretation."[29] Public and private spheres are not a simple construct but places of ambiguity and instability.[30]

CULTURAL CHANGE AND THE STATUS OF WOMEN

The twentieth century was a time of considerable cultural change in the United States. Culture interacts in a reciprocal fashion with political institutions and events and with economics. The increased role of the mass media in the lives of ordinary citizens, two world wars, and a major economic depression followed by a period of sustained prosperity, to name just a few influences, have contributed to profound changes in attitudes. Ronald Inglehart argues that as a result of the rapid economic development and the expansion of the welfare state following World War II, young people have had fundamentally different experiences than previous generations had.[31] Daniel Yankelovich notes the influence of sustained affluence on culture.[32] He catalogs a variety of ways that culture in the United States has changed, for example, an increased emphasis on self-fulfillment and expressing individualism, a broadened definition of the family, and belief in sharing family responsibilities between both partners.

These analysts have asserted that the diminution of the threat of severe economic deprivation has resulted in a shift from values emphasizing economic and physical security to those that emphasize self-expression and the quality of life. Included in these values are a declining confidence in religious and other traditional authorities and an increasing tolerance for diverse lifestyles. A shift in attitudes toward gender roles has been one component of this changing value set.

Changing attitudes toward women have also been affected by the women's movements that began in the nineteenth century. The fight for suffrage led early by Susan B. Anthony and Elizabeth Cady Stanton and later by Anna Howard Shaw and Carrie Chapman Catt reached a successful conclusion with the passage of the Nineteenth Amendment to the U.S. Constitution in 1920. In 1949 Simone de Beauvoir's work *The Second Sex* argued that liberation for women would liberate men as well. Her book became an international best-seller. In the 1960s and 1970s Bella Abzug, Betty Friedan, and Gloria Steinem led the fight for the Equal Rights Amendment and for a change in attitudes toward women. The prevailing stereotype of women as passive, delicate individuals who were unsuited to participation in the public realm of politics and work was gradually replaced as more women entered the workplace.

Social science surveys support a change in cultural attitudes toward the role of women in society. The General Social Survey has featured a series of questions concerning the role of women. One question that has been asked repeatedly is: Do you approve or disapprove of a married woman earning money in business or industry if she has a husband capable of supporting her? From 1972 to 1998 there has been a steady increase in the percent that approve and an accompanying decline in those who disapprove of women working outside the home. Slightly more than a third of respondents in 1972 (34.6 percent) opposed employment for women with husbands to support them. By 1998 this number had shrunk to 17.5 percent.

Other questions relating to women in public life and particularly in politics have been asked over time and with similar results. The proportion of the public who would support a qualified woman candidate for president has increased from 73.6 percent to 90.2 percent. Meanwhile the number who argue that everyone would be better off if women stayed home and left running the country to men dropped by 20.2 percent from 1974 to 1994.[33]

At the same time that public opinion shows increasing support for equal treatment of women, ambivalence concerning gender roles remains. In 1998, 21.6 percent agreed that men are better suited emotionally for politics than women, and although in 1998 there was solid support for women working outside the home, a substantial minority (34 percent) expressed the view that families are better off when the men are the achievers outside the home and the women remain in the home to care for family members. Twenty-nine percent agree (and another 18 percent neither agree nor disagree) that family life suffers when the woman has a full-time job. Inglehart argues that even as the economic and social functions of the family have been eroded, the emphasis on the psychological role of the family has received greater emphasis.[34] The family is seen as a key agent in promoting love and self-esteem, values highly prized in the postmaterialist culture. On the one hand are the cultural changes that favor women's entry into the public world, namely the erosion of traditional authority and an emphasis on self-fulfillment. Women are perceived as deserving the same opportunities as men to pursue careers and self-actualization and are no longer seen as the property of men. However, on the other hand there is an emphasis on the family as the locus for promoting psychological well-being—much more difficult to achieve when both parents are busy pursuing careers. In 1994, 54.7 percent of respondents in the General Social Survey believed that a woman with children under school age should not work outside the home.

GENDER ROLES AND FIRST LADIES

One would expect the increasing support for women in the public sphere to apply to the role of first lady. In fact by 1987–88 the press seemed confident of impending changes in the first ladyship. *U.S. News and World Report* noted that the candidates' wives were notable for their achievements outside of marriage and that the public was increasingly aware that in electing a president they were choosing a team.[35] *Ms.* magazine noted that Nancy Reagan would probably be the last first lady for whom being the president's wife was her ultimate achievement.[36] The new first lady was expected to reflect the trend of women pursuing careers of their own and working outside the home. Yet the next first lady, Barbara Bush, was a career homemaker who was seen as deferential, unassuming, and apolitical. That she has been one of our most popular first ladies suggests that attitudes toward the status of women have not changed quite so much as some thought.

In regard to the first lady there is still a dichotomy between public and private spheres. People expect her public actions to be consistent with her private role. Major expectations revolve around responsibilities in four different but related areas. These include supporting and nurturing her husband, the president; choosing public causes that are "appropriately" women's concerns; not trespassing the boundary between her private role and policy making; and fulfilling the idealized image of traditional womanhood most notably by not expressing controversial opinions and by being a good homemaker.

Nurturing and Supporting the President

First ladies usually receive their best press coverage for actions viewed as supportive of their husbands. Although she was sometimes criticized for her overly adoring attitude, Nancy Reagan received considerable sympathy and her image was improved by her devotion to her husband after he was shot and during his bout with cancer. She was seen as fiercely protective of her husband and fiercely devoted. She noted, "I'm a woman who loves her husband and I make no apologies for looking out for his personal and political welfare. We have a genuine sharing marriage. I go to his aid. He comes to mine."[37]

First ladies generally agree that this is their most important role. Lady Bird Johnson said, "It's up to you [the first lady] to create a zone of peace, of comfort, within the White House where your husband can regain his equilibrium, restore his spirit."[38] Hillary Clinton observed, "It's more than being a political partner. I don't think there's any job like it in the world. You have to be a partner in the fullest sense of the word—someone who's trying to support the President in a personal way that's not available to him elsewhere."[39] Jackie Kennedy noted that her main role was to "take care of the president."[40]

Lady Bird was praised for being a good wife, while Eleanor Roosevelt was criticized for not being supportive enough. Eleanor's son described the Roosevelts' relationship as an armed truce that endured until FDR died. Ultimately, while Eleanor is praised for many of her actions as first lady, she receives low marks as a wife.[41]

Boundary Trespass

At the same time that she is to support her husband, the first lady must not overshadow him. Although not expected to be passive, she is expected to take an active role during her tenure as first lady, and first ladies who failed to do what was expected of them have been criticized. President Andrew Johnson's wife, Eliza, received visitors only twice in four years. Jackie Kennedy hated the title first lady and forbade her staff to use the term.[42] She made it a point to do little of what was expected of her and was often absent from the White House. She argued that her duties to her children came first, but her husband was often embarrassed by her failure to attend functions. In contrast, Dolley Madison, seen as a great asset to her husband, disavowed any interest in politics and noted that she cared only about people. Nevertheless her abilities as a hostess were seen as crucial at times to her husband's success. She and other political wives have advanced their husbands' careers by pursuing social connections.[43]

First ladies have attracted their greatest negative publicity when they have trespassed into areas viewed as inappropriate. As Karen O'Connor, Bernadette Nye, and Laura Van Assendelft note, any first lady who goes beyond what the public or the press considers an appropriate role for women suffers.[44] Our most recent example is that of Hillary Rodham Clinton in her role as chair of the President's Task Force on National Health Care Reform. Not only was she severely criticized in the media, but she was even taken to court for the way in which she carried out this role. The case concerned whether meetings of the health care task force should be opened to the public. The Federal Advisory Committee Act (FACA) requires that meetings must be open to the public unless all the members of the committee are U.S. government officials. The key issue was whether the first lady was a government official or a private citizen. The lower court ruled that she was a private citizen, but the appeals court reversed this ruling, arguing that the first lady is a "full-time officer or employee of the government" because of the services she performs for the president.[45] Throughout Clinton's tenure as first lady, a sizable proportion of the population felt that she had too much influence in the administration. Between January 1993 and January 1997 disapproval of her influence ranged from a low of 37 percent to a high of 53 percent. She was criticized as a copresident and for using the term "we" when referring to herself and her husband. In response to this criticism Clinton sought to redefine herself as a benign spokesperson for women and children as her husband's term continued.[46]

Clinton was hardly the first to be criticized for undue influence.

Abigail Adams's enemies called her the presidentress. Mary Todd Lincoln was called Mrs. President by the men around her husband who resented her attempts at influence. Nancy Reagan was referred to as the dragon lady. Rosalynn Carter was labeled a steel magnolia.

Although Nancy Reagan was admired for protecting her husband, she was vilified for interfering with his staff. She was blamed for the firing of Don Regan during the Iran-Contra controversy. Her main image during this period was of "a pushy harpy who participates inappropriately in her husband's job."[47] Regan's subsequent book portrayed Nancy Reagan as a skilled political infighter who engineered his dismissal.

Rosalynn Carter was criticized for sitting in on and taking notes during cabinet meetings and for allowing her young daughter to attend state dinners (Amy was ten when her father became president). As Rosalynn's image as presidential partner grew, it caused problems. Troy notes, "It made Jimmy appear too weak, Rosalyn[n] too aggressive."[48] In contrast, Barbara Bush was careful to exercise influence discreetly and hence was not viewed as overstepping the boundaries prescribed by the office of first lady. In fact, her selection to give the commencement address at Wellesley was criticized by some students on the grounds that she had achieved nothing on her own. In her address she defended women who had chosen to stay home and tend to their families.

Issues

Because first ladies are expected to be active and yet not overstep the boundaries between appropriate and inappropriate behavior, they must choose the issues they champion with care. The days when a first lady, for example Dolley Madison, could be expected to contribute to her husband's career primarily in her role as hostess are over. The first lady is expected to choose a substantive issue or cause with which to associate herself. However, that cause must be appropriately feminine, should not be controversial, and ideally should revolve around traditional female concerns such as the family, the home, or aesthetics. Lady Bird Johnson's involvement with highway beautification appealed to her constituency, women involved in their communities. She considered using other terms, but the word "beautification" was chosen; as Troy argues, "It was punchier, yet more feminine than its clinical-sounding rivals."[49] Although Johnson's involvement with the Highway Beautification Act had clear policy implications, her image as a southern lady helped her avoid widespread criticism. When Richard Nixon was elected to the presidency, Pat Nixon abandoned her earlier involvement with job training and welfare and took up volunteerism. Barbara Bush espoused the cause of family literacy. "Long before family values became a campaign war cry, she believed that if more people could read and write there would be fewer problems with drugs and violence and unwanted pregnancies."[50]

The first lady is expected to work for an appropriate cause in the same way that socially prominent women have long been expected to take part in volunteer work and charity fund-raising. Nancy Reagan's early image was that of socialite, out of touch with ordinary Americans, who attended glitzy parties and associated with the wealthy. Once she took up her "Just Say No" campaign, her popularity increased significantly, particularly as the campaign was judged effective—drug use dropped during this time.

In contrast, Hillary Rodham Clinton's involvement in health care policy was seen as crossing a line. Instead of advocating a cause, she was directly involved in policy making. Since she had not been elected to or formally installed in public office, her actions were viewed by many as inappropriate and her influence on policy was seen as too great. In response, Clinton later associated herself with less controversial issues such as women's health and child rearing.[51] Like Hillary Clinton, first lady Eleanor Roosevelt was called an instigator for her effect on public policy. However, unlike Mrs. Clinton, Mrs. Roosevelt often acted on issues without her husband's endorsement or encouragement, and she had her own independent agenda. She is viewed today independently of her husband, particularly as she remained politically active after FDR died. As U.S. delegate to the United Nations, she was deeply involved in the drafting of the Universal Declaration of Human Rights. With her election to the U.S. Senate, Hillary Clinton's post–White House life also may eventually overshadow her tenure as first lady.

Image

The first lady is expected to fulfill the traditional images of womanhood. She should be a devoted wife and mother for whom family comes first. Jackie Kennedy agreed with this conception when she said, "If you bungle raising your children, I don't think whatever else you do matters much."[52]

Not only does the public appear to desire this role for the first lady, quite often their husbands do also. Examples abound—Calvin Coolidge, John Kennedy, Dwight Eisenhower, Herbert Hoover, Richard Nixon. From the beginning of their marriage, Calvin and Grace Coolidge agreed that they would operate in two separate spheres, with Lou running the household and Calvin serving as breadwinner. John Kennedy had to be persuaded to allow Jackie even to redecorate the White House. Pat Nixon noted that Richard Nixon never asked her opinion on anything.

One indicator of the extent to which the role of devoted parent is valued publicly is that in the midst of all the controversy surrounding the Clintons, they were consistently praised for their devotion to their daughter, Chelsea. Their requests for privacy concerning her were respected. Hillary enjoyed a close relationship with her daughter and was known to put business aside to attend Chelsea's school activities. They also vacationed together and both wrote and telephoned each other frequently when apart.

First ladies are criticized when they are seen as neglecting family duties. When Rosalynn Carter was on the campaign trail, she was criticized for leaving Amy behind with relatives. During the campaign in 1992 Hillary Clinton caused controversy when she noted that she was not the kind of woman who stayed home to bake cookies. Later, sensitive to the controversy she had created, she took part in a cookie-baking contest sponsored by a popular women's magazine. Notably, while the cookie comment contributed to a negative image for Clinton, her popularity ratings soared when Bill Clinton was accused of sexual involvement with Monica Lewinsky. Clinton gained sympathy from the public for standing by her man. In fact, during that time her approval ratings were higher than her husband's.

What many people do not realize is that none of this is new. Over one hundred years ago cookies were not the controversial issue, but butter was. The wife of presidential candidate Henry Clay was praised for being a model wife who could make butter. Sarah Polk noted that if her husband were elected, she would "neither keep house nor make butter."[53]

Keeping a good house was not the only controversy to plague Hillary Clinton. Many viewed keeping her maiden name as inappropriate. "I kept my maiden name. You would have thought that I had decided to do some terrible deed equivalent to killing the firstborn," she commented.[54] Twenty-one percent of the public thought that it was a bad idea for the first lady to refer to herself as Hillary Rodham Clinton.[55]

An important part of the feminine image is to avoid controversy. The perfect first lady is apolitical and nonassertive. When Betty Ford gave her opinion on premarital sex and abortion, she was pilloried in the media. The resulting criticism caused a later first lady, Barbara Bush, to conceal that her views on abortion differed from her husband's. In contrast, when Betty Ford and Nancy Reagan were forthright about their battles with breast cancer, there was a groundswell of public support and sympathy.

A first lady's actions will be judged in relation to her image. Rosalynn Carter, viewed by many as having too much influence in her husband's administration, was criticized when she journeyed to Latin America on Jimmy's behalf. Columnists Meg Greenfield and Bob Wiedrich accused her of conducting diplomacy without constitutional authority.[56] Meanwhile, Pat Nixon, who was seen as unassuming, received praise for similarly representing her husband abroad.

At the same time that first ladies must adhere to a traditional feminine image, they must be careful to avoid negative female images, as these may reflect poorly on their husbands. For example, they should not be spendthrifts or flighty, particularly if they are seen as influential. Not only did Nancy Reagan attract bad publicity for her habit of borrowing expensive designer gowns and for buying expensive china at a time of economic distress, but she also received considerable negative coverage in the media for her reliance on astrologers. During this controversy the number of people believing that she had too much influence on the president rose to 43 percent and the president's overall job approval rating declined. Any number of factors may have influenced this approval rating, but there is evidence that some members of the public were affected by the negative publicity generated by the first lady's actions.[57]

CONCLUSION

While there is no longer an evident dichotomy between the public and private spheres with women relegated to the private sphere, the American public is not yet certain what gender roles are to be. U.S. first ladies find themselves in a difficult position largely because of the circumstances behind their prominence. Two factors are important here. First, the first lady enters the public political realm because of her private role as wife. Carolyn Heilbrun quotes Heywood as writing over four hundred years ago that "wedding is destiny, and hanging likewise"—i.e., weddings, like hangings, were the end of experience.[58] Heilbrun notes that few works of fiction make marriage their central concern. "The heroine who becomes a bride, and eventually, one assumes, a mother, on the last page of a romance, has accommodated herself to the cyclical movement: by her marriage . . . she completes the cycle and passes out of the story."[59]

In a sense the first lady's existence as a separate individual ends at her marriage, but it is precisely because of their marriages that the public is interested in first ladies. First ladies rise to prominence not because of any accomplishments of their own, but rather because of whom they married. As Margaret Truman wrote, "No matter how political she becomes, the First Lady will always be a woman, married to a specific man."[60] Her existence, and our interest in her, is anchored in another person. As such her actions are judged in that light. She is evaluated as a domestic partner at the same time that she is judged as a public figure. It is inevitable, then, that she will be expected to adhere to standards for women that would normally be associated with an earlier era—namely those concerning women's roles as wives and mothers.

A second important factor is that a first lady's situation is made all the worse by the absence of any clearly defined formal role. The Constitution specifies clearly the duties of the president but makes no mention of the first lady. She does not have formal duties associated with her office and is not paid for her activities.

Watson notes that while Hillary Clinton's activism was not new, it stirred debate. She put a face to questions such as how society views women in public life, what the balance is between career and family, and other issues concerning the meaning of feminism.[61] According to Edith Mayo, "It is disheartening to find that virtually every First Lady who has used her influence has been either ridiculed or vilified as deviating from women's proper role or has been feared as emasculating."[62]

The quote by Rosalynn Carter that begins this essay was chosen because she expresses well the tension and ambiguity in perceptions of the first lady. Carter is correct in noting that the public wants women to have opportunities outside the home and to have their own careers. Yet she notes that first ladies are criticized for expressing their individuality and for trying to achieve on their own terms. This seeming inconsistency could be explained by the particular situation within which each first lady emerges into the public sphere. She is judged first and foremost as a wife because she is first and foremost a wife. And while the public supports equality for women in the abstract, when conflicts between that independence and the home are perceived, many tend to resolve those conflicts in favor of preserving home and family at the expense of women's independence. Although many women have escaped the public/private dichotomy to take up active and respected roles in the public sphere, the first lady remains locked in a sort of cultural limbo. This is reflected most recently in a statement by Laura Bush. When asked what expectations the American people have of her, she said, "I don't know that. I don't have any idea."[63] This cultural limbo will continue until such time as a woman is elected president and talk will be not of first ladies but of first spouses.

NOTES

1. Robert Watson, *The Presidents' Wives: Reassessing the Office of the First Lady* (Boulder, Colo.: Lynne Rienner, 2000), 34.

2. Margaret Truman, *First Ladies: An Intimate Group Portrait of White House Wives* (New York: Random House, 1995), 138.

3. Gil Troy, "Mr. and Mrs. President? The Rise and Fall of the Co-Presidency," *The Social Science Journal* 37 (Oct. 2000): 4.

4. Robert P. Watson, "A Review Essay: Hillary's Legacy? Recent Literature on the First Ladies," *The Social Science Journal* 37 (Oct. 2000): 4.

5. Mary Ann Tétreault, "Frontier Politics: Sex, Gender, and the Destruction of the Public Sphere," *Alternatives* 26 (Mar. 2001): 53–72.

6. As Hillary Rodham Clinton once said, "I like having a role as a private citizen making a public contribution," quoted in Donnie Radcliffe, *Hillary Rodham Clinton: A First Lady for Our Time* (New York: Time Warner Books, 1993), 216.

7. Kay Knickrehm and Robin Teske, "Attitudes toward Domestic Violence among Romanian and U.S. University Students: A Cross-Cultural Comparison," *Women and Politics* 21 (2000): 34–39. Part of the discussion here is taken from this article.

8. Daniele Archibugi, David Held, and Martin Köhler, eds., *Re-imagining Political Community: Studies in Cosmopolitan Democracy* (Stanford, Calif.: Stanford University Press, 1998), 236.

9. Ibid., 237.

10. Frances Olsen, "International Law: Feminist Critiques of the Public/Private Distinction," in *Reconceiving Reality: Women and International Law*, ed. Dorinda G. Dallmeyer (Washington, D.C.: American Society of International Law, 1993), 157.

11. Donna Sullivan, "The Public/Private Distinction in International Human Rights Law," in *Women's Rights, Human Rights: International Feminist Perspectives*, ed. Julie Peters and Andrea Wolper (New York: Routledge, 1995), 128.

12. Susan Moller Okin, *Justice, Gender, and the Family* (New York: Basic Books, Inc., 1989), 110, 8–9.

13. Olsen, "International Law," 158–59.

14. Okin, *Justice,* 30.

15. Ibid., 19, 116.

16. Shelley Wright, "Economic Rights, Social Justice and the State: A Feminist Reappraisal," in *Reconceiving Reality: Women and International Law,* ed. Dorinda G. Dallmeyer (Washington, D.C.: American Society of International Law, 1993), 127–28.

17. Carolyn G. Heilbrun, *Writing a Woman's Life* (New York: Ballantine Books, 1988), 85.

18. Heilbrun, *Hamlet's Mother and Other Women* (New York: Ballantine Books, 1990), 147.

19. Okin, *Justice,* chap. 7, quoted in Tétreault, "Frontier Politics." Attitudes on this point may not have changed much. Tétreault offers a reminder of the 1998 Southern Baptist Convention resolution that wives should submit graciously to their husbands.

20. Heilbrun, *Hamlet's Mother,* 127.

21. As quoted in Karen Engle, "After the Collapse of the Public/Private Distinction: Strategizing Women's Rights," in *Reconceiving Reality: Women and International Law,* ed. Dorinda G. Dallmeyer (Washington, D.C.: American Society of International Law, 1993), 152–53.

22. Wright, "Economic Rights," 121.

23. Okin, *Justice,* 129–31.

24. Ibid., 131.

25. As quoted in Olsen, "International Law," 163.

26. Engle, "After the Collapse," 146.

27. Tétreault, "Frontier Politics."

28. Mary Ann Tétreault, "Formal Politics, Meta-Space, and the Gendered Construction of Civil Life," in *Philosophy and Geography II: The Production of Public Space,* ed. Andrew Light and Jonathan M. Smith (Lanham, Md.: Rowman and Littlefield, 1998), 81–97.

29. Ibid.

30. Engle, "After the Collapse," 152–53; Olsen, "International Law," 164.

31. Ronald Inglehart, *Modernization and Postmodernization: Cultural, Economic, and Political Change in 43 Societies* (Princeton, N.J.: Princeton University Press, 1997).

32. Daniel Yankelovich, "How Changes in the Economy Are Reshaping American Values," in *Values and Public Policy,* ed. Henry Aaron, Thomas Mann, and Timothy Taylor (Washington, D.C.: Brookings Institution, 1994), 16–53.

33. In 1974, 34.3 percent agreed that the country would be better off if women stayed home and left running the country to men. In 1994 only 14.1 percent agreed.

34. Inglehart, *Modernization.*

35. Rainie Harrison, "The Other Hot Race for the White House," *U.S. News and World Report* 103 (Sept. 1987): 34–36.

36. "Stargazing," *Ms.* 17 (July 1988): 66.

37. Quoted in Troy, "Mr. and Mrs. President," 4.

38. Truman, *First Ladies,* 13.

39. Ibid., 332.

40. Kristen Rae Paynter, "The Evolution of the First Lady" (B.H. honors thesis, James Madison University, 2000), 31. See also *Association of American Physicians and Surgeons, Inc., et al. v Hillary Rodham Clinton et al.*

41. Marine H. Beasley, Holly C. Shulman, and Henry R. Beasley, *The Eleanor Roosevelt Encyclopedia* (Westport, Conn.: Greenwood Press, 2001), 323–27.

42. Thomas E. Cronin and Michael A. Genovese, *The Paradoxes of the American Presidency* (New York: Oxford University Press, 1998), 299.

43. Watson, "Review Essay," 654; Jay Tolson, "First among Ladies," *U.S. News and World Report* 130 (15 Jan. 2001): 38.

44. Karen O'Connor, Bernadette Nye, and Laura Van Assendelft, "Wives in the White House: The Political Influence of First Ladies," *Presidential Studies Quarterly* 26 (summer 1997): 835–53.

45. Paynter, "Evolution," 71–72.

46. O'Connor et al., "Wives," 848.

47. Linda Marie Delloff, "Irangate: Stereotypes as Side Effects," *The Christian Century* 104 (Mar. 1978):18–25.

48. Troy, "Mr. and Mrs. President," 593.

49. Gil Troy, *Affairs of State: The Rise and Rejection of the Presidential Couple Since World War II* (New York: The Free Press, 1997), 153.

50. Radcliffe, *Hillary Rodham Clinton,* 248.

51. O'Connor et al., "Wives," 847.

52. Paynter, "Evolution," 31.

53. Truman, *First Ladies,* 98–99.

54. Radcliffe, *Hillary Rodham Clinton,* 177.

55. *Gallup Poll Monthly* (Feb. 1993).

56. Gary D. Wekkin, "Role Constraints and First Ladies," *The Social Science Journal* 37 (Oct. 2000): 4.

57. Watson, *Presidents' Wives,* 144, 152, 156–57.

58. Heilbrun, *Hamlet's Mother,* 131. It is interesting to note that Nancy Reagan has been widely quoted as saying, "My life began when I met my husband"; see Truman, *First Ladies,* 162.

59. Heilbrun, *Writing a Woman's Life,* 86.

60. Truman, *First Ladies,* 14.

61. Watson, "Review Essay," 655.

62. Edith Mayo quoted in Cronin and Genovese, *Paradoxes,* 300.

63. Ann Gerhart, "Learning to Read Laura Bush," *Washington Post,* 22 Mar. 2001, C1.

TWELVE

Copresident or Codependent?

The Rise and Rejection of Presidential Couples
since World War II

GIL TROY

INTRODUCTION

Americans of all political parties have followed the scandals of presidents and first ladies, some criticizing and others pitying them. One first couple appeared to pity themselves, talking about the unfair standards imposed on them. In another case the second-term mandate withered away amid daily headlines bemoaning the president's assault on the dignity of his office and condemning the first couple for "lower[ing] the standard of good taste, which we American people have a right to expect from the family who represents our great country to every other country in the world."[1]

Life as a U.S. first couple could not be easy. During past presidential administrations the media justified gossiping about a first couple's marriage by claiming to open some Freudian window into the soul of the most powerful man in the world. Wags chuckled about a president's supposed affair with an aide. In one case the West Wing staff prepared a mock briefing paper prepping the president for a meeting with his jealous wife "to try to explain" a photograph "showing you about to give an enthusiastic kiss to an attractive young lady member of the Longview rangerettes"; the three "talking points" were "Yes dear," "Yes dear," and "Yes dear."[2] It seemed, in fact, that whatever normal marital tensions the various presidents and first ladies have faced were often exacerbated by having dueling palace guards, some devoted to him and some devoted to her.

While the president may have the toughest job in America, the first lady clearly has the toughest undefined, unsalaried position in the world. After all, there is no constitutional mandate for the position, and the title itself is an improvisation. For instance, in mid-October 1945 the first lady received a letter from Los Angeles begging, "I do hope that you as our First Lady will take some sort of a stand politically or as a human individual. A woman in your position can be a positive example to this world, if she so desires."[3] Just four days earlier a letter received from a Rochester, Minnesota, woman had approved the same first lady's homemaker incarnation, saying, "We are so proud that you are an example of a good wife, mother, and hostess for the Nation. We do not want a First Lady who gets into every issue that arises from the many groups of thought in the nation."[4]

Another first lady wanted to be constructive, as she tried to fulfill her campaign vow to make health care more just. Alas, the post–Robert Kennedy antinepotism law barring a public official from appointing close relatives, even if they received no pay, complicated her attempts to run the task force. As a way around the law, the Justice Department's Office of Legal Counsel suggested that she take the role of honorary chair and therefore remain "sufficiently removed from the commission's official function." She should "avoid being the moving force" but could attend hearings, submit her ideas, offer her support, and solicit support from others.[5] This was unsuccessful, and many wondered why the first lady bothered to play an active role. For all her attempts to be substantive, the mail told what Americans valued most in a first lady. Christmas cards, birthday wishes, and pleas for photographs and personal blessings came in by the thousands. Requests for help with various personal and bureaucratic problems came in by the hundreds. Issue-oriented letters came in only by the dozens. Less than a fifth of the 428,282 letters delivered in four years addressed issues, and barely 5 percent concerned the health crusade.[6] No wonder she said, privately, "I could stay here and pour tea and entertain the guests all day and I would be criticized."[7]

In addition to being terrorized by such mixed messages, a first lady is also the lightning rod for the president. Critics justified even shrill attacks because the "ears" of the president and his wife "are somewhat isolated from expressions of what the people really feel."[8] The many cartoons picturing, for example, a first lady brandishing a sword to protect her husband while he shuffled off to bed, or holding cue cards as he delivered a speech, or wearing her husband's pants, and so on suggests how unnaturally society has viewed women who wielded the kind of power traditionally held by men.

At one Washington gala a ventriloquist had his dummy point toward the presidential couple. The dummy asked, "Do you know who that is?" The ventriloquist responded, "The Leader of the Free World," to which the "dummy" added, "and she brought her husband."[9] The president, of course, attacked the "despicable fiction" that his wife was "running the government."[10] The first lady found many of the criticisms sexist. When Phil Donahue convened a panel of experts who condemned her, she harrumphed that none of the panelists was a woman.[11]

Remarkably, none of the preceding passages has anything to do with Bill and Hillary Clinton; all refer to their predecessors. The self-pitying couple struggling with scandal was the Nixons. The undignified couple was the Kennedys; he was being attacked for "lowering the dignity of his office by submitting to interviews in the White House on television programs that are commercially sponsored," and she for being featured on the cover of *Modern Romance* with the caption, "How Jackie Kennedy Fell in Love."[12] The tryst rumor concerned George Bush. The jealous wife was Betty Ford, although in every modern White House the East Wing and West Wing staffers have clashed. The conflicting letters were from October 1945 and were written to Bess Truman. Rosalynn Carter was the stymied health care reformer who was tempted simply to drink tea. The man justifying attacks on the first lady was Martin Luther King Jr. after the entertainer Eartha Kitt blasted Lyndon Johnson's Vietnam policy at a first lady's luncheon. Finally, the feminist first lady attacked and mocked for being powerful and defending the rights of all women to wield power was Nancy Reagan.

The story of Bill and Hillary Clinton in the White House reflects the rise and rejection of the presidential couple in the half-century since World War II. The first lady, in particular, is bound by her position's shackles—she is given extraordinary opportunities but also suffers from great, if often unstated, restrictions. When Hillary Clinton acted like a copresident, she was criticized—as Nancy Reagan, Rosalynn Carter, and Eleanor Roosevelt had been. When Hillary Clinton acted more traditionally, she was also criticized—as Barbara Bush, Jackie Kennedy, and Mamie Eisenhower had been. At the end of the day many Americans marveled at the mysteries of the Clintons' codependency. Scrutinized, analyzed, even brutalized by critics, Hillary Rodham Clinton, like her predecessors, experienced many White House days that were not easy.

The Clintons, along with every presidential couple since the Roosevelts, stood at an awkward crossroads where three central institutions clashed: the presidency, the quintessential American institution; marriage, the quintessential human institution; and the media, perhaps the most influential institution in America today. The story of ten couples and three critical institutions unfolds on two levels: the personal level in which presidents and first ladies lived their lives as couples inside the White House; and the public level, through the way the media conveyed and the public perceived those lives. The stories of the Trumans, the Eisenhowers, the Kennedys, and the Johnsons illustrate some of the forces that led to the rise of the presidential couple; the stories of the Nixons, the Fords, the Carters, and the Reagans help explain the rejection.

THE POST–WORLD WAR II WHITE HOUSE

In many ways the rise of the presidential couple was prefeminist. By 1960 the *Ladies' Home Journal* proclaimed: "Politics today is a husband-wife partnership."[13] Such cooperation was seen not as a mark of liberation but as an appropriate extension of wifely duties.

The ten presidential couples discussed need to be understood in context, as products of three distinct generations. The Clintons were the first of the baby-boomer generation to enter the White House. The World War I doughboy generation produced two presidential couples, the Trumans and the Eisenhowers. The most remarkable generation was the generation between those two, the "GI Joe" generation. This is represented by the fourteen White House occupants from 1961 through 1993, the Kennedys through the first Bushes. All were born in the first three decades of the twentieth century and married on the cusp of World War II. They were children of the Depression and war. The couple that married most recently of the seven was the Kennedys, who tied the knot in 1953, one year after the Reagans were married.

This was a generation raised on common ideals, united by dramatic experiences, mentored in many ways by one precedent-shattering and standard-setting presidential couple: Franklin Delano and Eleanor Roosevelt. Even if these individuals did not always do the right thing, they entertained few doubts about what the right thing to do was. These fourteen Americans—along with millions more—embarked on their lifetime marital adventures with detailed road maps uniquely committed to a vision of their country as a place of middle-class prosperity, genteel sensibilities, bourgeois morality, and democratic principles. Yet they presided over the nation as all those values were challenged.

Of course, yesteryear should not be romanticized. The lives of Harry and Bess Truman indicate that U.S. citizens of the previous generations experienced the gamut of what Americans now call "family dysfunction." However, the moral consensus let them cope with such traumas differently. Bess Wallace's father committed suicide when she was eighteen. Her traditional code of conduct taught her to manage her feelings in silence, rather than process them in public. The Trumans' daughter, Margaret, grew up thinking that her grandfather died of a heart attack.

While in the age of Oprah Winfrey keeping any such family secrets is condemned as repressive or stigmatizing, such silences worked for the Trumans. Their small-town discretion proved especially useful in the White House when the Trumans hid the fact that they were experiencing great marital strain. In fact, when Harry Truman was in Potsdam in 1945 helping to create the postwar world with Winston Churchill and Josef Stalin, he and Bess were squabbling. Bess "wasn't happy about my going to see Mr. Russia and Mr. Great Britain—neither am I," Truman noted in his diary.[14] After one tense phone call from Berlin, Germany, to Independence, Missouri, he confessed, "I spent the day . . . trying to think up reasons why I should bust up the conference and go home."[15]

The Trumans

Bess Truman entered the White House hostile to Washington life and committed to her privacy. Even then reporters' focus on the presidential couple was overwhelming. When Harry's mother visited from Missouri and saw the press hordes stampeding toward her at the airport, she yelled: "Harry, if you are President, why can't you shoo all these people away?"[16]

Especially after Franklin and Eleanor Roosevelt extended the federal government—and the presidency—into so many facets of American life, the Trumans would rarely have the tranquillity they craved. This became abundantly clear in October 1945 when the new congressman from Harlem, Adam Clayton Powell, blasted Bess Truman for agreeing to attend a Daughters of the American Revolution (DAR) tea. Powell's wife, the pianist Hazel Scott, had been barred because of her race from performing at the DAR's segregated Constitution Hall.

Bess sidestepped civil rights questions to defend her privacy and gentility. Of course, a lady never addressed the details of any unpleasantness directly. She told Powell "that the invitation to which you refer was extended and accepted prior to the unfortunate controversy which has arisen."[17] When Powell called Mrs. Truman "the last lady," Harry Truman exploded.[18] The salty but usually fair-minded Missourian, who integrated the armed forces with one pen stroke, blasted Powell in a staff meeting as "that damned nigger preacher."[19] Truman also barred Powell, a fellow Democrat, from the White House.

Unwittingly the Trumans had played into Powell's hand. They ignited a nationwide debate about segregation—and about the shifting boundaries between the presidential couple's private and public lives. Eleanor Roosevelt's fans, African Americans, World War II "widows," and northeastern ethnics, especially Jewish women, led the attack against Mrs. Truman for "failing to" uphold American "ideals."[20] By contrast, Bess Truman's most ardent defenders came from the South and the West. "Thank God for your . . . womanly attitude in being JUST THE WIFE of the President . . . and not trying to enter politics," a woman who was no fan of Eleanor Roosevelt's activism wrote.[21]

The Powell-Truman showdown served up a warning to all occupants of 1600 Pennsylvania Avenue. In the coming decades the first couples' personal examples would become more relevant as presidents tackled complex personal issues such as racial discrimination. Presidents and their wives could not crusade for freedom in public while perpetuating the problem in private. Nor could first ladies hide as easily behind a frilly veil of feminine prerogative to avoid the challenges of modern politics.

The Eisenhowers

The Eisenhowers also discovered that the job of the first couple was becoming more public and more complex. Mamie Eisenhower was uninterested in her husband's official tasks. "Ike runs the country, and I turn the lambchops," she would say.[22] During Dwight Eisenhower's eight years in the White House, Mamie entered the Oval Office only four times, "and each time I was invited," she boasted.[23]

Each day Mamie sent out dozens of frilly notes to her friends. Royalty came and went, and wars were declared and averted, but Mamie ignored them. "The latest news is that [grandson] David has lost his first tooth," she reported on 31 March 1954 as her husband faced an outcry over American hydrogen bomb tests and the Russians agitated in East Berlin.[24] Many of these were thank-you notes, as Mamie's social office was a clearinghouse for thousands of dollars' worth of goods rolling into the White House—Norwegian salmon, cases of scotch, heads of cattle for the Eisenhowers' Gettysburg farm. Most Americans delighted in this homage to a hero and did not see the ethical dilemmas their successors would see today.

Yet even Mamie, this happy 1950s homemaker, found herself in the eye of a public storm. Every week hundreds of widows, mothers, daughters, and grandmothers sent letters asking the first lady to help search for men who were missing in action, to increase their elderly mothers' public assistance, or to urge the continuation of rent control. Each request was duly forwarded to a government agency, many of which had not existed the last time Republicans ruled, including the Economic Stabilization Agency, the Selective Service

System, and the Federal Security Agency, to name a few. After two decades of Democratic rule and world war, Americans relied on the federal government in unprecedented ways. They turned to the first lady as first mother, a crucial ally in making the federal government more nurturing and more human.[25]

The Kennedys

The Eisenhowers and the Trumans are unfairly caricatured as passive and traditional in comparison to their predecessors, the Roosevelts, and their successors, the Kennedys. Jacqueline Kennedy proved just how formidable a popular first lady could be as a public relations asset. The Kennedys dazzled the world from the start of their magical thousand days in office. And after that awful day in November 1963 Jackie Kennedy almost singlehandedly created, then burnished, the Camelot myth—which was her phrase. It was arguably the most influential contribution of a first lady to modern American history.

Still the Kennedys mystify. How did they dazzle the world with this Camelot myth when the reality was so tawdry? Surprisingly, the Kennedys first doubted that Jackie would be a political asset. Jackie, said her husband, had too much status and not enough quo.[26] A picture in *Life* magazine of the thin, lithe debutante next to a rotund Democratic National Commiteewoman with floppy midwestern hat and cat's-eye glasses proved the dangers of letting Jackie loose on the public.[27]

Nevertheless, Jackie's celebrity buoyed her husband's political standing. In this new age of the televised celebrity presidency, the president's power base was shifting, thus making the first lady all the more important. Professor Richard Neustadt's thesis from this era that the power of the president is the power to persuade soon became outmoded. In the "celebridency" the power of the president is the power to entertain.[28]

The Johnsons

The Kennedys' successors, Lyndon and Lady Bird Johnson, had a deep political partnership. Their tenure in the White House shows how the rise of the presidential couple was rooted in the expansion of the "nanny state," the growth of the presidency, the politicization of the personal, the rise of the media, and the emergence of the celebrity presidency. All this came together in Lyndon Johnson's Great Society, of which Lady Bird's beautification crusade was a centerpiece. Beautification is unfairly remembered today as a frilly, feminine, prefeminist project dedicated to wisteria and wildflowers. In fact, it spurred the nascent environmental movement and cleverly domesticated and boosted the Johnsons' domestic agenda.

The Johnsons' experience, which was upended by the Vietnam War, also provides harbingers of the rejection of the presidential couple. Presidents and their wives would be challenged by the shattered consensus about marriage, the mixed messages and only partial successes of the feminist revolution, the overwhelming power of media in the television age, and the attendant ever-intensifying and trivializing scrutiny.

The trends and movements grossly summarized as the 1960s bedeviled the presidential couple. The job description of the political spouse—or any spouse—changed, especially among the nation's elite, which increasingly included reporters. What the historian John Demos calls the "anti-image" of the American family took hold.[29] Much of America's "chattering class" bought the feminist and countercultural argument that "the traditional family structure is not good for human beings."[30] For first ladies the pressure to take an active role was severe. Still, overall the message was clear: the American people wanted joint image making, not power sharing, in the White House.

The Nixons

In the 1950s Vice President Richard Nixon and his wife, Pat, were America's suburbanites in chief. Pat was named Outstanding Homemaker of the Year in 1953, Mother of the Year in 1955, and the "nation's ideal wife" by the Homemakers' Forum in 1957.[31] But by 1968 political spouses could no longer be benign. Pat's stamina, her self-sacrifice, and her poise now seemed to stem from "low self-esteem."[32] Mrs. Nixon became "Plastic Pat," the "tragic epitome of the captive political wife."[33] Wags joked that Mrs. Nixon traveled with her hairdresser and her embalmer. In criticizing the first lady, reporters also attacked the president. Had the marriage changed? Hardly; it was the 1952 Checker's speech that altered the protocols of the Nixon relationship, because the speech made Pat Nixon a recognizable public figure as the ideal housewife. From the 1950s to the late 1960s it was the values of the onlookers that changed most. Despite it all, Pat Nixon was popular with the masses.

The Fords

The gap between the media agenda and the American people became even clearer during the Ford administration. Thanks to her adoring press, most Americans fondly remember Betty Ford as a brash, zesty woman who faced her mastectomy courageously and helped ease the transition from the repressive 1950s to our more open era. Mrs. Ford was a media favorite when the media was growing ever stronger in the wake of Watergate.

The 1970s witnessed a dramatic shift in the media agenda, as reporters plunged ahead of the social curve. Encouraged by the new first lady and the sexual revolution, reporters posed questions they never had dared to ask before. A proposed interview with President Gerald Ford for *McCall's* illustrated just how "political" and "personal" questions had become. Winnie McLendon wanted to ask about hiring women in government, whether Mrs. Ford's feelings of worthlessness were "the very root of the women's movement," and then whether the president had ever been approached by "women attracted to men of power."[34]

While the president wisely avoided such inquiries, his wife was less discreet. A *Newsweek* cover story about the Fords quoted Betty Ford telling a friend, "I've been asked everything except how often I go to bed with my husband." Asking for trouble, she added, "If they had asked me, I would have told them." A week and a half later, when she used the same line on Myra MacPherson of the *Washington Post,* MacPherson asked, "What would you have said?" The sassy first lady replied, "As often as possible!"[35]

Such talk disgusted millions of Americans. As a result, Mrs. Ford's first ladyship helped derail her husband's presidency. Her blithe comments on *60 Minutes* that her children had probably tried marijuana and that she "wouldn't be surprised" if her eighteen-year-old daughter, Susan, had had "an affair" outraged the president's core constituents.[36]

More than thirty thousand letters reached the White House commenting on Mrs. Ford's *60 Minutes* remarks, with 23,308 letters "con" and 10,512 "pro."[37] It alienated the Republican conservative core in the South and the West just as Ronald Reagan was contemplating a presidential run against his fellow Republican Gerald Ford. "We think this error is much more serious than anything that President Nixon did," a southerner wrote Ford's campaign manager.[38] As one of Betty's critics wrote, "Your statements on 60 Minutes cost your husband my vote. . . . Until now I thought we had someone in the White House who thought along the same lines that I did."[39] On the other hand, Betty's fans tended to wish that she were running for president or that her husband were a Democrat, implying that she had earned their love if not their votes.

Jerry Ford's loss in 1976 by fewer than two million votes out of eighty million cast could easily have resulted from the backlash against Betty's candor. Millions of Americans did not want a first lady who sounded like the boozy wife who speaks the unspoken at her husband's office party.

The Carters

While the Fords illustrate the dangers of a first lady being too outspoken—even if she charms reporters—the Carters reflect the problems that arise when a first lady is too powerful—especially if the husband stumbles. At the height of the feminist revolution Americans seemed to have had the ideal egalitarian couple in the White House. The Carters worked and played together. Once a week they met for a working lunch, Rosalynn attended cabinet meetings, and the Carters loved to jog, play tennis, swim, and bowl together.

But Mrs. Carter's loyalty, selflessness, and humility were passé in the 1970s. Gloria Steinem fumed, "More than any other president's wife I have seen there is no independent thought or phrasing separate from him."[40] Frustrated by Rosalynn Carter's desire to help her husband however she could, reporters complained about the first lady's "fuzzy" image.[41] Rosalynn's predecessors, "whether or not they had an impact at least had a clear image." Jackie Kennedy renovated, Lady Bird Johnson beautified, Pat Nixon volunteered, and Betty Ford spoke out. "But when one mentions the name of Rosalynn Carter, many people draw a blank," reporters said, annoyed that they could not stereotype Mrs. Carter easily. The reporters wanted the first lady to be independent rather than loyal.[42]

Reporters were also uncomfortable because of Mrs. Carter's obvious discomfort with them. Especially at the start of the administration Jimmy was the media star. In December 1976 Barbara Walters interviewed the first-couple-to-be on ABC. The two were dressed casually and lounged on their living room couch in Plains, sitting side by side. Jimmy's right arm rested on the headrest behind his wife. They appeared open, with Jimmy protective of his wife. Jimmy's relaxed body language and his willingness to jump in and help Rosalynn deflect difficult questions underlined the political miracle he had just accomplished.[43]

In the White House, while her husband suffered and saw his hair turn gray and his face become lined, Rosalynn Carter flourished. She traded in her no-nonsense, polyester, drip-dry dresses for stylish outfits; her hair-spray helmet blossomed into a well-coiffed hairdo; her halting litany of "Jimmeh-thinks" and Jimmeh-says" became a smooth testimony to the Carters' joint accomplishments and loving partnership.

Rosalynn Carter's growing prominence in 1978 and 1979 made President Carter appear weak. "Goddam it. I voted for Carter, not his wife!" one businessman seethed.[44] By the fall of 1979 Jack Anderson's syndicated column declared, "The First Lady . . . is now co-president, with a tremendous impact on U.S. policy."[45]

This image was nothing but trouble, as it would be for Hillary Clinton two decades later. Americans were becoming used to strong women—if they remained unmarried. Four of the top ten television shows from 1979 to 1980 featured independent, sassy, and single women: *Three's Company, Alice, Flo,* and *One Day at a Time.* In a cover story on "The President's Partner," *Newsweek* asked whether "Lady Macbeth" lurked "beneath" Rosalynn's "soft voice."[46] The comparison conjured up a long line of powerful, seductive women back to Jezebel and Eve.

In a *60 Minutes* interview on the eve of the 1980 Democratic National Convention, the dynamic between the Carters had changed. Rosalynn Carter was pleased with herself and looked comfortable, stylish, and relaxed. Jimmy sulked. Rosalynn Carter acknowledged their competition when she admitted, "I don't like interviews with him where he does all the talking and I sit and look at him, . . . but when you ask me questions I enjoy that."[47] Now it seemed that Rosalynn, not Jimmy, was the star.

The Reagans

Ronald Reagan was always the star of his administration; it took his wife over a year to learn how to be an effective costar. Nancy Reagan cast herself as a traditional homemaker whose "life didn't really begin until I met Ronnie."[48] Such rhetoric pleased her husband's conservative constituents but made reporters cringe, especially women reporters.

Eventually the Reagans figured out how to please their constituents and reporters. Nancy's crusade against drug abuse built on a key insight of the Reagan presidency: the centrality of popular culture in modern politics. Nancy used what she called her "white glove pulpit" as first lady to advance her ideas and harmonize with her husband's "bully pulpit."[49] The antidrug crusade cast the Reagans where they were most comfortable, perched above the crowd setting an example as moral leaders. Much of the Reagan drug crusade was a public relations attack on the Reagans' own show-business community for glamorizing drugs. The crusade helped change the moral tone in the nation and may have been the most important first-lady project ever. It satisfied reporters by allowing them to write about something more substantive than Nancy's lunch companions or outfits.

By 1983 the Reagans were the most popular presidential couple since the Kennedys, showing that happy marriages were possible in the divorce-happy modern age. This was a remarkable achievement for a president whose marriage began rather hastily. (When Patti Davis confronted her father "about the lies" surrounding her miracle birth seven and a half months after the wedding, he said, "Well, if the studio hadn't made us change the wedding date, you wouldn't have been premature."[50] Reagan remained wedded to his illusions.) Still, America's excitement about the Reagan love affair helped sustain the administration even amid policy disasters and personal embarrassments. White House aides often preferred feeding reporters personal or patriotic stories rather than controversial policy lines.

Through her antidrug crusade, and her increasing comfort with asserting power, Nancy Reagan had her consciousness raised; she became perhaps the first effective feminist first lady. At a time when much of the feminist movement was sounding shrill and distancing itself from the needs of American women, Nancy Reagan hijacked the most popular elements of feminism. She coopted the feminist argument for equality and self-determination. "Feminism is the ability to *choose* what you want to do," she said; "I'm doing what I want to do."[51] In the 1990s younger "Third Wave" feminists such as Naomi Wolf became frustrated that their movement was no longer "seen as guaranteeing every woman's choice."[52] The middle path they sought brought them surprisingly close to Nancy Reagan's position.

Unfortunately for them, much of the goodwill Nancy Reagan painstakingly cultivated vanished when Nancy, like Rosalynn Carter before her and Hillary Clinton after her, overstepped. During the last two years of the Reagan presidency, especially during the ugly battle to depose Donald Regan as chief of staff, Nancy Reagan appeared too powerful and became a lightning rod for attacks. Indeed, some feminists came to her defense. But it was a losing battle. The feminist movement was not about to champion its bête noire, and millions of Americans remained uncomfortable with a too-powerful first lady, especially when they feared that her husband was faltering.

The Bushes

The Bushes learned from the Reagans' mistakes, at least in this arena. Barbara and George cast themselves as the people who actually lived the values the Reagans championed so eloquently yet often trampled in their tumultuous family life. Barbara played the role of "Mrs. Not Nancy" to the hilt, turning the cruel jibes about her excess pounds and her gray hair into a badge of honor and authenticity.[53] At the time even feminists such as Gloria Steinem and Jane Fonda looked fit and lovely, and everyone was being told that they had to be as perfect as the 1985 John Travolta movie by that name showed. As a result millions of women applauded this grandmother in the White House.

In reality Barbara Bush was a sharp-tongued, intimidating woman who frequently earned the right to be called "barb," not Bar. Yet she sensed that the American people wanted a warm, fuzzy, grandmotherly type as first lady. By exhibiting those characteristics she silenced the stories from reporters, aides, and secret service agents who endured her wrath. Barbara Bush's phenomenal popularity—the fact that the less interested she seemed in power, the more she seemed to get—proved that presidential couples have to build a joint image but should beware of power-sharing.

The Bushes were able to square the circle so effectively at first and were able to charm Americans and subdue reporters because they had one built-in advantage: they came from the right class. While it is not a subject people like to talk about in our democracy, it is no coincidence that the most successful first ladies in recent history, from Eleanor Roosevelt to Mamie Eisenhower to Jackie Kennedy to Barbara Bush, came from America's aristocracy.

Of course, there had to be some distancing from their upper-class roots as well, as evidenced by the Bushes' sojourn to Texas, where George Bush proved that he could have earned the silver spoon he was born with in his mouth. Still, once in office, upper-crust women had an easier time navigating some of the peculiarities of the position, and Americans accepted them in that position more easily. In fact, the whole idea of a first lady is a class-bound, aristocratic notion.[54]

The Clintons

This twisted tale helps explain why being first lady proved to be so frustrating for Hillary Clinton. The Clintons' initial "two-for-the-price-of-one" copresidency gambit was doomed to fail. There were too many restrictions and too many ambiguities surrounding the position for such a bold approach to work. Throughout her eight years in the White House, Mrs. Clinton discovered that she was most popular when the public perceived her to be most distant from serious policy making. In 1996 she neutralized her negatives before the reelection campaign by transforming herself from health care czarina into a warm and fuzzy "soccer mom" who giggled, baked, and happily smooched with Oscar the Grouch on *The Rosie O'Donnell Show*. In 1998 and 1999 her role as the stiff-upper-lip, stand-by-your-man kind of woman during the Monica Lewinsky scandal made her an American popular idol.

THE BLURRING OF PERSONAL-PUBLIC (AND POLITICAL) BOUNDARIES

Reviewing the last half-century helps explain how the Clintons' marital crisis mushroomed into a constitutional crisis. In America not only has the personal become political, as feminists wanted, but the political has become exceedingly personal. The excesses of the Clinton-Lewinsky spectacle resonated with the broader excesses of the celebrity culture. In modern America everything the president does, everything he touches, and everyone he knows is transformed by his celebrity. Thus, if even the most intimate details of a president's life are flattering, they are broadcast by that president and his friends to humanize and popularize the president. If the intimacies are less flattering, the president's enemies will do the job.

Sharing little tidbits of behind-the-scenes first-family life often charms the public. But such publicity is a double-edged sword. The scandal showed that the blurred lines between the personal and the political, between the popular culture and political culture, make the president at once a rock star and a rogue. The media magnifying glass aggrandizes and trivializes, making the president, his sins, and his virtues at once larger than life and also vaguely pedestrian. Our presidents and their wives have never been so famous, so personally influential, so glorified, but also so scrutinized, so devoured, so demeaned.

Unfortunately celebrity is a highly unstable currency. This is the age of the manic-depressive presidency in which the first couple zigzags from high highs to low lows, making them as great and as terrible as the latest headlines and news leads. Bill Clinton succeeded a president who won a world war but lost reelection. Four years later, the same week that Clinton became only the third Democrat in the twentieth century to be inaugurated for a second time, the Supreme Court allowed Paula Jones's sexual harassment suit against him to proceed. Hillary Clinton was the first first lady to win a Grammy award and also the first first lady to testify before a grand jury.

Ironically, the Monica Lewinsky episode underlined the cooperative nature of this modern and often dizzying presidency. With the first lady so deeply involved in the president's political life, only Hillary Clinton could save her husband from the charges that he had betrayed her by committing adultery with an intern. Mrs. Clinton's performance on *Today* just after the scandal broke, wherein she dismissed the whole Kenneth Starr investigation as part of a "vast right-wing conspiracy," was the most influential action by a first lady since Mrs. Kennedy defined her late husband's reign as "Camelot."[55]

The cooperative nature of the modern presidency has been good for most presidential marriages. Most couples saw that once in the White House, living "above the store," as it were, and working intensely together, their marriages often healed and even thrived. First couples often felt that they could only trust each other in what Mr. Clinton called a "very isolating" job.[56] Both Betty Ford and Lady Bird Johnson said that they were thrilled finally to have their peripatetic congressional husbands home for dinner more often; Mamie

Eisenhower, who felt so abandoned when Dwight Eisenhower was running World War II from London, loved being in the White House so that she could reach out "and pat Ike on his old bald head anytime I want to."[57] It seems that even the Clintons, who had suffered severe marital ruptures in the past and some humiliations in the White House, had found the White House crucible to be a bonding experience until the Lewinsky scandal.

The tawdry story of the president and the intern once again highlighted the ambiguous and often thankless nature of the first lady's job. As she struggled to keep up with her husband's stream of lies and half-truths, Mrs. Clinton found her own credibility threatened. For eight months Bill Clinton vehemently denied that he ever had "sexual relations with that woman."[58] When he finally confessed to the affair, even the formidable Clinton spin machine did not know how to position the first lady.

"Two irreconcilable story lines began seeping out" of the White House, *Time* would note, "one so painful it was hard to hear, the other so cynical it was hard to believe." Was it "worse for Hillary to appear as a stupid, duped wife or as a conniving wife who had been covering for her husband all year?"[59]

Mrs. Clinton had her press secretary call one hundred reporters and insist that the president had "misled" his wife. "It was an extraordinary spectacle," the media critic Howard Kurtz would write, "a president and First Lady peddling competing accounts of her awareness that he was cheating on her."[60]

Similarly, the first lady's critics sometimes contradicted themselves. When Americans discovered in March 1997 during the Clinton fund-raising scandals that the first lady of the United States had also raised funds, Republican congressman David M. McIntosh said of Mrs. Clinton: "As a quasi-governmental official working out of the White House, the West Wing, there's a responsibility to make sure that line is maintained between Government functions and campaign functions."[61] Thus the same conservatives who cried foul when Mrs. Clinton tried to take on a governmental role with health care were now trying to treat her like a federal official.

Such contradictory messages made many first ladies, especially Mrs. Clinton, feel that they would be condemned no matter what they did. Mrs. Clinton won wild applause from working women by universalizing her plight. She insisted that she suffered from the sexist fear of powerful women and the mixed message imposed on all modern American women to be powerful career women and traditional moms.

That assessment was only partially true. In her characteristically Clintonesque self-pity, Mrs. Clinton missed the degree to which she made things worse. Even more relevant, Mrs. Clinton overlooked the peculiarities of the first lady's role. It is historically misleading to say that the odyssey of the presidential couple mirrors women's history. And it is politically unwise to pin hopes for feminist fulfillment on the "wife of" the president. The first lady is not a typical woman nor a typical woman politician. Unlike women politicians who openly stand for election and reach for power, the first lady derives power through her husband. As first wife she is burdened by a host of cultural demands to uphold the traditional American home during culturally tumultuous times. Furthermore, the first lady has an unelected, undefined, pseudo-monarchical position monitored by a media addicted to controversy in a democracy terrified of government power. The Constitution vests presidential power in "a" chief executive; Americans do not want "two" chiefs, even "for the price of one" in the Oval Office.

In addition to the problems of the celebrity presidency, the copresidency, and the modern first ladyship, the Lewinsky scandal revealed the moral crisis modern America faced. One of the great ironies of the Monica Lewinsky episode was that it showed how one of Bill Clinton's greatest successes became one of his greatest failures. During the 1992 campaign Clinton did a brilliant job of distinguishing his character from his other qualifications to lead. This laid the groundwork for the free pass most Americans gave him to act amorally as long as the stock market continued to soar. Polls in the second term consistently showed that many Americans approved of the man's job performance but disliked the man. Yet as president, again and again Clinton recoupled moral concerns with political concerns, showing that personal character flaws can have vast policy implications. The Clinton years illustrated the complexity and ubiquity of America's moral crisis.

Even though reporters often treated the central cultural story in modern America as a tug-of-war between the Christian Right and the secular Left, the American people were more confused than polarized. Baby-boom Democrats also yearned for an America of faith and values and moral certitude. Yuppies had values too. Hillary Rodham Clinton's best-seller, *It Takes a Village*, was a milestone in American cultural history. With equal parts of Eleanor Roosevelt, Nancy Reagan, and Martha Stewart, it reflected the odyssey of an elite that rejected traditional mores only to rediscover that divorce harms kids, drugs are destructive, promiscuity is degrading, and that "every child" needs an "intact, dependable family."[62] At the same time Dole country witnessed churchgoing midwesterners divorcing, having abortions, wearing Nikes, and watching Tim Allen, a recovering drug addict whose 1994 Disney blockbuster, *The Santa Clause,* portrayed Saint Nick as a bumbling, remote, materialistic single father whose son helped him get in touch with his own "inner child."

Bill Clinton, in all his contradictions, was an accurate barometer of the country he led, illustrating the yearnings, the excess, the orthodoxy, and the ingenuity that was and is America. While America's manic-depressive, media-drenched, celebrity culture has been addicted to false polarities, it is necessary to recognize these paradoxes. Unfortunately Hillary Clinton too often confirmed the stereotype that women were either hotshots or homemakers. That is why her crack in 1992 that she could have baked cookies and served tea caused such a firestorm. And that is why her reincarnation as a Barbara Bush–like helpmate was so disturbing—but popular.

CONCLUSION

So what is a first lady to do? Mrs. Clinton's final incarnation as a Senate candidate showed that the first lady should try to transcend the simplistic polarities that shackle too many modern women. Hillary Clinton learned, as so many of her generation did, how to let her warmer "okey-dokey artichokey" side emerge in public and still be respected. Just as *It Takes a Village* showed that a progressive could still champion tradition; just as her relationship with her daughter, Chelsea, proved that a career woman could be a good mom; and just as her ongoing marriage with her husband showed that marriages are not merely good or bad but ebb and flow, rupture and heal, Hillary Rodham Clinton as Senate candidate set out to prove that a modern woman— and first lady—could be feminist and feminine, substantive and fun-loving, neither supermoms nor "just" housewives.

Reporters must help by embracing complexity. Too often journalists reduce first ladies to one box or another. In 1997 the *New York Times* found it incongruous that "on the same day that [Mrs. Clinton] made her confectionary appearance on Ms. [Rosie] O'Donnell's syndicated show . . . she delivered a speech at a development conference" on "Microcredit."[63] Yet that was the reality for many modern women who rush from boardrooms to playrooms, from cutting-edge deal making to traditional mothering.

Similarly, scholars have to develop a more sophisticated language for assessing first ladies—and first couples. The gushing tributes to first ladies in most "first-lady scholarship" is striking considering how much criticism first ladies often endure in office. Books that deviate from that norm are often condemned as antifeminist, suggesting that critical historical conversation about the first ladies remains in its infancy.

Even if the Clinton experience ended up being more of a codependency than a copresidency, observers need to appreciate the value of viewing the president and first lady as a couple. Too much analysis artificially separates the president and the first lady into separate boxes. Discussion of the couple as a couple can be an illuminating prism that clarifies, among other things, the role of the first lady and the complexity of the modern presidency, the way changing attitudes toward marriage affect standards for judging both roles, the changing agenda and growing importance of the media in shaping politics, and the implications of blurring popular culture and political culture.

In the United States today the presidency and marriage are undergoing similar crises, suffering from a loss of authority, of credibility. Modern American culture is hooked on cynicism. This must change. Just as husbands and wives choose to build useful fictions about each other and about their relationships, so too can citizens choose to build useful fictions about their leaders and their government. A step back toward a culture of appearances, away from the culture of the exposé, would be a welcome one. Strong marriages and successful democracies require a leap of faith and an occasional suspension of disbelief motivated by the confidence that ideals such as love, justice, and virtue can and will ultimately triumph.

NOTES

1. *Boston Globe*, 15 Apr. 1961, 1.

2. The Staff to Gerald R. Ford, 1 May 1976, Box 132, Ron Nessen MSS, Gerald R. Ford Library, Ann Arbor, Mich.

3. Goldie Bull to Bess Truman, 18 Oct. 1945, Box 125, Social Correspondence Files, Harry S. Truman Papers, Harry S. Truman Library, Independence, Mo.

4. Susie M. Baird to Bess Truman, 13 Oct. 1945, Box 125, Social Correspondence Files, Harry S. Truman Papers, Harry S. Truman Library, Independence, Mo.

5. John M. Harmon to Douglas B. Guron, 18 Feb. 1977, p. 1; Edwin S. Kneedler to John M. Harmon, 17 Feb. 1977, p. 7, in Harmon to Guron, 18 Feb. 1977, FG 287, White House Central Files, Jimmy Carter Library, Atlanta, Ga.

6. Rhonda Bush to Kit Dobelle, 8 Feb. 1980, Box 7, Daniel Malachuk Files, White House Office of Administration, Jimmy Carter Library, Atlanta, Ga.

7. Lisa Meyers, "Behind the Smiles," *Family Weekly,* 12 Oct. 1980, 5.

8. *Variety*, 24 Jan. 1968, 71.

9. *NBC Special: The First Lady, Nancy Reagan,* 24 June 1985, R2729B, Audiovisual Archives, Ronald Reagan Library, Simi Valley, Calif.

10. Tom Shales, "Reagan, in Command," *Washington Post*, 5 Mar. 1987, B1, B2.

11. Nancy Reagan, *My Turn* (New York: Random House, 1989), 335.

12. *Boston Globe,* 15 Apr. 1961, 1; *Modern Romance,* Aug. 1962, cover.

13. Beatrice Blackmar Gould, "Because Women Care," *Ladies' Home Journal,* Oct. 1960, 73.

14. Robert H. Ferrell, *Harry S. Truman Diary* (New York: Norton, 1980), 49.

15. Ferrell, "Harry S. Truman to Bess Truman, July 29, 1945," in *Dear Bess: The Letters from Harry to Bess Truman* (New York: Norton, 1983), 522.

16. "Truman's Mother Home," *New York Times*, 23 May 1945, 21.

17. Bess W. Truman to Adam Clayton Powell, 12 Oct. 1945, Box 43, Social Correspondence Files, Harry S. Truman Papers, Harry S. Truman Library, Independence, Mo.

18. "Trumans Condemn D.A.R. Negro Ban," *New York Times*, 13 Oct. 1945, 17.

19. Robert J. Donovan, *Conflict and Crisis: The Presidency of Harry S. Truman, 1949–1953* (New York: Norton, 1977), 148. See also, Charles V. Hamilton, *Adam Clayton Powell: A Political Biography of an American Dilemma* (New York: Atheneum, 1991), 165.

20. Mrs. Edwin S. Schweig to Bess Truman, 13 Oct. 1945, 1–2, Box 125, Social Correspondence Files, Harry S. Truman Library, Independence, Mo.

21. Mrs. Boell to Bess Truman, 18 Oct. 1945, Box 125, Social Correspondence Files, Harry S. Truman Library, Independence, Mo.

22. Lester David and Irene David, *Ike and Mamie: The Story of the General and His Lady* (New York: World Publishing, 1981), 17.

23. Julie Nixon Eisenhower, *Special People* (New York: Simon and Schuster, 1977), 203.

24. Mamie Eisenhower to Louise Caffey, 31 Mar. 1954, Box 5, Mamie Doud Eisenhower Papers, White House Social Office Files, Dwight Eisenhower Library, Abilene, Kans.

25. See file: "February 1953," Box 540, PPF2, White House Central Files, Dwight Eisenhower Library, Abilene, Kan. See also Paula Baker, "The Domestication of Politics," *American Historical Review* 89 (June 1984): 620–47.

26. Ralph Martin, *A Hero for Our Time: An Intimate Story of the Kennedy Years* (New York: Vantage, 1983), 144.

27. Donald Wilson, "John Kennedy's Lovely Lady," *Life*, 24 Aug. 1959, 80.

28. Samuel Kernell, *Going Public* (Washington, D.C.: CQ Press, 1986); Richard Neustadt, *Presidential Power and the Modern Presidents* (New York: Free Press,1990), 28; Stephen Skowronek, *The Politics Presidents Make* (Cambridge: Harvard University Press, 1993).

29. John Demos, *Past, Present, and Personal* (New York, 1986), 37.

30. Barbara Sinclair Deckard, *The Women's Movement: Political, Socioeconomic and Psychological Issues* (New York: HarperCollins College Division, 1975), 73.

31. "Mrs. Nixon Hailed As 'Ideal Wife,'" *New York Times,* 11 Dec. 1957, 10.

32. Flora Rheta Schreiber, "I Didn't Want Dick to Run Again," *Good Housekeeping,* July 1968, 188; "She Also Ran; Now She's Home," *Newsweek,* 2 Dec. 1968,

31; *Time,* 29 Feb. 1960, 25; "Women: The Silent Partner," *Time,* 24–27; James A. Linen, "A Letter from the Publisher," *Time,* 19.

33. Lenore Hershey, "Compassion Power: On Tour with Mrs. Nixon," *Ladies' Home Journal* (Sept. 1969): 88.

34. Winnie McLendon to Jerry TerHorst, n.d. [circa Aug. 1974], pp. 1–3, in Ron Nessen to Jerry Jones, 10 July 1975, Ron Nessen MSS, Box 130, Gerald Ford Library, Ann Arbor, Mich.

35. "Betty: The New First Lady," *Newsweek,* 19 Aug. 1974, 30; "Seven Days in August, 13–34; Betty Ford, *The Times of My Life* (New York: Harper and Row, 1978), 168.

36. CBS, *60 Minutes,* 10 Aug. 1975, F388 Transcript, pp. 1–13, Box 6, Sheila R. Weidenfeld MSS, Gerald R. Ford Library, Ann Arbor, Mich.

37. Staff secretary to Gerald Ford, 1–29 Aug. 1975, Box 3, WH 4–1 Mail, White House Central Files, 12975, Gerald Ford Library, Ann Arbor, Mich.

38. William J. Gordy to Harold Calloway, 13 Aug. 1975, Box 80, President Ford Committee Record, Gerald Ford Library, Ann Arbor, Mich.

39. Mrs. John Richard Ghilon to Betty Ford, 11 Aug. 1975, Box 458–459, "Con" Bulk Mail Samples, White House Social Office Central Files, Gerald R. Ford Library, Ann Arbor, Mich.

40. Sally Quinn, "Have You Heard What They're Not Saying about Rosalynn?" *Washington Post,* 25 June 1978, K2, K3.

41. *Atlanta Constitution,* 1 Aug. 1978, A6.

42. Quinn, "Have You Heard," 25 June 1978, K1–K5.

43. ABC, *Barbara Walters,* 14 Dec. 1975, C16, Audiovisual Archives, Jimmy Carter Library, Atlanta, Ga.

44. *Washington Star,* 3 Aug. 1979, A11.

45. Jack Anderson, "Rosalynn Carter: Co-President's Role," *Washington Post,* 4 Oct. 1979, 19.

46. "The President's Partner," *Newsweek,* 6 Nov. 1979, 38.

47. CBS, *60 Minutes,* with President and Mrs. Carter, 10 Aug. 1980, C1184, Audiovisual Archives, Jimmy Carter Library, Atlanta, Ga.

48. Reagan, *My Turn,* 92–93.

49. Nancy Reagan, "Remarks for Associated Press Publishers' Luncheon," 4 May 1987, p. 6, F95–109, White House Office of Records Management, Ronald Reagan Library, Simi Valley, Calif.

50. Patty Davis, *The Way I See It: An Autobiography* (New York: Putnam, 1992), 329.

51. Bernard Weinraub, "Mrs. President," *McCall's,* Nov. 1985, 178.

52. Katie Roiphe, *The Morning After: Sex, Fear, and Feminism on Campus* (Boston: Little, Brown, 1993), 5, 121; Naomi Wolf, *Fire with Fire: The New Female Power and How It Will Change the Twenty-first Century* (New York: Random House, 1993), 68.

53. Quoted in *Washington Post,* 15 Jan. 1989, F6.

54. Gil Troy, *Affairs of State: The Rise and Rejection of the Presidential Couple since World War II* (New York: Free Press, 1997); Margaret Truman, *Bess W. Truman* (New York: Macmillan, 1986).

55. NBC, *Today Show,* 27 Jan. 1998.

56. Michael Isikoff, *Uncovering Clinton: A Reporter's Story* (New York: Three Rivers Press, 1999).

57. Stephen E. Ambrose, *Eisenhower: Soldier, General of the Army, President-Elect, 1890–1952* (New York: Simon and Schuster, 1984), 2:29.

58. Isikoff, *Uncovering Clinton,* 351.

59. "Clinton Defenders, Clinton Foes," *Time,* 28 Dec. 1998, 74.

60. Howard Kurtz, "What War?" *Vanity Fair,* Jan. 1999, 39.

61. James Bennet, "White House Memo," *New York Times*, 7 Mar. 1997, 1.

62. Hillary Rodham Clinton, *It Takes a Village* (New York: Simon and Schuster, 1996), 41.

63. James Bennet, "First Lady Talks of Mice and Men on 'Rosie' Show," *New York Times,* 4 Feb. 1997, 3.

Thirteen

Hillary's Choices

The First Ladyship of Hillary Rodham Clinton and the Future of the Office

Myra G. Gutin

Introduction

For many years it was common to hear scholars, historians, and journalists conclude a conversation about American first ladies with the words, "Well, since Eleanor . . ." or "Because of Eleanor. . . ." For a younger generation, and those who witnessed the Clinton presidency, the phrases might eventually be modified to read, "Well, since Hillary . . ." or "Because of Hillary. . . ." In fact, media scholar Betty Houchin Winfield has pointed out that Hillary Clinton has been "the most salient, controversial, and arguably one of the most politically powerful women of the end of this century."[1]

When Hillary Clinton became first lady in January 1993, the role had already evolved from a strictly ceremonial function to an institution called the Office of the First Lady, complete with a sizable staff and attendant political, social, and advocacy dimensions. It is always important to keep in mind that the first lady has no official duties but that the American public expects her to be a good wife, a good mother, and the epitome of the American woman. She is expected to have some sort of project or area of concern (if she has been involved in the project prior to coming to the White House, so much the better), but that project should not cross over into the area of public policy. If the first lady does become involved in matters of public policy, she risks expending some of the president's political capital and the public's affection and support.

Hillary Clinton served in this dynamic and challenging role from 1993 to 2001. Her tenure as first lady saw both the continuation of traditions and expansion of the nature and scope of the office. Mrs. Clinton's first ladyship, like Eleanor Roosevelt's before her, marks a turning point in the office, one requiring closer inspection and one that surely will long be debated.

Hillary Clinton's First Ladyship in Perspective:
Key Moments in the History of the Office

Some of the more interesting changes to the institution include the following innovations. Edith Kermit Roosevelt hired the first first lady's staff person when she enlisted Isabelle "Belle" Hagner to serve as the first social secretary in 1902.[2] No future first lady would be without a social secretary.

Grace Coolidge had been offered the chance to speak over the radio, but she declined because her husband insisted on a no-interview, no-quote policy for the first lady. Her successor, Lou Hoover, however, enthusiastically embraced the new medium. On 29 April 1929 she became the first first lady to speak over a nationwide hookup, and it was the first time that a large number of Americans had heard the first lady speak. Eleanor Roosevelt would become a regular on the airwaves as a result of Lou Hoover's actions. In addition to speaking over the radio, Lou Hoover became the first first lady to give formal speeches.

Eleanor Roosevelt expanded the office in a number of ways. Perhaps more than any first lady before her or since, she understood the value of communication and worked to maintain an ongoing conversation with the American people. During her thirteen years as first lady she gave over one thousand speeches.[3] Beginning on 31 December 1935 and continuing until a few weeks before her death in 1962, she wrote a four-hundred-word newspaper column titled "My Day" (see Susan Roth Breitzer's essay on Eleanor Roosevelt in this book). She went on the lecture circuit and was involved in a number of commercially sponsored radio broadcast speeches. She was the first first lady to testify before a congressional committee and the first first lady to address a national nominating convention, the Democratic National Convention in 1944.

In 1961 Jacqueline Kennedy appointed the first first-lady press secretary, twenty-three-year-old Pamela Turnure. United Press International's Helen Thomas was far from impressed with Miss Turnure, however, stating that she "had about as much business being press secretary as I would have directing the space agency."[4] Despite Thomas's ridicule and Mrs. Kennedy's advice to Turnure not to create news and to protect her from the press, Turnure's appointment was important in that it spoke to the growing importance of the media. Reporters would frequently complain that Mrs. Kennedy would bring them in on stories relative to her refurbishment project but would push them aside on stories that might have a larger readership or that they might find of interest.[5]

While she was not enthusiastic about the press, Jacqueline Kennedy was enthusiastic about the refurbishment of the White House. The long-overdue restoration of the public rooms of the executive mansion became the first "special project" by a first lady. No future first lady, with the exception of Betty Ford, who had a shortened tenure, would be without a White House project. On 14 February 1962 Mrs. Kennedy shared her triumph in a nationally televised program, *A Tour of the White House with Mrs. John F. Kennedy.* Forty-six million people tuned in to the program, the first time that a first lady had utilized television.[6]

In November 1963 Lady Bird Johnson, recognizing that the first lady could benefit from effective press relations, appointed Elizabeth S. "Liz" Carpenter as staff director and press secretary. The appointment of Carpenter, a former newswoman, guaranteed greater expertise in delivering the news to reporters. It might be argued that news management of the first lady began with Carpenter, as she suggested potential stories to those covering Mrs. Johnson. Carpenter was probably one of the early "spin doctors," sharing her perspectives on a story with members of the fourth estate. Reporter Marie Smith of the *Washington Post* commented favorably on Carpenter and her propensity to manage news when she said, "We know that if there's a story, Liz will call us, and if she calls us, there is a story."[7] Lady Bird Johnson enjoyed positive press relations during her tenure as first lady, in marked contrast to her husband, who had a difficult time with the press.

Lady Bird Johnson became the first first lady to campaign by herself for her husband when she undertook a controversial whistlestop tour through the South during the 1964 presidential campaign. When asked why no other first lady before her had campaigned for her husband, not even the venerable Eleanor Roosevelt, Mrs. Johnson commented, "For many years it wasn't considered seemly for a wife to go out on behalf of her husband."[8]

Betty Ford was diagnosed with breast cancer a little over a month after moving into the White House in August 1974. She required a radical mastectomy and made the decision to go public with her cancer. Mrs. Ford's action heralded the beginning of national conversations about women's health issues, and never before had a first lady's personal life become such a topic of public attention (see Mary Linehan's essay on Betty Ford in this book).

Rosalynn Carter established a first when she became a regular attendee of cabinet meetings. She never participated in discussions; she only took notes, as she wrote later, "so that when I traveled around the country . . . and was questioned by the press and other individuals . . . I'd know what was going on."[9] In addition she had regular working luncheons with the president to review projects and initiatives.

Nancy Reagan became the first first lady to address the United Nations, choosing this forum for a discussion on drug abuse prevention. Barbara Bush was the first first lady to campaign for members of her husband's party during mid-term elections. This was the role and office that Hillary Clinton stepped into in January 1993.

HILLARY'S POLITICAL EMERGENCE

While Mrs. Clinton's biography is well known to most Americans, a summary of her education and achievements will help to frame later events. Hillary Diane Rodham was born in Chicago, Illinois, on 26 October 1947. The Rodham family, which included younger brothers Hugh and Anthony, moved to conservative, white Park Ridge, a suburb of Chicago, when Hillary was three years old. Early on, Hillary demonstrated that she was an intelligent, serious child. By the time she reached Maine East High School she had evolved into a gifted student who felt comfortable sharing her opinions in her classes. Articulate and logical, she was able to "state her opinions in complete sentences, reeling off the main points of her argument in logical order."[10] She had great academic success and won a National Merit Scholarship.

A particularly important event in Hillary's young life occurred when Don Jones became a youth pastor at the United Methodist Church to which the Rodhams belonged. Jones had a strong social conscience and exhorted Hillary and others to be aware of social issues. In 1962 he took Hillary and other members of their church youth group to hear a speech given by Dr. Martin Luther King Jr. After the speech Hillary had a chance to meet Dr. King, a significant moment in her life. In addition Jones introduced Hillary to the writings of Reinhold Niebuhr and Paul Tillich, which, along with Jones and other readings, further developed her social philosophy.[11]

Hillary enrolled at Wellesley College in 1965 and established a reputation there as a vocal, opinionated campus leader. When she was elected president of her college's student government during her junior year, Ruth Adams, Wellesley College's president, observed that Hillary was a reformer: "She was, as a number of her generation were, interested in effecting change, but from within rather than outside the system."[12] The reformer made national headlines in 1969 when she became the first-ever student commencement speaker at Wellesley.

Sen. Edward Brooke was the invited commencement speaker. In Hillary's words, his speech was a "defense of Richard Nixon . . . the world awaits you, we've got great leadership. America is strong abroad."[13] To many listeners it seemed like a pro forma commencement address. When he had finished his remarks Hillary discarded her carefully written text and told Brooke and the audience that her generation had grown tired of promises for change. She said, "The challenge now is to practice politics as the art of making what appears to be impossible possible."[14] Some who heard her were shocked, and others were dismayed, but her classmates seemed to support Hillary's scolding of a U.S. senator. Her audacious response landed Hillary in the pages of *Life* magazine, her first mention in a national publication.

While at Wellesley, Hillary made the switch from Republican to Democrat. She had been a "Goldwater Girl" in 1964 and had worked for the House Republican Conference in 1968. However, with the winds of political change blowing, she worked for Democratic senator Eugene McCarthy during the New Hampshire primary in 1968 and said that she would have voted for Sen. Hubert Humphrey during the 1968 general election if she had been old enough to vote.[15]

Hillary continued her education at Yale Law School. Influenced by Marian Wright Edelman, founder of the Children's Defense Fund, she developed an abiding interest in protecting the rights of children. A serious, diligent student, she served on the board of editors of the *Yale Review of Law and Social Action*.

In 1970 Hillary met Bill Clinton. He was a year behind her in school, as a result of having spent one year in England on a Rhodes Scholarship. In an interview Mrs. Clinton recalled that she knew of Bill Clinton but had not been introduced to him until one day in the Yale Library when she was trying to study and noticed Clinton staring at her. After a while she walked up to Clinton and said, "If you're going to keep looking at me and I'm going to keep looking at you we ought to at least know each other's names. I'm Hillary Rodham."[16] One biographer writes that for Hillary Rodham it was love at first sight.[17] Hillary decided to delay her graduation from Yale by one year so that she would have a chance to develop a relationship with Bill. She applied for and was accepted into a law school program devoted to children's rights. In the summer of 1972 Bill and Hillary, both political activists, went to Texas to work on George McGovern's presidential campaign. Though McGovern lost the election, the duo was building the friendships that would eventually "give them a network of supporters throughout the Democratic party."[18] Clinton and Rodham graduated from Yale Law School in 1973.

When Bill Clinton returned to Arkansas to teach law at the University of Arkansas Law School and plan his initial run for public office, Hillary went to Cambridge, Massachusetts, to work for the Children's Defense Fund. In early 1974 Hillary was hired as a staff attorney for the House Judiciary Committee, which was considering impeachment proceedings against President Richard Nixon. Her employment ended when Nixon resigned the presidency in August 1974.

In spite of a promising career, Hillary decided to try life in Fayetteville, Arkansas, teaching law and continuing her relationship with Bill Clinton. Her friends never thought she would be happy in Arkansas, but Hillary made the decision that she was going to follow her heart. "My friends and family thought I had lost my mind," Hillary admitted; "I was a little bit concerned about that as well."[19] Bill and Hillary were married in October 1975, and Hillary decided to retain her maiden name.

Bill Clinton was elected attorney general of Arkansas in 1976. After they moved to Little Rock, Hillary received a job offer from the Rose Law Firm, arguably the most prestigious law firm in the state. At the same time the Carter administration appointed her to the board of the Legal Services Corporation. She eventually became chairman of that board. Moving from attorney general to governor in the election of 1978, Clinton became the youngest governor in the country. The new first lady of Arkansas worked continuously for children, families, and education. While maintaining a busy law practice, she founded the Arkansas Advocates for Children and Families and served as chairwoman of the Arkansas Education Standards Committee. Hillary became a partner at the Rose Law Firm in 1979, and the couple's only child, Chelsea Victoria, was born on 27 February 1980.

Clinton was reelected to the Arkansas governorship five times. There was a period of two years after his first term, however, when he had been voted out of office. In a postmortem of that loss it was learned that the people of Arkansas thought it was disgraceful that their first lady did not have the same last name as her husband. In the next election Hillary became Mrs. Bill Clinton.

All this was a prologue to a run for the presidency for Bill Clinton, and his wife figured strongly into his plans. During the 1992 presidential campaign all was going well for the candidate until it was reported that Gennifer Flowers had made public her alleged twelve-year affair with the governor. When confronted with the situation, both Bill and Hillary Clinton responded to the allegations by appearing on the CBS program *60 Minutes,* which was aired immediately following the Super Bowl. During the interview Mrs. Clinton stated, "I'm not sitting here because I'm some little woman standing by her man. . . . I'm sitting here because I love him and respect him and I honor what he's been through and what we've been through together, and you know, if that's not good enough for people, then heck, don't vote for him."[20]

Republican strategist Mary Matalin observed, "There was nothing pitiful or beleaguered about Hillary. In fact, she was defiant, tough and sassy. She likely saved the day, and clearly was going to be a force—not background noise—in the campaign."[21] The motif that had been seen before in the Clinton marriage would be repeated countless times during the Clinton presidency. Bill Clinton would err; Hillary would go on the attack and help formulate a strategy to resurrect her husband; he would survive; and all would be forgiven.

The Clintons told America that they would get "two for the price of one" if they elected Bill Clinton, and many believed that this comment portended a copresidency. Political commentator Maureen Dowd expressed the opinion that "the notion of a coequal couple in the White House is a little offensive to men and women."[22] More than any other prospective first lady, Hillary Clinton found herself continually answering questions about her views and her possible role in her husband's administration. While many voters may have been wary of the duo and their plans, Clinton soundly defeated President George Bush in 1992.

THE PRESIDENT'S PARTNER

It is doubtful that any first lady experienced more highs and lows during her first ladyship or was more polarizing—both loved and despised—than Hillary Clinton. Shortly after taking office, Mrs. Clinton was named to head the President's Task Force on National Health Care Reform. Bill Clinton had campaigned on this theme and had said that he would put Hillary in charge of the efforts in this arena. At the outset 65 percent of the public had no problem with her appointment.[23] There was some precedent for the move, as Eleanor Roosevelt had served as assistant director of the Office of Civilian Defense and Rosalynn Carter had been honorary chair of the President's Commission on Mental Health. However, neither of the earlier first ladies had the staff or resources at their discretion that Mrs. Clinton had; nor did the outcome of their work begin to have the significance on the nation's economy as the proposed Clinton health care initiative would.

Almost immediately the whole enterprise became an organizational nightmare. There were over six hundred people working in various subgroups. Since a management style that favored secrecy was utilized, many meetings were closed to the media and the public.[24] Frustration and fear mounted, and the Association of American Physicians and Surgeons brought suit in federal court to open the meetings and question the appointment of the president's spouse as a violation of federal nepotism laws. A federal judge ruled that the task force was guilty of misconduct in withholding documents.[25] The United States Court of Appeals for the District of Columbia would eventually rule that Mrs. Clinton was a full-time federal official and that the commission was not obligated to open its hearings. They ruled: "Congress itself has recognized that the President's spouse acts as the functional equivalent of an assistant to the President. . . . We see no reason why a President could not use his or her spouse to carry out a task that the President might delegate to one of his White House aides." The judges concluded that "it is reasonable to treat the President's spouse as a 'de facto officer or employee' of the government."[26]

The new plan that was unveiled was as unwieldy as the committee that had assembled it, complete with bureaucracy, regulations, rules, and requirements. It seemed that there was something to offend every constituency. Congress reacted unfavorably, and those legislators who had initially indicated that they supported the plan now deserted it. Compromises were offered that might have gained support from both Democrats and Republicans. Hillary, however, refused to compromise, especially on the idea of universal coverage. She lost her high-stakes political gamble.[27] Though well intentioned, the health care plan collapsed completely in August 1994. The health care debacle was not the most important cause, but it was cited as one of the factors in the Democrats' loss of majorities in both houses of Congress during the midterm elections of November 1994.

For a time Hillary Clinton took a step back and embraced a more traditional first-lady stance. She addressed conferences on women's issues and toured Asia with her daughter, Chelsea. She began to write a weekly syndicated newspaper column, "Talking It Over," that was similar to Eleanor Roosevelt's celebrated column, "My Day."

During the health care project other problems that would evolve into scandals were taking place. Among them were firings at the White House Travel Office, also known as Travelgate.[28] Other scandals included the disappearance and reappearance of Hillary's billing records from the Rose Law Firm, where she had worked back in Arkansas. One of the most devastating events was the suicide of Deputy White House Counsel (and Hillary's former partner at the Rose Law Firm) Vincent Foster on 20 July 1993. One of the most damaging of all the scandals was the failed Arkansas land deal known as Whitewater. Questions had first arisen about Whitewater during the 1992 presidential campaign, but the Clintons managed skillfully to deflect them. The Clintons and their partners, Susan and Jim McDougal, had borrowed almost two hundred thousand dollars in 1978 to buy into the Whitewater development deal. The deal unraveled amid allegations of a failed savings-and-loan bank owned by the McDougals, conflicts of interest in the financing of the deal, Hillary's handling of the McDougals' business at the Rose Law Firm, and efforts to thwart an investigation into the matter by the Resolution Trust Corporation.[29] At the same time questions surrounded Mrs. Clinton's commodities trading in 1979, when, with the help of a friend, she parlayed a one-thousand-dollar investment into one hundred thousand dollars.[30]

Mrs. Clinton emerged in a different incarnation in September 1995, when she attended the United Nations Fourth World Conference on Women in Beijing, China. There was a question as to whether Mrs. Clinton would attend the Beijing conference. Tensions between the United States and China had been exacerbated by protests about China's poor human rights record, Chinese nuclear testing, and the detention of well-known human rights activist Harry Wu. It was not until a few days before her scheduled departure that the first lady was given permission to attend the conference.

Considering the firestorm that had preceded the trip to China, it might have been expected that Mrs. Clinton's remarks would be innocuous, but her speech took on a strong accusatory tone as she castigated the governments of China, India, Bosnia, and a number of Middle East nations for practices that she considered abhorrent and unacceptable for women: "It is a violation of human rights when babies are denied food, or drowned, or suffocated, or their spines broken, simply because they were born girls. It is a violation of human rights when women and girls are sold into slavery or prostitution. . . . It is a violation of human rights when women are denied the right to plan their families, and that includes being forced to have abortions or being sterilized against their will. . . . If there is one message that echoes forth from this conference, let it be that human rights are women's rights. And women's rights are human rights, once and for all."[31]

There was virtually no coverage of the first lady's speech in China, but in the United States it was a page-one story in virtually every newspaper. Both Democratic and Republican delegates to the conference lauded the first lady for her remarks. Other observers believe that Mrs. Clinton complicated U.S. relations with China. After the health care retreat, however, the speeches at the conference were victories for Hillary Clinton.

Another victory occurred in January 1996, when Hillary published *It Takes a Village*. Drawing on her lifelong interest in children and her experiences as a mother, Mrs. Clinton wrote about the way in which children develop and their relationships to their parents and society. The title of the book, taken from an African proverb, suggests that a child needs many people to become a healthy, well-adjusted adult. The book was well received in spite of criticism from 1996 Republican presidential nominee Robert Dole. An unexpected bonus for the first lady was a Grammy award she received for her oral reading of the book.

When she appeared at the 1996 Democratic National Convention, Hillary seemed to have regained some political momentum and spoke eloquently about families. For the next two years she traveled the country, calling attention to the plight of children, highlighting the various historical sites, and speaking on behalf of a myriad of Democratic candidates.

But the successes would again give way to crisis. In January 1998 Bill Clinton woke his wife to tell her that stories about his purported affair with a White House intern were about to break in the national media. Many would recall the image of an angry president pointing his finger and saying, "I did not have sexual relations with that woman, Miss Lewinsky." The next day Hillary was interviewed on *The Today Show* by cohost Matt Lauer. The first lady told Lauer that Clinton had been the target of a lengthy and vicious campaign to discredit him.[32]

The president maintained his innocence until August 1998, when he admitted that he had lied and had, in fact, had a sexual relationship with Lewinsky. Public opinion surveys taken at the time indicated that in spite of the fact that they had questions about Bill Clinton's moral character, respondents still approved of his performance as president. In addition, "respondents said that they admired how Mrs. Clinton had stood by her husband since he admitted his relationship."[33] His admission that he had lied moved forward plans to impeach the president. After months of strategy and delaying tactics, on 19 December 1998 Bill Clinton was impeached in the House of Representatives on charges of perjury and obstruction of justice.[34] But he survived the charges of high crimes and misdemeanors and the action of the Senate. Again the Clintons would experience both the highs and lows of political life, and again Mrs. Clinton would play a role in her husband's career.

First Lady–Politician

In April 1999 *Time* magazine ran a cover story that featured a painting of Hillary Clinton with the words "Senator Clinton?" written below her name.[35] Most people reacted with disbelief, but Mrs. Clinton was considering pursuing the New York Senate seat soon to be vacated by Daniel Patrick Moynihan.

Again the Clintons surprised and Hillary forged yet another first for the first ladyship. But there seemed to be compelling reasons why the first lady should not run for the U.S. Senate. She was called a "carpetbagger," a reference to the fact that she had never lived in New York and had few, if any, connections to the state. She might lose the race, which would be seen as an embarrassment and rejection of both Clintons' careers in public service and Hillary's accomplishments as first lady. Her opponent was Rudolph Giuliani, mayor of New York City, who was a tough competitor and a worthy foe. While it was thought that Mrs. Clinton would probably do well in New York City, there were concerns about other, more conservative areas in the state. Ironically, if elected, she had to face the prospect of serving in a Senate presided over by Trent Lott of Mississippi, a man active in the impeachment initiative against her husband. She also faced an aggressive press, one more demanding of a Senate candidate than a first lady. Moreover, when asked in a 1995 interview if she would run for elective office, she responded, "Probably not. . . . I think that there are so many ways to serve and I would be involved in my community . . . but I don't know that I would have pursued an elective [office], no."[36]

Yet, Mrs. Clinton did choose to run and was an enthusiastic, albeit cautious, candidate. Before she would commit to running for office, Mrs. Clinton announced that she would undertake a "listening tour" of New York State during the summer of 1999 to test the waters and learn if the voters would support her candidacy. The tour yielded generally positive results, but the always-cautious first lady still avoided throwing her hat into the ring until as late as possible. Speaking to reporters during the tour, she said, "It is a different feeling to be the person who is in the spotlight . . . speaking on my own behalf." She said that the listening tour "was the first time I have ever done it. . . . I loved what I did. I had a wonderful time."[37]

The public took the first lady's campaign seriously, especially after she purchased a home in Chappaqua, New York. The formal announcement for the campaign came in November 1999 when Hillary Clinton made it official by stating that she was in the race "to stay."[38] This posed yet another challenge: that of functioning as both candidate for public office and first lady at the same time. Starting on New Year's Day in 2000 she became the first part-time first lady because of her own political career. Then on 6 February 2000 she entered the race full-time with a speech and biographical video. In the speech she challenged the charge that she was a carpetbagger and provided a rationale for her run for office. In her words, "Now I know some people are asking why I'm doing this here and now, and that's a fair question. Here's my answer and why I hope you'll put me to work for you: I may be new to the neighborhood, but I'm not new to your concerns."[39]

The remainder of the first lady's speech was devoted to establishing credibility with her audience by citing her White House work on certain key issues and her plans for dealing with the national debt, targeted tax cuts, hate crimes, gun control, privacy, and education. She concluded her comments by saying, "New York defined what was possible in the twentieth century and New York can make what seems impossible today possible in the twenty-first century. And that's why I want to be your senator from New York."[40]

Conclusion: Hillary Clinton's Legacy

Unique in the annals of first-lady history is the fact that so many popular and scholarly books have been written that assess various aspects of Hillary Clinton's eight-year tenure as presidential spouse. Although Eleanor Roosevelt was the topic of many writers, the range of coverage and scholarly nature of the coverage was nothing like that devoted to Mrs. Clinton. Moreover, while it is not unusual for a first lady to be the topic of a book, it is extraordinary for her to be the subject of so many books while still in the White House and for the books to be so negative. There were a few books published on Eleanor Roosevelt and Nancy Reagan while they were still serving in the White House, but neither first lady was the object of such vicious criticism. Most authors have waited until the first lady has exited the White House before penning biographies. However, a survey of titles on Amazon.com in late 2000 indicated that there had been over twenty-five books written about Hillary Clinton since 1993 and that several more were slated for 2001 release. The books range from polemics to carefully researched and documented studies of her first ladyship. The titles cover her marriage, her political views, and the scandals associated with the Clinton administration. In keeping with Hillary Clinton's polarizing first ladyship, they run from the complimentary to the critical. A sampling of ten of the many titles reveals the interest and controversy she generated:

1. *The First Partner*
2. *State of a Union: Inside the Complex Marriage of Bill and Hillary Clinton*
3. *The Case against Hillary Rodham Clinton*
4. *Hell to Pay*
5. *The Unfolding Story of Hillary Rodham Clinton*
6. *The 10 Year Campaign to Destroy Bill and Hillary Clinton*

Still absent from the plethora of Hillary Clinton books are scholarly stud-ies that utilize White House files and documents. Of course, these documents are not likely to be available and cataloged until the Clinton Presidential Library opens its doors. The idea of waiting "until the dust settles" from Mrs. Clinton's first ladyship will provide necessary perspective, an opportunity for thoughtful analysis, and the passing of sufficient time in order to better assess her legacy and the direction of her post-first-lady political career.

After the eight turbulent years of the Clinton administration, the ques-tion of Hillary Clinton's legacy on and contribution to the first ladyship has yet to be fully considered. Her White House tenure was fraught with con-troversy and scandal but also included impressive achievements. Mrs. Clin-ton seemed to recover from each setback, be it marital or political, and learn from each misstep.

At this point in time her legacy appears to be twofold. First, there are no longer any limits on what the first lady has attempted to do. Hillary Clinton moved the Office of First Lady from relative noncontroversy to embracing controversial issues. While previous first-lady projects included just saying "no" to drug abuse, literacy, and mental health, Mrs. Clinton's projects included, among other things, health care reform. President Clinton offered his wife executive responsibility and made her the point person on perhaps his major legislative initiative. In the White House, where perception is criti-cal, Mrs. Clinton occupied an office in the West Wing within proximity of the Oval Office and the major policy and advisory staff offices. There was lit-tle question about her power or influence. At the same time she evolved from personal adviser to public spokesperson and point person on policy issues. Future first ladies may elect to take less public roles, but the opportunity to be actively and publicly involved in discussions of the national agenda— whether right or wrong—is now a possibility.

Second, Hillary Clinton further pushed the boundaries of the role of first lady by running for public office and doing it *prior* to the conclusion of her husband's term in office. By taking this action, she decided that she would devote her energies to *both* her campaign and her duties as first lady, becom-ing a part-time first lady. Her daughter, Chelsea, and others assisted in ful-filling the duties of the office during Mrs. Clinton's absences from the White

House. The only other first lady to be involved in a public office was Eleanor Roosevelt, who temporarily held an office in the Civil Defense Agency and assumed a post as a member of the United States delegation to the United Nations in her post–White House years, where she chaired the United Nations' Committee on Human Rights.

The decision to be a full partner in her husband's presidency, the decision to head the health care initiative, the decision to fight charges about Bill Clinton's indiscretions, and the decision to run for the Senate were all Hillary's choices. Bold, creative, and tenacious, she chose to take a storied institution and give it new directions and limitless possibilities. Those who succeed her may not care to follow the trail that she blazed, but that trail, and with it the potential for accomplishment, will remain.

NOTES

1. Betty Houchin Winfield, "Introductory Notes: Hillary Rodham Clinton's Image: Content, Control, and Cultural Politics. A Symposium," *Political Communication* 14 (1997): 221.

2. Lewis L. Gould, "Modern First Ladies: An Institutional Perspective," *Prologue* 19 (summer 1987): 73.

3. Myra G. Gutin, *The President's Partner: The First Lady in the Twentieth Century* (Westport, Conn.: Greenwood Press, 1989), 86.

4. Helen Thomas quoted in Winzola McLendon and Scottie Smith, *Don't Quote Me! Washington Newswomen and the Power Society* (New York: Dutton, 1970), 70.

5. Bonnie Angelo quoted in Robert P. Watson, *First Ladies of the United States* (Boulder, Colo.: Lynne Rienner Publishers, 2001), 240–42.

6. Mary Ann Watson, *The Expanding Vista: American Television in the Kennedy Years* (New York: Oxford University Press, 1990), 142.

7. Marie Smith quoted in Foreman, *The First Lady,* 134.

8. Mrs. Lady Bird Johnson, interview by author, 2 Feb. 1979, Department of Communication, Rider University, Lawrenceville, N.J.

9. Rosalynn Carter, *First Lady from Plains* (Boston: Houghton Mifflin, 1984), 176.

10. Joyce Milton, *The First Partner: Hillary Rodham Clinton* (New York: Perennial, 1999), 17.

11. Lewis L. Gould, "Hillary Rodham Clinton," in *American First Ladies: Their Lives and Their Legacy,* ed. Lewis L. Gould (New York: Garland, 1996), 17.

12. Gail Sheehy, *Hillary's Choice* (New York: Random House, 1999), 56.

13. David Brock, *The Seduction of Hillary Rodham* (New York: Free Press, 1996), 22.

14. Hillary Rodham Clinton quoted in Brock, *Seduction,* 22.

15. Gould, *American First Ladies,* 632.

16. Hillary Rodham Clinton, interview by Carl S. Anthony for "The Role of the First Lady," televised on C-SPAN, 1 Jan. 1995.

17. Milton, *First Partner,* 48.

18. Gould, *American First Ladies,* 634.

19. Donnie Radcliffe, *Hillary Rodham Clinton: A First Lady for Our Time* (New York: Time Warner Books, 1993), 136.

20. Hillary Rodham Clinton quoted in Gould, *American First Ladies,* 639.

21. Mary Matalin and James Carville, *All's Fair: Love, War, and Running for President* (New York: Random House, 1994), 116.

22. Maureen Dowd, cited in Darlaine C. Gardetto, "Hillary Rodham Clinton, Symbolic Gender Politics and the *New York Times,*" *Political Communication* 14 (1997): 232–33.

23. Betty Houchin Winfield, "The Making of an Image: Hillary Rodham Clinton and American Journalists," *Political Communication* 14 (1997): 247.

24. Peggy Noonan, *The Case Against Hillary Clinton* (New York: Regan, 2000), 61.

25. Winfield, "Making of an Image," 247.

26. Robert Pear, "Court Rules That First Lady Is 'De Facto' Federal Official," *The New York Times,* 23 June 1994, A19.

27. Michael Wines, "First Lady's Health Strategy: Accept Less or Gamble It All?," *The New York Times,* 5 July 1994, A1.

28. Originally Mrs. Clinton said that she had nothing to do with the firings at the White House Travel Office. Later information seems to indicate that she was involved to a certain extent. See John Solomon, "Date Shows First Lady Pushed for Travel Office Firings," *The (South Jersey) Courier-Post,* 11 Jan. 1996, A7.

29. The most comprehensive coverage of Whitewater can be found in James B. Stewart, *Blood Sport* (New York: Simon & Schuster, 1996). A chronology of Whitewater events can be found in *Time* (18 Mar. 1996): 54–62.

30. Mrs. Clinton's commodities trading is examined in Stewart, *Blood Sport,* 240. For an interesting discussion of Mrs. Clinton's role inside the Clinton administration, see Bob Woodward, *The Agenda: Inside the Clinton White House* (New York: Simon & Schuster, 1994), 250–60.

31. Remarks to the United Nations Fourth World Conference on Women, Beijing, China, 5 Sept. 1995, official White House transcript. Transcripts of speeches and manuscripts of the conference can be obtained through the United Nations Division for the Advancement of women. See website at http://www.undp.org. To access documents, see http://www.undp.org/fwcw/dawoff.htm

32. Joe Conason and Gene Lyons, *The Hunting of the President: The Ten Year Campaign to Destroy Bill and Hillary Clinton* (New York: St. Martin's Press, 2000).

33. *The New York Times,* 22 Aug. 1998, 1.

34. Alison Mitchell, "Clinton Impeached: He Faces Senate Trial, 2nd in History: Vows to Do Job Till Term's 'Last Hour,'" *The New York Times,* 20 Dec. 1998, 1.

35. "Senator Clinton? The First Lady Gets into a New York State of Mind," *Time* 153 (26 Apr. 2000): 20.

36. Hillary Rodham Clinton, interview by Carl S. Anthony for "The Role of the First Lady," televised on C-SPAN, 1 Jan. 1995.

37. Fred Kaplan, "In Upstate NY, Mrs. Clinton Exults in Campaign Spotlight," *The Boston Globe,* 10 July 1999, A18.

38. Adam Nagourney, "Moving to Ease Doubts, First Lady Says She Will Enter Senate Race," *The New York Times,* 24 Nov. 1999, 1.

39. "Hillary's Announcement Speech," Purchase College (SUNY), 7 Feb. 2000, http://www.hillary2000.org

40. Ibid.

Fourteen

Sharing the Bully Pulpit

Breast Cancer and First Lady Betty Ford's Leadership

MaryAnne Borrelli

Introduction

On the evening of 27 September 1974 a presidential spokesman informed the nation that a routine physical had led to the discovery of a lump in the right breast of first lady Betty Ford. The first lady would have a biopsy the following morning; if the tumor was malignant, she would undergo a radical mastectomy. The news was difficult for the public to comprehend. After all, the first lady had appeared strong and vigorous earlier that day while dedicating the LBJ memorial grove and speaking at a Salvation Army meeting.[1]

Yet there was much more to the public response than surprise that a seemingly healthy person could be confronting a life-threatening disease. Prior to this announcement, the illnesses of first ladies had been handled discreetly throughout the history of the presidency.[2] Presidents' wives were usually presented as thoughtful and resilient, and any association with hardship seemed more romantic than real. A radical mastectomy, however, was very real. Polls indicated that cancer was the "most dreaded" disease of the time. In 1974 there were few support groups or advocacy organizations for cancer patients. Medical research advances notwithstanding, some people still held to the germ theory of cancer, so that having cancer was cause for shame and embarrassment.[3] To state publicly that the first lady had been diagnosed with breast cancer, therefore, was to identify a revered symbol with a subject of fear and superstition. Would Betty Ford's mortality lead to public rejection and humiliation? Or would her honesty and openness help to destigmatize cancer? These questions begin to indicate the ways in which the public announcement of Betty Ford's cancer diagnosis and treatment was a test of her reputation. This publicity forced the public to reconsider their expectations of and standards for first ladies. What symbolic significance would the public attach to a first lady who had been a breast cancer patient? What would it mean to have the "icon of American womanhood" be a woman who had had one breast amputated?[4]

These are also questions that ask about the connections between the first lady's reputation and her leadership role. As chief of state, the president embodies the spirit of the nation. Gender scholars have described the chief executive as modeling gender roles and political relationships, undertakings that are shared with the first lady.[5] Moreover, recent first ladies have translated their political philosophies into policy stances with increasing frequency. In order to be an effective leader, however, the first lady must be regarded as credible and legitimate. Did cancer rob Betty Ford of these resources? After all, cancer patients have suffered various kinds of discrimination. In the workplace, they have been fired, denied promotions and salary increases, and lost health and life insurance benefits. In their private lives, they have lost spouses and friends, and sometimes have been asked to leave their homes by those who fear contamination.[6] Was this alienation—or its political equivalent—experienced by the first lady?

These issues will be considered through a careful study of the letters that were received by Betty Ford immediately following her surgery. Particular consideration will be given to letters written by cancer survivors. In subsequent decades these women and men would mobilize and establish a powerful cancer movement. In 1974 their letters reveal how a first lady may facilitate political participation by those whom society has ostracized. Betty Ford's decision to dismiss tradition and to be open about her health problems challenged public perceptions about the first ladyship and about the disease. To appreciate this aspect of the first lady's leadership fully, however, it is necessary first to understand the policy and presidential context in which Betty Ford publicized her breast cancer diagnosis and treatment.[7]

THE FIRST LADY AND BREAST CANCER TREATMENT

By the time Betty Ford faced her cancer ordeal, funding for medical and cancer research was receiving significant government support. However, a cure remained in the distant future. Patient support and advocacy were in their earliest stages and were more an expression of individual impulses than of professional dedication. Fear of the disease and its consequences remained strong. This was the environment in which the White House announced that Betty Ford had breast cancer.

In late September 1974 Betty Ford had been first lady for approximately seven weeks. She was not yet well known to the ordinary citizen. As a congressional wife, her first priority had been raising her four children; in effect she had been a single parent throughout her husband's thirteen terms in the House. The year that Gerald Ford entered the presidential office was supposed to have been the year he retired from public life. Instead, there were new and extraordinary demands.

In the weeks between the president's swearing-in and Betty Ford's cancer operation, the first lady had hosted a state dinner (within forty-eight hours of becoming first lady), lobbied on behalf of the Equal Rights Amendment (ERA) with state legislators, conducted the first East Wing press conference since 1952, delivered speeches to political and public-interest organizations, and presided over numerous meetings pertaining to her policy concerns and interests.[8] When Betty Ford was diagnosed with breast cancer, it was presumed that her activism was at an end. One ERA lobbyist, for example, remarked that the breast cancer was a twofold tragedy: It would deprive the women's movement of an influential spokesperson and advocate, and it would deny the first lady the opportunity to realize her political talents and capitalize on her political opportunities. Such pessimism seemed more than justified by the medical treatments to which she was subjected.

Within forty-eight hours of the routine physical that had discovered the lump in her breast, the first lady underwent a biopsy and a radical mastectomy of the right breast. The radical mastectomy procedure had originally been developed by Dr. William Halsted of Johns Hopkins and had been the standard surgical treatment for breast cancer since the late nineteenth century. It was (and is) a serious medical procedure, involving the removal of the entire breast, the lymph nodes, and the pectoral muscles with all connecting ligaments and tendons. Even when it arrested the cancer, a radical mastectomy was likely to affect the individual's health negatively. Loss of the lymph nodes impaired the immune system and lowered resistance to disease. Loss of the pectoral muscle dramatically altered upper-body strength, especially in the arm. By the late 1970s and 1980s the radical mastectomy was being challenged by patients and doctors as "unnecessary mutilation" in all but extreme diagnoses. In 1990 the National Institutes of Health agreed that the radical mastectomy could be reserved to those cases, recommending lumpectomy and radiation therapy as effective alternatives that were far less intrusive and disfiguring.[9] These reconsiderations were made long after Betty Ford was treated, however. She underwent a radical mastectomy, radiation, and chemotherapy. Information about each of these treatments was made public, and there was extensive media coverage.[10]

The popular response was immediate and intense. Rather than stigmatizing and rejecting the first lady, the public seemed to empathize with her and with the first family. Women began going for preventive examinations in much greater numbers; many credited the first lady with saving their lives when malignant tumors were discovered and removed.[11] Among these women was the wife of the vice president, whose examination resulted in a double mastectomy. That both Betty Ford and Happy Rockefeller could have breast cancer seemed proof that everyone was vulnerable, a perception that gave added impetus to preventive care and helped destigmatize the disease.

Evidence that Betty Ford's reputation was not injured by the diagnosis can be seen in the public correspondence. The first lady received an estimated ninety-two cubic feet of mail wishing her a safe recovery and good health. The approximately 55,800 letters, cards, and messages received by the East Wing made frequent mention of her courage and strength, suggesting that her handling of this event actually bolstered her reputation.[12] In order to understand the source and character of this support, however, this correspondence must be analyzed in detail. The lengthier letters, in particular, reveal how the first lady was perceived, who most identified with her experiences and why, and how a first lady and the public might influence one another's political activism.

If an individual's skills and talents as a leader are to be judged by the changes that she effects, then consideration should be given to the ways in which Betty Ford and the letter writers influenced one another. In other words, it is important to think about the ways in which the public responded to her announcement about her breast cancer diagnosis and treatment in order to determine how that response evidenced a change in popular beliefs and perspectives. Leadership, after all, is typically measured by its results. These may be policy changes and institutional developments, as when the president draws on the executive or legislative powers assigned by Article II of the Constitution. Or these may be shifts in popular opinions and beliefs, as when the president draws on the more informal resources of the office to mobilize and motivate the public. In the case of Betty Ford's breast cancer experience, the first lady evidenced that second form of leadership in altering public understanding of cancer.

"Dear Mrs. Ford . . ."

The public correspondence to Betty Ford about her breast cancer diagnosis and treatment took the White House by surprise. When flowers also began to arrive, the Fords requested that any gifts be given to the American Cancer Society and then found that they were forwarding thousands of dollars to that organization.[13] Careful records were kept of all the gifts, which included books, religious articles, and various handmade remembrances. When all of these materials arrived at the presidential library, the archival staff requested and received permission to keep a random sample of the complete collection.

The archival inventory determined that approximately 70 percent of the correspondence was comprised of commercially produced get-well cards. The remaining 30 percent were, in approximately equal proportions, divided between handmade cards and personal letters. Only a few of the commercial cards were retained in the 5 percent sample, which therefore consisted primarily of letters and handmade cards.[14] Once sampled, each document was reviewed and "sanitized"—the author's name and address were removed—whenever it conveyed private information. Letters in which medical case histories were recounted, for example, were sanitized.

This study examined each of the "letters" in the sample. For the purposes of this work, every piece of correspondence that conveyed more than a brief phrase or sentence from its sender was considered a "letter." By this definition, there were 228 letters in the breast cancer public correspondence sample. The other sampled documents, which were not analyzed, were cards and other pieces of artwork. A coding schema was prepared and administered, making it possible to describe patterns across the letters in more quantitative terms. As already indicated, two sets of questions were particularly interesting. First, who was writing to the first lady? The writers were classified according to their sex and their self-described experience with cancer. Second, why were these individuals writing to the first lady about breast cancer? The letters were virtually unanimous in their efforts to encourage and support the first lady, but the character of that reassurance merited careful study.[15]

The vast majority (84.8 percent) of the letters to the first lady came from women. Most were written within a comparatively narrow time frame, from the evening of the president's initial announcement of the diagnosis through mid-October.[16] This information should not, however, be viewed as evidence that the letters were superficial or spontaneous. Several authors described themselves as being hesitant or uncertain about writing, feelings that they attributed to the subject matter, to their lack of a personal relationship with the first lady, or to the broader implications of writing to a public official. These and other passages indicate that writing to the first lady about breast cancer was a form of political participation that involved considerable risk taking. As the passages demonstrate, the letters were thoughtful, testifying to their authors' intellectual and emotional investment in their contents.

What patterns of identity and motivation can be discerned from the letters? Three distinct categories were identified, each of which is briefly described below.

(1) *Breast cancer survivors: 57.6 percent (n=131).* These individuals wrote to share their experiences and to reassure the first lady. Within this category, 44.3 percent (n=101) had personally dealt with breast cancer, while 10.1 percent (n=23) had seen the effects of breast cancer in family members and friends. This category also included the 3.1 percent (n=7) of letters from survivors of other cancers.

(2) *Religious witnesses: 20.2 percent (n=46).* As one individual wrote: "In various speeches and especially in his Inaugural Address, Mr. Ford made reference to God and to prayer. I thus conclude that your family possesses a firm belief in God and that you acknowledge Him as Supreme in your lives. It is for this reason that I have enclosed some non-denominational, purely Scriptural pamphlets which will help."[17] Letters such as this stressed the need for faith in difficult times and expressed confidence in God's enduring love. Bible verses were quoted and cited. Correspondence directly addressed the theological question of why a loving God would permit pain and suffering. Yet there was also a dose of politics mixed into the theology, as writers quoted or commented on the president's speeches.

(3) *Well-wishers: 22.4 percent (n=51).* The following passage reflects the tone of many of these letters: "Allow me to join with millions of others in wishing you a complete and speedy recovery from your illness. Your misfortune touched me as a woman—and your openness in dealing with the harrowing situation is an inspiration to countless other women. I'm not in the habit of writing to First Ladies. That you seem so accessible and, indeed, that you are such an individual is so refreshing. I look forward to happily reading about continued courage on your part as an active First Lady."[18] Letters such as this offered generalized good wishes and hopes that the first lady would fully recover from cancer and from the associated treatments. As in the quoted passage, the writers also commented on aspects of Betty Ford's public persona and politics.

Each category carries its own messages about the public perceptions of and responses to the first lady. The religious witness letters are interesting for their theological messages, but their connections between religion and politics also offer insights on political culture in the United States. Given the increasing electoral influence of the "Religious Right," this understanding is of considerable importance.[19] The well-wishers, in contrast, offer a more generalized commentary about the first lady and the first ladyship. In writing to express their sympathy for Betty Ford, these individuals also discuss the roles and responsibilities that they expect a first lady to fulfill. Thus, these letters are revelatory of the standards to which the first lady was held in the mid-1970s. However, the letters by cancer survivors—most specifically the letters by those who had personally dealt with the disease—are of most interest. These documents allow us to step beyond broad expressions of human sympathy and to see the deeper implications of the first lady's experiences. To reprise an important question, What does it mean for a woman in the position of first lady to have had breast cancer and a radical mastectomy?

The Power of Narrative

The letters written by the cancer survivors are personal narratives. In order to appreciate their content, therefore, an understanding is needed about what it means to share one's life story. This kind of knowledge has often been dismissed by scholars as too individualistic or too emotional, precisely because it is a personal and intimate record. Yet feminist scholars have argued that the rich subjectivity of women's and men's lives offers extraordinary opportunities for reflection and learning. These scholars add that so-called scientific objectivity is a dangerous mask for biases and presumptions that themselves merit close examination.[20]

There is a good philosophic foundation, then, for studying the survivors' letters as chronicles of personal and political meaning. These writers broke with prevailing societal strictures to share their understandings of a "dreaded disease," of surgical amputations, and of physical disfigurement. The letters, therefore, are complex essays. The presidential library considered this information so personal that it was "sanitized," an action rarely undertaken with public correspondence. The writers echoed the archivists' sentiment in commenting that relatives and friends had forgotten—if they ever knew—about their radical mastectomies. Thus, the writers reflect the contrasting forces of propriety and compassion, strength and fragility, privacy and confidence.

Breast cancer activism is seldom perceived as political activism.[21] And yet, in reading survivors' letters to Betty Ford, it becomes hard to understand this correspondence as anything other than political participation. The letter writing was communication with an officeholder at an intimate level, calling upon shared values and commenting on a shared concern. Certainly the letters mirrored Mrs. Ford's communication style, following the first lady's lead in publicly sharing a health condition that had previously been hidden.[22] In style and substance, then, the letters indicate Betty Ford's influence as a first lady.

Survivors, Not Victims

Illness is routinely associated with dependency and a loss of personal autonomy. In most instances it is also accepted as something for which no one is directly responsible—it occurs at the whim of fate or through mysterious biochemical interactions. For these reasons individuals diagnosed with life-threatening diseases are typically considered, at best, as victims. They are absolved of responsibility and viewed (or ignored) as reminders of human mortality and scientific ignorance. Cancer patients and others, however, have increasingly rejected the status of victim for that of survivor: victims are passive; survivors are proactive. A diagnosis of cancer brings extraordinary change but no reason to presumptively deny someone human dignity.[23]

These were the sentiments of the survivors who wrote to Betty Ford about their own breast cancer experiences and medical treatment. The letters indicated that the writers were undergoing a significant personal and political conversion. Quite clearly, most of the writers had previously viewed cancer as an essentially personal and private matter. For example, only 8.3 percent of the survivor letter writers mentioned having any contact with such programs as the Reach for Recovery Program of the American Cancer Society, which was then the most extensive network of post-radical-mastectomy women in the United States. Why were breast cancer survivors now changing their behavior in regard to this sensitive and personal issue? Why were they writing to the first lady?

Though some writers expressed their hope that Mrs. Ford would see their letters, media coverage about the flood of correspondence must have made them well aware that this was unlikely. Yet Betty Ford's correspondents could have hidden their thoughts and feelings in a journal. Instead they sent letters to a public official, forsaking a valued anonymity, even though the public official might never hear their voices. This was an act of considerable confidence, a kind of political activism that was revelatory of its participants' personal and political worth.

> The reason for my writing is to thank you for making your recent surgery public. I know this was a very difficult thing to do for a mastectomy is both a painful and private experience. I would think you had hoped to help someone in some way. . . . Because of you and my new knowledge of many other women my anxiety pushed [my doctor and I] to biopsy and the unbelievable news that the cyst was a malignant breast tumor. It could have been months before either my anxiety or my doctor's concern would have suggested biopsy.[24]

> The reason for this letter is to assure you both [the president and the first lady]—and anyone in like circumstances—that all this horror

and trauma is not the end of the world—you can make a complete recovery and lead normal, happy, productive lives. At the time of my own crisis, this was the assurance I most craved. I wanted someone to go out and "beat the bushes" to find survivors of over 5 years period from the date of their mastectomies.[25]

At a consistent minimum, the cancer survivors identified themselves as having had radical mastectomies (88.0 percent, n=95). They also indicated in some way the length of time that had passed since their operations (92.6 percent, n=100). Finally, they described their health at the current moment (65.7 percent, n=71) and their accomplishments (39.8 percent, n=43). The following is an example of a such a letter written to Betty Ford:

This time last year I, too, was in the hospital recovering from radical mastectomies on both breasts. It is a shock to one's entire system to go to sleep thinking a small knot is to be removed, and you wake up and both breasts are gone! In January, I was back in my classroom teaching full time and I never missed a day the rest of the year! This year I have been named assistant principal in addition to my regular teaching duties and I relish the additional work and responsibilities.[26]

The letter writers thus mirrored Betty Ford's own disclosure, pushing aside a strong societal taboo by talking about a personal health issue. They also rejected popular conceptions of cancer as a death sentence by noting the number of years they had lived since their diagnoses and treatments. These were claims of medical and psychological success. The subsequent descriptions of relationships, family life, and careers then resolved any concerns about the quality of a postmastectomy life. The letter writers treated years of life as an obvious "threshold goal" but then recited personal accomplishments in that period of time with great pride. In so doing, they described their transformation from victims to survivors.

Fundamentally the letters are reflections on the writers' identities. The physical, social, psychological, and sexual elements of the letter writers' self-understanding are considered and shared. Considering that the loss of a breast at that time was often popularly equated with a loss of femininity and sexuality, the power of these narratives is even more striking.[27] These women rejected those descriptions and proclaimed themselves productive and creative adults. In so doing, they revealed the impact of the first lady's action and example in making public her own cancer experience.

The Physical Body, Faith, and Life after Breast Cancer

Having set out the basic contours of their lives, the survivors diverged in their further assessments of how breast cancer affected their lives. For some (27.8 percent, n=30), providing this basic information was sufficient. For others (34.3 percent, n=37), there was a self-evident need to comment in greater detail on the physical aspects of their experiences. For still others (38.0 percent, n=41), there was a need to examine the religious meaning and significance of their suffering.

The Physical Body

Though a few of these writers (4.6 percent, n=5) said that they had been chronically ill before their cancer diagnoses, survivors more often implied that cancer had interrupted a healthy and active life. This circumstance undoubtedly contributed to the importance associated with the medical aspects of their cancer diagnoses and treatments.

A small number of the letters discussing the physical impact (4.6 percent, n=5) described misdiagnoses or other difficulties with their medical care. More often doctors were praised for their healing skills; individual doctors and hospitals were recommended (17.6 percent, n=19). As a rule, however, medical details and data were quickly passed over. These letters were personal accounts of physical experiences, not scientific reports. Consider, for example, the following accounts of the writers' postoperative recoveries.

> One of the first things we think of is, what am I going to look like, what will I wear? Believe me we can wear almost anything. The Prostheses they have are wonderful. I was most flattered when asked to model after I was back on my feet as I had always done a lot of it locally. They did not think I had changed and I am still modeling.[28]

> I drive every day, I swim (even backstroke), clean my windows, clean and move the furniture and just about everything.[29]

Each writer's goal was to regain her (or his in one case) preoperative lifestyle. Each letter, therefore, commented on the most important aspect of the writer's lifestyle—bodily appearance for the model, strength and agility for the amateur athlete, and so on. The writers recognized that their former routines were now achievements, but they refused to see cancer as diminishing them in any meaningful way. This mind-set was sustained even when the radical mastectomy did affect the writer's lifestyle. For example,

> I am right-handed and before the operation I was very active, (I am a 27 year old high school chemistry teacher, and I enjoy bicycling, tennis,

basketball, etc.) and I was anxious to return to normal activities. . . . The chinning bar helped me so much that I was playing light tennis again in six weeks, much sooner than the doctor had predicted. . . . I have regained complete use of my arm, (though it will never be as strong as before, I have free movement).[30]

The grassroots cancer movement of the 1980s and 1990s would encourage people to appreciate the courage required for recovery from cancer and a radical mastectomy. In the mid-1970s, however, people generally preferred to hide this experience. It was important to be able to "pass" for "normal" and to avoid the stereotyping often directed at cancer patients. Individual strength was not yet associated with a constructive and collective identity for breast cancer survivors or for post-radical-mastectomy women and men.

Faith

The physically centered letters celebrated the writers' quality of life by secular standards. The religiously centered correspondence, in contrast, had a biblical and evangelistic tone. The following is an example of a religiously centered letter: "May I share with you the thoughts I had when I came out of surgery. In 2 Corinthians 12:9–10 it says, My grace is sufficient for you. My strength is made perfect in weakness. Most gladly therefore will I rather glory in my infirmities so that the power of Christ may rest upon you. At that time I experienced a power that I had never had before. These verses were great source of strength to me. He really gave me peace at that time and I am praying that he will give you that peace too."[31]

Although these writers viewed cancer as a test of faith, they did not depict it as one imposed by a harsh or vindictive God. Instead, the writers responded to the "why me?" question in terms that counseled trust in God's love and confidence in one's own resources. For example: "When I was ill my sister used to pray that my life would be used to glorify Christ. In all honesty I will admit there were many days when I used to wish she would just concentrate on asking God for my good health and forget the rest. Her prayer has been answered and I am happier than I have ever been in my life, and I am *so glad* she prayed as she did. I especially will be praying that same prayer for you knowing as I do that God will answer."[32]

The more secular survivors' letters described healing in terms of activities resumed. This focus on personal accomplishments was entirely congruent with the individualistic and rights-centered orientation of Lockean liberalism, the political philosophy that has underlaid mainstream political culture in the United States. The religious witnesses among the survivors, however, described their healing in more relational terms. Their sense of wellness and of reconciliation with God was more inclusive of others than it was centered on self. In this sense the survivors who were religious witnesses posed a double challenge to established standards. First, they self-identified as breast cancer and radical mastectomy survivors, breaking taboos about discussions of the "dreaded disease" and of women's health. Second, they recommended less individualistic and more collectivist standards for the quality of life.[33]

Sharing the Bully Pulpit?

The letters sent to Betty Ford in response to the public announcement of her breast cancer diagnosis and radical mastectomy indicate that the first lady did help to destigmatize this disease. Her willingness to acknowledge her cancer publicly sparked a similar response from women and men who had previously remained silent. This sharing of experiences, already a hallmark of the women's movement of the 1960s and 1970s, would become an essential element of the grassroots cancer movement.[34]

A leader will always be judged, at least in part, by her or his effect on followers. In this particular instance Betty Ford led a number of women and men into a more public understanding of who and what they were. But was this merely confessional? Was she drawing on her celebrity status or was she acting as a political leader? Was Ford delivering a substantive message and sharing the president's bully pulpit?

Those who argue that Betty Ford was not a political leader vis-à-vis breast cancer can quote from two of the first lady's writings in support of their contentions. In her first memoir, which tells about her life up through her years in the White House, she writes, "If I hadn't been the wife of the President of the United States, the press would not have come racing after my story, so in a way it was fate."[35] This statement implies that her contribution was passive, as opposed to the activism of a leader. A passage from her February 1975 article in *McCall's* seems to reinforce this perspective: "This is the last time I will discuss the mastectomy. I want to go back to the support for fields I have previously committed myself to. I can't afford to let this episode become the focal point of my life. I had no choice; it was something I *had to do*. It is over now."[36] These words are interpreted as silencing further discussion, reversing the transformational effects of her earlier public statements about cancer. Betty Ford noted to White House aides that she was tired of having people study her chest, trying to remember which breast had been removed. However, once her words have been put in the context of the breast cancer letters, and in the context of ongoing policy and political developments, it becomes clear that the first lady was exercising leadership in this issue area.

First, it is necessary to study the critics' evidence more thoroughly. Betty Ford does seem to remove herself from the cancer issue network in the *McCall's* article. Yet she continued to deliver speeches about cancer and participated in American Cancer Society events, even receiving several awards from that organization. Her daughter Susan has continued this commitment in more recent years.[37] Why, then, would the first lady claim that she would no longer discuss her breast cancer diagnosis and treatment? This author believes that the *McCall's* article is properly understood as a reclaiming and a reassertion of autonomy by the first lady. As such, the article echoes the writings of breast cancer survivors whose letters encouraged the first lady to establish her own standard of healing and to resist being identified with her disease. This reinterpretation is buttressed by passages in the first lady's memoir that reflect on her breast cancer diagnosis and treatment. For example, "Lying in the hospital, thinking of all those women going for cancer checkups because of me, I'd come to realize more clearly the power of the woman in the White House. Not *my* power, but the power of the position, a power which could be used to help."[38]

Mrs. Ford describes the Office of the First Lady as having "power." She thereby concludes that the woman in this office has the ability to make things happen directly and immediately. She does not write, for example, that the first lady can exert influence, which would connote a more indirect and less autonomous effect. "Power" raises concerns of accountability and responsiveness, whereas influence merely leads to questions about the decision-making process and its participants.

Betty Ford seems aware of this distinction and its implications. Evidence of this conclusion is seen in her descriptions of the first lady's power as being drawn from, and therefore appropriately returned to, the people. This is "a power which could be used to help." Notwithstanding her use of the conditional verb tense, Mrs. Ford's writings and actions suggest that she actually viewed this possibility as a normative imperative: The power of the first ladyship *should* be used to help. These were conclusions she articulated in association with her recovery from the radical mastectomy. They were also ideals that she set in the historical context of her office's development and that she implemented during her White House years.

Because her husband had not been elected to the presidency, Betty Ford readily acknowledged that her first weeks in the White House plunged her into situations for which she had little preparation. That "learning by doing" approach was interrupted by her breast cancer diagnosis and surgery, which involved a two-week postoperative hospital stay. A life-threatening illness often causes a person to undertake a personal reassessment, but Betty Ford extended her reflections to her public responsibilities. Without confusing her self and her "position"—indication that she perceived herself as an office-holder and not merely as a celebrity—she thought through the role of the first ladyship.

Ronald Heifetz's discussion of adaptive authority is highly relevant to Betty Ford's experience with breast cancer and her consequent learning about the Office of the First Lady. Rather than exercising power through command-and-control, which presumes omniscience on the part of the leader and complete obedience on the part of the followers, the adaptive leader exercises authority interactively. The leader and the followers exchange ideas, and every participant is changed through that sharing. The leader's effectiveness is then demonstrated through the emergence of a new consensus.

Heifetz illustrates the working of adaptive leadership through a case study of Lyndon Johnson's management of events surrounding the passage of the 1965 Voting Rights Act: "We often think that leadership means having a clear vision and the capacity to persuade people to make it real. In this case, Johnson had authored no vision. Events acted on him to shape the vision to which he then gave powerful articulation. He *identified the nation's vision* and put it into words. As the nation clarified its values, so did he. . . . Along with the nation, he wrestled with its fundamental and enduring values. He gave those values the power of his voice and his presence. And he seized the moment to turn the nation's emerging values into potent legislation."[39] The same conclusion could be written about Betty Ford and breast cancer, though the new social consensus would not be marked by formal policy for several years. Both LBJ and Betty Ford stated that they only fully understood their power *after* confronting their responsibilities as leaders. They then described themselves as becoming aware of their moral obligation to "appeal to the best in our people," to "help." Subsequently they both worked to forge new alliances throughout society. Johnson secured landmark legislation. Mrs. Ford altered popular perceptions of a disease and its survivors. The president moved from the exercise of informal power to the exercise of formal power, while the first lady consistently exercised informal power.

Informal power, of course, is the hallmark of the first lady. Yet leadership exercised informally is still leadership. In fact, the full measure of first lady Betty Ford's leadership can only be appreciated if one takes seriously President Johnson's contention that "the moral force of the presidency" has real effects in altering public perceptions and opinions. Johnson spoke of the presidency, not merely the president; and the first lady is most definitely a member of the presidency.[40] Betty Ford's public announcement of her cancer diagnosis and treatment led to an outpouring of support, suggesting that the public was ceasing to view cancer as reason for shame or guilt. Also in response to this announcement, women altered their health care priorities to give greater attention to preventive care, and many were saved through the early diagnosis of malignant tumors. Yet cancer survivors were not the only individuals whose identity the first lady sought to recast or whose lives she sought to improve.

Always supportive of the women's movement, Betty Ford wrote in her memoirs that her breast cancer led her to reinvigorate her commitment to women, children, the elderly, and the mentally handicapped. In particular she claimed a public and authoritative role for a gender previously confined to the private sphere. She would even revise statements in order to emphasize this point (previous wording in brackets): "I'm in favor of the equal rights amendment not only for equal pay for equal work, but because I feel every woman should have the right to decide the direction of her life. Whether a woman chooses a career in the home or outside the home, what is important is that she make that decision herself—without [the] any pressures [that] to restrict her choice. This is what real liberation is about! A liberated woman is one who feels confident in herself and is happy in what she's doing. She's a person who has a sense of self."[41] In this speech, made to the members of the Homecoming and Identity Conference, Betty Ford insisted that she and other women be allowed to construct their own identities. This intensely political message was the foundation of her alliance with and contribution to the women's movement of the 1970s.[42] It also became the distinguishing feature of her leadership and tenure as first lady.

Conclusion

Betty Ford did enter and share the bully pulpit with Gerald Ford, delivering a political message that was substantive and significant. Her actions in regard to breast cancer exemplified the adaptive exercise of authority, as they were both proactive and responsive. Her decision to make public both her diagnosis and her treatment prompted many women to alter their medical practices. In a number of cases preventive health care measures resulted in lifesaving medical interventions, as examinations revealed otherwise undetected cancers. Women and men also responded to the first lady by writing to her about their own experiences with cancer. As careful study of these letters has revealed, Betty Ford's example led to a powerful assertion of strength and resilience by these writers. Their complex narratives reject societal standards of silence and insist on new standards of personal autonomy and political engagement.

In response to these actions and writings, Betty Ford reassessed the first ladyship and its "power . . . to help." As detailed in her memoirs and as evidenced in her speeches, her reflections caused her to renew her efforts on behalf of women, children, the elderly, and the mentally handicapped. She became even more frank and forthright about her views, a tactic that sometimes generated great controversy. Later, as a former first lady, Betty Ford again went public with personal disclosures about her health, this time in regard to alcohol and drug addiction. Becoming a spokesperson for recovery programs, she again rejected prevailing societal standards to insist that illnesses be destigmatized and treated.

The effects of Betty Ford's conclusions about the first ladyship and her actions as a first lady had implications far beyond her own career or the Ford administration. As she noted, the first lady's power was derived from an office, not a personality, and that office was evolving through history. Betty Ford's public announcement of her breast cancer and radical mastectomy altered conceptions of the first ladyship. No longer would a first lady be judged principally by decorum or discretion. Courage and individualism also entered the mix. Beauty and strength became more complicated ideals. Subsequent first ladies began to address issues that went beyond being controversial (as was Lady Bird Johnson's beautification program) to those that were difficult for and even frightening to the popular imagination. Rosalynn Carter would lead a presidential commission and secure notable legislative advances in mental health. Nancy Reagan would mobilize and support networks dedicated to the prevention of and recovery from drug addiction. First lady Hillary Rodham Clinton would address women's rights as human rights.

Betty Ford's demographic profile made her an unlikely breast cancer survivor. She and her husband held highly stressful and time-consuming positions. Her familial support system was further limited by the absence of all but her youngest child. She had suffered chronic pain for years, the result of a pinched nerve and severe arthritis. Previously those medical conditions had sometimes caused depression and necessitated psychiatric care. A former dancer, her physical appearance was important to her. In brief, she had few of the advantages typically associated with a good recovery from a radical mastectomy.[43] She was, further, a first lady in an unelected administration struggling to reestablish the credibility and legitimacy of the presidency. Betty Ford therefore had many more reasons to accept than to resist societal standards and political norms. Yet having issued a challenge, she both led and followed. She empowered and was empowered. She held the pulpit and she shared it—with the president and with a people.

NOTES

1. Marjorie Hunter, "Mrs. Ford Faces a Breast Biopsy," *New York Times,* 28 Sept. 1974, 30; Hunter, "Ford's Wife Undergoes Breast Cancer Surgery," *New York Times,* 29 Sept. 1974, 1.

2. Gil Troy, *Mr. and Mrs. President, from the Trumans to the Clintons,* 2d ed., revised (Lawrence: University Press of Kansas, 2000), 209.

3. James T. Patterson, *The Dread Disease: Cancer and Modern American Culture* (Cambridge: Harvard University Press, 1987), 232–41.

4. Barbara Burrell, "The Office of the First Lady and Public Policymaking," in *The Other Elites: Women, Politics, and Power in the Executive Branch,* ed. MaryAnne Borrelli and Janet M. Martin (Boulder, Colo.: Lynne Rienner Publishers, 1997), 169.

5. See Georgia Duerst-Lahti, "Reconceiving Theories of Power: Consequences of Masculinism in the Executive Branch," in *The Other Elites: Women, Politics, and Power in the Executive Branch,* ed. MaryAnne Borrelli and Janet M. Martin (Boulder, Colo.: Lynne Rienner Publishers, 1997).

6. Patterson, *Dread Disease,* 236–41, 271.

7. The author thanks Dr. Harold J. Burstein of Harvard Medical School and Professor Stephen H. Loomis of Connecticut College, who graciously shared their expertise in the history of science and human physiology. Two archivists at the Gerald R. Ford Library were especially helpful in conducting this research: Lessa Tobin supported this project in its earliest stages and Geir Gundesen helped bring it to a conclusion. Finally, the author would like to acknowledge the support of the Gerald R. Ford Foundation, whose research grant program partially funded this study.

8. Betty Ford, *The Times of My Life* (New York: Harper and Row, 1978), 157–81.

9. Marilyn Yalom, *A History of the Breast* (New York: Alfred A. Knopf, 1997), 228–29; Jane E. Brody, "Fast Action Vital in Cancer Cases," *New York Times,* 29 Sept. 1974, 23; Brody, "Report Intensifies a Breast Cancer Dispute," *New York Times,* 2 Oct. 1974, 29; Brody, "Mrs. Ford Facing Tests to Determine Treatment," *New York Times,* 1 Oct. 1974, 1.

10. Betty Ford, *Times of My Life,* 182–94.

11. Brody, "Inquiries Soaring on Breast Cancer," *New York Times,* 6 Oct. 1974, 21.

12. Disposal Request #6, 21 Oct. 1977, Gerald R. Ford Library, Ann Arbor, Mich.

13. At least one correspondence objected to this recommendation; a florist wrote to President Ford that "people send flowers because it's a warmth in their hearts,

money is cold." See Wallace Peterson to President Ford, 29 Sept. 1974, "Box 326, 20 letters," Folder, Box 26, Breast Cancer Bulk Mail, White House Social Files, Gerald R. Ford Library, Ann Arbor, Mich.

14. Disposal Request #6, 21 Oct. 1977, Gerald R. Ford Library, Ann Arbor, Mich.

15. Included in the breast cancer correspondence collection was one letter, written on 8 Mar. 1975, that commented on a recent report of the first lady's arthritis. This letter, which was the only critical letter in the collection, offered the following counsel: "my Christian Science aunt . . . always used to tell me that feelings of guilt cause most illnesses. Consequently, I write to suggest that you try to rid yourself of any feelings of guilt that may have arisen from your practice of abusing your husband's office and the prestige of the White House to push women's lib." See Edward De Jongh to Mrs. Gerald Ford, 8 Mar. 1975, "Box 322, 20 letters," Folder, Box 25, Breast Cancer Bulk Mail, White House Social Files, Gerald R. Ford Library, Ann Arbor, Mich.

16. However, breast-cancer-related mail continued to arrive at the White House through Dec. 1974. See White House Social Files, Gerald R. Ford Library, Ann Arbor, Mich.

17. Mrs. Karen Snidar to Mrs. Betty Ford, 1 Oct. 1974, "Box 429," Folder, Box 31, Breast Cancer Bulk Mail, White House Social Files, Gerald R. Ford Library, Ann Arbor, Mich.

18. Lisa Schwarzbaum to Mrs. Ford, 1 Oct. 1974, "Box 330, 20 letters," Folder, Box 26, Breast Cancer Bulk Mail, White House Social Files, Gerald R. Ford Library, Ann Arbor, Mich.

19. The influence of the "Religious Right" and its power to check the first lady would be particularly evident in the White House response to public criticism following Betty Ford's *60 Minutes* interview in 1975. See Gerald R. Ford, *A Time to Heal: An Autobiography of Gerald R. Ford* (New York: Harper and Row, 1979) 306–7; and Sheila Rabb Weidenfeld, *First Lady's Lady: With the Fords at the White House* (New York: G. P. Putnam's Sons, 1979), 162–88.

20. Sandra Harding, *Feminism and Methodology* (Bloomington: Indiana University Press, 1986). For an early and popular consideration of subjectivity, see Gloria Steinem, *Outrageous Acts and Everyday Rebellions* (New York: New American Library, 1983).

21. Ulrike Boehmer, *The Personal and the Political: Women's Activism in Response to Breast Cancer and the AIDS Epidemic.* (Albany: SUNY Press, 2000).

22. For a discussion of one individual's recognition of cancer as a feminist issue, see Susan Shapiro, "Cancer as a Feminist Issue," in *Frontline Feminism, 1975–1995: Essays from Sojourner's First 20 Years,* ed. Karen Kahn (San Francisco: Aunt Lute Books, 1995).

23. Audre Lorde, *The Cancer Journals* (San Francisco: Aunt Lute Press, 1980); Leatrice H. Lifshitz, ed., *Her Soul beneath the Bone: Women's Poetry on Breast*

Cancer (Chicago: University of Illinois Press, 1988), xvii. Two further points should be connected with this issue of self-identification: first, three of the breast cancer letter writers did describe themselves as "victims." However, they articulated the same themes seen in the correspondence of other survivors; they were neither passive nor accepting of a terminal diagnosis. Second, during the mid-1970s, some continued to believe that cancer could result from an immoral or otherwise flawed lifestyle. For this reason, some cancer survivors did favor self-identification as victims in order to stress their blamelessness and innocence.

24. [sanitized] Letter to Mrs. Ford, 29 Nov. 1974, "Box 326, 20 letters," Folder, Box 26, Breast Cancer Bulk Mail, White House Social Files, Gerald R. Ford Library, Ann Arbor, Mich.

25. [sanitized] Letter to Mrs. Ford, 25 Nov. 1974, "Box 326, 20 letters," Folder, Box 26, Breast Cancer Bulk Mail, White House Social Files, Gerald R. Ford Library, Ann Arbor, Mich.

26. [sanitized] Letter to Mrs. Ford, 28 Sept. 1974, "Box 330, 20 letters," Folder, Box 26, Breast Cancer Bulk Mail, White House Social Files, Gerald R. Ford Library, Ann Arbor, Mich.

27. Lorde, *Cancer Journals,* passim; Yalom, *History of the Breast,* 270, 278.

28. [sanitized] Letter to Mrs. Ford, no date, "Box 330, 20 letters," Folder, Box 26, Breast Cancer Bulk Mail, White House Social Files, Gerald R. Ford Library, Ann Arbor, Mich.

29. [sanitized] Letter to Mrs. Ford, 11 Oct. 1974, "Box 429, 20 letters," folder, Box 31, Breast Cancer Bulk Mail, White House Social Files, Gerald R. Ford Library, Ann Arbor, Mich.

30. [sanitized] Letter to Mrs. Ford, 13 Oct. 1974, "Box 357, 20 letters," Folder, Box 27, Breast Cancer Bulk Mail, White House Social Files, Gerald R. Ford Library, Ann Arbor, Mich.

31. Phodoris Wallested to Mrs. Ford, 30 Sept. 1974, "Box 429, 20 letters," Folder, Box 31, Breast Cancer Bulk Mail, White House Social Files, Gerald R. Ford Library, Ann Arbor, Mich.

32. [sanitized] Letter to Mrs. Ford, 1 Oct. 1974, "Box 429; 20 letters," Folder, Box 30, Breast Cancer Bulk Mail, White House Social Files, Gerald R. Ford Library, Ann Arbor, Mich.; emphasis is in the original.

33. See Carol Gilligan, *In a Different Voice, Psychological Theory and Women's Development* (Cambridge: Harvard University Press, 1982).

34. Ulrike Boehmer has noted that some view this movement as a "cancer movement" while others identify it more specifically as a "breast cancer movement." Because the movement is inclusive in nature, notwithstanding the high profile given breast cancer, it has been described as a "cancer movement" in this piece. See Boehmer, *Personal and the Political.*

35. Betty Ford, *Times of My Life,* 186.

36. Quoted in Troy, *Mr. and Mrs. President,* 210; emphasis is in the original.

37. In 1976, for example, Betty Ford received the Communicator of Hope Award from the American Cancer Society. In her acceptance speech she reiterated her determination not to let cancer divert her attention from other projects and noted the need for greater public awareness of preventative care. Both themes in the speech had extensive markups from the first lady, indicating that she had taken a personal interest in how they were articulated. See "Communicator of Hope Award, American Cancer Society, December 1, 1976," 1976/12/01, American Cancer Society's Communicator of Hope Award Folder, Box 4, Speech Reading Copies File, Frances Kay Pullen Files, Gerald R. Ford Library, Ann Arbor, Mich.

38. Betty Ford, *Times of My Life,* 194.

39. Ronald Heifetz, *Leadership Without Easy Answers* (Cambridge: Harvard University Press, 1994), 148–49.

40. See Public Law 95-570, White House Personnel Authorization—Employment. Section 105 (e).

41. "Mrs. Ford's Remarks before Participants in the Homemaking and Identity Conference, 26 Sept. 1975," "Homemaking and Identity Conference, White House, September 26, 1975," Folder, Box 3, Frances Kay Pullen Files, Gerald R. Ford Library, Ann Arbor, Mich.

42. On the frequent occurrence of this theme in Ford's speeches, see Myra G. Gutin, *The President's Partner: The First Lady in the Twentieth Century* (New York: Greenwood Press, 1989).

43. For a discussion of the literature pertaining to these variables, see Doris T. Penman et. al., "The Impact of Mastectomy on Self-Concept and Social Function: A Combined Cross-Sectional and Longitudinal Study with Comparison Groups," in *Woman and Cancer,* ed. Steven D. Stellman (New York: Haworth Press, 1987).

PART SIX

Conclusion

Presidential scholars have long noted that the most important asset to any successful president is his wife. First ladies have performed a variety of functions and roles to help further their husbands' political and public policy fortunes. First ladies have been extremely active in campaigning for their husbands and their respective parties' nominees for congressional and senate seats. They have been active in social and charitable causes either on their own or in conjunction with their husbands' policy agendas. Many first ladies have been among the elite social hosts of their era. Perhaps the two most notable social hosts of their times were Dolley Madison and Jacqueline Kennedy. First ladies have also branched out on their own in search of public policy causes. Modern first ladies including Lady Bird Johnson, Rosalynn Carter, and Hillary Rodham Clinton contributed to the professionalization of the Office of the First Lady and its integration with the White House Office. They also championed their own public policy causes, from the beautification of America to mental health awareness to the increased protection of children at risk. Modern first ladies have become so involved in the policy process that they have frequently appeared before congressional committees to testify for legislation sponsored by the White House. They have also engaged in lobbying and, in Hillary Clinton's case, the development of health care policy and the recent successful conclusion of a New York Senate race.

When surveying the various roles and functions that first ladies perform, it quickly becomes clear that the most important role for any first lady is presidential adviser. First ladies are in a unique position with respect to the presidency. While they have no constitutional role, they often see the president upon arising for the day and retiring at night. No other presidential adviser or lobbyist can hope to match this arrangement. The relationship that a president develops with a first lady can go a long way in deciding her influence. This type of relationship has changed as society has changed.

First ladies today are more overtly active socially and politically than in the early days of our nation. The suffragette, equal rights, civil rights, and the women's movement have all contributed to a new society for women, and first ladies have strongly influenced these movements and causes. In this century, for example, both Betty Ford, Rosalynn Carter, and Hillary Rodham Clinton actively supported the proposed Equal Rights Amendment to the Constitution. To truly understand the relationship between a first lady and a president, an exploration of the type of partnership they have developed and the impact of changing societal roles concerning women upon this relationship is necessary.

PREMODERN FIRST LADIES

As the various essays in this work establish, modern first ladies were not the only influential ones. The accomplishments of earlier first ladies cannot simply be analyzed as those of their more modern counterparts would be. The first ladies of the founding period were instrumental in establishing the position of first lady. As Patricia Brady has demonstrated, Martha Washington's commitment to duty and her ability to forge a partnership with her husband literally launched the first ladyship. Catherine Allgor's analysis of the early first ladies, especially Dolley Madison, helps us view these extraordinary women through a new lens. First ladies have always been influential. We may have missed just how influential they were by failing to place ourselves within their social context. These early occupants of the office utilized tools that were available to help advance their husbands' agendas. Thus, Dolley Madison's social gatherings possess a distinct public quality. This was the tool that she used to make the Washington contacts that would advance President Madison's agenda. Seen in this light, activist first ladies have always been influential. In more recent times, as Mary Linehan points out in her essay, Betty Ford and other first ladies captured the public's attention and through their high-profile first ladyships transformed the office into the highly visible, public institution it is today.

Personalities, social contacts, hostessing, management of the White House, and partnerships with their husbands were the early tools that first ladies had in their arsenals. As the essays here indicate, the more activist of these ladies used these tools well. As Elizabeth Lorelei Thacker-Estrada notes, while these tools were exercised behind the scenes, their effectiveness cannot be denied, especially when placed in the hands of first ladies such as Dolley Madison, Sarah Polk, Margaret Taylor, Abigail Fillmore, and Jane Pierce.

In fact these behind-the-scenes influences were used most effectively by Edith Wilson and Bess Truman, as James McCallops and Raymond Frey, respectively, note in their essays. Mrs. Wilson, Mrs. Truman, and other first ladies, acting as concerned spouses, sought to support and protect their husbands and in so doing emerged as trusted confidantes. Gil Troy suggests that even traditional modern first ladies such as Mamie Eisenhower and Barbara Bush have had their impact upon public policy and social causes. The accomplishments of the more traditional first ladies should not be dismissed.

Modern First Ladies: Lessons Learned

The essays in parts 4 and 5 represent an attempt to add to the analyses in the relatively new field of modern first ladies studies. Historians have pioneered the field, but in recent years the disciplines of political science, psychology, communications, and sociology have contributed to this emerging area. These disciplines have been interested in the modern era of first ladies, but this era presents some problems. Since Eleanor Roosevelt was first lady, only eleven first ladies have occupied the office, and the tenures of seven of them were less than two terms. Two, Jacqueline Kennedy and Betty Ford, served less than one term. Only Mamie Eisenhower. Nancy Reagan, and Hillary Clinton have served two terms. Only three can be classified as strong activists: Lady Bird Johnson, Rosalynn Carter, and Hillary Rodham Clinton. Only one of these strong activists, Hillary Clinton, has served two terms. With such an uneven base concerning first-lady tenure, it becomes difficult to detect trends and assess reforms to the first ladyship. What are the lessons learned from these essays?

First, any influence that a first lady has will be, in part, conditioned by the type of relationship she has with her husband. Many of these essays include references to Robert Watson's categorization of presidential partnerships in his work *The President's Wives: Reassessing The Office of the First Lady*. Presidential partnerships range from first ladies being nonpartners, partners in marriage, behind-the-scenes partners, partial partners, and full partners. The most influential and powerful first ladies achieved full partnerships with their husbands. In this type of relationship the first lady is perceived by the president as a copartner and trusted adviser. Her insights are not only solicited but welcomed by the president.

Second, influence is also conditioned by the backgrounds first ladies bring to their job. Generally the more independent and professional the background, the more influence she will wield. Post–Eleanor Roosevelt first ladies who had jobs or significant professional responsibilities have generally been activists. For example, Lady Bird Johnson ran her husband's congressional office while he was serving military duty. Rosalynn Carter virtually ran the Carter peanut business. Hillary Rodham Clinton was a practicing lawyer and advocate for many issues long before she became first lady. Betty Ford was a professional dancer. As the roles and status of women change, it is likely that more of these types of first ladies will serve.

Third, as Eleanor Roosevelt's experience demonstrates, activist and independent first ladies with their own social public policy agendas will inevitably become lightning rods for controversy. An example can be seen in the recent experiences of first lady Hillary Rodham Clinton. In fact, many observers compare Mrs. Roosevelt with Mrs. Clinton for these very reasons. The essays in part 5, such as those by Kay M. Knickrehm and Robin Teske, as well as those by Gil Troy and MaryAnne Borrelli, demonstrate the problems associated with the public/private divide for modern first ladies. It seems that this is a transition period concerning women's roles and that U.S. first ladies are still caught in this transition. Thus, first ladies have faced and will face paradoxical expectations from the public and the press. This is evident in the varying public perceptions of Betty Ford and Hillary Clinton, as pointed out in the essays by Borrelli and Myra G. Gutin, respectively.

Fourth, all of the above variables have affected the formal Office of the First Lady. There has been a trend toward professionalization of the office. For example, staffers are better paid today than at any previous period. Many advisers to the first lady have presidential adviser status. The office has been organized more professionally throughout the post–World War II era. As a result, modern first ladies were and are able to take on new and different responsibilities, including foreign policy responsibilities.

Fifth, the Office of the First Lady is now highly integrated with the various divisions of the White House Office. Such integration is tempered by the type of relationship a first lady has with the president. It is also affected by the compatibility of the policy agendas of the first lady and the president. If compatibility is high, then integration will also be high. During the last fifty years there has been a noticeable movement of office space for the first lady from the East Wing to the West Wing and currently the Old Executive Office Building of the White House. Geographical proximity is but one indication of integration.

Sixth, greater responsibility for policy development and agenda setting go hand in hand with such office integration. As noted in the essay by Colton C. Campbell and Sean E. McCluskie, first ladies today are testifying more frequently before congressional committees. Mrs. Clinton has pushed the boundaries here by not only testifying but also serving as a prime architect of health care policy. As integration and professionalization continue and as full partnership between first couples intensifies, this trend will increase. Indeed, it may already be institutionalized by the actions of modern first ladies. Just as in presidential studies scholars note the increasing powers left by one president for their successors, the same principle holds true for first ladies. Part of the expansion of influence and policy roles has involved foreign policy and international affairs, where first ladies, as examined in the essay by Glenn Hastedt, have emerged as forces in international goodwill and diplomacy.

Seventh, the Office of the First Lady may be seen as a potential stepping stone toward continued public service. The path blazed by Mrs. Clinton's historic Senate victory may be but an indication of future possibilities for first ladies. If this turns out to be the case, there will be a wealth of scholarly activity and perhaps a newfound and well-deserved interest in first-lady studies. Susan Roth Breitzer notes in her essay on Eleanor Roosevelt that such post–White House political careers—and many other facets of the modern office—stemmed in large measure from the trailblazing first ladyship of Eleanor Roosevelt.

Eighth, this implies that the time is ripe for the development of a new explanatory model for first ladies, a more independent/integrative model conditioned by the marital relationships and professional backgrounds and interests of first ladies. There might be some predictive elements associated with such a model. For example, by examining the marital relationship and history between first couples and the professional backgrounds and personalities of first ladies along with their dedication to social issues and causes, it might be possible to predict generally how active these first ladies will be. It may also be possible to judge how they might best utilize their office.

These essays have merely scratched the surface of first ladies studies. For example, much more work needs to be done on the role and involvement of first ladies in foreign policy. This is true not only for the modern era but also for the eighteenth and nineteenth centuries. Scholars and journalists need to make an effort to include first ladies and their office in books on the presidency. This should be a normal procedure, considering the potential influence first ladies possess. Professional and scholarly associations should sponsor workshops and conferences on the subjects of first ladies studies. Students should be encouraged to do research on the various topics associated with first-lady studies. Finally, if it is true, as Ted Sorensen noted about the presidency long ago in his *Decision Making in the White House,* that the office affects the man as much as the man affects the office, then the same holds true for first ladies. This sentiment should provide the impetus for more professional and steady assessments of first ladies, their office, and their accomplishments.

APPENDIX

Chronological List of First Ladies

President	First Lady	First Lady Birth–Death	Pres. Years

indicates a spouse who died prior to her husband's service as president

President	First Lady	First Lady Birth–Death	Pres. Years
George Washington	Martha Dandridge Washington	1731–1802	1789–1797
John Adams	Abigail Smith Adams	1744–1818	1797–1801
Thomas Jefferson	Martha Wayles Jefferson	1748–1782	1801–1809*
James Madison	Dolley Payne Madison	1768–1849	1809–1817
James Monroe	Elizabeth Kortright Monroe	1768–1830	1817–1825
John Quincy Adams	Louisa Johnson Adams	1775–1852	1825–1829
Andrew Jackson	Rachel Donelson Jackson	1767–1828	1829–1837*
Martin Van Buren	Hannah Hoes Van Buren	1783–1819	1837–1841*
William H. Harrison	Anna Symmes Harrison	1775–1864	1841
John Tyler	Letitia Christian Tyler	1790–1842	1841–1845
	Julia Gardiner Tyler	1820–1889	1841–1845
James K. Polk	Sarah Childress Polk	1803–1891	1845–1849
Zachary Taylor	Margaret Smith Taylor	1788–1852	1849–1850
Millard B. Fillmore	Abigail Powers Fillmore	1798–1853	1850–1853
Franklin Pierce	Jane Appleton Pierce	1806–1863	1853–1857
James Buchanan	Harriet Lane (niece)	1857–1861	
Abraham Lincoln	Mary Todd Lincoln	1818–1882	1861–1865
Andrew Johnson	Eliza McCardle Johnson	1810–1876	1865–1869
Ulysses S. Grant	Julia Dent Grant	1826–1902	1869–1877
Rutherford B. Hayes	Lucy Webb Hayes	1831–1889	1877–1881
James A. Garfield	Lucretia Rudolph Garfield	1832–1918	1881
Chester A. Arthur	Ellen Herndon Arthur	1837–1880	1881–1885*
Grover Cleveland	Frances Folsom Cleveland	1864–1947	1885–1889 1893–1897
Benjamin Harrison	Caroline Scott Harrison	1832–1892	1889–1893
William McKinley	Ida Saxton McKinley	1847–1907	1897–1901
Theodore Roosevelt	Alice Hathaway Lee Roosevelt	1861–1884*	
	Edith Carow Roosevelt	1861–1948	1901–1909

President	First Lady	First Lady Birth–Death	Pres. Years
Howard Taft	Helen Herron Taft	1861–1943	1909–1913
Woodrow Wilson	Ellen Axson Wilson	1860–1914	1913–1921
	Edith Bolling Wilson	1872–1961	1913–1921
Warren G. Harding	Florence Kling Harding	1868–1924	1921–1923
Calvin Coolidge	Grace Goodhue Coolidge	1879–1957	1923–1929
Herbert Hoover	Lou Henry Hoover	1874–1944	1929–1933
Franklin D. Roosevelt	Eleanor Roosevelt Roosevelt	1884–1962	1933–1945
Harry S. Truman	Bess Wallace Truman	1885–1982	1945–1953
Dwight D. Eisenhower	Mary Geneva "Mamie" Doud Eisenhower	1896–1979	1953–1961
John F. Kennedy	Jacqueline "Jackie" Bouvier Kennedy	1929–1994	1961–1963
Lyndon B. Johnson	Claudia "Lady Bird" Taylor Johnson	1912–	1963–1969
Richard M. Nixon	Thelma "Pat" Ryan Nixon	1912–1993	1969–1974
Gerald R. Ford	Elizabeth "Betty" Bloomer Ford	1918–	1974–1977
Jimmy Carter	Rosalynn Smith Carter	1927–	1977–1981
Ronald Reagan	Anne "Nancy" Frances Robbins Davis Reagan	1921–	1981–1989
George W. Bush	Barbara Pierce Bush	1925–	1989–1993
Bill Clinton	Hillary Rodham Clinton	1947–	1993–2001

BIBLIOGRAPHY

Allgor, Catherine. *Parlor Politics: In Which the Ladies of Washington City Help Build a City and a Government*. Charlottesville: University Press of Virginia, 2000.

Ambrose, Stephen E. *Eisenhower: Soldier, General of the Army, President-Elect, 1890–1952*. New York: Simon and Schuster, 1984. Reprint, New York: Touchstone Books, 1991.

Anderson, Alice E., and Hadley V. Baxendale. *Behind Every Successful President: The Hidden Power and Influence of America's First Ladies*. New York: Shapolsky, 1992.

Anthony, Carl Sferrazza. *First Ladies: The Saga of the Presidents' Wives and Their Power, 1789–1961*. New York: Quill/William Morrow, 1990–1991.

————. *First Ladies: The Saga of the Presidents' Wives and Their Power, 1962–1990*. New York: Quill/William Morrow, 1992.

Anthony, Katharine. *Dolly Madison: Her Life and Times*. Garden City, N.J.: Doubleday, 1949.

Archibugi, Daniel, Davil Held, and Martin Kohler, eds. *Re-imagining Political Community: Studies in Cosmopolitan Democracy*. Stanford, Calif.: Stanford University Press, 1998.

Arnett, Ethel Stephens. *Mrs. James Madison: The Incomparable Dolley*. Greensboro, N.C.: Piedmont Press, 1972.

Baker, James T. "To the Former Miss Betty Bloomer of Grand Rapids." *Christian Century* 93 (13 October 1976): 864.

Baker, Paula. "The Domestication of Politics." *American Historical Review* 89 (June 1984): 620–47.

Banning, Lance. *The Jeffersonian Persuasion: Evolution of a Party Ideology*. Ithaca, N.Y.: Cornell University Press, 1978.

Barber, Ellen J., David B. Mattern, J. C. A. Stagg, and Anne Mandeville Colony, eds. *The Papers of James Madison*. Charlottesville: University Press of Virginia, 1992.

Barzman, Sol. *The First Ladies*. New York: Cowles Book Co., 1970.

Beasley, Maurine H., Holly C. Shulman, and Henry R. Beasley. *The Eleanor Roosevelt Encyclopedia*. Westport, Conn.: Greenwood, 2001.

"Behind Mrs. Truman's Social Curtain: No Comment." *Newsweek* 30 (10 November 1947), 16.

"Betty Ford: Facing Cancer." *Time* 104 (7 October 1974): 14.

"Betty Ford's Operation." *Newsweek* 84 (7 October 1974): 30–33.

"Betty Ford's Role on the Election Circuit." *U.S. News and World Report* 84 (7 October 1974): 31.

"Betty: The New First Lady." *Newsweek* 84 (19 August 1974): 30.

"Betty Versus Rosalynn: Life on the Campaign Trail." *U.S. News and World Report* 81 (18 October 1976): 24.

Bibby, John F., and Roger H. Davidson. *On Capitol Hill: Studies in the Legislative Process.* New York: Rinehart and Winston, 1967.

Black, Allida M. *What I Hope to Leave Behind: The Essential Essays of Eleanor Roosevelt.* Brooklyn, N.Y.: Carlson Publishing, 1995.

Black, Ruby. *Eleanor Roosevelt: A Biography.* New York: Duell, Sloan and Pearce, 1940.

Blumstein, James. "A Land Mine on the Path from First Lady to Senator." *Wall Street Journal* (7 June 1999): A23.

Boller, Paul F., Jr. *Presidential Wives: An Anecdotal History.* New York: Oxford University Press, 1988.

Boyd, Julian P., ed. *The Papers of Thomas Jefferson.* 29 vols. to date. Princeton, N.J.: Princeton University Press, 1950–.

Brant, Irving. *James Madison: The President, 1809–1812.* Indianapolis, Ind.: Bobbs-Merrill, 1959.

Brock, David. *The Seduction of Hillary Rodham.* New York: Free Press, 1996.

Brooks, Geraldine. *Dames and Daughters of the Young Republic.* New York: Thomas Y. Crowell, 1901.

Buckley, William F. "Pity Mrs. Ford." *National Review* 27 (12 September 1975): 1008–9.

Burrell, Barbara. *Public Opinion, the First Ladyship, and Hillary Rodham Clinton.* New York: Garland, 1997.

Burstein, Andrew. *The Inner Jefferson: Portrait of a Grieving Optimist.* Charlottesville: University Press of Virginia, 1993.

Bushman, Richard L. *The Refinement of America: Persons, Houses, Cities.* New York: Alfred A. Knopf, 1992.

Campbell, Colton C., and Roger H. Davidson. "U.S. Congressional Committees: Changing Legislative Workshops." *The Journal of Legislative Studies* 4 (1998): 124–42.

Caroli, Betty Boyd. *First Ladies.* 1987. Reprint, New York: Oxford University Press, 1993.

———. "First Ladies." In *Encyclopedia of the American Presidency,* edited by Leonard W. Levy and Louis Fisher. New York: Simon & Schuster, 1994.

———. "The First Lady's Changing Role." In *The White House: The First Two Hundred Years,* edited by Frank Freidel and William Pencak. Boston: Northeastern University Press, 1994.

———. "First Lady's Office." In *Encyclopedia of the American Presidency,* ed. Leonard W. Levy and Louis Fisher. New York: Simon & Schuster, 1994.

Carter, Rosalynn. *First Lady from Plains.* Boston: Houghton Mifflin, 1984. Reprint, Fayetteville: University of Arkansas Press, 1994.

Chadakoff, Rochelle. *Eleanor Roosevelt's "My Day": Her Acclaimed Columns, 1936–1945.* New York: Pharos Books, 1989.

Clark, Allen C. *Life and Letters of Dolly Madison*. Washington, D.C.: W. F. Roberts, 1914.

Clinton, Hillary Rodham. *It Takes a Village*. New York: Simon and Schuster, 1996.

Cobb, Roger, Jennie-Keith Ross, and Marc Howard Ross. "Agenda Building as a Comparative Political Process." *American Political Science Review* 70 (1976): 126–38.

Collier, Peter. *The Roosevelts: An American Saga*. New York: Simon & Schuster, 1994.

Colman, Edna M. *Seventy-Five Years of White House Gossip from Washington to Lincoln*. Garden City, N.J.: Doubleday, Page, 1925.

"Contest of the Queens." *Time* 108 (30 August 1976): 31.

Cook, Blanche Wiesen. *Eleanor Roosevelt: 1884–1933*. New York: Penguin Books, 1992.

Cooper, John Milton Jr. "Disability in the White House: The Case of Woodrow Wilson." In *The White House—The First Two Hundred Years,* edited by Frank Freidel and William Pencak. Boston, Mass.: Northeastern University Press, 1994.

Cooper, Joseph. "Organization and Innovation in the House of Representatives." In *The House at Work,* edited by Joseph Cooper and G. Calvin Mackenzie. Austin: University of Texas Press, 1981.

———. "The Origins of the Standing Committees and the Development of the Modern House." *Rice University Studies* 56 (1970): 3.

Cott, Nancy F. *The Bonds of Womanhood*. New Haven, Conn.: Yale University Press, 1977.

Crapol, Edward, ed., *Women and American Foreign Policy: Lobbyists, Critics, and Insiders*. New York: Greenwood Press, 1987.

Cronin, Thomas E., and Michael A. Genovese. *The Paradoxes of the American Presidency*. New York: Oxford University Press, 1998.

David, Lester, and Irene David. *Ike and Mamie: The Story of the General and His Lady*. New York: World Publishing, 1981.

Davidson, Roger H. "Leaders and Committees in the Republican Congress." In *New Majority or Old Minority? The Impact of the Republicans on Congress,* edited by Nicol C. Rae and Colton C. Campbell. Lanham, Md.: Rowman and Littlefield, 1999.

Davidson, Roger H., and Walter J. Oleszek. *Congress Against Itself*. Bloomington: Indiana University Press, 1977.

———. *Congress and Its Members*. 7th ed. Washington, D.C.: CQ Press, 2000.

Davis, Patti. *The Way I See It: An Autobiography*. New York: Putnam, 1992.

"Dear Mrs. Ford." *McCall's* 102 (December 1974): 66.

Deckard, Barbara Sinclair. *The Women's Movement: Political, Socioeconomic and Psychological Issues*. New York: Harper and Row, 1975.

Deering, Christopher J., and Steven S. Smith. *Committees in Congress*. Washington, D.C.: CQ Press, 1997.

Demos, John. *Past, Present, and Personal: The Family and the Life Course in American History.* New York: Oxford University Press, 1986.

DePauw, Linda Grant, and Conover Hunt. *"Remember the Ladies": Women in America, 1750–1815.* New York: Viking Press, 1976.

Diller, Daniel C., and Stephen L. Robertson. *Presidents, First Ladies, and Vice Presidents: White House Biographies, 1789–1997.* Washington, D.C.: CQ Press, 1997.

Donovan, Robert J. *Conflict and Crisis: The Presidency of Harry S. Truman, 1949–1953.* New York: Norton, 1977.

"Dr. Mitchill's Letters from Washington, 1801–1813." *Harper's New Monthly Magazine* (April 1879): 752.

Eisenhower, Julie Nixon. *Special People.* New York: Simon and Schuster, 1977.

Eksterowicz, Anthony J., and Kristin Paynter. "The Evolution of the Role and Office of the First Lady: The Movement toward Integration with the White House Office." *Social Science Journal* 37 (2000): 547–62.

Elkins, Stanley, and Eric McKitrick. *The Age of Federalism: The Early American Republic, 1788–1800.* New York: Oxford University Press, 1993.

Ellet, Elizabeth F. *Court Circles of the Republic: or the Beauties and Celebrities of the Nation.* Hartford, Conn.: Hartford Publishing, 1871.

Ellis, Joseph J. *American Sphinx: The Character of Thomas Jefferson.* New York: Alfred A. Knopf, 1993.

Engle, Karen. "After the Collapse of the Public/Private Distinction: Stargazing Women's Rights" and "International Law: Feminist Critiques of the Public/Private Distinction." In *Reconceiving Reality: Women and International Law,* edited by Dorinda G. Dallmeyer. Washington D.C.: American Society of International Law, 1993.

Erskine, Helen Worden. "The Riddle of Mrs. Truman." *Collier's* (9 February 1952): 12.

Eulau, Heinz, and Vera McCluggage. "Standing Committees in Legislatures: Three Decades of Research." *Legislative Studies Quarterly* 9 (1984): 195–270.

Faber, Doris. *Life of Lorena Hickok, E.R.'s Friend.* New York: William Morrow, 1980.

"A Family Affair." *Newsweek* 86 (25 August 1975): 20.

Feldman, Trude B. "The New First Lady." *McCall's* 102 (October 1974): 88.

Felsenthal, Carol. *Alice Roosevelt Longworth.* New York: G. P. Putnam's Sons, 1988.

Fenno, Richard F. *Congressmen in Committees.* Boston: Little, Brown, 1973.

Ferrell, Robert H. *Dear Bess: The Letters from Harry to Bess Truman.* New York: W. W. Norton, 1983.

———. *Off the Record: Harry S. Truman Diary.* New York: W. W. Norton, 1945.

———. *Truman: A Centenary Remembrance.* New York: Viking, 1984.

"A Fighting First Lady." *Time,* 3 March 1975, 20.

"First Lady." *Newsweek* (7 January 1946): 26.

Flemion, Jess, and Colleen M. O'Connor. *Eleanor Roosevelt: An American Journey.* San Diego, Calif.: San Diego State University, 1987.

Ford, Betty (with Chris Chase). *The Times of My Life.* New York: Harper and Row, 1978.

Ford, Gerald. *A Time to Heal.* New York: Harper and Row, 1979.

Ford, Paul Leicester. *The Writings of Thomas Jefferson.* New York: G. P. Putnam's, 1892–99.

Freeman, Joanne B. "Dueling as Politics: Reinterpreting the Burr-Hamilton Duel." *William and Mary Quarterly* 53 (April 1996): 289–318.

———. "Slander, Poison, Whispers, and Fame: Jefferson's 'Anas' and Political Gossip in the Early Republic." *Journal of the Early Republic* 15 (spring 1995), 25–27.

Fremont, Jessie Benton. *Souvenirs of My Time.* Boston: D. Lothrop & Co., 1887.

Furman, Bess. "Independent Lady from Independence." *New York Times Magazine,* 9 June 1946, 19.

———. *White House Profile.* New York: Bobbs-Merrill, 1951.

Garcia, Rogelio. *Travel Costs of the President, Vice President, and First Lady.* Washington, D.C.: Congressional Research Service Report RS20111, 1999.

Garland, Susan B. "First Lady, and No Second Fiddle." *Business Week* 19 (18 July 1999).

Garrett, Elisabeth Donaghy. *At Home: The American Family, 1750–1870.* New York: Harry N. Abrams, 1990.

Gibbs, Nancy, and Michael Duffy. "Just Heartbeats Away: The Proposal That the First Lady Aspirants Hold a Debate Suggests How Much the Role Has Changed." *Time,* 1 July 1996.

Ginsberg, Benjamin, and Martin Shefer. *Politics by Other Means.* New York: Basic Books, 1990.

Goodwin, Doris Kearns. *No Ordinary Time; Franklin and Eleanor Roosevelt: The Home Front in World War II.* New York: Simon & Schuster, 1994.

Goodwin, Maud Wilder. *Dolley Madison.* New York: Charles Scribner's Sons, 1896.

Gould, Lewis L. *American First Ladies: Their Lives and Their Legacy.* New York: Garland, 1996.

———. "First Ladies." *The American Scholar* 55 (autumn 1986): 528–35.

———. "Modern First Ladies: An Institutional Perspective." *Prologue* 19 (summer 1987): 73.

———. "Modern First Ladies and the Presidency." *Presidential Studies Quarterly* 20 (1990): 677–83.

Grayson, Cary T. *Woodrow Wilson: An Intimate Memoir.* New York: Holt, Rinehart and Winston, 1960.

Green, Harvey. *The Light of the Home: An Intimate View of the Lives of Women in Victorian America.* New York: Pantheon Books, 1983.

Gross, Bertram M. *The Legislative Struggle: A Study in Social Combat.* Westport, Conn.: Greenwood Press, 1953.

Gutin, Myra G. *The President's Partner: The First Lady in the Twentieth Century.* Westport, Conn.: Greenwood Press, 1989.

Hamby, Alonzo. *Man of the People: A Life of Harry S. Truman.* New York: Oxford University Press, 1995.

Hamilton, Charles V. *Adam Clayton Powell, Jr.: The Political Biography of an American Dilemma.* New York: Cooper Square Publishers, 1991.

Hamilton, Holman. *Zachary Taylor: Soldier of the Republic.* Indianapolis, Ind.: Bobbs-Merrill, 1941.

Haraven, Tamara K. *Eleanor Roosevelt: An American Conscience.* Chicago: Quadrangle Books, 1968.

Harris, John F. "For First Lady, a Controversy in Plane Terms." *Washington Post,* 3 July 1999, A8.

Harrison, Rainie. "The Other Hot Race for the White House." *U.S. News and World Report* (September 1987): 28.

Hastedt, Glenn. *American Foreign Policy: Past, Present, and Future.* 4th ed. Upper Saddle River, N.J.: Prentice-Hall, 2000.

Hatch, Alden. *Edith Bolling Wilson: First Lady Extraordinary.* New York: Dodd, Mead & Co., 1961.

Hay, Peter. *All the President's Ladies.* New York: Penguin Books, 1988.

Heilbrun, Carolyn G. *Hamlet's Mother and Other Women.* New York: Ballantine Books, 1990.

———. *Writing a Woman's Life.* New York: Ballantine Books, 1988.

Hershey, Lenore. "Compassion Power: On Tour with Mrs. Nixon." *Ladies' Home Journal* (September 1969): 88.

Hickok, Lorena A. *Eleanor Roosevelt: Reluctant First Lady.* New York: Dodd, Mead & Co., 1962.

Holloway, Laura Carpenter. *The Ladies of the White House.* New York: U.S. Publishing, 1870.

Hoover, Irwin Hood. *Forty-Two Years in the White House.* Westport, Conn.: Greenwood Press, 1934.

Hosford, David. "Exile in Yankeeland: The Journal of Mary Bagot, 1816–1819." *Records of the Columbia Historical Society of Washington, D.C.* 51 (1984): 35.

House, Edward. *The Intimate Papers of Colonel House.* Boston: Houghton Mifflin, 1930.

Howard, Jane. "Forward Day by Day." *New York Times Magazine,* 8 December 1974, 86.

Howe, John R., Jr. "Republican Thought and Political Violence of the 1790s." *American Quarterly* 19 (1967): 147–65.

Huitt, Ralph K. "The Congressional Committee: A Case Study." *American Political Science Review* 48 (1954): 340–65.

Hunt-Jones, Conover. *Dolley and the "Great Little Madison."* Washington, D.C.: American Institute of Architects Press, 1977.

Hurd, Charles. *Washington Cavalcade.* New York: E. P. Dutton, 1948.

Inglehart, Ronald. *Modernization and Postmodernization: Cultural, Economic, and Political Change in 43 Societies.* Princeton, N.J.: Princeton University Press, 1997.

In Memoriam: Mrs. Jas. K. Polk (Nashville, Tenn.: S. N., 1891).

Isikoff, Michael. *Uncovering Clinton: A Reporter's Story.* New York: Three Rivers Press, 1999.

Jacob, Kathryn Allamong. *Capital Elites: High Society in Washington, D.C., after the Civil War.* Washington, D.C.: Smithsonian Institution Press, 1995.

Jervis, Robert. *Perception and Misperception in International Relations.* Princeton, N.J.: Princeton University Press, 1976.

Kearney, James R. *Anna Eleanor Roosevelt: The Evolution of a Reformer.* Boston: Houghton Mifflin, 1968.

Kent, Deborah. *Jane Means Appleton Pierce, 1806–1863.* New York: Children's Press, 1998.

Kernell, Samuel. *Going Public: New Strategies of Presidential Leadership.* Washington, D.C.: CQ Press, 1986.

Kingdon, John W. *Agendas, Alternatives, and Public Policies.* Boston: Little, Brown, 1984.

Kirk, Elise Kuhl. *Music at the White House: A History of American Spirit.* Urbana: University of Illinois Press, 1986.

Klapthor, Margaret Brown. *The First Ladies Cookbook.* New York: Parents' Magazine Press, 1969.

Knickrehm, Kay, and Robin Teske. "Attitudes toward Domestic Violence among Romanian and U.S. University Students: A Cross Cultural Comparison." *Women and Politics* 21 (2000): 34–39.

Kraditor, Aileen S. *Up from the Pedestal: Selected Writings in the History of American Feminism.* Chicago: Triangle Books, 1968.

Krehbiel, Keith. *Information and Legislative Organization.* Ann Arbor: University of Michigan Press, 1991.

Lansing, Robert. *The Big Four and Others of the Peace Conference.* Boston: Houghton Mifflin, 1921.

Lash, Joseph P. *Eleanor and Franklin: The Story of Their Relationship Based on Eleanor Roosevelt's Personal Papers.* New York: W. W. Norton, 1971.

———. *Eleanor Roosevelt: A Friend's Memoir.* Garden City, N.Y.: Doubleday, 1964.

———. *Love, Eleanor: Eleanor Roosevelt and Her Friends.* New York: Doubleday, 1982.

"Letters of Abijah Bigelow, Member of Congress to His Wife, 1810–1815." *Proceedings of the American Antiquarian Society* 40 (October 1930): 312.

Logan, Logna. *Ladies of the White House.* New York: Vantage Press, 1962.

Martin, Ralph G. *A Hero for Our Time: An Intimate Story of the Kennedy Years.* New York: Fawcett Books, 1984.

Marty, Martin E. "Our Moral Arbiters." *Christian Century* 92 (17 September 1975): 807.

Maass, Arthur. *Congress and the Common Good.* New York: Basic Books, 1967.

Matalin, Mary, and James Carville. *All's Fair: Love, War, and Running for President.* New York: Random House, 1994.

Mayo, Edith. "The Influence and Power of First Ladies." *Chronicle of Higher Education,* 15 September 1993, A52.

———. *Smithsonian Book of the First Ladies: Their Lives, Times, and Issues.* New York: Henry Holt and Co., 1996.

McCullough, David. *Truman.* New York: Simon and Schuster, 1992.

McDonald, John W. "Ten of Truman's Happiest Years Spent in Senate." *Independence (Mo.) Examiner,* Truman Centennial Edition, May 1984.

McLendon, Winzola. "Betty Ford Talks about Homemaking." *Good Housekeeping* 183 (24 August 1976), 65–67.

McLure, Ruth K. *Eleanor Roosevelt, an Eager Spirit: The Letters of Dorothy Dow, 1933–1945.* New York: W. W. Norton, 1984.

McPherson, Myra. "The Blooming of Betty Ford." *McCall's* 102 (September 1975): 134.

Means, Marianne. *The Women in the White House: The Lives, Times and Influence of Twelve Notable First Ladies.* New York: Random House, 1963.

"Meet Harry's Boss, Bess." *Collier's* (12 February 1949).

Meyers, Lisa. "Behind the Smiles." *Family Weekly* 12 (October 1980): 12.

Milton, Joyce. *The First Partner: Hillary Rodham Clinton.* New York: William Morrow, 1999.

Minton, Lynn. "Betty Ford Talks about Her Mother." *McCall's* 103 (May 1976): 74.

Moore, Molly. "First Lady 'Moved,' 'Overwhelmed' on Asian Journey of Self-Discovery." *Washington Post,* 6 April 1995.

Moore, Thomas H. "First Ladies on the Hill." *Congressional Quarterly Weekly Report* (2 October 1993): 2641.

"Mrs. Ford and the Affair of the Daughter." *Ladies' Home Journal* 92 (November 1975): 118.

Nelson, Anson, and Fanny Nelson. *Memorials of Sarah Childress Polk.* New York: Anson D. F. Randolph & Co., 1892.

Nelson, Michael. *The Presidency: A to Z.* Washington, D.C.: CQ Press, 1998.

Neustadt, Richard. *Presidential Power and the Modern Presidents.* New York: Free Press, 1990.

Nichols, Roy Franklin. *Franklin Pierce: Young Hickory of the Granite Hills.* Philadelphia: University of Pennsylvania Press, 1958.

"No Secret, Truman Says of Wife's Job in Senate." *New York Times,* 27 July 1944, 11.

Noonan, Peggy. *The Case Against Hillary Clinton.* New York: Regan, 2000.

Oberderfer, Dan. "Carter Addresses OAS, Stresses Human Rights." *Washington Post,* 15 April 1977.

O'Connor, Karen, Bernadette Nye, and Laura Van Assendelft. "Wives in the White House: The Political Influence of First Ladies." *Presidential Studies Quarterly* 26 (fall 1996): 835–53.

Okin, Susan Moller. *Justice, Gender, and the Family.* New York: Basic Books, Inc., 1989.

Olson, Barbara. *Hell to Pay: The Unfolding Story of Hillary Rodham Clinton.* Washington, D.C.: Regnery, 1999.

"On Being Normal." *Time* 106 (25 August 1975): 15.

"On to the Showdown in Florida." *Time* 107 (8 March 1976): 11.

Pearson, Richard. "A Republican Congress, an Embattled First Lady; It Happened Before, with Mary Todd Lincoln." *Washington Post,* 27 January 1996, A12.

Pemberton, William E. *Harry S. Truman: Fair Dealer and Cold Warrior.* Boston: Twayne, 1989.

"Political Wives with Different Styles." *U.S. News and World Report* 81 (8 March 1976): 24.

Polk, William R. *Polk's Folly.* New York: Doubleday, 2000.

Polsby, Nelson W. *Congress and the Presidency.* Englewood Cliffs, N.J.: Prentice-Hall, 1981.

Radcliffe, Donnie. *Hillary Rodham Clinton: A First Lady for Our Time.* New York: Time Warner Books, 1993.

Reagan, Nancy, with William Novak. *My Turn: The Memoirs of Nancy Reagan.* New York: Random House, 1989.

"Record 30 Women's Bills Passed in 1993 as Ranks Grow in Congress." *Minneapolis Star Tribune,* 3 December 1993, A5.

"The Relentless Ordeal of Political Wives." *Time* 104 (7 October 1974): 16.

Rios, Delia M. "Goldgate? Wife of an Earlier President Had Problems with Congress." *St. Louis Post-Dispatch,* 24 January 1996, C5.

Ripley, Randall B. "Congressional Party Leaders and Standing Committees." *Review of Politics* 36 (1974): 394–409.

Ritchie, Donald A. "Eleanor Roosevelt and Congress." In *The Eleanor Roosevelt Encyclopedia,* edited by Maurine Beasley and Holly C. Shulman, pp. 103–5. Westport, Conn.: Greenwood Press, 2001.

Robbins, Jahn. *Bess and Harry: An American Love Story.* New York: G. P. Putnam, 1980.

Roiphie, Katie. *The Morning After: Sex, Fear, and Feminism on Campus.* Boston: Little, Brown, 1993.

Roosevelt, Eleanor. *The Autobiography of Eleanor Roosevelt.* New York: Curtiss Publishing, 1958.

———. *This I Remember.* New York: Harper & Bros., 1949.

———. *This Is My Story.* New York: Harper & Bros., 1937.

———. "Women Must Learn to Play the Game as Men Do." *Red Book Magazine* 50 (April 1928): 78–79.

Roosevelt, Elliot. *FDR: His Personal Letters (1905–1928).* New York: Duell, Sloane and Pearce, 1948.

Rosebush, James S. *First Lady, Public Wife: A Behind-the-Scenes History of the Evolving Role of First Ladies in American Political Life.* Lanham, Md.: Madison Books, 1987.

Rosenau, James. "Pre-Theories and Theories of Foreign Policy." In *Approaches to Comparative and International Politics,* edited by R. Barry Farrell. Evanston, Ill.: Northwestern University Press, 1966.

Rosenau, James, and W. Michael Fagan. "A New Dynamism in World Politics: Increasingly Skillful Individuals?" *International Studies Quarterly* 41 (1997): 655–86.

Ross, Ishbel. *First Lady of the South: The Life of Mrs. Jefferson Davis.* New York: Harper & Bros., 1958.

———. *Power with Grace: The Life Story of Mrs. Woodrow Wilson.* New York: G. P. Putnam's Sons, 1975.

Rubin, Alissa J. "Mrs. Clinton Conquers Hill, Sets Debate in Motion." *Congressional Quarterly Weekly Report* (2 October 1993), 2640–43.

Ryan, Mary C., and Nancy Kegan Smith. *Modern First Ladies: Their Documentary Legacy.* Washington, D.C.: National Archives and Records Administration, 1989.

Salter, J. T., ed. *Public Men in and out of Office.* Chapel Hill: University of North Carolina Press, 1946.

Sapiro, Virginia, and David T. Canon. "Race, Gender, and the Clinton Presidency." In *The Clinton Legacy,* edited by Colin Campbell and Bert A. Rockman. New York: Chatham House, 2000.

Schreiber, Flora Rheta. "I Didn't Want Dick to Run Again." *Time* (29 Feb. 1960): 25; *Good Housekeeping* (July 1968): 188; *Newsweek* (2, 31 December 1968), 31.

Schwartz, Maralee. "Hillary Gets off GOP Case: Clinton Assails Rivals' Portrayal of Her Views." *Washington Post,* 1 August 1992.

Scott, Ann Firor. *The Southern Lady: From Pedestal to Politics, 1830–1930.* Chicago: University of Chicago Press, 1970.

Seale, William. *The President's House: A History.* Washington, D.C.: White House Historical Association, 1986.

Shannon, Elaine. "Building That Bridge to a Special Relationship." *Time* (8 December 1997): 22.

Sharp, James Roger. *American Politics in the Early Republic: The New Nation in Crisis.* New Haven, Conn.: Yale University Press, 1993.

Sheehy, Gail. *Hillary's Choice.* New York: Random House, 1999.

Shelton, Isabelle. "I Feel Like I've Been Reborn." *McCall's* 102 (February 1975): 142.

Shulman, Holly Cowan. "Dolley (Payne Todd) Madison." In *American First Ladies: Their Lives and Their Legacy,* edited by Lewis L. Gould, 45–68. New York: Garland, 1996.

Skowronek, Stephen. *The Politics Presidents Make.* Cambridge: Harvard University Press, 1993.

Smelser, Marshall. "The Federalist Period as an Age of Passion." *American Quarterly* 10 (winter 1958): 391–419.

Smith, Gene. *When the Cheering Stopped: The Last Years of Woodrow Wilson.* New York: William Morrow, 1964.

Smith, Margaret Chase. *Declaration of Conscience.* New York: Doubleday, 1972.

Smith, Scottie. *Don't Quote Me! Washington Newswomen and the Power Society.* New York: Dutton, 1970.

Smith, Steven S. *The American Congress.* Boston: Houghton Mifflin, 1995.

Solomon, Burt. "The First Partner." *National Journal* 19 (June 1993): 1472.

Sontag, Susan. *Illness as Metaphor.* New York: Farrar, Straus, and Giroux, 1978.

Sorensen, Theodore. *Decision Making in the White House: The Olive Branch or the Arrows.* New York: Columbia University Press, 1963.

Sperling, Godfrey. "New First Ladies, in 1960 and Today." *Christian Science Monitor* 8 (December 1992): 19.

"Stargazing: Presidents' Wives and Careers." *Ms.,* July 1988, 17.

Stoessinger, John. *Why Nations Go to War. 7th edition.* New York: St. Martin's Press, 1998.

Sullivan, Donna. "The Public/Private Distinction in International Human Rights Law." In *Women's Rights, Human Rights: International Feminist Perspectives,* edited by Julie Peters and Andrea Wolper. New York: Routledge, 1995.

Sylvester, Christine. *Feminist Theory and International Relations in a Postmodern Era*. Cambridge: Cambridge University Press, 1994.

"Tea for Fifty Ladies." *Newsweek* (22 October 1945): 36.

Tétreault, Mary Ann. "Formal Politics, Meta-Space, and the Gendered Construction of Civil Life." In *Philosophy and Geography II: The Production of Public Space,* edited by Andrew Light and Jonathan M. Smith. Lanham, Md.: Rowman and Littlefield, 1998.

———. "Frontier Politics: Sex, Gender, and the Destruction of the Public Sphere," *Alternatives* 26 (2001): 53–72.

"There's No Gilded Cage for Betty." *Time* 106 (1 December 1975): 22.

Thimmesch, Nick. "Ten-Four First Mama." *Saturday Evening Post* 248 (September 1976): 120.

Trollope, Frances. *Domestic Manners of the Americans.* Barre, Pa.: Imprint Society, 1969.

Troy, Gil. *Affairs of State: The Rise and Rejection of the Presidential Couple since World War II.* New York: Free Press, 1997.

————. *Mr. and Mrs. President: From the Trumans to the Clintons.* New York: Free Press, 1997; rev. ed. Lawrence: University Press of Kansas, 2000.

Truman, David B. *The Governmental Process: Political Interests and Public Opinion.* New York: Alfred A. Knopf, 1971.

Truman, Harry. *Memoirs.* Vol. 1, *Year of Decisions.* New York: Doubleday, 1955.

Truman, Margaret. *Bess W. Truman.* New York: Macmillan, 1986.

————. *First Ladies: An Intimate Group Portrait of White House Wives.* New York: Random House, 1995.

"Truman Ladies.." *Newsweek* (8 November 1948): 13.

Tumulty, Joseph P. *Woodrow Wilson as I Know Him.* Garden City, N.J.: Doubleday, Page & Co., 1921.

Tyler, Patrick. "Hillary Clinton in China, Details Abuse of Women." *New York Times,* 6 September 1995.

Unekis, Joseph K. "Committee Hearings." In *Encyclopedia of the United States Congress,* edited by Donald C. Bacon, Roger H. Davidson, and Morton Keller. New York: Simon & Schuster, 1995.

U.S. House of Representatives, House Committee on Education and Labor, *Health Care Reform,* 103d Cong., 1st sess., 29 Sept. 1993, 3.

U.S. Senate, Senate Committee on Labor and Human Resources, *Health Security Act of 1993,* 103d Cong., 1st sess., Sept. 29, 30, Oct. 5, 6, 15, 19, 1993, S. Hrg. 103–216, pt. 1.

Walsh, Kenneth T. "Hillary's Resurrection." *U.S. News and World Report* (20 October 1997): 26–29.

Ware, Susan. *Beyond Suffrage: Women in the New Deal.* Cambridge: Harvard University Press, 1981.

————. *Partner and I: Molly Dewson, Feminism, and New Deal Politics.* New Haven, Conn.: Yale University Press, 1987.

Watson, Mary Ann. *The Expanding Vista: American Television in the Kennedy Years.* New York: Oxford University Press, 1990.

Watson, Robert P. "The First Lady Reconsidered: Presidential Partner and Political Institution." *Presidential Studies Quarterly* 27 (fall 1997): 805–18.

————. *The Presidents' Wives: Reassessing the Office of First Lady.* Boulder, Colo.: Lynne Rienner Publishers, 2000.

————. *First Ladies of the United States: A Biographical Dictionary.* Boulder, Colo.: Lynne Rienner Publishers, 2001.

Weaver, Judy L. "Edith Bolling Wilson as First Lady: A Study in the Power of Personality, 1919–1920." *Presidential Studies Quarterly* 15 (winter 1985): 51–76.

Weidenfeld, Sheila Rabb. *First Lady's Lady: With the Fords at the White House.* New York: G. P. Putnam, 1979.

Weinraub, Bernard. "Mrs. President." *McCall's* (November 1985): 178.

Weinstein, Edwin A. *Woodrow Wilson: A Medical and Psychological Biography.* Princeton, N.J.: Princeton University Press, 1981.

West, J. B. *Upstairs at the White House.* New York: Warner Books, 1974.

Wharton, Anne Hollingsworth. *Social Life in the Early Republic.* Philadelphia: J. B. Lippincott, 1902.

Whitton, Mary Ormsbee. *First First Ladies, 1789–1865: A Study of the Wives of the Early Presidents.* Freeport, N.Y.: Books for Libraries Press, 1948.

Wilson, Edith Bolling. *My Memoir.* 1939. Reprint, New York: Arno Press, 1981.

Winfield, Betty Houchin. "Introductory Notes: Hillary Rodham Clinton's Image: Content, Control, and Cultural Politics. A Symposium." *Political Communication* 14 (1997): 221.

———. "Madame President: Understanding a New Kind of First Lady." *Media Studies Journal* 8 (1994): 59–71.

Wolf, Naomi. *Fire with Fire: The New Female Power and How It Will Change the Twenty-first Century.* New York: Random House, 1993.

"Woman of the Year." *Newsweek* 86 (29 December 1975): 19.

Woodward, Bob. *The Agenda: Inside the Clinton White House.* New York: Simon & Schuster, 1994.

Wright, Shelley. "Economic Rights, Social Justice and the State: A Feminist Reappraisal." In *Reconceiving Reality: Women and International Law,* edited by Dorinda G. Dallmeyer. Washington D.C.: American Society of International Law, 1993.

Yankelovich, Daniel. "How Changes in the Economy Are Reshaping American Values." In *Values and Public Policy,* edited by Henry Aaron, Thomas Mann, and Timothy Taylor. Washington D.C.: Brookings Institution, 1994.

Young, James Sterling. *The Washington Community, 1800–1828.* New York: Columbia University Press, 1966.

Youngs, J. William T. *Eleanor Roosevelt: A Personal and Public Life.* Boston: Little, Brown, 1985; 2d ed. New York: Longman, 2000 (Library of American Biography).

About the Contributors

Catherine Allgor received her Ph.D. from Yale, where she received the Yale Teaching Award. Her dissertation on women and politics in early Washington won prizes both for the best dissertation in American history at Yale and for the best dissertation in U.S. women's history in the country. She is assistant professor of history at the University of California–Riverside and author of *Parlor Politics: In Which the Ladies of Washington City Help Build a City and a Government* (University of Virginia Press, 2000). Allgor spoke at the White House Historical Association celebration of the capital city's bicentennial in November 2000.

MaryAnne Borrelli is an associate professor of government and Connecticut College. Her research is concerned with the connections between gender, decision making, and organizational culture in the United States presidency. She has authored articles analyzing the cabinet nomination and confirmation processes, and the position and office of the first lady. She is coeditor of *The Other Elites: Women, Politics, and Power in the Executive Branch* (Lynne Rienner Publishers, 1997) and author of *The President's Cabinet: Gender, Power, and Representation* (Lynne Rienner Publishers, 2002).

Patricia Brady earned her Ph.D. in history from Tulane University and is the former director of publications at the Historic New Orleans Collection. She is the author of dozens of essays on southern history and editor of *George Washington's Beautiful Nelly: The Letters of Eleanor Parke Custis Lewis to Elizabeth Bordley Gibson, 1794–1851* (University of South Carolina Press, 1991) and *Nelly Custis Lewis' Housekeeping Book* (Historic New Orleans Collection, 1982).

Susan Roth Breitzer is a Ph.D. candidate in history at the University of Iowa. She received her B.A. from Grinnell College, her M.L.S. from the University of Pittsburgh, and her M.A. from Eastern Illinois University. Her research interests include U.S. social, political, and labor history, and she has written works on first ladies Eleanor and Edith Roosevelt.

Colton C. Campbell is assistant professor of political science at Florida International University (the State University of Florida at Miami), and served as visiting assistant professor of government at American University, and visiting research fellow at the Center for Congressional and Presidential Studies. He is coeditor of *New Majority or Old Minority? The Impact of Republicans on Congress* (Rowman and Littlefield, 1999), *The Contentious Senate: Partisanship, Ideology and the Myth of "Cool" Judgment* (Rowman and Littlefield, 2001), *Congress Confronts the Court: The*

Struggle for Legitimacy in Lawmaking (Rowman and Littlefield, 2001), and author of *Discharging Congress: Government by Commission* (Praeger, 2001) and *Congress and the Internet* (Prentice-Hall, 2002). He served as an American Political Science Association Congressional Fellow in 1998–99, working in the office of U.S. senator Bob Graham (D-Fla.), and is the associate editor and book review editor of the journal *White House Studies.*

Anthony J. Eksterowicz is professor of political science at James Madison University, where he teaches courses on the presidency and Congress. He has published approximately thirty articles on various subjects in American government. Eksterowicz is coeditor of *The Post–Cold War Presidency* (1999) and *Public Journalism and Political Knowledge* (2000), both from Rowman & Littlefield Publishers. He is the associate editor of the journal *White House Studies.*

Raymond Frey is associate professor of American history and dean of the faculty at Centenary College in New Jersey. He has published works on Bess Truman and is completing a biography of Mrs. Truman (Nova Science Publishers, 2003).

Myra G. Gutin is professor of communications at Rider University in New Jersey. She is the author of *The President's Partner: The First Lady in the Twentieth Century* (Greenwood, 1989) and numerous articles on first ladies. A frequent consultant to and commentator on the media on the topic, she also teaches a course titled "The American First Lady in the Twentieth Century" at Rider.

Glenn Hastedt is professor of political science at James Madison University. He received his Ph.D. from Indiana University and is the author of *American Foreign Policy: Past, Present, and Future* (Prentice Hall, 4th edn., 2000) and the Dushkin—McGraw-Hill *American Foreign Policy Annual Edition* (7th edn., 2001).

Kay M. Knickrehm is professor of political science at James Madison University. Her main research interests lie in the fields of comparative politics and international relations. She has published four books and a number of articles in journals such as *Women and Politics, Journal of Refugee Studies, Journal of Political Science,* and *Southeastern Political Review.* For the last several years she has worked as a consultant with the Mine Action Information Center at James Madison University on a number of contracts related to the global land mine crisis.

Mary Linehan is associate professor of history at Spalding University in Louisville, Kentucky. Her research interests include the interplay between politics and social action movements, United States women's history, and popular culture. She has written articles and chapters on several first ladies.

James S. McCallops is associate professor of history at Salisbury State University in Maryland, where his primary focus is on women's history and gender studies. His essay on Edith Wilson originated from his research and writing on peace activists and World War I. McCallops is currently writing a book about Edith Wilson for Nova Science Publishers (2002) and essays on Edith Wilson and Florence Harding for *American First Ladies,* an encyclopedia on the first ladies (Salem Press, 2001).

Sean E. McCluskie received his Ph.D. from the University of Maryland and law degree from George Washington University and is an aide to U.S. representative Fourtney "Pete" Stark (D-Calif.). He was a Presidential Management Intern and previously worked for U.S. senator Bob Graham (D-Fla.). McCluskie has published numerous articles on international relations and American politics.

Kristen Paynter graduated as an honors student from James Madison University, where she wrote her thesis on the first ladies.

Robin Teske is a professor of political science at James Madison University, where she teaches courses in international law and organizations, international relations, and peace studies. Her academic background and her research interests are interdisciplinary. She holds both a law degree and the Ph.D., and her current research focuses on feminist theory, and international law issues. Prior to joining the faculty at JMU she was a human rights attorney in Washington, D.C., and a Peace Corps volunteer in the Republic of Korea.

Elizabeth Lorelei Thacker-Estrada is a librarian and a department director at the San Francisco Public Library. She is researching and writing the first scholarly books on Abigail Powers Fillmore and Jane Means Appleton Pierce. Thacker-Estrada was educated at the University of California, Santa Barbara, where she studied political science and women's history, and she earned a master's degree in library science and information studies from the University of California, Berkeley.

Gil Troy received his Ph.D. from Harvard University and is professor of history at McGill University in Montreal. He is the author of *Mr. and Mrs. President: From the Trumans to the Clintons* (University Press of Kansas, 2000; previously published as *Affairs of State* by Free Press in 1997) and *See How They Ran: The Changing Role of Presidential Candidates* (Harvard University Press, 1996).

Robert P. Watson has published thirteen books and more than a hundred scholarly articles and essays and is editor of the journal *White House Studies.* He has edited several projects on the first ladies, including a special issue of *Social Science Journal*

(2000), the encyclopedia *American First Ladies* (Salem Press, 2001), the thirty-five-book Presidential Wives Series (Nova Science Publisher, 2001–2004, and *Report to the First Lady—2001* (National First Ladies' Library & Nova Science Publishers, 2001). Watson's works on the first ladies include *Martha Washington: "Mother of Her Country"* (Longman Publishers, 2003), *First Ladies of the United States: A Biographical Dictionary* (Lynne Rienner Publishers, 2001), and *The Presidents' Wives: Reassessing the Office of First Lady* (Lynne Rienner Publishers, 2000). Watson teaches at Florida Atlantic University.

Name Index

Subject Index